LOOK BACK AND CHEER

Also by Wallace Vickers Kaufman

Nurse Buster

Invasive Plants (co-author with Dr. Sylvan Kaufman)

Coming Out of the Woods: The Solitary Life of a Maverick Naturalist

No Turning Back: Dismantling the Fantasies of Environmental Thinking

Amazon

Finding Hidden Values In Your Home

The Beaches Are Moving (co-author with Dr. Orrin Pilkey)

LOOK BACK AND CHEER

The Legacy of Small Towns

And A Small School

As Seen Through The Lives

Of

The Last Senior Class of Sea Cliff School

1957 – 2010

Written and Compiled

by

Wallace Vickers Kaufman

Much of this work was first published on CD by Wallace Kaufman, 2009.

Library of Congress Cataloging in Publication Data:

Kaufman, Wallace Vickers.   1939 –

    Look Back and Cheer: non-fiction/ Wallace Vickers Kaufman

    ISBN 1453722211

    EAN-13 is 9781453722213.

Cover photos: Nik Epanchin, Fred Feingold, a few others

For information address:

Wallace Kaufman
34251 Mt. Tom Dr.
Harrisburg, OR 97446 USA

DEDICATION

Learning is the most important fact of growing up. Learning is growing up. In writing this history I found myself again learning from our many teachers—at school, in our community, and at home. I also learned something from every person mentioned in this book. This book is for those who taught us and a celebration of everything we taught each other.

TABLE OF CONTENTS

BECOMING

Moving Up Day 1957, photo V. Epanchin

Most teenagers are preoccupied, if not obsessed, with becoming—all sorts of becoming-- professional, sexual, athletic, social, domestic, economic, political. In Sea Cliff High school from 9th grade on students would memorialize and tease those ambitions in that early June assembly called Moving Up Day. Everyone dressed in bleached white pants, skirts, blouses and shirts, sat in the hard wooden seats of the auditorium and awaited the final act when every class stood and began to sing. In 1956 I watched my brothers Art and Bill rise from the front rows and lead the way out of the school and I wanted to run after them into the "wide, wide world" we were singing about—that moment, not a year later.

A year later we seniors, some glad, some sad, (some glad *and* sad) sang for the last time the song that had become the sentimental year-end celebration and our passage into a higher class at the end of school:

Weaving in and out the rows
Every class now slowly goes

Who remembers which senior sat in the far left seat of the front row and was first out the door? We were all on our way out. Behind us, the three lower grades moved one stage forward in their becoming—juniors stopping in our rows, sophomores moving into the junior seats, and the freshman becoming sophomores. As seniors we sang our way

to the doorway down the stair
soon to start another pattern

in the fabric started here.

The finished pattern was 18 years of lives tended by parents, guardians, relatives, and teachers.   And often, in moments even as serious as suicide, by each other.   Looking back, I see more clearly now than I did then, that we had become a class.   Our numbers, 110 in the yearbook, were small enough that everyone knew each other, and knew something about each other.   As we made our way out of the auditorium into the fresh air, sunlight and expansive blue skies of late spring, we left behind the rest of the student body in their new seats singing to our backs the familiar chorus:

Symbolic of our lives ahead
As the shuttle weaves the thread.
Building fabrics of the life
Strong enough to stand the strife.
Onward, onward, ever on
Till the cloth of life is done.
(Moving Up Day Song Chorus)

Such fine sentiment deserves the counterweight of reality.   Fifty years after the classes behind us sang that the "grand old seniors" had "gone out from their alma mater, safe now in the wide, wide world," each of us had learned that the cloth of life had ended for one out of ten who sang that song with us.   Some had not survived "the strife."   In the song strife rhymes with life, and if we didn't know why then, we know now.   Every year now will end both life and strife for several more.   Before the today's 6th graders now assembling in those same auditorium seats reach the age of 45, we will all be gone.   That is biological reality and not a particularly happy one when stated so abstractly.   This book, however, is not a prepared epitaph or even an elegy for the dead and the increasingly mortal remainders.   It is a celebration.   How so?   Let's skip the theory and go to the facts.

The first fact is that I may not be frivolous enough.   I have always identified with the guilty party in the fine play, "A Walk In The Woods."   During drearily stalemated Cold War negotiations on reducing nuclear weapons, an older Russian diplomat and a young American negotiator go for a walk in the woods for a welcome change.   The American pleads with the Russian to tell him why the talks are stalemated.   The dour Russian tries to avoid this serious subject, then agrees to talk on one condition.   He tells the earnest young American, "You must say something frivolous."   How the play ends is beside the point.   I am too often too intensely focused on the serious.   So, when John Broderick and Dave Schweers noted in the spring of 2007 that it looked like our class would have no 50th reunion, but maybe we should still try to get together, I answered that I was not up for something merely frivolous.   I think I said that I didn't want to go to the East Coast for a cocktail party and five minutes with this old friend, ten minutes with another and learning nothing but who had how many spouses, who had a heart by-pass and who had become filthy rich.

Jane Sessler, '57   Fran Henke, '56   Barbara Gilson, '57   Buster & Art Kaufman, '56
(first 3 photos by Fred Feingold)

HISTORY—IS THAT WHAT WE ARE?

"The fact that I never write to anyone does not indicate in any way that I do not think of them often over a period of forty years." Fred Feingold, August 1996

Our lives in the 40s and 50s are history. I love history. I love reading good history. I've tried to write history. History tells us our address in time and space. It gives us our cultural DNA. The history that we've lived, the stories in which we appear personally, tell us the most about ourselves. Wouldn't we be different people if grandparents or parents had not fled Europe for America—fled the Irish potato famine, the English factories and class system, the murderous anti-Semitism of Russian pogroms, the Bolshevik Revolution, the Nazi regime, or the misery of post-war refugee camps? Wouldn't we be different if our parents had not lived through the Great Depression? Wouldn't we have learned in a different school if Sea Cliff had not once been a Methodist campground and then a popular summer town whose housing and assets were torn up by hurricanes and left behind by the ever extending reach of the automobile? How many of us would have become classmates and friends except for the forces of world history and family history?

I'm the over-confident, do-it-yourself type who thinks he can build his own house and also thinks he can be his own psychologist. I finally got rid of the house I built to someone who thought my grade C carpentry quaint and didn't mind a washing machine in the dirt floored crawl space. Having recognized and rid myself of my lumber and stone building dreams, in 2001 I decided to go into historical reconstruction, requiring nothing heavier than mind-craft and word-craft. I began gathering material for a small history of the 40s and 50s in Sea Cliff. Call it a house or home for the soul. Once built, I thought, I might get a better idea of who I am and what Sea Cliff and our school meant. Maybe the story would mean something to other people too. I found a few old friends and coaxed, beguiled, badgered and bullied them into writing what they remembered. I envisioned bolting the pieces together in something like Thornton Wilder's "Our Town." Several people sent interesting pieces of history, but I was not good at coaxing, beguiling, badgering or bullying. The project fizzled. It came to mind again, in a new form, when John and Dave proposed a reunion.

Yes, that's a confession—the program I proposed for the reunion was not entirely new and was self-serving. I was and I am presumptuous to assume that what interests me might also interest others in the class and even people who were never in our class or our communities. In 1957, as co-editor of the *Cliffonian*, I wrote many of the staccato summaries that accompanied each senior picture. They were little formula pieces that didn't do much justice to the person. Who didn't dislike "snobby, conceited people?"

Twenty or thirty people were to be "found at Dobkins." Half the class was some version of quiet and easy going, the other half liked pizza or had a "good sense of humor." Ho hum. We were individualized mainly by our nicknames—Knox, Porky, Brud, Sam, Mickie, Lo-Lo, Cappi, Bones. A reunion and a follow-up "yearbook" I thought, would give me a chance to try again to avoid the clichés that Dr. Shulman had constantly warned against, and I'd try to write more interesting profiles and a fuller story of the class.

I thought that my hope for a fruitful reunion had a chance because I had heard often enough from people who had enjoyed a class reunion far more than they expected. Some of them had gone to a reunion as Sourpuss and returned as Mr. or Ms. Smiley. When I began to sound out people in our class, I heard such stories. In July 2007 Fred Feingold replied, "It will be strange. I'm up for it. . . . . I never went to these things, but about three years ago my college love took me to her 40th at Barnard, and it was as though only a month had passed when I saw all her roommates. Similarly at 40th cousins' reunion last summer which I almost (typically) was not going to attend. . . . Both were wonderful."

Our class had not gathered since our Carole Brown (Muttee) spearheaded the effort that created our 25th in 1982. Since then we had scattered even more, changed names, and begun to succumb to age. Yet when I began sounding people out on a 51st Reunion, only one person was not interested in coming—too many unpleasant memories. On the weekend of September 12, 2008 forty-three of our class ages 69 to 71 came to the reunion in Sea Cliff. Guests brought the total to 69. In most minds, however, we arrived not as senior citizens, but as we were when last seen and heard as a group of 110. Many of us were simultaneously near 70 and still seventeen. Fred Feingold also wrote at the end of his first response, "Slow to mature; I am now a fairly sound 17 year old." Maybe no matter how much we do mature, we are always still that earlier person. We could go from here to what theoretical physicists say about the nature of time (or its non-existence), but psychology might be more fruitful. Or maybe we might just note that as one wit has written, "I never thought I'd grow up to be an adult."

In thinking about what we might get from reflection on our lives, I asked Allan Schwartz, our salutatorian and a distinguished psychologist at the University of Rochester, for a few thoughts. Allan happens to be an expert on suicide, but that still requires an appreciation of life. He referred me to "The Up Series" of documentaries in which Michael Apter follows the lives of 15 British children from 7 into their 30s, one film for each 7 years. The repeated opening of each film quotes, "Give me the child at seven and I will show you the man…"

Apter makes a good case for the truth of that formula, but as the number of classmates I talked to grew large, the less they seemed like my fellow students in 1957. Sure, Barbara Gilson may still be the class wit and Ro Greenfield is certainly one of the most enthusiastic, and Pete and Carole who were "cutest couple" and who may not be described now as cute, but they are still a couple that hunts and shoots together and gives each other presents like tickets to climb glaciers in the Swiss Alps.   But even they are quite different than the students they were.   If we had been cruel enough to vote "most likely to commit suicide," the two who did would have received no votes at all.   And yours truly, once "most likely to succeed," can only look back the last 51 years of dabbling in careers and geography and ask, succeed at what?   In my best Dickensian-Victorian   prose I can say only, Dear Reader, I will dust off the superlative if this book becomes a success for you.

Cherry Campbell   Janice Painter   Pete Swanson   Tom Wolfe   Sue Frost

Cherry w/husband (left)   Janice Painter   Charles (Pete) Swanson   Tom Wolfe   Sue Frost

2nd Grade Sea Cliff

Sea Cliff: One In Three

The number people who gathered in Sea Cliff School as the Class of '57 grew suddenly in our freshman year, 1953 when students from St. Boniface chose the nearby public school over more distant Catholic high schools, and when graduates of Glen Head and Glenwood middle schools came to the district's one high school.   I should include here a short history of each community, but "a little knowledge is a dangerous thing" the poet said, so for the most part I write about Sea Cliff which I know best.   The following I wrote in 2001 as an introduction to stories of Sea Cliff that I was trying to collect from classmates.   I did not collect enough, but some are woven into this history from time to time.

OUR TOWN, OUR LIVES

1939

This is the year a few men in the town of Glen Head, in New York City, in Roslyn and Sea Cliff villages, and in the provincial city of Nice, France waited impatient and worried while their wives gave birth.   The events were special to each man and woman—their personal difficulty and pain, joy and hope, burden or pride, and their surprise wanted or unwanted.   Beyond a few close friends and relatives, no one else in a world of two or three billion other citizens cared or even knew.   The babies were no one unusual--no savior, no genius, no baby with two heads or three eyes, no twins inseparably joined, no quintuplets.   These babies were us, or most of us, the writers of this collection of memories about the village in which all of us would soon be living if we had been born there.

In 1939 the village of Sea Cliff was adrift in time between its loud and hymn-joyous beginning not long after the Civil War as a Methodist campground and summer colony and today's upscale, prosperous and fashionable village whose main streets are punctuated by galleries, antique shops, crafts stores, studios, cafes, and delicatessens.   It was a village where almost every block had several homes whose turrets, porches, carriage ports, stained glass windows, gables or gingerbread trim were often hidden in soot, covered in heavy layers of peeling paint, or aged to soft decay by years in rain and sun.   The homeowners' burdens of the time had not yet been valued as antiquities.   Sea Cliff's decaying and unfashionable housing made for affordable living, illustrating the unpleasant fact of the ages that vastly more affordable housing is created by decay than by planning.

Intersection Sea Cliff and Central Ave; photo V. Epanchin

Unlike many of the Gold Coast towns that surrounded it, Sea Cliff was a town built for and catering to Americans just beginning to aspire to lives beyond work and survival. Methodists, we should remember, were not far removed from their origins in England and the American South as a somewhat radical church for the lower classes. Sea Cliff covered a square mile on top of a ridge of sand and rock rubble left 10,000 years earlier as the afterthought of a glacier. That the land of Sea Cliff was a on the high lip of this geological garbage meant little to its founders. The view from that lip of rubble and the usually quiet waters below being within an hour by train and a few hours by ferry from New York meant everything. Most important was its availability to the masses of people craving relief for body and soul from the New York City's tenements, factories, crowds, crime, and streets littered with garbage and always ripe with horse manure. Churches were the first to meet the needs of working class city people with prayer camps in the country. After the Civil War their popularity soared. Where demand is high and supply low, entrepreneurs step in with capital. A group of New York City investors organized the Sea Cliff Grove and Metropolitan Camp Ground Association, appointed four pastors to their board, raised over a half million dollars and bought 240 acres from the heirs of James Carpenter whose family had held the land since 1677 under the Musketo Cove Patent issued by the English king.

By 1871 public records contain maps for the entire community of Sea Cliff Grove from Littleworth Lane to Glen Cove with thousands of 50 foot by 100 foot lots, a tenting park centered on a chapel, an amphitheatre tabernacle, and bath houses scattered along. The Association benefitted handsomely from the sale of lots, and used its capital and profits to build a $270,000 Tabernacle, an Old Ladies' Home, a chapel for clergy, a steamboat dock, boardwalk, water reservoir, and bath houses along the beach. Soon Sea Cliff had a Catholic church, the Plymouth Brethren, and a large Salvation Army house of worship on 12th Avenue between Main and Roslyn. Worshippers at these places tended to come from the ranks of America's working poor—sometimes simply the poor. The first presence of the Episcopal Church, the church of the later labeled WASPs, were cottages and dining halls in the then malarial swampland around Scudder's Pond to accommodate poor children it sponsored from New Jersey and New York City. (Episcopalians, please take no offense—history is what it is and the risk of malaria was more than offset by the benefits and pleasures of a cottage by swamp, pond and beach.)

Many of the village's first residents first came as worshippers and tent dwellers, arriving by steamboat or train, then taking a horse drawn stage to their destination. Soon they were buying lots. While America's super rich built their mansions in Sands Point, Glen Cove, Brookville, Oyster Bay, and Roslyn, several newly affluent families chose the water view sites in Sea Cliff. Others combined the small lots into plots suitable for fine homes.

By the end of the 'Gilded Age' New Yorkers had built large summer homes around the edges of the old campground where they could have larger lots. A steamboat came and went daily from a busy pier where Shore Road turned and ran flat along the water to Glen Cove. A cog railway ran up and down the bluff for those who did not want to walk hundreds of stairs. Several large hotels did a thriving business. For two miles along the shorefront visitors sauntered along a wide wooden boardwalk with the waves at high tide lapping under their feet. On weekends hundreds of tourists and occasional residents arrived by train at Sea Cliff station and were carried into town by coach or taxi.

The explosion of automobiles and parkways in the 1920s began to siphon away some of the visitors. They could now motor to ocean beaches or farther out on the Island to new attractions. Sea Cliff had never been a town for the very rich, and when the stock market crash of 1929 gave way to the Great Depression even fewer visitors came. Stores closed. Hotels failed or became rooming houses. Apartments were abandoned. The upkeep of the big old homes became a burden. Prices dropped. A few city people still came for the summers, but not many. Then, in 1938 a powerful hurricane, in those days before the naming of storms, roared in from the Atlantic, crossed Long Island, churned Hempstead Harbor into a raging sea. Oceanic waves chewed up piers and the decaying boardwalk. When the sun came out little remained except a few leaning bulkheads and pilings supporting only air.

If anyone were inclined to rebuild very much, war soon diverted their attention. By 1945 if you said 'Sea Cliff' in New York City or on the South Shore of Long Island, people almost always asked, "Where is that?"

It was where many of our parents, during or after the Depression or World War II found housing working people and veterans could afford to rent or buy. Sea Cliff is where we grew up in the three decades between its ruin as a resort and its reincarnation as combination live-in museum and comfortable affluent suburb. Our Sea Cliff had boundaries that were not yet blurred by television and Internet, a consolidated school district, the ease of jet flight, and a car in every garage. People commuted, of course, to Wall Street and the factories of Long Island City, and now and then a family left for a vacation in Florida or the Catskills. Most of the time and especially until you finished school, you lived almost entirely within the boundaries of Sea Cliff. Maybe we were provincial, but in those years Sea Cliff had almost everything necessary to sustain life and the imagination.

As we grew up many of us grew restless with the boundaries. We left for college and then for places much farther than those places our parents or grandparents had come from. Some of us stayed. All of us recognize the truth that Vachel Lindsay wrote about small towns:

> Let not our town be large, remembering
> That little Athens was the Muses' home,
> That Oxford rules the heart of London still,
> That Florence gave the Renaissance to Rome.

Sea Cliff gave us much and we have taken it with us to many other places. The time has come for us to give something back to Sea Cliff.

Sea Cliff Station, photo V Epanchin

ARRIVAL: AMERICA MOVING

Malkin, Brown, Sprague, Allen, Berroyer

Very few of us were born in Sea Cliff, Glenwood, or Glen Head. Our families came with a purpose. After the Great Depression and after the War, Americans were on the move. They could choose where to live. And soon immigrants, displaced persons and refugees from Europe began to arrive. They often had little choice and settled where they had friends or family or where someone said they should go. For most young families these communities were part of getting ahead, settling down, or to use a phrase in vogue today—of hope and change. If you wanted to get out of an apartment in Queens, Brooklyn, or the Bronx, housing in a these little commuter towns was cheap. The air was clean, the streets lined with trees and green lawns, and in summer there was the beach. They were havens of affordability surrounded by Fitzgerald's "Gold Coast" towns of Port Washington and Sands Point, Locust Valley, and Brookville.

Sea Cliff's Victorian "cottages" had seen better days and the stores on its once thriving main streets were mostly boarded up. At Glenwood Landing the large resort and bathing spa call Keratsoni's had given way to the Long Island Lighting Company's brick power plant, its smoke belching stacks, and its giant mounds of coal. My parents bought our home on 12th Avenue from Roy Hendrickson whose father had run a stable in Sea Cliff--$4,000 and Hendrickson held the mortgage. The 75 year old house had been moved to its small lot to make way for Levine's paper and candy store. The side and back yards were no more than 10 ft wide, with Hendrickson's welding shop on one side. Our dining room window looked into business teacher Eleanor Zipperian's kitchen window. Across 12th Avenue a large weed filled lot had once held a hotel, and it was fine for kids to play ball or build snow forts until it became the town parking lot.

Buster Kaufman pitching to brother Art in lot between 12th Ave and Sea Cliff Ave. 1947

Sports fans at Clifton Park.   Photo by Nik Epanchin

From left: Feingold, ___, Bob Cunningham, Ian Ronald, Lee Berroyer, Ceil Snayd, Ro Greenfield, Denny Gallagher, Jimmy O'Donnell, Ed Bolitho, ___; Back: Gail Capobianco, Ruth Ahearn (?)

"I Dare Us" (from Diane Schweikert, Class of '60)

Although my family had a long history in Sea Cliff and I was born there, my first real memory is of our return from a two year sojourn in California during WWII. We returned, my father, mother, sister and baby brother in the dead of night after a three day bus ride across country. It was a snowy starry night with air so crisp and clear that it took my breath away and excited me at the same time. Standing in the street in front of my grandparents' house at 76 Main Avenue on that night thrilled me; I was barely five years old. The only thing since that has come close to the magic of that sky is Van Gogh's Starry Night ; I once had a dream as an adult that I had arrived back in Sea Cliff again in the middle of just such a snowy starry night. I jumped off the train and got on a sled and proceeded to wind my way down and around the many hills and lanes of Sea Cliff with my long white hair flowing behind me. Finally I came to what I thought must be my house. My husband and children were inside. I knocked on the door until they came but they immediately told me that I must go back, I couldn't come in and they shut the door. I cried, but they didn't open the door again.

Consider this theory: My tears, my wild mane of hair flowing freely, my excitement on the sled in the night, all expressions of ecstasy.   The door closing was not shutting me out of Sea Cliff, it was shutting them out.   They are locked in the present and unable to enter the Sea Cliff that I can never leave.   I believe that when people speak of not being able to " go back " they are mistaken.   If where they want to go was instrumental in their forming, they can never really leave.   What they are longing for is the comfort of their own identity.   "The human heart is like a wild bird seeking shelter in remote places ". We can go back, if we accept ourselves back.   I dare us, in this collaborative book, to go back, to us again.

A few families like the Spragues had been in Sea Cliff for several generations, their lives woven into the town's fabric. Betty, Dorie and Buzzy Sprague were 4th generation Sea Cliff residents, descendants of great grandfather Sprague, a mason who plastered the ceiling in the Methodist church (now town hall and museum). His son "Gramps" Sprague started life in 19th Century Sea Cliff as a cook for the "Oyster House" by the power plant. He was also an oysterman when oysters grew abundantly in the harbor, and he caught eels on the sand flats off Laurel Avenue. Next he worked at the old water company, then with his wife opened "Sprague's Fish Market" near Longo's bar. Betty's father played basketball, became the school's premier track star, and drove a Bohack's delivery wagon taking fish and groceries all over Sea Cliff and up and down all the hills for 10 cents a wagon load.

A Veteran's Family

From Judy Brown

When World War II ended, my parents were among the hundreds of thousands of Americans who found that they had conquered not only Japan and Germany but the Great Depression and that conquest had blessed them with new choices. While my father served in France for three and a half years, my mother, my baby sister Jessie and I lived in an army camp in Lacey Park, Hatboro, Pennsylvania. My parents chose to live near the water and among the many old houses fallen from grace in Sea Cliff they found a tall, brown-shingled house at 134 7th Avenue with 3 porches stacked one above the other and facing Hempstead Harbor. My father's wages could not cover the mortgage on the $7,000 home so he rented the third floor as an apartment until we became more prosperous. I was eight and had never been in such a big house, but with the tenant on the third floor, the attic being the fourth, our own space became the above ground basement and the main floor. My parents used one room of the first floor for their bedroom, the others being our living room, bathroom, kitchen, and small pantry. I was assigned a room in the finished basement/ground floor with clanking and hissing pipes over my head. In time, they actually lulled me to sleep. When the coal truck came to deliver for the furnace the loads roared down the chute into the bin next to the furnace. Every night and morning my father came down to the basement, opened the cast iron door to the fire box, scooped up great shovels of shiny black coal and pitched them onto the flames.

The porches of the main floor and the third floor were my favorite places. Several concord grape vines grew up to the third floor and filtered the world outside through their green shade. I could look out from the second porch to the harbor and see a tiny piece of Appleby's, the start of the channel to Wah Chang's tungsten plant and some of the boats moored inside the jetty that reached far out into the harbor from the J.P.Morgan Estate in Glen Cove, separating the harbor from the winds and seas of Long Island Sound.

CITY TO SEA CLIFF: THE KAUFMANS

1944

In 1938 my father had already been promoted from a runner to a clerk for a broker on Wall Street, but he and my mother could barely afford to pay the rent on his $19 a month.   They could not afford twins.   When the doctor came out of the delivery room and told my father, my father shot back, "You're a dammed liar."   Maybe because my mother could not breast feed the twins, by fall she was pregnant again.   A week after she gave birth to me in April 1939 the Wall Street broker cut my father's salary by $5 to $14 a month.

During the war we had moved two or three times from one row of anonymous city apartments in Queens to another.   The war was sucking up single men like a vacuum cleaner.   For married men with children, like my father, it offered new opportunities with real pay.   He had dropped out of high school in the 10th grade, but he had already learned algebra and geometry, and he enrolled in Delahanty Institute and learned to run a metal lathe and a milling machine.   He took a job in a munitions factory making bomb fuses. He brought one home--a brass cylinder the size of his index finger with large holes in it. The bombs were going to Germany to kill Germans.   My grandmother, my father's mother, was German, but she lived in Manhattan.   Hitler was the only other German we had heard of.   He stood for all Germans—the enemy.   We were going to beat him.   My parents were sure of that.   God was on our side.

My brothers and I had our own war in the alley behind our apartment block.   We had already lost.   The one time my mother put us into the alley behind our house alone, bigger kids from up the alley came and beat us up.   We already knew a better place to live--the country.   The country was where my mother's mother and several uncles and aunts lived.   It was 'the country' because it had green trees and green lawns and across from my grandmother's house a swampy park with ducks on the ponds.   The country was the village of Roslyn on the north shore of Long Island.

My mother, the source of food and justice, rag dolls with buttons for eyes, and bed time stories, had grown up in the country with a dog named Jud who walked around the village with her delivering newspapers.   As the generals were planning D Day at Normandy, we moved to a row of crumbling stucco apartments with tiny lawns in Roslyn Heights.   We had a tree in front of our apartment.   We played alone in a vacant lot, and we played with other kids in the alley between the two rows of apartments.   We sifted the coal ashes thrown into the gravel side street and brought home chunks of coal and coke for the furnace in the cellar.   We tried to plant a Victory Garden in the back yard to help the war effort.   Roslyn was good for two years.   Then the landlord decided to sell the apartments.   My mother and father were outraged by the price.   "The walls get so damp," my mother said, "moss grows out of the cracks."

Second grade had been going only a month when we moved away from Roslyn.   If Roslyn had been good, Sea Cliff was a boy's dream--at least this boy's.

"Why is it called Sea Cliff?" I asked my mother.

"Because it is on the harbor and it has steep bluffs by the water," she said.

My brother Art, a year older and a twin of my brother Bill, said, "Maybe when the discoverers first saw it they were in a boat, and they pointed and said, "See cliff?"

What mattered most to me was that we were moving up in the world.   The first up was our apartment.   It was not *up* because it was fancy.   In fact the apartment was in a house like most houses in Sea Cliff, on the way down.   The narrow spiky Victorian house at 158 Prospect Avenue had been divided into upper and lower apartments.   The lower apartment began with the partly above ground basement and included all of the first floor and porch except what used to be the main entry hall.   That hall had been blocked off to become the entry landing from which we climbed to our apartment on the second and third stories.   The original Victorian banister ran broad and dark and slick from bedrooms to entry hall.   A narrow steep stair between two bedrooms led up again to a small square widow's watch with a narrow window that offered a view over the tops of other houses and trees to a faintly discernable patch of water where Hempstead Harbor opened into Long Island Sound.   To see for such a distance, to see over the water to a horizon to places we could not go, was the same as seeing the future.   It was out there, ahead of me.

That first day in Sea Cliff, a sunny day in October, my mother walked with the three of us down 14th Avenue. It ended at the top of the bluff, the cliff of Sea Cliff. We descended and counted the 83 stairs of the wooden stairway that ended at the beach by an old pier, Newell's Pier. We stood on the sand and looked under the pier and north up the widening funnel of Hempstead harbor toward Long Island Sound. I asked my mother if the Sound was the Atlantic Ocean. She said, no, it led to the ocean and across the ocean was England and Europe.

I knew about England. During the war we received letters from my mother's young second cousin, a girl named Daphne, who described the sound of German bombs falling around the hospital where she lay with a broken leg. Europe was where the war ended. I looked at the harbor and out to the Sound and imagined England and Europe. My mother promised that when summer came she would teach us to swim. I wanted to swim out into the harbor. My mother had an octagonal bronze medal showing a powerful swimmer plowing through waves. My mother could not run because when she was six, crossing a street with her new set of paper Dolly Dimple dolls, she had fallen and been stepped on by the horse drawing a milk wagon, but she could swim, and my father could not. She swam so well that she had won that medal in a swimming competition in this same harbor when she was fifteen. I believed she would teach me to be the swimmer on that medal. Nothing was more important to me during the fall of 1946 and the winter and next spring than the coming of summer and learning to swim.

Many times we walked up Prospect Avenue and at its summit into the small park that had a panoramic view of the harbor and beyond to J.P. Morgan's breakwater at the shore of the neighboring town of Glen Cove. Morgan had been the richest man in the world, my mother told us. She also told us of the time my her father, a feisty little English immigrant who had risen from being a stable boy for lawyer Townsend Scudder to the proprietor of his own newspaper and antique shop, had rowed a boat onto the shore of Morgan's estate. Morgan's guards had ordered him off, but he had refused to leave because he knew the beaches were public land.

A seven year old boy absorbs stories without thinking about them. He absorbs a place and imagines what he can do in it, but he doesn't understand what it will do to him until he's long gone and looking back as I am now. Sea Cliff was not just a town. It was a place with a view. Nothing about Sea Cliff would ever hold you back. From that first view over the water to places unseen, to school, to Scout leaders, teachers, friends, the parents of friends, and neighbors Sea Cliff would become for me a place with an ever widening view of the future.

◆ ◆ ◆

A NEW AMERICAN COMES TO SEA CLIFF

Nik Epanchin

Vladimir, Nik, Nadine, and Paul Epanchin, France, 1949

I hated Thursdays that summer of 1951 when I was 12.   On Thursdays, *Newsday*, Nassau County's suburban paper, was extra thick and heavy with the weekly advertising insert.

I was not only a new newspaper boy, I was a new American, or at least an immigrant.   Shortly after V-J day in 1945, my Russian born parents had submitted applications to the American consul in France, asking permission to emigrate to the USA. We were living on the Mediterranean coast of France in the country's fourth largest city, Nice.   My Uncle Nicolas, father's brother, who had immigrated sometime before 1910 and lived in Cleveland, sponsored our application.   After some 6 years of   trials and tribulations, we   received permission to enter the USA.   This would be my parents second and last move of their lives.   They had fled Saint Petersburg, Russia in 1920, part of the great flood of "White" Russians fleeing the Bolshevik Revolution.

Everything had been set for a March 1951 departure, a few weeks before I would turn twelve and my parents would have to dig into their scant savings to pay full fare for me.   However the aging and problem-riddled SS America, which we were to board on her next crossing to the USA, experienced a major break down with an unknown repair schedule in New York.   The dark cloud over my parents cleared when agreements between transatlantic ship lines permitted, in cases of *force majeure*, to change vessels at no extra charge.   We switched to the HMS Queen Elizabeth whose scheduled departure was several weeks before the birthday.

In those last few weeks my parents still had to negotiate the tense last minute illegal sale of our apartment lease.   For weeks before boarding the train to Paris my mother's tears flowed freely as she bid farewell to her parents and to the friends with whom she had shared thirty years of immigrant life.   She also had left her secretarial work which had added to father's part time work as photographer and earned just enough to feed us. Father, at age 52, was going to have to start looking for work again.   To add to the general upheavals, he almost missed our train from Paris to Cherbourg.

The weather in Cherbourg was atrocious with 120 km per hour winds.   The harbor, damaged by World War II bombings, could not accommodate docking the Queen Elizabeth.   The huge black and white ship lay anchored offshore and her mass dragging her anchors dangerously.   At the port Cunard and French officials discussed whether she might leave without picking up her French passengers.   We were eventually ferried to her side and transferred into her holds.   Heavy seas followed us across the Atlantic, making the ship roll and pitch in long slow stomach floating see-saw movements which I enjoyed immensely.   My parents also worried that immigration officials in New York would take note of the scar tissue in the X-rays of father's lungs and forbid our entry into America.   In the Port of New York, we stood our turn in long lines.   Having arrived on board the Queen Elizabeth may have helped our image since she was a classy and posh vessel which did not usually transport poor immigrants.   An immigration official examined our papers, pounded each with his stamp and waved us through into New York City, not Ellis Island.

At the dock, on a dreary afternoon in late April, Uncle Nicolas waited to meet us. With him was the sister of father's first wife who had died in childbirth—Aunt Sonia. Aunt Sonia lived not too far from the New York City docks in a place called Sea Cliff. She suggested that since our voyage from Nice had been long and hard, we should rest a few days in Sea Cliff before proceeding to Cleveland.

Aunt Sonia had made arrangements with her Sea Cliff Russian community friends to take us in.   This community, she told us, comprised almost ten percent of Sea Cliff's population of 5,000.   It included some members of Russian aristocracy including the wife and several descendants of General Vrangel who had been the commander in chief of the White Russian Army during the Bolshevik Revolution.

Our entire possessions consisting of 7 or 8 trunks were off-loaded that day, and our caravan, resembling something out of *Grapes of Wrath*, proceeded to Sea Cliff.   We arrived after dark and settled in a house on 8th Avenue on the corner of Park Way.   The owners were away on vacation.   After several days of meeting various Russians, many of whom had lived for years in France, our parents decided not to proceed to Cleveland, but to try their fortune in Sea Cliff.

What amazed me about Sea Cliff was its greenery and even more its numerous gray squirrels. Despite many hours of attempting to feed them, they never permitted me to get close to them. This kind of exposure to nature was unheard of in Nice.

After a month in the house on 8-th Avenue, we split up. Paul, age 6, stayed with my parents who moved in with a Russian family on Glenlawn Avenue behind the Schweers'. Alex, age 9, was taken in by the Hartmans on 15-th Avenue where he shared a room with their son George who became his bosom buddy. I was given a private room in the Tatishchev residence on Glen Avenue. Mrs. Tatishchev and her sisters had been mother's friend in Paris in the 20's when they were all young refugees. My room at Tatishchev's was in the attic and stifling hot as summer came on. Our family saw each other frequently and we spent Sundays together, first at church, then for meals at my parents' place.

In July 1951 we moved into a street level apartment at 309 Sea Cliff Avenue, one of the two streets of Sea Cliff lined with small stores and wide enough for parking on both sides. Created on the ground floor of an old store, our Sea Cliff Avenue apartment was not choice real estate. The ceilings were 12 foot high and 8 foot partitions separated the three rooms. I could hear my parents in their room which also served as living room and they could hear my brothers and me. Only the bathroom walls rose to the ceiling for full privacy. The back room had been made into a kitchen. Its window faced the very small asphalted backyard. In our living room two big store display windows faced the street. These had pull down shades which father had to adjust almost daily. The dark and damp basement was shared with the upstairs tenants. Despite the apartment's short comings, it was a great pleasure to live as a family again.

While my father, a medical doctor, unsuccessfully searched for work, my mother began giving private French and Russian lessons. I too wanted to work. Boys my age were carrying sacks of newspapers around town for *Newsday*. Delivering newspapers would not only earn pocket money but also improve my English.

In Nice I had acquired a smattering of English. I had had one semester of it taught by a teacher who, my mother said, spoke English with a horrible southern French or Niçois accent. Since arriving, my English had improved slightly. Upon our arrival, my mother had enrolled us in the local school on Carpenter Avenue. Despite her efforts to keep me with my peers, I was transferred from a technical French 6th grade into 3rd grade where I was a head taller that my class mates. The teacher used flash cards to teach simple arithmetic. Knowing the correct number in French, my challenge was to say it in English before the rest of the class could solve the problem.

My parents who spoke English flawlessly, but with an accent, contacted *Newsday*. The distribution manager assigned me a route. I had no choice. My route took me up and down the steepest hills in Sea Cliff - Adams, Brown, Franklin and Dayton Streets, with their interconnecting streets west of Glenlawn Avenue, plus portions of Littleworth Lane, Laurel and Highland Avenues. Whether on foot or on bicycle, most boys carried cloth newspaper bags over their shoulder. This bag option was not practical for my route. Luckily, using my meager savings, I had recently bought a five dollar Clipper bicycle, quite old and not as responsive and light as the skinny tired bike with hand brakes I had left four months earlier in my native France. The Clipper was what I had and it served. I tore it down and reassembled it, discarding all non-essential parts such as fenders, top tube bubble, kick stand and various decorative items. I attached a large wire basket over the front wheel.

Usually I could deliver the papers to my 80 plus customers in two trips. With the Thursday supplement almost doubling the paper's bulk, I needed at least three and more often four. On rainy Thursdays I took extra care and made up to five trips.

In the early afternoon the Newsday supervisor dropped off the papers at our apartment. On Thursdays the paper came in multiple bundles. The separate bundle of advertising sections had to be inserted into the center of the news section, more than doubling the weight of the newspaper. I usually did this in our back yard. Upon completion I would load the papers into my basket and pedal off with them riding heavy over the front wheel. I rode down Central Avenue, turned by the Youth Center, around Central Park, then up 17th Avenue, across Glen Avenue to the beginning of my route.

I already knew the names of the trees in Central Park and rehearsed them as I cruised by. To better integrate into the local fabric and learn English as quickly as possible, my parents had Alex join Cub Scouts and me Boy Scouts. I became a member of Sea Cliff Troop 43. Scoutmaster Ed Bolitho, or Mr. B, as we called him, assigned me to the Wolf Patrol led by patrol leader Arty Kaufman. Arty, his brother Buster (now Wallace) and their friend Howie Goldick, all future Eagle Scouts, tried to teach me the names and the identification clues of the various trees in Central Park for an upcoming contest during a campout Jamboree in that park. They looked at me, frustrated and astonished, as I fumbled for these names in my broken English.

Once on my route, I was often struck by the size of the homes on those hilly streets, their fresh paint, their trimmed shrubs, their soft green lawns, the big shady trees. Some had driveways and garages. An occasional shiny car stood in the drive. A few had swimming pools. Usually I was the only person on the quiet streets. I thought about our life in the three room old store. I swore to myself to never talk about these beautiful homes to my parents. They did not need to know.

I delivered my papers quickly and hoped I would not meet and have to speak to my customers.   I had little to say I thought, and I was sure I would say it wrong.   To my relief I seldom saw anyone while making my deliveries between 2 and 4 in the afternoon, the delivery period required by Newsday.   The streets at that time of day were usually empty and though I passed through front gates to reach the front porches of many customers to drop off the paper, rarely did I see children in the yards.   The occasional dog charging me from a yard or barking from behind a fence did not worry me.   The more unpleasant encounters with dogs while riding my bike did.   The dogs would chase me and attempt to nip my ankles causing me to erratically steer my heavily loaded and delicately balanced bike, but I served my time without a bite.

The one person on my route who I talked to was not a customer.   Madame Castelli had come from France several years before my family.   She actually came from Nice, the city of my birth.   She was about my mother's age and when she would spot me she would walk out of her yard where she was hanging up laundry and we would chat in French with our southern French accents.   Occasionally, she would offer me some bread with a hard piece of chocolate which reminded me of the typical "gouté" or snack French kids were given upon returning from school in the afternoon.   I loved the bread and chocolate, but did not look forward to our chats.   Her house was on Adams Street near the beginning of my route and chatting with her meant I would deliver my last paper at the bottom of Laurel Avenue at least half an hour later than I had hoped.

Only one person would interrupt the solitary work of a shy delivery boy.   Towards the bottom of Laurel Avenue whenever Mr. Cadiz saw me, he would make it a point of starting a conversation. No subject was too trivial, ranging from simple school questions to my impressions of Sea Cliff.   Yes or no answered most of these questions.   When he asked if my parents read Newsday, I emphatically replied, "No, it's not a very good paper you know".

Fridays were the exception to my silence.   That was collection day when I had to bolster my courage and attempt to tell customers how much they owed.   I hated this task, but it improved my English as invariably I had to argue with several customers.   They would claim the paper had not been delivered at all or had been placed in the wrong spot and that therefore they did not owe anything for that particular day.   The subscription was 60 cents a week and though many of my customers had big homes and new cars even they could fall behind in their payments.   Since I had to pay Newsday on time, I had to carry the delinquents' payment from my occasional ten and twenty cents tips.   Others I never saw as they worked in the "City" and came home late.   They left the moneys due in a predetermined spot, a milk box or under a mat, and usually payment came with a very generous tip.

Collection of subscription money had a hidden benefit.   As apprehensive as I was about meeting Americans, collection time gave me the opportunity to glance inside my customer's homes, even if it was only the front parlor. While I waited for the lady of the house to find her purse and then count the correct change usually including a small tip, I glimpsed the way these people lived. Many had mats by the front door declaring "Welcome". In the foyers hung framed "God Bless This House" embroideries and colored prints of jagged peaks of distant mountains. Many had something I had never seen in ordinary people's houses, natural wood paneling.

By the end of the summer, at the beginning of the new school year, it became clear that continuing with this paper route was going to interfere with my school work. This was a happy conclusion to my first American job. I had done it well enough and saved some money, but I had no love for selling or pedaling up and down hills with heavy loads. Some boys expanded their routes or took on an extra one. I was glad to have none. The last person I had to talk to in this business venture was my route supervisor. It was a short painful conversation for me, but one he had participated in many times. Lacking a replacement for me, the supervisor urged me to stay on saying that my English had improved so much that now I would be able to recruit new subscribers and be awarded prizes. (From time to time *Newsday* sponsored subscription contests with successful sales boys receiving prizes from pens to tickets to Yankees, Giants and Dodgers baseball games. Lacking the self-confidence required to approach potential customers, I had not participated in these circulation expansion programs.) I listened patiently but refused his enticing offers. When I walked away with my last week's earnings I was glad to be free again. I had asked for a job, done it well enough and quit. I was becoming an American.

Nik on his paper route, photo by Vladimir Epanchin

WHO WERE WE?

"God bless our memories as they sustain us when the moments are not just right."   Ruth Ahearn Loeber, spring, 2008.

"For the most part, we are no longer 'climbing' to be anywhere, to seek higher aspirations, or to look for 'greener grass.'"   Sandi Freedman

Senior Class Trip to Washington, DC in April 1957.   (Photo scan by Nik Epanchin)

It's worth remembering what we were in 1957 the year when we thought becoming stopped or had at least come under our own control.   Each of us lives inner and outer lives that distinguish us from everyone else in our class of 110, and even from the world of 7 billion.   We graduated as some 100 diverse and very different people.   (We had 110 yearbook photos, but a few had moved, others would graduate after summer school.)   Time worked its changes.   If this reunion had happened by accident in an airport waiting lounge, most of us would have flown off without having recognized each other.   Yet in the process of our deliberate reuniting 51 years later, it was clear that we still thought of ourselves as a group with our own common identity.   So why does that identity remain important so long after it dissolved physically?

Here at the beginning, I apologize to you for writing is largely my personal answer. I do not have the resources or the training to give you a statistical, sociological, or psychological analysis.   I do promise that what I write will be fully informed by the many hours of conversations I've had with members of the class and by the hundreds of letters and e mails we've exchanged.   Enough said. I stink at apologies and seldom read lengthy introductions.   Let's start with something like E pluribus unum (out of many, one).

We came from poor, middle class and rich families.   We were new or relatively new American families.   Less than a quarter of us had ancestors here before 1880.   Most came from Irish, German, Latin, Russian, French, English, and Polish parents and grandparents.   At least nine of us were born as citizens of foreign lands.   We attended Jewish synagogues or churches that were Catholic, Episcopal, Russian Orthodox, Friends, Plymouth Brethren, Methodist, Baptist or Lutheran, and a few claimed no religion.

From Jane Allen
I remember looking at the kids from St. Boniface very warily and also a bit snobbishly. After all, they were the intruders.   They were coming to 'my' school.   I think lines were drawn up quickly with "them" and "us".   It took a year or two to break down those barriers.

From Pete Marnane ('55):
I think both groups had a mistrust of each other until we became better acquainted.   Jane Allen's description was on the mark; although I don't think it took most of us a year to fully accept each other.   There were several factors that facilitated the assimilation.   For me, the pavilion provided a place to grow up with many contemporaries from SCHS and elsewhere and as a result I knew many of my freshman classmates both from the beach and St. Boniface.   That was probably the reason I was elected freshman class president. I think the boys who played freshman sports were very rapidly accepted into the freshman class. On the down side, St. Boniface never really had a physical ed. program and we suffered in comparison for that.   My first attempts at gymnastics were comical.

If you think about these origins, we represented lines of humanity that had been constantly at war with each other for centuries.   We too had moments of tension and war on our own scale.   As a grade schooler I walked home across the vacant lot opposite St. Boniface, and bigger boys from that school, their uniforms making them an army, shoved me around, tripped me, threatened worse.   I had the impression Catholic boys were tougher, meaner.   Meanwhile Ruth Ahearn notes, "my first love was a boy down the street, and a protest from my mother who reminded me that this was not to be.....Mom would chime that Catholics date Catholics!"

I don't recall that we set many, if any, boundaries on romance--ethnic or religious, in any case.   Our parents did.   Parents often got uneasy, outright upset, and sometimes near hysterical   when romance crossed the major religious lines: Catholic, Protestant, and Jew.   Or "the wrong kind."

My brother Art, president of the Student Council in his senior year ('55-6) first crossed the line when he began to date a girl my parents and many teachers considered "loose" and licentious. She was Mary Etta Belch whose father tended to the C.W. Post family's properties in the Carolinas and where Post College would soon arise. I recall only that Mary Etta could drink and swear comfortably and that she and my brother spent a lot of time in his car and on the Post Estate. In the summer of '55 when I was in South Dakota working as a digger on an archeological project, my mother's letter contained the following typical parental worry:

"We are trying our best to break up that Marietta combination. After talking with the teachers, we feel it quite necessary. All the boys refuse to take him to Brookville and Ellie, Clancy and Paul [my older cousin, her friend and boyfriend] were quite mad at her Sunday. So why don't your brother get wise to himself. Maybe he would like the job as cook next summer. (Really don't think he would although he might like the chance to get out there.) Don't mention this to him as both Dad and I have been talking to him very seriously, more Dad than I as you know I get very upset."

I suspect some parents were not happy about my brother dating their daughters after he attended a PTA meeting about parent-student conflict and announced that if a parent would not allow a girl to stay out at least an hour after a night movie so he and she could park at the beach and neck, then he would not take her out.

A couple of years later my brother was romancing Barbara Wade, a Catholic. Her parents and ours had as little influence on the lovers as the Montagus and Capulets had on Romeo and Juliet. So, they decided to blame each other. The Wades sent Barbara off to Georgetown Visitation in Washington, DC. They underestimated the power of love. Or was it rebellion? My brother triggered a red alert for our parents and hers when he drove his nosed and decked and glass-packed '50 Ford down to DC, sprung Barbara, and went to South Carolina intending to get married because that state had no waiting period. The four parents quickly united in common cause. They called out the police to stop this Episcopal-Catholic transgression. On their own free will Barbara and Art decided not to tie the knot. They returned home. Art quickly left for the U.S. Air Force.

We were a more tolerant generation than our parents, at least in our younger years. This was clear in the way we dealt with our prejudiced peers. Rosalie Greenfield remembers a number of anti-Semitic taunts, and Sandi Freedman feared a boy who would shout, "Dirty Jew" as she walked to school. Jane Allen said, "My dad quite a heated argument with a next door neighbor who didn't think that America was nice to open our doors to anyone, especially the Russians who were fleeing Communism. Our neighbor accused the Russians of being Communists and 'wanted to run them out of town on a rail'."

But Rosalie also recounts how her Irish Catholic boyfriend, Jimmy O'Donnell, showed up at her house with a black eye because he had fought another boy who mocked him for dating a Jew.   Sandi sometimes walked to school with Artie Hall or Pat Mills as a defense against the boy who called her Dirty Jew.   "Pat would beat him up."   This particular problem was solved ecumenically when Sandi's mother enlisted the priest's help.   Jane Allen became fast friends with two nearby Russian families who lived untroubled by their bigoted neighbor.   The distance and fear between Catholic school kids and public school kids evaporated quickly when we mixed in junior high.   Pete Marnane ('55) whom I once dreaded became my boss and mentor as chief lifeguard, and I began to try to imitate his cool and quick thinking in emergencies.

History, size, and location conspired in Sea Cliff, Glen Head, and Glenwood to frustrate and redirect the human tendency to live among "our own kind."   Glen Cove had its ethnic and racial neighborhoods.   Most larger towns had rich, middle class, working class and poor neighborhoods. Estates and the desire for privacy and status dominated places like Muttontown, Old Brookville, Locust Valley, the Shore Road of Roslyn, and Sands Point. In high school my brother Art dated Mary Etta Belch, whose father looked after the hounds and grounds on the C.W. Post (as in Post cereals) estate before we expected any of us would attend a commuter college there.   Within our own communities black people were so few a neighborhood was impossible.

We didn't have a race relations problem, but tolerance was not universal.   Our new art teacher, Katherine "Kitty" Strohe remembered into her 90s the prejudice she saw when the Mezzrow family moved to Sea Cliff for a few years.   Miss Strohe, a freewheeling young Greenwich Village veteran, found herself in a small minority of teachers uncomfortable among the old-timers.   Among the people who became her friends was Mae Mezzerow, the wife of jazz critic Milt Mezzerow and mother of my friend Milton who lived a few houses down 17th Ave from our first apartment.   Jazz was Negro music in the 1950s and Milt had tightly curled wiry reddish hair and tan skin and we considered him part Negro.   Strohe says that other teachers asked her, "Why do you go down to their house?"

"Because I'm very fond of Mae," she told them.   "I was so mad at the teachers who were nasty to Milton."

For elementary school kids the more interesting fact was that Milt's father was famous, not that he might be black.   But Milt's first days in school with the Class of '54 were not entirely smooth.   Jay Siegel remembers them well.   "Milton came to Sea Cliff School in sixth grade, the grade in which we had our first male teacher, Mr. Davis. . . . Milton was the first (and probably the only) black classmate that we ever had--at least I can't think of any others.   He hadn't been in our class very long--perhaps a day or two--when we had some sort of activity (perhaps a spelling bee) that required us to line up along the blackboard in the front of the room.   We all started to line up, and no one wanted to stand next to Milton.   I can still see the shuffling and re-shuffling of places as one after another of my classmates moved away from him.   For whatever reason I went and stood next to Milton, he probably on the end, and me next to him.   I probably haven't done many bold things in my life, but I have always been proud and happy that I did that.   The prejudice and segregation faded away quickly in the next several days.   I very seriously doubt that what I did had anything to do with it--everyone just adjusted, as school kids do. Milton became accepted as a friend and playmate by most of the class.   If anyone ever gave his color another thought I didn't see it."

Religions, nationalities, ethnic groups lived everywhere.   So did the rich and poor, never concentrated enough to create divisions.   Within our communities we had a faint sense of "us and them."   "Them" usually meant another town, school, or maybe a group in another town.   But in America where everyone can dream of making it, almost everyone knows or thinks he knows who has "made it."

The differences that money made became obvious even before we understood money or knew how to count it.   But the poorer did not always envy the richer.

From Judy Brown.

Sea Cliff school and the village parks were all farther than our parents would let us wander, so the long steep narrow hill of 7th Avenue and ending at Prospect Avenue together with Eighth Avenue above and Central Avenue below became our playground. Few drivers except neighbors used 7th Avenue and we played there or on the old concrete stairs whose weed bordered escalades connected the three streets.   In the winter we would ride our sleds down the steepest flight of stairs starting at 8th Avenue, trying to cross 7th and go all the way to Central.   In the warmer months we played on the street itself—Kenny and Lenore, Tommy, Ellen, Buzzy, Jessie and I. Ellen and Buzzy lived on 8th Avenue and our parents became good friends.   Kenny and Lenore lived across the connecting path from us on Central Avenue.   I thought they were rich because a maid looked after them. Their parents were not home very much.   I felt sorry for them because, although they had a maid and expensive furniture in their house, I had an at-home mommy and Daddy.   They had boxes and closets overflowing with toys but the neighborhood kids were seldom allowed in.   Tommy lived directly across the street. He had a baby sister named Laurie who was too young to play with us. We rarely saw Tommy's mother and when we did, she always seemed cross.

*   *   *

A few well-known and admired homes spoke of acquired wealth and a different class of citizen, but they were more the objects of curiosity than envy.   A few were at the bottom of 17th and 18th Avenues sat on the bluff between Bay Avenue and the beach and barely visible from the street or from below. Any object of curiosity that is not visible, of course, becomes richer by that fact alone. South Sea Cliff, outside the original 240 acres of Sea Cliff Grove and its small lots, was the closest to an exclusive neighborhood that the village had. The citizen least seen (at least by this writer) and most famous for riches lived in a house behind a wall at the corner of Downing and Glenlawn opposite the North Shore Country Club. The owner, Norvin Rieser, was said to have invented the hair net. He did own the Venida Hair Net company. When bobbed hair made hairnets impractical in the early 20s Rieser branched out successfully into cosmetics and hair lacquer. As soon as the war ended and hair nets were back, Rieser was off to China to restart the delicate handwork industry of making hair nets from real human hair. Rieser's son Norvin or "Norvi", almost a generation older than us, enjoyed sailing and parties at the Sea Cliff Yacht Club and being seen around town in his Messerschmidt 3 wheeled car.

The Rieser home was fine, and its semi-hidden setting inspired speculation, but even that neighborhood was far from exclusive. The Ronald family (Ian, '55) lived cattycorner across the intersection in the caretaker's cottage of St. Christopher's home for children. The closest Sea Cliff had to a solid blue collar neighborhood was the core of the village along 12th to 17th Avenues, an area then and now dominated by the smallest lots and smallest homes in town. (Thanks to Jay Siegel and Pete Marnane, '55, and to Dave Schweers for Rieser information.)

School was a microcosm of the American "melting pot", but we melted into one school and one class with a speed that may be possible only to the clay of childhood and adolescence seeking an identity in which they might sometimes forget the often painful process of becoming more responsible for who they are and what they do.

We had diversity before the word became a social and political goal, and we are even more diverse now. School was the first time we belonged to and functioned, apart from our families, in a society of strangers. Admitted, school was a very small society, but it was also a microcosm that had citizens, a political system, departments, teachers, administrators, recreation, civic organizations, businesses, and even a simple health service. Schools then, and maybe now, are societies with training wheels.

IN THE BEGINNING

"In his book, Childhood and Society, Erikson articulated in the western 20th century idiom what many much older cultures had grasped: the task of every society is to prepare the next generation to assume the responsibilities that allow the society to exist Failure to do so dooms the society to extinction. To the extent that as a culture we have come to depend upon formal primary and secondary schooling to do this, Sea Cliff can claim to have done that wonderfully well for the Class of 1957.   Said with greater balance, the environment that was the school did contain what we needed to survive and thrive, and we brought that basic trust in the OKness of the environment that supported our taking from it what we needed and wanted."   Allan Schwartz, remarks at the class reunion.

Why do parents choke up when they deliver their child to school on the first day of the first year, and why do the children often cry and cling?   When children begin school they enter for the first time a society apart from the family, where rules are set by powers over which parents have little control.   And parents can do little to control the people who surround the child and protect, challenge, help and abuse him or her.   So it was that when I first entered Sea Cliff School in the second grade, my mother signed whatever papers she had to sign as I stood by in Principal Furlong's office wondering about my fate.   Someone took me to the door of a room in a corner of the first floor, opened it and announced to the teacher and to twenty some strange kids who all turned to stare at me, "This is Buster Kaufman, a new student."   The door closed behind me. I don't remember what the teacher said.   I do remember my thoughts in that instant.   As the teacher was speaking, I was surveying all the students who had turned to examine me.   I examined them with one question in my mind, "Which one of these boys can beat me up?"   I decided that only one looked threatening enough, a boy with a slightly olive skin and dark round eyes in a round face, a T-shirt and bare arms--Bobby Solon.   Most of us felt vulnerable the first day in school or in a new school.   My first thought in entering that new society was, "Who has power that can hurt me?"

* * *

A school is where they grind the grain of thought,
And grind the children who must mind the thought.
It may be those two grindings are but one,
As from the alphabet come Shakespeare's plays,
As from the integers comes Euler's Law,
As from the whole, inseparably, the lives,

The shrunken lives that have not been set free
By law or by poetic phantasy.
But may they be. My child has disappeared
Behind the schoolroom door. And should I live
To see his coming forth, a life away,
I know my hope, but do not know its form
(from "SEPTEMBER THE FIRST DAY OF SCHOOL, by Howard Nemerov)

* * *

Every student enters school with questions or fears, but I doubt if any begin school without understanding in some way that the class they enter is a new society with new opportunities for joy and pain, friends and enemies, glory and shame.   Whether we entered school first in Sea Cliff, Glen Head, Glenwood, or another town, entering school was our first entry into a society separate from our family.   Over the years we adapted in our own ways.   By 1957 we had become a society of 110 individuals (plus a few who had left before graduation).   The Class of 1957.   Our class, of course, was also a part of the society of Sea Cliff High School.   That school, in turn, was part of a district, and a state, and so on, but beyond the other 12 classes that made up the school, we cared little for the wider world, and didn't have to care, even if the aim of social studies, history and citizenship courses was to make us aware and caring.   The more immediate presence of a wider world was "duck and cover", slipping under our desks and covering our heads to avoid the flying glass that would be blown from the windows if a Soviet nuclear blast hit Manhattan—or maybe the closer towns of Bethpage or Farmingdale where Grumman and Republic built fighter planes and bombers.   But even these drills were often more like recreation and a time to pass notes than a lesson in international tensions.

What we did to and for each other, what we said to and about each other were much more important than nuclear annihilation.   Ruth Ahearn has summed up our view of ourselves and each other: "As a teenager, most everything was a big deal (good or bad)."

Pat Mills Describes Her First Day In Sea Cliff Elementary:

Miss Shelland's First Grade Class at Sea Cliff School

September 1944.   I am five and a half years old.

Labor Day ends another summer season in Sea Cliff.   Cool weather has come. The Pavilion on Shore Road has closed its doors and will soon haul in the two floats.   "No, you can't go to the beach any more, Patty," my mother says.   The deep dark green leaves on most trees lining streets and yards are fading to shades of gold, muted reds, soon to turn brown and fall.   My parents still talk about "the war", Japan and Germany.   In the dark night the air raid sirens wail, we pull the dark shades down our windows and the streetlights go out.   Working fathers are air raid wardens at night, mothers and wives of service men are busy writing letters and working in aircraft factories.   Grown-ups talk all the time about people they know who are fighting 'the Japs'.   My Father hopes my older sister Phyllis' husband, Jimmy Mc Avoy, will be safe.   He is a sailor in the Navy on a ship in the Pacific.   My sister took her little girls, Karen and Ditty far from Sea Cliff to wait for him to come home.   They live near my big brother, Paul, who goes to college in California.   My parents and other grownups worry about the war.   I am worried about my first day in kindergarten.   It is two days away.

Wednesday, September (?), 1944.   My mother comes into my room and gently shakes me.   I remember immediately, this is school day.   I jump out of my bed onto a cold floor. I am a different girl. I am going to school. Up until this point, I'm a kid whose world has been mostly confined within my yard and home. I am thinking about the children who are going to be in my class. I'm not sure if I will know anyone. I wonder what my teacher will look like. What will I say to her? "Can I take Judy?" I ask my mother. My mother says, "No, Judy must remain at home."

Judy is my doll. She has a soft body made of material, but her head, hands and feet are hard and look real. She has blue eyes and brown painted on hair. She is a baby doll. I make believe she is my friend. We have tea parties and make mud cakes and pies in my yard. Judy comes on walks in the yard with me by the lilac bushes, in the garden, and sometimes we listen to the children playing in the lot behind the woods in back of our house. When my mother is unhappy with me for talking fresh or not doing what she asks, I hold Judy on my lap and talk to her. When my sister broke Judy's head my Mother glued it together for me. She told me Judy was still beautiful and the cracks in her head should make no difference in the way I love her. My Mother told me "Pretty soon you won't even notice the cracks because you will love her so much." We couldn't find all the pieces and Judy had a hole in her head but no one knows it. My mother sewed her a hat that she wore all the time. The only time I feel bad about the cracks is when I show Judy to someone and they say "What's the matter with her face?" My Mother says I should just tell people she was in a bad accident. That's what I do.

I don't have friends among other children, only Judy. I see other kids when my mother takes me to the store or when I attend Sunday school occasionally at the Methodist Church for an hour a week.

My sister Janet will start third grade this year. My older sister, Lois, will go to high school. She is fifteen years old and very pretty. I watch her while she gets ready and wish I could have penny loafers like she has. She says she doesn't like school, but my father tells her she shouldn't say that in front of Janet and me. My mother bought Janet and me brown shoes that have shoelaces. She says "these shoes are good for feet and should hopefully hold up for the school year." Both of my sisters are leaving before me, carrying their notebooks and pencils. I have watched my sisters go to school for years now. I have been waiting for MY first day, for a long time! I can't go with them. I have to wait, my mother says, until all the older kids are inside. I don't want to go alone like this.

The house is quiet now as we begin to get ready. My mother is combing out my long hair. I plead, "please don't make me wear braids to school today." She has braided my hair all summer to keep it out of my face. She parts it in the middle and braids it tightly. It hurts my head and I think it looks horrible. She thinks for a moment and decides I can wear it differently. "Just for today," she says. She braids only the two sides, leaving it long in the back. The two side braids are joined in the back of my head with a single rubber band and red, white and blue plaid ribbon.   I am very happy.   I wish I could wear it that way every day.   My mother has made me a medium-blue corduroy jumper and a white cotton blouse with a Peter Pan collar.   She has carefully sewn some white lace on the collar that I know is for this day.

I sit down to the kitchen table to eat breakfast.   My mother pours me a bowl of Rice Krispies, my favorite cold cereal, adds milk and a spoon of sugar.   I don't even take time to listen to them snap, crackle and pop.   I'm not too hungry, but know I have to finish.   I eat very fast and my mother tells me to slow down.   She promises we won't be late for school.

I run to my room where my clothes are laid out.   In my effort to dress in a hurry, I get my jumper on backwards.   It doesn't feel right, but I'm not sure what I've done.   During the summer, I learned to tie my shoes.   I proudly present my finished self to my mother.   She is sitting at the dining room table having her coffee.   I notice the vase of red, yellow and orange flowers she has placed in the middle of the table.   I ask her what kind of flowers they are and she says a long word I can't repeat.   She tells me they are autumn flowers and I can call them mums for short.   I tell her they are pretty, but I like the purple ones that smell pretty better.   She agrees, the spring lilacs are her favorite also.

My Mother steps back to look at me, dressed in new school clothes from hair ribbon to my shoes and I'm feeling very important.   She has that look that says she is very pleased with me.   She helps me get my turn my jumper around, brushes my hair, and buttons the single button that I couldn't reach on the back of my blouse.   I turn around one more time for her.   Smiling softly, she gives me a hug and gentle kiss on the cheek and gets me into my jacket and puts on her coat.   We finally leave the house and I skip joyfully down the path past two big hydrangea bushes that we call "snowball" bushes, onto the sidewalk. This time I am not going with my Mother.   She is going with me.   I am going to school.

Our house is on the corner of Main Avenue and Sea Cliff Avenue.   We walk out of the yard I have called "home" for the past five years.   We turn left on Main Avenue (which has never been the real main avenue of the village) and across Sea Cliff Avenue.   We pass the narrow streets – 12th Avenue, Maple Avenue, 14th Avenue.   My mother has taken me down these avenues to the center of the village and I like the little houses with tiny yards.   I love walking down these streets because they are small, have no sidewalks and I am comfortable with the closeness I feel from the porch steps, the porch chairs I can almost touch.   We continue on Main Avenue, past St Boniface Catholic School, a large, light tan brick building.   The kids coming home from that school walked past my yard. The Catholic kids wore dark blue and bright white every day, blue socks and jumpers and white blouses for the girls, blue pants and white shirts for the boys, also, ties like my dad when he went to work.

My sisters never wore the same thing every day, and I am glad I am not a Catholic. My mother is holding my hand more tightly than when we go shopping in the village. I ask her "Why are you holding my hand so tight?"

She says, "Because you are my last child to bring to Kindergarten, and I'm not sure I'm ready to let you go."

"Please, Mommy, let me go?" I beg her and I pull my hand away. She assures me that "going to school is the Law, Annie-Patrish, and I don't have a choice."
I ask her "what's the law"?

She explains that laws are the same as rules. I think I am happy that going to school is a law then, because I know my parents don't break rules. They make rules. A crossing guard in a blue police uniform stands in the middle of the intersection at Main and Glen Avenue. I know that busses to Glen Cove go down this street, and Officer Kelly helps kids get across safely. She introduces me to him and says that I will need assistance in crossing this busy street that runs parallel to Sea Cliff Avenue. One more block up Main Avenue, and there is Sea Cliff School. MY school! I am smiling broadly. I tell my mother I can't wait to meet my new teacher. My mother tells me I will need to listen carefully to her, do as she asks and always be polite. I smile up at her, our eyes meet and I promise I will do all that. We turn left onto the sidewalk that takes us by the school. We must pass by the small cinder covered, oval running track on the backside of the school. Some high school boys are running around the track and my mother tells me that my brother, Paul was a track star for Sea Cliff when he went school here. I was three and remember him lifting me to the ceiling of our house before he went to college. He is married now, I think.

I notice there is a lot of greenery growing up the sidewall of the school, all the way to the roof. I ask my mother why the school is made out of a plant, and she tells me the ivy makes it more beautiful. We continue past the double doors that open into the auditorium. I was in there once to see my sister Janet in a play. We sat upstairs and watched big maroon curtains sweep open. I want to be in a play and stand on the stage behind the curtains and watch them open so the audience can see me. We continue to a door where I see other mothers bringing their kids. I tug on my mother's hand to slow down and she says, "This is the door you will be going in when you come to school every day."

As we enter double doors, we climb a flight of wide stairs to the beginning of a very long hallway with very shiny wooden floors. When we walk we can hear our footsteps and everyone else's, too. We are in a stream of mothers and children. In a small yellow room on our left as we proceed down the hall is the children's library with low bookshelves and round tables. The next room is a larger, blue room with tall bookshelves, regular size tables and chairs. My mother tells me it is the library used by the high school students.

We pass the Principal's office where we came before to register.   Mr. Furlong, the principal is standing in the door watching as we parade by.   He is a tall man with dark curly hair and dark intense eyes in a narrow face.   He smiles.   The mothers say hello, but they are not smiling.   They are holding on till the last minute.   . . .

I sit down at the table in the kid size chairs and look at the faces of the others.   We say nothing.   They look back at me and at each other.   We wait.   I guess a box in the corner of the room with all color blocks is for boys to build things.   On a small table I see a metal tea set like mine.   I think I might be able to have a real tea party with a real friend. I notice a girl with long braids and eyeglasses sitting at another table, and a boy is pulling on one of her braids.   She begins to cry and I feel sorry for her.   I'm glad I don't have braids and will remember to ask my mother if I can wear my hair different so they won't get pulled.   My mother still stands at the door looking in at us.   She waves good-bye and I wave back and try to smile but my mouth is still.   She waves again, turns, and disappears.

Suddenly, I am a stranger among strangers in a strange place.   I am lost.   Tears begin to well in my eyes and I think I may cry except two children are crying already and I promised I wouldn't be a baby.   I use my sleeve to carefully blot my eyes and remember I'm in kindergarten now, and I'm here to make friends, have fun and learn.   I'm thinking I would like to be in my yard right now, making mud pies or helping my mother in the garden.   I am about to cry when I see someone I know across the room at the opposite table – my friend from Sunday school, Betty Sprague.   I smile as our eyes meet and she smiles back.   She is sitting next to a blonde girl who I also recognize from the same Sunday school class.   Joan Sharp.   Betty tells Joan to look at me and Joan looks over and smiles and we wave to each other.   I have two friends already.

The Moving Up Day song had it all wrong when it answered the question, "*Where, oh where, are the Grand old seniors?*" and answered, "*Safe now in the wide wide world.*" That world would not be as dangerous as the Great Depression and World War II, but that sudden independence beyond school and family has never been very safe, and several of our class would risk their lives in Vietnam. It's worth remembering, however, that the communities we grew up in and lived in during school years shared with other small American towns perhaps the greatest natural security this country has ever known. As teenagers most of us found that security boring, but before adolescence it was a security that nurtured independence and creativity.

Maybe people speak of childhood as wonderful or blessed because of what comes next—adolescence. Childhood before adolescence is a period of often zany experimentation before the hormones of adolescence kick in and most kids' interest in identity, sex and social escalates to somewhere between pre-occupation and obsession.

Nancy Meyer ('56) captured it in her comments about a piece of 50s nostalgia circulating on the Internet.

We all enjoyed growing up in those days with a freer lifestyle. The kids these days don't have that. They are all caught up in their computer games and rarely play outside as a group. We used to make up our own games and have fun doing it. That wouldn't make it today. There were countless games of hopscotch, kick the can, ringaleavio, baseball, basketball on our street all the time. I hate to even mention it but for a while a bunch of us would even spend the day at the Glen Cove dump rummaging through all the junk and treasures. We would find lots of discarded "stuff" from Columbia Carbon & Ribbon and thought it was great.

I can remember making our own golf course in the neighbors' front lawn. We used all my dad's paint cans and sunk them into the ground. Made our own golf clubs. We had a grand time until their dad came home from work and saw it. Then we decided to make a slide in my back yard since we had a large steep hill. We took my dad's new planks of wood and ran them down the hill. Then when we didn't slide too well we went inside and got my mother's can of Crisco and greased the wood. What a mess that was with the whole neighborhood covered with grease and dirt from when we landed. Then we decided to dig a large hole in the back yard and line it with my dad's boat tarps before filling it with water. Another disaster when my dad came home and found all the neighborhood dogs in the 'pool'. It took us a while to fill that hole back in. You can't say that we were not innovative. A group of us packed a sandwich for lunch and rode our bikes over to Oyster Bay. Another time up Glen Cove Rd. past where the L.I.E.[Long Island Expressway] was later built. We made it home in time for supper sound and safe, luckily. How did we survive? Thankfully most of us did. Everything was so much different growing up in the 50's. I'm glad to have been a part of it. Things are not as easy or safe these days. I miss those carefree, fun days.

From Judy Brown
Seven heads produced all the entertainment we could use. We wore out hundreds of

hopscotch diagrams color chalked in the middle of the street. It was not easy to hop the boxes either up or downhill. We played red light, green light where one of us stood facing up the hill with the others below. With the cry of "green light", we advanced, running up hill as fast as we could until the cry of "red light" stopped us. The object was to try and tag the leader first and take a turn at calling out the signals.

Giant Sep was similar. Again the leader stood with her back to the rest and each of us asked permission to proceed up the hill by taking giant steps. We disguised our voices when asking so as not to give ourselves away and we invariable took one or two extra steps. The object of the game was similar to red light-green light, to become the leader. On the level cement floor of my basement porch, we threw jacks, shot marbles, and played pick-up sticks. This was also a place to hit rolls of exploding paper 'caps' with a rock-one cap at a time to make them fire. We had cap guns, but they often misfired and failed to hit the little black pill of powder. One rock in a quick hand could hit every cap faster than pulling a trigger.

For any eight year old a few streets and a strip of beach in Sea Cliff had all the adventure, joy and danger we needed or our minds could imagine. Our childhood was not formed by television in our living rooms but from what our neighborhoods in Sea Cliff offered. The offering was abundant from the long horizon from the third floor porch, the blank palette of black top streets, to the esplanade of weed lined steps. We were becoming Sea Cliff and Sea Cliff was becoming us.

Betty Sprague's random list of childhood memories in Sea Cliff also suggests that kids were very capable of finding their own entertainment, usually in simple things, but things that appealed to their senses. Here is her list:

Playing "bottle-tops" and ringaleevio on bikes, hopscotch, pretending I was Wonder Woman, playing with paper dolls,   listening to the radio - no TV.

Playing games at home with Mom - while Dad traveled - hang-man and Bunco, making shell jewelry and candles from mold.

Living on Laurel Avenue - the town's greatest sleigh-riding hill before they started sanding and plowing it.   Popping tar bubbles.   Porter Place – the only cobblestone street Sea Cliff.   Walking to the beach in our PJs for Mom to tell us bedtime stories.

Loving hurricanes.

Halloween trick or treating - costume contest in school auditorium.   Later sock flour fights and writing on cars with soap.

Yucky lard with yellow dye to mush and make look like (notice I didn't say taste like) butter. My great grandparents' house with old Victrola and wood stove.

The milkman, Dugan's goodies and Mike the Good Humor man.

Roller skating with the old key skates that never wanted to stay on - tripping on a crack in the school sidewalk and chipping my front tooth - with Bizzy Morse.

Riding bikes to Bailey's Stables and sneaking (yeah sure) back behind the barn to ride an old gray mare. The school riding club in Hempstead - getting a "good" horse and yelling when it galloped, usually in a hurry to get back to the barn and be rid of me!

Loving the quiet of waking up to fresh snow - I truly miss that. Sucking on icicles, making angels, and snowmen. Putting on and taking off all those winter sweaters, coats, scarves, gloves, boots, earmuffs. New ice skates every year - my favorite Christmas present. Scudder's Pond, falling in, walking home with dungarees and me - frozen.

Going to Bayville Beach to ride the merry-go-round with the "brass ring". The porpoises jumping in the water. Horse-shoe crabs and jellyfish. Polluted water. Too much seaweed. The wonderful salt water that cured just about everything.

From Scott (Fred) Hughes:

Pete [Merkel] and I became good friends when he came to Sea Cliff High. I remember renting rowboats at Glenwood Landing for so-called "fishing" on the harbor, but were more about smoking cigars and drinking beer. One time, we actually caught a nice bluefish, which my Dad cleaned up and Mom cooked for a nice dinner. We also got a bit too far away once, and couldn't row against the tide and wind, and ended up walking the boat back to the Landing.

I remember us walking the golf course at North Shore Country Club, and one time laying down on one of the greens, looking up at the stars and contemplating parallel universes. I wonder if Pete remembers any of this.

From Diane Schweikert ('60)

In the spring the actors would come to the boarding house adjoining the Summer Theatre. They would stay in the three story boarding house and drink lots of cokes. Although we never had a soft drink in our house, we knew we could turn the bottles in for pennies so we feverishly collected the bottles . The boarding house smelled like cheap perfume and grease paint makeup and old costumes. It was wonderful in every way. It was cheezey and bizarre and dramatic; in direct opposition to the otherwise conservative European Sea Cliff citizenry. Sometimes, when there were empty seats we could sneak in to a matinee. The productions were completely beyond my comprehension but the whole atmosphere of theater was intense.

Often, on summer evenings, we were allowed to sit on our front porch catching fireflies and watching the parade of glamorous New Yorkers strolling by on their way to the theater which was shaped like a large Quonset hut painted light bluish gray with round blue mirrored glass windows decorating the front like a rainbow.

The Sea Cliff Methodist Church and the Sea Cliff Public Library were both on Sea Cliff Avenue and I spent a lot of time at both, especially in the winter. Our house was cold and dark and lonelier each year as my grandparents slipped into an alcoholic fog. The church provided choir practice and various activities and the library provided stimulation to mind and spirit. But mainly, both were warm. I often did not return home until after dark. Even though I froze all the way home, I was in love with the snow and the moonlight together and the contrast of warmly lit homes along the way. I must have been a bit of a voyeur. Years later, back in California in high school and not performing very well, I was diagnosed by the counselor for the gifted as having low expectations. It hurt somehow to be thought of that way. The point was, compared to what? My expectations were for what I had painfully lacked. Simple as those expectations may have seemed to a well fed educated educator, they were glorious to me. How can one ever understand the present state of mind without the point of reference?

* * *

To be fair, our freedom was the result of a variety of facts, not all of them pleasant. We had our share of parents who didn't care or who were too busy or tired or even drunk to care much where we were and what we were doing. In elementary school I spent a lot of time with Richie Loftus. His mother was worn down with kids and marital problems. They lived in a tiny bungalow that smelled of old food and diapers and loud with children shouting and crying. She wanted us out of there and Richie was always happy to go. He took out his anger on other kids and in senseless violence. "Let's go break windows," he said to me one afternoon. We sneaked through wooded areas behind houses near Central Park and heaved a rock through the back window of the Storojev garage. We ran until we reached Rum Point.

Adrenalin was Richie's addiction. Adrenalin and power. The power could be bullying as in the time we went to catch frogs and garter snakes at a little pond in the woods near Glen Cove's Orchard section. We found a boy our age at the pond and Richie immediately started bossing him around and threatened to beat him to a pulp if he didn't wade into the water with his clothes on. The boy looked at the fire in Richie's blue eyes, his wild curls, his clenched fists and then waded obediently into the water and stood there while we left.   His adrenalin addiction, his anger, his love of power made Richie a fierce competitor on the baseball field or basketball court.   He was a city street player without a city.

The security and safety of our communities was a matter of geography, size, and maybe the proximity of people and houses.   In that time before surveillance cameras neighbors and pedestrians did the surveillance and recording.   Human nature was the same as anywhere in America, and it included the usual range of unwelcome or dangerous behavior--criminals, drunks, bullies, and sexual predators.

From Pat Mills

A Sea Cliff Story - 1943

I am four. It is a sunny, spring morning. in Sea Cliff.   I have eaten my usual breakfast of Rice Krispies with milk and sugar while sitting at the kitchen table with my mother.   She is having her second cup of coffee and says, "I had a cup earlier and got one eye open, now I shall have my second cup to open the other."   I smile and wonder what that means. I say, "Both of your eyes look like they are open all the time, Mommy."

My sister, Janet and Lois left earlier for school.   Janet is in second grade arid Lois is in high school.   I ask if I can play in the yard and my mother cautions me to "stay in the yard."

I go to my room, get Judy, my doll-friend, and head out the back door.   A butterfly catches my eye, and I follow it to the snowball bushes that are located at the end of the path entering Main Avenue, which never became a main avenue.   The dirt is soft and it will be good for mud cakes, so I run back and fetch my cup and spoon.   I also have a mayonnaise jar lid my mother gave me to make cookies with, too.   I haven't done that yet, so I'm anxious to try it out.   I sit down in the shade of the snowball bush, sit Judy leaning on the bush, and proceed to play in the soft dirt underneath it.   The shade from the overgrown bush doesn't allow the grass to grow. It provides me a very nice mixture for making my dirt pies or cakes.   I say to Judy "we will be baking cookies, today."   Suddenly, a man appears on the path from the street.

"Hi, " he says.   I look up at him.   He is smiling and looks like a nice man.

"Hi", I reply.

"What are you doing?" he says.

"Judy and I are making cakes and cookies," I reply.

"Can I buy one of your cakes?" he says.

"I don't sell my cakes, just make them."

He holds out three very shiny, new pennies and tells me if I will go for a walk with him, he will give them to me.

"I have to ask my mommy if I can go ", I tell him.

He says, "Oh, we are just going to walk on the sidewalk, you're mommy won't mind."

I think about the wonderful, shiny pennies and believe it will be alright.   "Okay, I am allowed to go on the sidewalk sometimes," I say. He takes my hand, and we start walking up Main Avenue towards Eighth Avenue.   He says, "Your mother won't mind if we just go for a little walk," and once more, I believe him.   We turn left on 8th Avenue.   He asks me if I would like some cookies.

"I like cookies a lot", I tell him.   He takes me into a garage in the yard of a house on Eighth Avenue and there is a ladder. He tells me the cookies are up in the top and he will help me climb the ladder.   It looks like fun to me, so I start climbing.   He follows after me.   When we are up into the loft area, he shows me that he does have a box of cookies. We sit on the floor near the opening where the ladder is and I can see down the ladder to the floor below. I like these cookies.   They are the ones that are shaped like flowers with a hole in the middle.   As we are sitting up there talking, I am putting the cookies on my fingers, like rings.   The man is talking softly to me when I hear a bark below, and look down the hole where the ladder is.   My dog Sport is at the bottom of the ladder barking.   I say "that's my dog, Sport and I think he must be looking for me to bring me home.   I think my mommy is worried because I'm not supposed to leave the yard.   She is probably looking for me with Sport."

The man looks at me, and quietly says, "Will your dog bring you home?"

I say "I think so, Sport is a good dog."

I know it is time for me to be home, and hurry to go down the ladder while he steps away from where we are sitting.   I am holding the three pennies he has given me, but they drop as I hurry down the ladder.   I pick them up as he comes down, and I just start running for home, following Sport who is running ahead.   The man doesn't bring me home; in fact when I look back he isn't anywhere.

My mother is waiting on the sidewalk when I start running down Main Avenue with Sport. She runs up to meet me, frantically asking "Patty, where have you been. I'm so worried?" I tell her breathlessly, "A nice man took me to his house and gave me cookies and three pennies." My mother picks me up and carries me. She never carries me anymore, because I'm four and much too big to carry. I think she is very angry because she is holding me very tight and moves very quickly into the house.

She is very upset with me. I am beginning to cry, because I know I am not allowed to leave the yard. She places me on the sofa in the sun parlor. I hear her calling my father in NY City and she is talking to him very quietly, almost like she is going to cry. I'm really crying myself now, but quietly, because I know my Daddy will be angry with me for disobeying the rules.. I hear her call someone else and give him our address. She says, "I will wait for you to come." She checks me to see if I am okay, and I tell her through my tears that "The nice man gave me cookies, three pennies, and said Sport could walk me home. He was really nice, mommy, and said you wouldn't mind." She sits me on her lap and holds me tight for a long time. I try to speak again, and she just holds me and says, "Shhh. It will be okay". I love it when my mother holds me on her lap like this. She is warm, soft and smells good. I finally stop sobbing. There is a knock on the door. "Patty, sit here quietly until I get back", she whispers.

I am waiting in the sun parlor for my mother to come back. She finally comes into the room with another man. I don't know who he is. He is nice, though, and says, "Patty, I hear from your mommy that you like looking at the things on your sister's dresser." Smiling, I say, "I don't get to go into my sister Lois' room and look at the things she has on her dresser because she gets mad if I do " He looks at my mother. She nods affirmatively, and he says, "I think we might just go up to Lois' room and look around, okay?" I am very happy about this, because I am never allowed in Lois' room. My mother smiles reassuringly at me and says, "It's okay, Annie-Patrish, we can go on up to look around just today if you'd like. This man is going to ask you some questions and I'd like you to tell him only the truth, okay?"

Lois has a dresser with perfumes, lipstick, nail polish, jewelry and a lot of other items that I've never been allowed to explore. As I pick up and fondle each item on this mysterious and forbidden dresser, the man asks me a lot of questions. He has a pad and pen and writes things.

I was four, and to this day, I do not remember one question or one answer I gave. I only know I told the truth.

The "man" was apprehended and arrested by the police the same day, and charged on child molestation. He was imprisoned for 6 months and as far as is known, went free. He was seen only one time in Sea Cliff, and it wasn't a definite identification.

My parents NEVER mentioned this event to me. It was never considered a "big deal" in our household.   I know and remember this occurred, but I have never been given the details.   Siblings have told me that I was sexually molested.   I do not remember anything of the kind.   It was handled in a very calm, quiet and gentle manner.   I was never allowed in my sister's room again, and I recall her being angry that my mother allowed me in there. My mother spoke to her of the event, and she wasn't angry anymore.

My parents scolded me for going out of the yard without permission and told me never to break their "rules" like that again.   I never did. I was still allowed to roller skate around the block by myself at age 6.   My parents did not seem concerned nor did they take any type of protection measures on me.   This was Sea Cliff and it was as safe as anywhere was.

* * *

For some of us the town itself, the place, the trees, the beach, the weather saved us from troubled families and even loneliness itself.

From Diane Schweikert:

If I had any foes I didn't know it. If I had many friends, it was always with the reservation of not being able to be a full participant, always with a little distance. The only intimate friend I allowed myself was the town. I was intimate with the wet fall leaves under my feet and the hot sand on the beach, with the sweetness of greener than green spring grass and the violets hiding under the hedges and with the moonlit snowy starry nights. With every winding path and lane, church yard, park and garden. I was intimate and confided to them only, the deepest secrets of my heart.   I loved Sea Cliff the way one loves a best friend who is true and trustworthy and accepting. It was a Rockwellian/Tolstoyan town and it rocked me and it cooed to me like a nurturing mother. God lived in Sea Cliff.   I hope he still does.

Regardless of the reasons parents had for giving us so much freedom, before we were teens we exercised that freedom in reasonably safe ways in very safe communities. Today kids are often abandoned by their parents to the anonymous adults who create television shows, electronic games, and computer web sites.   Today kids leave home in the morning psychologically and no one is able to reach them all day.

Americans who came of age during the war and in the next decade have been the country's greatest experimenters and innovators.   That suggests to me that we got a bum rap being called "The Silent Generation". Innovation Generation may be more accurate.

* * *

From John Broderick:
It has been my observation that the kids who "had it all" oftentimes struggled the

most with getting a good foothold in life while those challenged early on with family, financial and resource problems found the resolve to persevere and make a better go of it.

J Allen, A Maass, C Snayd, E Piat, B Sprague

Valerie Deveuve's (right) Sweet 16 Party
Bette Kreidemaker, Knox Norwich, ??, Valerie

Jane Allen, Sure Frost, Peggy Gremelsbacker

ON PARADE: MEMORIAL DAY

Charles Henry August Hicks on Parade.   Photo by Carol Vesicchio Griffin ('56)

Almost every community has a directory.   They used to be printed.   Today they are on the Internet along with community web pages.   Sea Cliff has one: http://www.seacliff-ny.gov/   (Glenwood and Glen Head apparently do not.)   Missing from Sea Cliff's "Recreation and Events" page is the greatest community event of our time—the Memorial Day Parade.   The Parade was a living, walking, singing, drumming, flag waving, gun shooting, praying directory of the village population and interests.

After a few years as spectator and one of the kids scrambling to pick up the shells ejected after the salutes to veterans, I marched in the Parade for several years as a Boy Scout.   I would rather have been watching.   Instead my parents watched.   Each year I had a few more merit badges on my sash, but we never had enough money for the full official uniform.   I had to wear the same khaki pants from year to year.   Even I, always a sartorial ignoramus, knew my pants were embarrassingly too short.

Sociologists might go on and on about the role of such an event in community life. Maybe some adults thought about it philosophically, but for most of the people in the

Parade and watching it, the event was pride and joy—the experience, not a symbol.

Betty Sprague captures both the community and the event in her recollection.

From Betty Sprague (Harnage):

Memorial Day.   I am 7, maybe 8 I have dressed in my brown skirt and blouse with Troop _____ on the shoulder patch.   I will march with the Brownie Scouts in the day's parade.   My house is two blocks from the overgrown cemetery next to the school yard.   A few dozen gray stones hold names of no one I ever heard of, people named Lugar and Carpenter, Lugar, and   I don't go in there among the tall grasses, the blackberry canes, and wild shrubs.

Years later, when I started working nights at Dobkins, that cemetery was between me and home.   No matter which way I went, I had to pass that darned cemetery.   Usually I would run as fast as I could, crinoline swishing - probably making way too much noise for all the ghosts and goblins that might have been hiding there (Charlie Hicks comes to mind, bless his soul).   Until recently, I would dream of actually running so fast, my feet barely touched the ground.   So I guess that cemetery affected my subconscious for a long, long time.

But for me that's where the Memorial Day and the parade starts.   I watch and a color guard of men in American Legion hats arrives and passes into the cemetery.   I listen absolutely still.   In the cool May morning with the sun still slanting into the tall unpruned privet around the cemetery the long slow notes of a bugle begin to rise, make their statement and fade.   This is "Taps" and it is played for some of the people in the cemetery, "the fallen."

When the color guard marches out, the parade begins for me and for everyone in Sea Cliff. The parade, at least for that day is Sea Cliff.   It is a half mile of Brownies, Cubs, Boy Scouts and Girl Scouts, firehouse band and school band, fire trucks, veterans, and women's auxiliary.   And it is the long gangly tall tan colored Charlie Hicks with his lantern jaw and joyous smile and waving arms who dresses like an Indian and calls himself the firehouse mascot.   The living will stop again at the chest high stone in Memorial Park and the names of the fallen from World War II, and one last time when the town assembles in Clifton Park in front of the great stone and its big bronze plaque and the names of the fallen.

Someone will talk about the fallen.   The Legionaire color guard will raise their rifles. "Ready, aim, fire!" and the guns sound at once.   Then again, and again.   Then as the smoke drifts away and boys scramble for the long copper shell casings the bugle sounds one last time.   No one in the crowd of hundreds of people says a word.   I know the words of Taps. I say them in my head, 'Gone the sun, from the hills, from the lakes, from the skies. Day is done. Safely rest."

* * *

The Memorial Day Parade passed by thousands of onlookers as a catalog of community groups, with the exception of one man -- Charles Henry Augusta Hicks, a member of the Class of '48. Charlie marched in every Memorial Day Parade dressed in a plains Indian war bonnet framing his lean and long face and raised above all the other marchers on his tall lanky frame. He said his family were Shinnecocks from the eastern end of the Island. Many said he was retarded, but he wasn't dumb. Anyone who spent time with him came to understand the difference between simple and dumb. Charlie's love for Sea Cliff and the organizations that made its civic life was simple and authentic. Some people in town laughed at him, some ignored him. Love doesn't last long, however, unless it's returned. Charlie's willingness to be what he was and to try hard to be what he could, won him friends even as a boy walking through town with his father, Hen Hicks.

Charlie held the attention of kids because he seemed an adult who was also one of us, and because he was what wanted not to be—a kid who never grew up. We heard how he had been a track star in our school, a long distance runner who had even run a race at Madison Square Garden. He should have been somebody as an adult, and we didn't understand that he was satisfied to be who he was. He lived alone in the dilapidated wooden apartment building behind the bakery shop on the corner of Prospect and 12th Avenue. We thought he was a sad case because he couldn't be any of the things we were sure we could be. In fact, he was mostly a glad case.

Unlike some student athletes, Charlie never insisted on being worshipped. In fact, he insisted on worshipping the village that had honored him and still provided for him. He volunteered to wash fire trucks. For years he raised and lowered and folded the flags at the firehouse and Memorial Park as he had learned to do in Boy Scouts. At Christmas he dressed up as an impossibly tall and lean Santa Claus and delivered candy and toys to village families.

He often worked as a part time handyman

in Mayor Richard Blauvelt's house, and on weekends the mayor, also a county Boy Scout leader, cooked and served Charlie breakfast and lunch.   Many others, both individuals and organizations, made sure Charlie had what he needed, including their appreciation.   In the winter of 1999 Charlie died.   He had lived 69 years.   Years before the Fire Department had made him an honorary member of the Enterprise Hose Company.   Former chief Butch Grella said, "His heart belonged to the Sea Cliff Fire Department."   The Department's chaplain, accompanied by ranks of firemen in full dress uniform, conducted Charlie's funeral service.   His familiar lanky figure lay unusually still before them, dressed in his fireman's uniform.

(I am indebted to Carol Griffin's ('59) fine obituary for much of the material and all the quotes about Charlie Hicks.)

Photo by Vladimir Epanchin

MINDING OUR BUSINESSES

Commerce in Sea Cliff went to sleep with the last of the tourists and the Great Depression. It slept through the Storm of '38 and World War II. and into the 1950s. The little commerce Sea Cliff had was conducted quietly in stores owned by local people serving local people. Only Bohack's Supermarket at the corner of Sea Cliff and Roslyn Avenues did not belong to a local owner though it was 'super' only by being larger than the corner groceries—Arata's at Central and Sea Cliff, Royal Scarlet at 12th and Roslyn and Chet's at 14th and Roslyn. Standing at Bohack's corner, a citizen could look up and down Roslyn and Sea Cliff Avenues and see every retail store in town with the exception of Munchin's Russian deli on Prospect and a few shops on the Sea Cliff side of Glen Cove Avenue. Below CentralAvenue the only commerce was the narrow steamy Chinese laundry and across from it Mama Longo's bar. Flanking the bar was Whearty's garage on one side, and next to the bar at the end of a short walk covered by a grape arbor, "Old Man Tenke's" closet-sized shoe shop and skate sharpening business with a rusty old taxi often parked under the arbor.

Though commerce slept, in that sleep a sleepy competition existed, like a dreamer's breath drawn in one nostril and exhaled through the other. Newspapers, candy, liquor, pharmaceuticals, insurance, hardware and bars came in pairs almost as identical in size and offerings as two nostrils. Ike Raff's newspaper and candy store in the middle of Sea Cliff Avenue was almost identical in size and contents to Levine's on Roslyn between Sea Cliff and 12th. Ike Raff's brother Sam next to the paper store sold the same liquor and wine as the liquor store in the small converted house on Roslyn Avenue. Schoelles Pharmacy and Schwartz's Pharmacy on opposite sides of Sea Cliff Avenue a half block apart both had soda fountains, though Schoelles' offered hamburgers and sandwiches. On opposite sides of Sea Cliff Avenue in the main block Hawes and Burns insured cars, homes, and lives.

Above Roslyn Avenue Vaccaro's barber shop charged the same $1 per cut as Bart's just below the library. Willie Kauffman's hardware store on Roslyn across from Levine's differed from Nelson and Rinas' Hardware a half block away on Sea Cliff only by being more chaotic and by the big round faced curly haired Willie being more talkative than Messrs Nelson and Rinas. A few people in town enjoyed life without competition, old man Tenke's battered maroon taxi being one of them. He was the de facto successor of the once lucrative business that Roy Hendrickson's livery stable enjoyed hauling a steady stream of visitors into town from the Sea Cliff railroad station in Glen Cove. The Whitting family enjoyed the other monopoly in town—beautifying and burying the dead.

When Sea Cliff had been alive with tourists and summer residents, the street level space in boarding houses and apartment buildings on the lower end of Sea Cliff Avenue had been occupied by stores. In the 40s and 50s, however, most were empty, a few boarded up, and some turned into cheap apartments for immigrants, transients, alcoholics or the impoverished old people with no family to support them.   Not nice places to live, but affordable.   Among the families that found a new start in life were the Epanchins. Nik, Alex, and Paul's father and mother had been born to Russia's nobility before communism and had fled to France.   After WWII, they became part of the flood of immigrants and refugees beginning life over in America.   The Epanchins settled into a grim apartment in an abandoned store building a short way down the avenue from Arata's.   (See Nik's story of his first years in America for more.)

Besides providing affordable housing, offices and store fronts, Sea Cliff's static economy meant residents, including kids, knew the business owners and the owners knew every customer, usually on a first name basis.

In our communities we learned an economics lesson that even some of us have forgotten—that business is people.   Even before we could count and before we had our own nickels and dimes or a dollar to spend, we went to local stores with our parents.   They knew the butcher, the barber, the druggist, the paper and candy store owner, the hardware store owner by name. Soon we did too.   They were on the other end of our first business transactions, and sometimes the victims of our first crimes.   Let's start there.

In the late 60s and early 70s I had many friends who were, or thought they were, radicals and revolutionaries.   In one form or another they embraced and proclaimed—"Screw the establishment."   They were people in their twenties, even early thirties, and they thought stealing something from a store or a business was a revolutionary act.   I understood the theory, but growing up in Sea Cliff, I had come to equate business with people, not an evil power.   Some of the business people could be unpleasant, but they were real people and not one of them seemed out to do me or my family or my friends any harm.   Yet, in talking to people for this history, I have been surprised by how many stole from local business people.   And sometimes it was a pre-cursor to the anti-establishment fad of the 60s and 70s—a sense that businesses were 'them' and everyone else was 'us'.   I recall a boy in the class of '56, a good friend, nice kid, creative family; he showed me with pride how he could steal comics and candy from Levine's store on Roslyn Avenue.   For him it was a trick like pulling a rabbit out of a hat.   Usually, a theft was a one time experiment, sometimes followed by an embarrassing forced march back to the store to return the stolen comic or candy with an apology.

Levine's seemed to be the easiest and preferred target, maybe because they were the least on guard and the least threatening of the store keepers.   For younger kids the stores had three or four objects of desire—candy, comics, models and maybe dolls.   The Raff brothers had two adjoining stores on Sea Cliff Avenue a few buildings up from what was then the Methodist Church and now the village hall and museum.

Both brothers were short, sallow, and gruff. Sam ran the liquor store. Ike sold candy, papers, tobacco, comics and miscellaneous. Ike chewed a cigar and usually stood in the door of his store, and drilled you with his eyes as you approached. Jay Siegel ('55) recalls the Raffs. "They owned the whole building, which also housed the U.S. Post Office. There wasn't nearly the collection of toys and games that Levine's had, but . . . the comic book selection was probably better. We used to go there for candy and gum. Ike Raff had two favorite teases: he would throw his voice and meow like a cat, then ask you where the cat was. And he would point to the floor and ask, 'Is that five dollar bill yours?' Of course there was nothing there. But the store was Spartan compared to Levine's, not nearly as much eye-candy."

Raff's was Jane Allen's favorite store. "When I was a child my grandfather would meet my brother and I at Raff's after school, and he bought us each the candy of our choice and mine was M & M's. I think it was a bribe because he then took us to Mom Longo's while he had a beer and this was so we did not tell my mother he was drinking. He was our caregiver while my parents, who owned a sort of Hallmark card and gift shop, worked in their shop in Manhasset. Ike Raff as he was known, knew everything about everyone in that town and my grandfather would stand there gossiping with Ike while Todd and I selected our candy."

Herman and Zelda Levine may have been less threatening because with their twins, David and Sandra graduating from Sea Cliff in the early 50s, they may have felt closer to students. As Jay Siegel noted, Raff's was sparse and Spartan compared to the overflowing clutter and crowding of Levines' offerings. "You could hardly find anything in the store by yourself--there was so much stuff piled on top of stuff. The Levines lived above the store, and I can remember going up to their apartment, to the bedroom, with Zelda, looking for some toy or game that I wanted. Sure enough, there it was, stored under the bed! What an inventory system."

I suspect the Levines knew as much about the town as the Raffs, but they were not nearly as cocky and outgoing. We lived just around the corner and went to the store frequently to buy cigarettes for our parents, a roll of scotch tape, a bottle of glue or something else we needed. On Fridays, pay day, my father would give my two brothers and I each a nickel for candy which we immediately took to Levines' along with ten cents to buy a Mounds bar that he would split with my mother. Before I was old enough to have working papers and a legal job, Levines' paid me to come in on Saturday afternoons and fold sections for the Sunday *New York Times*. I usually spent the money in their store—just as Henry Ford's workers bought Model T's from Ford's own factory.

Glen Head and Glenwood kids also had their local stores. My mother had grown up in Roslyn Village working in her father's candy, tobacco, and newspaper store, and her older brother Bill Pickering was surprised that his father's deathbed bequest turned that store over to his younger brother Jack.   Bill used his savings from Curtis Aircraft and opened a small store at the Glen Head railroad station.   He sold it shortly after the war, but John Broderick remembers the store with his name attached.   "We used to call it 'Picks.' All the commuters, and there were many, grabbed their morning papers and smokes there, and all the kids counted this location as their main daily stopping off place for candy, bubble gum (with cards) and soda."   My Uncle Bill sold the store to a couple—Bill and Janet and John remembers them as the proprietors.   "Bill had to be the 'stern' over-seer as shoplifting occurred amongst the urchins that plied his establishment.   Once apprehended, parents, rather than police were notified and apologies were the rule of the following day, maybe a few canings to boot!"

John and many others also frequented Hans and Katie's Ice Cream Shoppe located next to the First National Bank of Glen Head.   "Hans and wife Katie made great sandwiches, sundaes, floats etc and were very strict.   There was NO quarter asked nor given, so we were always on our best behavior during visits there.   NO SHOPLIFTING ALLOWED!"

"Across from Hans and Katie's Soda Parlour..Foss' was the original "grocery" store in Glen Head—Foss Fine Foods--complete with a "Widow's Walk" on the residential dwelling above it.   Foss had a "picker" to pull goods off the top shelves and into the grocer's apron, hence the term "can 'o corn" still evident in baseball parlance."   (In baseball a "can 'o corn" is an easily caught pop up ball that drops slowly into the glove.)

Every small town had to have a shoemaker's shop and while factory production had long ago turned most "shoemakers" into repairmen, the cost of repair labor versus new shoes had not yet made shoes the throw-away item they usually are today when soles or heels wear out.   The term "shoemaker," however, we still used.   In Sea Cliff the shoemaker was Mr. Somers, an old world craftsman who worked out of a tiny Roslyn Avenue shop next to the Royal Scarlet grocery.   He could reach almost anything on the crowded shelves from his stool.   He cut leather soles precisely with a hand held curved knife, then sanded them smooth on his grinder.   I used to like to go into the shop simply to watch him work while I inhaled the rich smell of neatsfoot oil, polish, and raw leather. Betty Sprague's parents and grandparents had known Somers and she remembers that he "repaired our shoes for free."   We lived just around the corner on 12th Avenue and Somers replaced all our heels and soles.   He often gave us a discount.

A few stores also served as informal educational institutions.   At Neice's Garage and Whearty's in Sea Cliff and at George Baker's garage on Glen Cove Avenue in Glen Head many boys and maybe a few girls took their first lessons in how to change oil, replace, gap, and time plugs, patch tires, and tune a carburetor.   George Baker, known to his friends as "Bake" knew so much of what happened in Glen Head and Glenwood that he was called "The Mayor of Glen Head."

Willie Kauffman seemed to love his Sea Cliff hardware business as much for its customers and his chance to be a teacher as for any profit he was making. I learned as much about fishing and fishing tackle and knot tying from him as I did from anyone on the water. The tuition was no more than the price of a fish hook, a lead sinker, or a 100 feet of drop line wound around a flat piece of wood. John Broderick describes a similar welcome at Glen Head Hardware. "It was owned then by Carol Wnuk (spelling?). I think he lived a long life and continued working daily into his 80's or thereabouts. A very good, decent, cheerful and helpful and knowledgeable man. It seemed they had everything you could possibly need in that very cool place with wood floors."

Sea Cliff was not big enough to support certain businesses, and that sometimes encouraged do-it-yourself production and even style. Jane Allen remembers Hawkshaw's, the equivalent of Kauffman's or Nelson and Rinas for girls and women. The sewing goods shop on Sea Cliff Avenue was "run by two old spinster sisters (I think). I had occasion to go in there for thread and sewing things for my mother. I don't remember if they sold anything else."

The absence of places like dress shops and craft stores were Glen Cove's bounty. Along with many boys I knew, I walked to Glen Cove and back to buy model air plane kits and to go to the movies. (Pete Marnane recalls the Saturday shows cost the odd figure of sixteen cents.) Jane Allen says, "There were no clothing stores in Sea Cliff and when I was old enough to buy my own clothes, Judy, Betty and I would go to Glen Cove by bus and buy our jeans in the Army - Navy store in Glen Cove. If there were any beauty parlors in Sea Cliff I don't remember since that would be something I would not frequent at my tender age. When I got older I just let my hair grow long. I also wore my hair in pigtails up until I was about 10 years old. I used to beg her to cut my hair and she refused so I just cut the pigtails off one day. I really chopped my hair up and she had to take me somewhere to get the damage repaired. My mother cried for days when I cut my hair. I still have the pigtails with the rubber bands still on the ends."

When we were old enough, local businesses often provided our first jobs. A few examples:

John Broderick

I learned lots as a clerk and delivery boy for the Glen Head Pharmacy. That was a fun job and I am still in limited contact with John Togneri, one of the owners during those days. Fond memories and a sense of accomplishment instilled there. Nancy Samuelson and Bill Livingston also worked there among others. One of my many fun jobs back then.

Jane Allen.

Other than babysitting and working in Dobkins I did not hold any other jobs.   My brother would slip me a few dollars for helping with his paper route but I don't think I remember doing any other job until my senior year, after graduation, working at the Sea Cliff Pavilion selling hot dogs and soda for the summer and that was because I was dating Nik at that time and wanted to be near him since all of you were life guards.

Soda Fountains and Drug Stores

Every small town in America has one or more stores that serve as informal, sit-down meeting places.   Today they are usually coffee shops, cafes or diners.   In Sea Cliff during the 40s and 50s first Schoelles' Drug Store, then Dobkins Drug Store hosted these small meetings.   In the 40s and early 50s Schoelles' had a large square soda fountain in the middle of the main room.   Men gathered here for morning coffee or a sandwich lunch.   Here business deals were struck, world problems debated, and new teachers recruited.   (See Katherine Strohe's account of meeting principal Rem Furlong and interviewing for the art teacher's job on her bio page.)   In the afternoons and evenings kids came to buy sodas or ice cream.   If you had enough money, maybe thirty-five cents, you could treat yourself to a banana split topped with toasted almonds, a ruby red cherry, and multi-colored sprinkles on top, and everything almost afloat in a sea of chocolate syrup. For kids that was the American dream.   How much I exaggerate may depend on how good your family income was then.

The second drugstore in town, halfway down the block from Schoelles' and on the other side was owned by our classmate Allan Schwartz's parents.   They lived above their store.   Inside the supporting posts were covered with mirror tiles and checkered black and white tiles covered the floor.   The Depression had killed Mr. Schwartz's dream of becoming a chemist, but he and his wife tried to pass on their dreams and ambitions to Allan and his older sister Laura or "Lolly."   They conducted their business seriously and brooked no nonsense from kids who came in.   In the mid 50s they sold the store to a young pharmacist, Emil Dobkins and his wife who promptly installed a soda fountain and hired high school girls to jerk sodas.   (One "jerked" a soda because the fountains, like beer bars, had handles to jerk to bring forth the gas, water and syrup.)   Dobkins' fountain may have thrived in part because Schoelles' removed its fountain and lunch counter.   Another reason may explain Dobkins' success.

Whether by intent or coincidence the girls behind the fountain attracted boys to the stools.   Jay Siegel remembers one of the first soda jerks and her admirer.   "Dennis Gallagher's sister, Patty, worked there behind the fountain.   Charlie Hicks (the tall, light-brown-skinned fellow who claimed to be a Shinnecock Indian and marched every Memorial Day in the parade in full war bonnet) was madly in love with Patty, and used to overstay his welcome at the soda counter just to watch her.   (Patty died of cancer many years ago--tragic.)"

Jane Allen had her first job in Dobkins.   "Mr. Dobkin hired me before I was 16 though.   I think I had only 2 months to go before my 16th birthday.   However, working in Dobkins was the "in" place to work.   That was where everything seemed to be happening except now in retrospect people only sat on stools, nursing a coke or whatever (you had to buy something or you got thrown out) and just talked.   Such gossip went on in there.   I bought my first lipstick there.   I used to run up a tab every week and sometimes ended up owing them money.   I don't remember how much we got paid but it couldn't have been more than 50 cents an hour.   We all used to help out in the back where the prescriptions were sold when the soda fountain was quiet.   I do remember Judy burning her foot quite badly climbing up to change the time on the clock over the counter.   There was a 2 burner stove there where we kept coffee and hot water and the counter gave way with her weight and tipped the hot water pot onto her foot.   She has quite a bad scar there to this day.   I worked in Dobkins for a few years as well as baby sitting for friends of my parents."

Betty Sprague says she landed a job at Dobkins at age 13, even before she was old enough to have working papers.   The pay was 35 cents an hour.   When the Health Department inspector came, Dobkins would hide her in the back room.   Jane Allen, Joan Imperiali, and Judy Brown also worked for Dobkins.   Among their duties were walking the Dobkins' poodle Peppi.   Among the benefits, says Betty, "eating the cherries out of the cherry vanilla ice cream."   Jane recalls what she learned there.   "We never had to worry about all the ice cream we ate in Dobkins because we all walked it off.   Dobkins was 'the' meeting place.   Joan Imperiali, Betty Sprague, Judy and I all worked there and I was so jealous of Joan because she got to baby sit Mr. Dobkin's new baby daughter and all I got to do was make egg creams.   Sometimes if we were good we even got to wait on customers in the back.   How times have changed though.   If any adults came in and refused to let us young girls wait on them then we knew they were buying condoms or some other sort of personal thing.   The customer would always ask for the owner so we knew what they were buying.   Judy and I would sneak in the back and check out the things we weren't supposed to see.   I spent more money in that store than I think I earned.   What a neat place to have your first job though."

◆ ◆ ◆

Open 3-5 and 7-9 Every day: Thompson's Book Store

In summers before we were old enough to work a steady job, my brothers and I and friends would put on bathing suits, throw towels over our shoulders and walk down Sea Cliff Avenue to the beach in the mornings and back in the late afternoons.   One afternoon when I was eleven and and walking home for supper from the beach with my brothers and Kevin Costello, something wondrous had occurred in the lowest block of Sea Cliff Avenue.   The double doors to the old store front on the ground floor of Willet Tilley's three story yellow home had been swung open for the first time in memory.   Inside the big room was dark but we stopped, leaned up the two cement steps between the empty display windows full of dead flies and wasps and tried to see into the darkness.   From the back of the room a man's voice--crisp, loud and severe—came at us like a ghost.

"Whaddaya looking at?"

We backed up, ready to run, but I think it was Kevin Costello who recovered first. With his curly red hair stiff with salt water and a towel wrapped around his waist, he looked in to where we could barely see a tall lanky man in short sleeves and a cap.   Kevin said smartly, "Well, what's going in here?"

"Nevva you mind, Buster," he said.   "You'll see.   Now go on and get outa here."

We did.   And every afternoon that summer when we passed late in the day we would look through the door or the windows to discover what was going on in there.   The old man was putting up rows of shelves made of the plainest bare pine boards.   One afternoon when I was alone and stopped to look in, the old man caught me.   "Come in here, Buster," he said.   Buster was my nickname but he couldn't know it.   He called most boys Buster.

I stepped through the doors.   He had boards stacked up along the walls and he was putting together a section of shelves in the back of the room.   "You wanna job?" he asked.

Of course I wanted a job.   I was too young to be lazy and young enough to equate work with growing up.   Everybody was supposed to have a job as soon as possible.   A job meant having my own money.   In the winters when it snowed with Richie Loftus or my brothers, I had already begun knocking on doors and making twenty-five or fifty cents shoveling walks, mainly for old people and widows.   In the summer I occasionally found someone who would pay a dollar for me to cut the front and back yard grass with an old push mower my father had salvaged, oiled and sharpened.   The old man in the store, however, looked to have a lot of work, a job.

"Hold this board for me," the old man ordered and I did.   As we worked he explained that the shelves were short because books were heavy.   "I'm going to fill every one of these shelves with books," he said.   "Whaddaya think o' that?"   I told him I thought it was good.   "How many books ya think I got?" he asked.

"Three hundred," I guessed thinking that was an enormous number.

"Three thousand, Buster, and that ain't all I'm going to have.   An' no cheap stuff either." After an hour he went next door to Mom Longo's bar and bought himself a coffee and brought me a lemonade and told me to sit on the front stoop and take a rest.   He asked me if I liked books and I told him I did.

I didn't know it, but that was his one-question job interview.   I was hired.   "When we finish work today you come back here tomorrow at three o'clock 'n there'll be more work."

    I came back the next day and many days that summer, and whenever the air was warm we would sit on the front steps and I would drink a lemonade from Mom Longo's bar.   The old man was Mark Thompson, always 'Mr. Thompson,' to kids and all but a half dozen people, mainly other book dealers who came by.   We sat on the stoop in summer and in winter at the big dark brown battered table that was his desk and sales counter, and he gave me his advice on business, work, and girls, and he would document each piece of advice with a story from his life—his work in a glove factory in Gloversville, New York; how he had been booted from Syracuse University for playing semi-pro basketball in the days when there were no out of bounds because they had nets at the sides of the courts; how he had run luxurious movie houses for Loews Theaters; and how he had got into the used book business when he was a waiter in New York walking home past the book stores and sidewalk stalls on 4th Avenue.   On his way to his room he would buy a few Louis L'Amour paperbacks or a detective novel from Bass's Bookstore's outdoors bin.   On his way to work a day or two later, he'd throw the books back in the bin.   Freddie Bass stopped him one day and said, "I'll buy them back for a nickel if they're in good shape." Freddie's willingness to pay for something he had been getting free appealed to Thompson. He became friends with Bass and learned how to buy books and quote them out to dealers who advertised every week in *Antiquarian Bookman*.

    Part of his life he left out and I never asked about because I knew if he left it out it, would be *'none o' your business, Buster.'*   I knew from his face and guessed from his advice that he had been for some years a ruined man, ruined by drink, money, women or maybe all of them.   I guessed too that in his recovery he had been humbled and hardened. He set the hours for the bookstore the first day he opened the doors—3 to 5 and 7 to 9 every day of the week.   It stayed that way for over thirty years.   It started that way because Mark Thompson earned his living as a lunch waiter in what he called 'the Dutchman's restaurant' in New York City.   Later he switched to waiting lunch at Rothman's on of North Shore Boulevard in the heart of the estate section. And then at Gerlich's German restaurant on Glen Cove Road.

    At the core of his success in the book business were two rules that he learned from Bass: *never buy a busted book,* and *let everybody make a dollar.*   Honesty for Mark Thompson was a kind of vengeance on the world that had hurt him with its temptations and deceptions.   If Vassar Alumni group in Nassau County or the University Women had a book sale, they invited Thompson to price their books.   He priced every one and guaranteed that he would not buy any until after the sale, and then he would pay half the marked price for anything not sold.   The other book dealers howled and suspected him of taking the best books before they were put on the tables but he did not.   If someone walked into the store with a box of books and willing to sell them for twenty-five or fifty cents a book, Thompson often picked out two or three first edition or scarce books and said, "Fifty cents a piece for the lot and five bucks each for these.   I'll make all my money back on just these three."   When the seller was gone he would repeat to me, "Let everyone make a buck, Buster.   It's better that way."

He stocked everything from comic books to encyclopedias, although I learned early that the only encyclopedias worth buying were the 'classic editions' of the Brittanica, the 14th and the 21st.   As with all of his books, even comic books had to be 'clean tight and unscuffed', the words I typed endlessly on postcard quotes to other dealers.   The comic books he sold for a nickel and bought back three for a nickel.   The fundamental economics and ethics that drive any great corporation, I learned in Thompson's book store.

I also learned charity.   From the thrift stores he visited Thompson always returned with boxes of ice skates and kitchen utensils that he put in the front windows with the books.   When winter came a kid who could not afford new skates came to Thompson's, and if he or she couldn't afford fifty cents or a dollar, Thompson gave the skates away and said, "Bring 'em back when you grow out of 'em."   He didn't have much good to say about the incoming tidal wave of Puerto Ricans filling New York City and beginning to spill into Sea Cliff's cheap old apartments but when they asked to look at an iron or pot in the window, he looked at the price he'd written and say, "It's a dollar fifty," then look at their faces studying the buy and most of the time he would say, "Gimme a dollar."

On into high school I worked for Thompson moving books, cleaning shelves, painting the windows, painting rooms at his home, typing the postcards on which he quoted books to other dealers, going to rummage sales and thrift stores to buy books.   He knew the workings of the rescue missions by heart—St. Vincent DePaul, Volunteers of America, Goodwill, Salvation Army—and he often knew the managers and the men and women in the back rooms by their first names.   He had nothing but good things to say about any of them.   I was convinced that in those years he never talked about, he too had been rescued not once but many times.

In a way he was rescuing me.   He overpaid me it seemed to me, but not by so much that I was embarrassed or felt patronized   With most of the money I bought books.   The books in the store were a huge feast, a world of escape from the frustrations of adolescence, from a home paralyzed by my parents' brief separation, then a suicide attempt by my mother, followed by her desperate battle to recover from electric shock therapy and the doom of depression. In eighth or ninth grade Dave Schweers, my closest friend, found a book that he read and insisted I read, a book that even today I can say was a turning point in my life and which today occupies a special place on my shelves. The book was *Transition*, the autobiographical novel by Will Durant, historian of ideas. I wanted his life and at least its beginnings seemed to be mine. Durant's fictional proxy begins life in a blue collar French Canadian family. As a seminary student he discovered philosophy and a world far deeper and wider than any he had imagined. I made a list of every book and philosopher he mentioned, and I began to search for them at Thompson's. Thompson knew everything about what books were worth but very little about what was in them except in the most general terms: Nietsche wrote about philosophy, Toynbee and Tuchman wrote about history, Edgard Guest and Dylan Thomas were both poets. When a customer asked him his opinion of a book he said, "Dammed if I know. I never read that stuff. I read westerns. I've read everything Louis L'Amour ever wrote. Great writer."

He seldom commented on the books I bought. Once in a while he would ask, "Whaddaya want with that, Buster?" This question never signaled a book he didn't think a boy should read because he never knowingly put a book on the shelves that would embarrass anyone, although he called some 'trashy.' When I wanted a book he had not priced yet, sometimes he would say, "You can't afford that." I remember a two-volume set of Nietzsche I wanted desperately. Durant had a lot to say about Nietzsche. "Four bucks, Buster," he said with his usual finality. I put them back in the box. He watched. "Take 'em," he ordered. "I don't know what you want that stuff for but if you want it, you take it and when you are through reading it, you bring it back."

I worked for Thompson through high school, through college, even as a graduate student in England, and later as a professor of English in North Carolina. In high school when I could drive he sent me to buy books at sales or he went himself and left me to run the store. When I was not in Sea Cliff he often called to ask me to do bibliographical work on a first edition or rare book. After I had moved to North Carolina he once sent me copies of the title pages of very rare incunabula (early printed books from the 15th century) and asked me to translate the Latin and Greek and find out how many editions had been printed, but most of all he wanted me to sell them to Duke or the University of North Carolina. "Buster," he said when I called him, "I could sell them here to Hofstra or NYU, but by Christ someone would just tear out the pages and ruin 'em." Duke University's rare book librarian, John Sharp, immediately flew to New York and came back amazed at the old waiter who was wanted to sell such treasures to a North Carolina university at a take it or leave it bargain price.

I had been living in North Carolina three or four years and had seen Thompson no more than once or twice a year when one of his best customers called me and said he had jumped off Roslyn Bridge to kill himself. The bridge is not high and the tide was out.

Two boys saw him go over and land in shallow water and mud.   They hauled him out and as soon as the hospital determined he had no injuries, he was assigned to the Meadowbrook mental wards.   He called me from there or maybe I called him.   "Buster, I tried to kill myself," he laughed.   He told me that he had never been to a doctor in his adult life and that he was sure that the intense pains he had started to feel in his groin was terminal cancer.   On a fine spring day he parked his old Buick sedan in the middle of Roslyn Bridge and jumped.   "You know, funny thing is they examined me all over after that and told me I don't have anything wrong but a hernia.   But they think I'm crazy and they won't let me outa here."

They did let him out and he ran the store on into his eighties when age and smoking caught up to him and he began to waste away.   I sat with him in the dim bedroom where he lay on his bed dying a quiet slow death.   He wanted me to take over the store.   I told him it was too early for talk like that.   This was the only lie I ever told him.

□□□

Bars: Mom's But No Pop's

England has its neighborhood pubs and the English who say America has nothing like them are right and wrong.   They mean our bars and taverns generally serve a variety of purposes marginal to everyday life of families and the community.   In that time when the drinking age in New York State was 18, Glen Head's Knotty Pine and its Wayside, for instance, were where younger people went for recreational drinking and pursuing the mating game. Sea Cliff's bars The Rail and The High Ceiling seemed to have an older clientele and the darkened windows marked them as hideouts.   Maybe the sour smell of smoke and stale beer wafting out the door made me think of them as places for lives in the decay of what I then thought of as old age.   One bar in Sea Cliff always seemed to have an air of celebration.   Again, maybe that was the indelible first impression of childhood.   To Mom Longo's (more formally the Pine Tree Bar and Grill), the firemen went after quenching a fire, and the American Legion's star baseball players retreated from our public adulation to celebrate their games there.   The main window on the street didn't hide the drinkers.   More than the character of the customers, the reputation and atmosphere was created by the owner, Mom Longo whose sons had been popular some years before us at Sea Cliff School.

Mom Longo as we knew her arrived in Sea Cliff in the spring of 1927 from her native Italy as 33 year old Mrs. Maria Cristina Longabucco.   She could not read or write and knew very little about America.   She loved to tell the story of the day she got off the boat in New York City and saw the biggest parade of her life with bands and floats and marchers stretching as far as the eye could see.   Someone, she says, told her the parade was to welcome her.   She knew better, but she liked to tell her Irish friends especially how the green marchers of St. Patrick's Day welcomed an Italian immigrant.

She and husband Gaetano opened a candy store not far from a grocery store run by one of the few Italian families then in Sea Cliff—the Arata's.   As soon as Prohibition ended, they converted the store into a tavern and enlisted George Arata to help at the bar on weekends.   They also made Sea Cliff their village, making secret night time grocery deliveries to the doors of poor families.   Like so many immigrants who arrived poor, the Longos became patriots and welcomed servicemen with free pasta and a drink.   Every Memorial Day she sat in a lawn chair on the sidewalk between the bar and Sea Cliff Avenue with her gray hair in curls, a flowered, a matronly flowered dress.   We waved to her from our Boy Scout troop and she waved back.   Brud Neice, who began tending bar for Momma Longo in the 1970s told the *Glen Cove Record Pilot*, "She was one of the most patriotic people I ever met in my life."   Brud also recalled that she understood loneliness. "At Christmas and Thanksgiving especially, she'd always remember the guys who had lost their wives or who were alone.   She always had something to eat for them." In that same article former fire department chief Bernie Harvey recalls that Gaetano and Momma staged a great party for returning servicemen in 1946.   "She had them block off the street from Central to Prospect Ave. and threw the biggest party you ever saw. Whenever somebody went back to camp, she'd give him a bottle of whiskey or a carton of cigarettes, it didn't matter who it was. When we were overseas, she'd send us packages. One time, we got a salami and a bottle hidden inside a loaf of bread. I still don't know how she managed to do that. "

When Gaetano's health began to fail in the 1940s Momma took over more and more of the work, and became sole owner when he died in 1949.   Although she seldom went far from the bar and the adjoining apartment where she lived, she became a community institution and guardian.   Long before lawyers began to sue bar owners for allegedly allowing patrons to get too drunk to drive, Mom Longo would take car keys left on the bar by young drivers.   If she felt they had drunk too much, she would tell them to walk home.   Many of those young men played on the baseball team she and Gaetano began to sponsor before his death.   She had such great respect for village firemen that when she died in September 1980 she became the first non-member to have her name displayed under the memorial light on the firehouse where the deaths of fire fighters are commemorated

"There's just so much this woman did, you forget more than you can remember," Neice said.
(For many of the facts and for the quotes from Brud Neice and Bernie Harvey, I am indebted to Joe Krupinski's October 2, 1980 article in the Glen Cove Record-Pilot and recommend it for a fuller account of Mom Longo and her business.)

ON THE WATERFRONT

All 118 miles of Long Island including Sea Cliff were dropped into place some twelve thousand years ago when the last glacier began to retreat and left behind a great ridge of topsoil, rock, and sand scraped from the face of New England. When only Indian villages sat on the hills overlooking Hempstead Harbor their founders preferred the low hills where they could get to and from the harbor quickly with their fish and clams or where fresh water ran into salt.

I may have excavated the last Indian burial in Sea Cliff. I found it where bulldozers were grubbing up stumps and leveling the land in the hills for Sea Cliff's first split level subdivision. The developer's land had been Eiler's Estate between Laurel Avenue and Prospect. In a flat meadow near the Prospect end of the property the dozers had exposed the telltale dump of oyster and clam shells. I had learned how to spot the Indian shell middens as a Boy Scout working with Ed Patterson, a man who paid his mortgage and supported his family as a design engineer with Oxford office products but who kept his spirit alive hunting Indian artifacts. (His passion would later make him the curator of Nassau County's Museum of Natural History.)

We had excavated two sites on Glen Cove's Appleby Estate that led to that land becoming part of the Nassau County Museum system. The first site had been exposed at the edge of a low eroding bluff beside the old Hempstead Harbor Club's two-room club house and it turned out to be the only intact pre-ceramic site ever found in the area. Just inland from the harbor alongside narrow barge channel called The Creek that led to Wah Chang's tungsten refinery we excavated another site from the "Orient Culture," Indians whose trademark was soapstone bowls and burials covered in ground red paint stones. At the Eiler's site I worked after school and on weekends screening pottery and a few arrowheads from the sandy soil and shells. And finally a skeleton that I took home and reassembled on my bed and called Moses. His people had occupied a promised land. Moses I sent to rest again in boxes at the Nassau County Museum of Natural History whose sole storage was then in Seaford on the South Shore.

Colonists bent on making a living from crops and livestock found little use in the narrow beaches at the bottom of the bluffs. Most of them preferred land closer to Manhattan, and later the flat lands of the Hemptstead Plains. The oldest homes in both Sea Cliff and Glen Cove were along the streams and creeks. The Downing farmhouse on the north side of Littleworth Lane took advantage of the low water table and had a cistern in the kitchen floor. Until the Methodists bought the 240 acres that became the center of a town, Sea Cliff was little more than scattered homes along Littleworth Lane and the stream that ran down from the hills to Scudder's Pond and into the Harbor.   A few campers pitched tents along the wagon road to Glen Cove in the summers.   Until 1905 all of the beach front continued to be private property dotted by private bath house and punctuated by the steamboat dock at "Pinnacle Point," yacht clubs and private bathing pavilions. When the town built a public boardwalk from the Glen Cove line to "Rum Point" at the foot of Prospect Ave and on past Scudder's Pond the Sea Cliff shoreline became one of the best known promenades and the golden age of Sea Cliff's shoreline began.

From Betty Sprague
Gramps was an oysterman at heart and loved to catch eels at the beach--bottom of Laurel Ave.   He owned a fish store in Sea Cliff and my Dad sold the fish – he hates fish – I do too.

My dad remembers the Tilley's beach stairs and boardwalk around the corner at the bottom of Prospect Avenue where all the "city folk" would come during the summer. The pavilion used to have a boardwalk out from the "porch" and at high tide Dad used to dive off the boardwalk that once stretched from the center of the Pavilion into the water to accommodate visitors arriving in boats.

The Depression, the direct hit of the 1938 hurricane and another in 1944 took away the Pavilion pier and left nothing of the golden age of the boardwalk except stubs of the steamboat dock pier, and scraps of bulkhead that had once kept the tides from undermining the boardwalk.   To stem erosion, short rock groins had been built out from the bluffs for the entire length of Sea Cliff beaches.   They collected little triangular pockets of sand on one side and the beach eroded on the other.   By the late 1940s the mile of beach where men and women had once strolled in high heels and suits had become impassible at high tide, and in lower water required slogging over tide flats and climbing the boulders in the groins.   The result was not one beach but several beaches, each with its own clientele. Yet even in its ruined state the shorefront brought to Sea Cliff people who found the rest of the village boring.   One of those who came after World War II was a young art teacher who had lived in Greenwich Village.

Kathryne Strohe (from an interview)

I was in my late twenties when I started teaching at the end of the Depression in a Dutch community near Patterson, New Jersey.   They paid me $1,300 a year but we had a hell of a good time.   I lived in Greenwich Village and early every morning I took the ferry to Jersey and the train to the town where I taught.   On the train home I would often fall asleep.   I smoked a little then and all my clothes had burns in them because I fell asleep smoking.   One day I read somewhere that a Prince George, Maryland district had an innovative new art program and after three years in NJ I applied and took the job in Maryland.   I found out they didn't have a program at all.   Nevertheless I was there the *three years required for tenure then began looking at the agency ads for teachers.   When you wanted a job in those days, you went to one of these agencies.   I had had it in Maryland.   They had a principal who was looking for teachers who might want to move back up north.*

Remington Furlong, the principal of Sea Cliff School that had classes K-12 invited me to come out for an interview.   That was in June or July and I put on the customary suit and stockings and hat despite the sweltering heat and I took the train to Sea Cliff.   I didn't know why I was to meet Furlong in Schoelles Drugstore, but that's where we met.   He had arranged for Sea Cliff's only taxi to meet my train and carry me up the hill and into town.

This old rattletrap car came up and this drunk got out in his overalls and I said to myself, 'Oh my God!'"   The driver was Mr. Tenke, a Greek immigrant who parked his taxi under the long narrow grape arbor beside Longo's Bar.   His small shoe shop stood at the end of the arbor and his small house for his big family stood behind the shop.

Furlong took me to see the school and when it was time for him to take me back to the train,   He took me down along the water, the long way.   He knew what he was doing. All the way back home on the train I said, 'Please let me have that job.'   I was thirty-three but I knew where I wanted to live and work.

There is something mysterious and awesome about seeing the sea or any portion of it from the midst of human structures, machines, noises, and motions.   It is like having the most untamed wilderness in your backyard, or the sensitive tip of a tentacle of an unpredictable wild beast resting at your feet.   Why else is it that when we are most bound and tortured by the squabbles and disasters of life, confronting the water seems to lend perspective?   Why else did every couple in Sea Cliff who were in love, both the infatuated young and the old feeling renewed love, go walking along the beach?   Almost everyone in town detoured once or twice a month on the way in or out of town to drive along the harbor road.   Any mild day in winter, spring, or fall at lunchtime you could see a dozen or so cars and trucks parked opposite the water—deliverymen, plumbers, linesmen, factory workers, hardhats, and businessmen eating a sandwich and gazing at the water.

When you are young, where you go to the beach, who you go with counts for almost nothing, and being there, on the sand and in the water counts for everything.   When I was seven or eight and suddenly found myself living in a town with a beach, I didn't know or care that where people went swimming indicated what later scholars came to call 'socio-economic status.'   Stevenson's Pavilion and pool at the Glenwood end of Prospect Avenue seemed to be the place for out of town visitors.   Pools were places where my parents believed you could get serious diseases, including polio.   Leave the pools to the city people.   Besides we could not afford the entry to the pool or even the beach, and at that narrowing end of the harbor at low tide the footing was little but mud and knee deep water for a hundred yards beyond the waterline.   It was not a beach for people who really wanted to swim.

Between Stevenson's and Rum Point, where Prospect Avenue reached the bottom of the hill, and turned south in a flat run to Glenwood Landing there was no beach at high tide and at low tide only a rocky muddy flat littered with cans and glass dropped from boats or thrown from the road or sidewalk.   Along the road on top of the seawall a sidewalk lined with sycamore trees provided a shady promenade, that substituted for the easy strolling of the 1920s boardwalk.   That stretch of beach also provided decent flounder fishing at high tide.

At Rum Point a triangular handkerchief of sand gathered against a short rock groin made a little beach at high tide where a few people from that end of town gathered.   From Rum Point to to "The Point" where Prospect Avenue made a hairpin turn and became the long flat Shore Road, the bluffs came right down to the water and the fences along property lines for houses on top of the bluff came down to the bulkhead and made passage at high tide impossible.   The next "public" beach after Rum Point was at the bottom of a long set of wooden stairs that descended from 17th Avenue and ended at the beach next to "Newell's Dock."   The Newell's had a summer home above on the bluff and the splintery old dock on its tall piers was there for anyone to use.   (The darkened pilings in the photo shows the level of normal high tide.   During hurricanes water would top the deck and waves often lifted planks off.)

Newell's Dock. Sea Cliff. 1956.
Photo by Wallace Kaufman

At high tide the small handkerchief of beach left next to the stairs and the bulkhead was big enough for a few families like ours who wanted a free beach.   At least for a few summers we played with Peter Newell and fished with him from the dock.   A few groins farther along the beach the next gathering place was The Shack, the Tilleys' one room boathouse with a small porch and a piece of flat dry sand beside it protected by a restored bulkhead.   This and Charley Tilley's house on the bluff above were all that remained of the Tilley shorefront holdings that once included the busy steamboat dock.

Willet Tilley, a slightly hunchbacked, hawk nosed roofer, presided over the shack. The Shack had a small membership of young men and a few wives or girlfriends who were as close as Sea Cliff had to working watermen--people who loved being by the water and rowboats, maintaining old outboards, sitting on the porch of The Shack telling stories, drinking beer, digging clams, and fishing for snappers in late summer and flounders in spring and fall.

The Shack's lack of rules and regulations and government authority also made it the place for experiments on shore and off shore. Want drinking water? Dave VanViorst and Don Deeks who had graduated in the early 50s drove a pipe horizontally into the clays at the bottom of the bluff and out came water believed to be pure, despite being only 100 feet below all the cesspools of Sea Cliff. On old pilings in front of The Shack, the habitués threw up some supports and nailed down old boards and created a dock good at least till the next hurricane. From that dock we launched a deep sea diving operation. The apparatus had been created by Rod Fyfield's ('56) older brother Corky. He had mounted a pump handle between two grapefruit juice cans, sealing the pistons in place with gaskets cut from inner tube gaskets, then uniting this air pump to a home-made helmet via a garden hose. With the helmet on our shoulders, a belt of lead weights on our waist, and a buddy on the dock pumping like mad, we could walk about the sea floor. I immediately got lost less than 100 ft from shore.

Pete Marnane ('55) says, "Tilley's Shack was, at times an 'all season resort'. In addition to the summer activities, in the winter when the harbor frozen over, the Tilley boys would use big saws to cut the ice in front of the shack into large blocks left floating in the water. The game was called 'Jumpin' Ice Kegs'. Since the ice kegs were large enough to support the weight of the jumper for only an instant, one had to move very quickly to stay dry. I seem to remember a fire on shore, where drift wood provided the fuel to keep us warm and make us think we were drying our wet shoes."

The unconscious but important character of The Shack was a seamless melding of generations and interests. Willet Tilley, the hunched and bucktoothed roofer who worked for Myles Roofing held what little authority governed the place and he always seemed reluctant to tell anyone what to do or not to do. His younger brother, the handsome, blond and married Charlie, lived in a house on the bluff above The Shack, but he was much less present than Willet. The

other older members were some single, some married, employed and sometimes unemployed.   Those I recall best included the powerful dare-devil tree surgeon Don Deeks and the quiet Dave VanVorst who knew everything about rowboats and fishing and docks.

The society of The Shack, however, was separated from another society by a set of wooden stairs extending down the bluff from the end of 14th Avenue to the stony beach. At high tide, its stairs ended in the water because the bulkhead that supported the Sea Cliff Boardwalk before 1938 had also reflected breaking waves back on the beach, causing all the sand to wash away.   Across the stairway from Tilley's a ten foot wide strip of sand behind the bulkhead became the preferred beach for Russian immigrants.   Word spread quickly that some of the women would sun themselves topless—'European style,' and that in the summer evenings girls, some in school with us, would swim topless.   Boys would try to be hidden in the trees of "The 18 Trails" above this little beach to watch.

From Rum Point at the bottom of Prospect Avenue to "The Point" where Shore Road made a hairpin turn to climb up into the village, all of the land behind the bulkheads was private land even if Newell's Dock and The Shack were the only structures visible.   In the days before Americans felt the world had to be made safe from fools and that suing each other was an acceptable path to riches, the haves were more willing to share with have-nots, at least along Sea Cliff's mile of shoreline.   At high tide we could walk on private land behind the bulkheads without being chased off despite a sign here and there declaring "Private Property" or simply, "Keep Out".

"The Point" or site of former steamboat dock in Sea Cliff. 1956 photo by Wallace Kaufman

"The Point" where people had once disembarked from the cog railway to eat at the fish house or board the ferry for Connecticut or New York, was Sea Cliff's handkerchief fishing park where kids and adults alike fished for flounders and blackfish (rockfish). Where Tilley's Steamboat Dock had been, in our time a broad triangle of rock punctuated by old pier pilings stretched out a hundred feet or so.   Like most kids from poorer families, I began fishing with a simple drop line wrapped around a wooden plank and weighted on the end with a lead sinker.   Richie Norwich and I often dug our sandworms or piss clams for bait from the black tidal muds that smelled of rotting seaweeds and clay.   Hooks and sinkers and swivels cost money, and we stalked the rocks of the point at low tide to find what others had snagged and broken off.

Between The Point and the Pavilion a few hundred yards down Shore Road a concrete bulkhead protected the road from the waves, but the trade off was that all the sandy beach that had been there before the road and first bulkhead was built had washed away long ago.   The town's drainage system also aided and abetted the beach erosion. Eighteen inch and two foot steel pipe carried storm water from all the streets and lots above the beach and discharged it like great water cannons during rain storms.   When they were dry, we discovered we could climb into the drainage system and hold private gatherings in the square concrete junction boxes below the street grills.   We could crawl up the pipes into the village.   Call it The Sea Cliff Underground.

Photo by Nik Epanchin. (edited by Jay Siegel from 2 pieces)

From Memorial Day to Labor Day most of Sea Cliff could afford to rent for $10 a season a wooden stand up locker in one of the two wings of the Pavilion, or a wooden locker with a door to the porch for $7.50 a season.   Pete Marnane, former chief lifeguard in the late 50s and early 60s, notes a particular advantage of the outside lockers.   "The owners of these lockers could use them after hours by either climbing the fence or coming in under the building.   One had to be quiet so that Kenny Kay, the manager who lived upstairs, did not discover the intruders and chase them away."   For better or worse the Village kept the Pavilion as a no-frills beach.   Several people who have remembered the Pavilion have shared Connie Roe's ('59, Miller) vivid impression of the showers.   "The showers were fun too.   Icy cold, of course, and we all used the left-over soap bars for body and hair.   As teenagers, in the mid '50's, we played cards, a lot of "Hearts" where we would strike our arms with the cards till they bled.

If the walk-in wooden lockers were too expensive, in a large second story room with board walls, floors and ceiling, a resident could rent for $5 a season a metal locker with the right to use of one of the two common dressing rooms.   This upstairs area in the

50s contained the cheap lockers and also on the street side had a bedroom and a kitchen for managers Kenny and Katherine Kay. If you couldn't afford the season fee, the day use of a metal locker cost 25 cents. In our family that was a week's allowance and the price of five boxes of Good 'n Plenty candy.

The Sea Cliff Yacht Club once occupied the upstairs floor of the Pavilion, and stairs and a runway had led from the seaward side of the Pavilion out to the Club's float. In the 40s, however, it had moved to its own building and built its own dock next door. The Yacht Club allowed members and guests only. It was the Sea Cliff waterfront's highest social status, having the best pier in Sea Cliff, a float for boat service at the end, and inside the club building a restaurant and bar. Its short beach, however, offered little room for swimming and a rocky bottom at low tide. (Thanks to Pete Marnane, '55, for many Pavilion particulars.)

That was how Sea Cliff divided its citizens among its beaches—the poorest (or stingiest) on little pockets of sand against the private bulkheads; next the renters of metal Pavilion lockers. To put the situation more accurately, the village's citizens made the choices that suited their circumstances, budgets and priorities and this is how they divided themselves. The choices they had to make sometimes chafed their beliefs.

Connie ('56) and Richard "Midgie" Roe ('59) used their grandmother Ryan's locker, for more than changing into bathing suits. Connie remembers, "You could not stretch your arms out; however, we managed to fit 3-4 girls into the locker to practice smoking. Smoking was prohibited in the lockers. And who were we fooling; the covering over the lockers was chicken wire." Connie ranks the Pavilion with the Youth Center, school, and the fence next Cozy Corner as creating for kids "the best of all worlds.

Her brother Midgie, who would later make his success in the financial world and business, says, "I made a lot of money there: How? I went below the floor boards with a scoop and found lots of coins. Lots!!! I never told anybody until this day because I did not want any 'poachers.' Then I would go upstairs to where they sold food, and play cards and win more money and eat hot dogs swathed with mustard and drink Cokes and have ice cream and go home with plenty of change left over in my pockets."

When I began gathering stories about our towns I extracted from them a conversation about beaches. Here it is.

Judy Brown

In the summer, we lived at the beach. Down 7th Avenue, past the house below us, across Prospect Avenue and down three series of concrete steps with landings in between and we were at the Yacht Club where my parents had become members. My father, with his salary as a supervisor at the Lily Tulip Company, bought a 22 foot open cruiser with a little cabin in the bow.   He named it Daisy.   The beach was paradise.   I would stay in the water for hours, swimming under water along the bottom looking for anything unusual. Colored pebbles, an odd shell, anything that glittered.   I followed the slow crawl of the horseshoe crabs, but carefully.   I believed if I were too close, at any moment they might suddenly raise their pointed tail and impale my leg, poisoning me with lethal fluid.

Betty Sprague

I hated the sun and the beach.   I would wrap up in towels, sit under an umbrella, and never go in the water.   I hated everything about it, sand, sun, salt water – even so far as to be allergic to it – broke out in hives and got sunburn on tops of feet.   But Mom made us all go – to Bayville Beach – with all the stones in the water.   One day, I was at the Pavilion – have no idea how old I was but would guess 5th or 6th grade, and decided that if everyone else could swim, so could I!   With that, I dove in the water – underwater – and said "this isn't so scary".   Same day started diving off the floats.   This was my new "can-do" attitude that you and Richie [Loftus] had inadvertently given me.   [After our grade school teasing left her swearing no boy would ever boss her around.]   After that, you couldn't keep me away from the sun, sand and salt water!

Wallace

My mother once or twice said, "We pay taxes.   I don't know why we can't use the Pavilion."

From a 1983 article by Barbara Thill (Schreiber, '54)

My family never came to the Pavilion and I never had my own locker.   My locker status was that of one-sixth Tenant in Common.   Different years, different tenants - but it always smelled the same.   A sheik's ransom couldn't buy the natural ingredients to recreate the exotic scent that permeated that locker.   To this day I can *still* smell the sweet aromatic blend of rubber bathing caps, "Skol" sun lotion and Evening in Paris dusting powder.

The lockers were segregated by scattered gender groups.   Very clever planning on the part of the assignment desk, I suspect.   Each year we had a whole new set of locker numbers to memorize with respect to who was where because if you didn't pay early enough, you ended up in a different spot than the year before.   Only fair.   Sometimes an unsuspecting new family would receive a startling knock from below.   The boys had a way of visualizing the floor plan and could accurately poke from beneath with an oar.   But sooner or later the new address was known either through squeal response or other clandestine detection methods.   Maybe it was the Evening in Paris powder after all?

Pat Mills

When I was little, we had a locker right by the door to the boardwalk.   When that could no longer be afforded, we got a locker upstairs.   Diana Gauld's mother went to the beach often, and we used their locker.   After my mother's death when I went to live with my sister Lois who was 10 years older than me, she had no money, but the beach was one of her indulgences and she rented a locker for us, and once again I was a full fledged participant.

Nik Epanchin

Several years after our arrival to Sea Cliff, my parents decided to rent a Pavilion locker.   It was definitely fun, but beyond our meager means.   So the following year, through friends at church, Our Lady of Kazan, we learned that the Kapustiansky family had a house on Shore Road a little east of Carpenter Avenue.   As it turned out many Russian families gathered there.   The beach was somewhat dirty, with debris strewed about, swimmable primarily while the tides were high and certainly not as nice as the Pavilion one.   In our first few summers in the US we did spend a great deal of time there.   It wasn't until I was well into high school that we again rented a Pavilion locker.   As I prepared to go to the Kapustiansky beach, my mother or someone else often asked "Куда идешь?   На Капустянский пляж!" [to Kapustyanki Beach]

Wallace.

Those of us who could not afford to rent lockers, could sneak in from the Point walking under the pavilion and slipping out onto the beach when no lifeguard was looking. One way or another the Pavilion, the only public beach, was accessible to everyone in town.   If your friends' went to the Yacht Club with their families, that was simply a luxury their families chose for them.   The Pavilion, however, was another matter.   It had the best sand beach, the longest deep swimming area, and First Float and Second Float to lie on or dive from.   The two floats were also the exhibition platforms where boys and girls showed off and flirted.   If you were a lonely or lusty teenager looking for a boyfriend or girlfriend, the Pavilion was the place to be.

Barbara Thill (Schreiber)

I'm sure there's not a square foot of the place we left unexplored.   Sometimes we even roosted on the roof in search of the definitive suntan.   I fried.   I was yet unaware that my Celtic hide lacked melanin and that peeling- pink would become a way of life. Everybody knew that Man-Tan gave you cancer, but the sun was good for you.   The more the better.   The Pavilion belonged to everyone.   For the most part, the various age groups harmonized with certain limitations.   The upper porch was dominated by the older (but not sedate) kids.   This became apparent to me very quickly one day when I appeared on that level only to be snatched up and dangled over the third story balcony.   I still remember promising Dean Scheu that if he spared my life, I would never return!

Connie Roe ('56, Miller)

At high tide, in the evening and being very quiet, I would sit on the 2nd float and watch my friend, Boots Reid, jump off the roof of the pavilion into the water.   Probably a

40-50' jump.

Wallace

Diving from the roof, of course, was prohibited but unusually high tides at full moon or

new moon combined with the absence of the Pavilion's manager Kenny Kay often proved too tempting even for chief lifeguard Pete Marnane who had a gift for knowing when and where rules could be broken.   (One reason the rest of the lifeguards respected him when he enforced the rules.)   Here's Pete in action:

Diane McAvoy Schweikert

The pavilion was home during the summer.   One walked down so early in the morning that the air was still cool and left exhausted when one could no longer stand the hunger.   The Green Steps; was a wooden staircase built to short cut the longer winding street route.   It started directly across the street from the pavilion and shot straight up the hillside through the trees and bramble to the street above.   Once you had dragged yourself up the Green Steps you had to further drag yourself up to the top of Prospect and turn left on Sea Cliff Avenue.   From there you continued to the Methodist church where you took the left fork around the peninsula and onto 10th Avenue, past Aunt Gertie Gill's house without stopping and finally to Bohack's Grocery.   From there it was only a short way home and you might even pick up the pace a little. The next morning you were right back down there ready to subject yourself to sunburn, sand from your scalp to your toe nails, and the glorious water.   There were two rafts, the close in raft for tenuous swimmers and the far out raft for jocks.   You could only dive off of the close in raft during high tide, so high tide was the nirvana beach experience.   Friends would come, friends would go, but few had the stamina to stay the course of an entire day, day after day. It all depends on your point of reference.

Wallace

The Pavilion also had beach food.   Before I knew what the word 'concession' meant, 'The Concession' had become the heart of the most important summer meeting place in Sea Cliff, at least for anyone under 21.   The place needed no name, but its business contract, a concession to do business, became the fiefdom under the absolute rule of the man and woman to whom the Village of Sea Cliff had conceded the right to sell hot dogs, hamburgers, grilled cheese sandwiches, coffee, ice cream and juke box music to the thousands of people who came every summer to swim, picnic, lay in the sun, to be seen and to see.   The Concession was a square in the middle of the square central room of the Pavilion, and inside the counters was a square room with supplies.   Between the

Concession and the wall of windows that gave a view of the water and the floats customers could sit on wooden chairs at wooden tables, eat, play cards, nurse a coffee   and talk.

Minnie and Frank Hall had the Concession as far back as I remember.   And they were old as far back as I remember.   They were not 'mom and pop' but brother and sister, small old people with white hair and keen eyes and a version of propriety tailored to summer life at the Pavilion.   In slow times they would come out from the Concession and sit on opposite sides of a small table by the wall.   Frank would cross his legs and lean back chewing a cigar.   To every greeting and most comments he would nod and say, "Yessir, yessir.   You said it brother."   Only sometimes he said it without taking the cigar from his mouth. Minnie took an active interest in everything and everybody.

Pat Mills
        I began to work for Minnie and Frank when I was 14.   On one wall opposite the grills and the ice cream freezers under the counter, with a view of the dining area and the front door stood a small table and on each side of it two chairs.   In those chairs Minnie and Frank would sit and watch me work all day.   Any dangerous behavior or the occasional drunk was a problem for the Pavilion's manager or the cop who occasionally stopped in. The crime Minnie took to solve herself was the tendency of teenagers and lifeguards to sit on the tables.   "Hey," she would yell in a sharp voice.   And when attention turned her way, she would rise from her chair, stare at the offending party and say to everyone present, "Tables are for glasses, not for asses."

Wallace
        Frank didn't shout, he grumbled.   He let Minnie shout and he shuffled around inside the concession counters and storeroom, chewing his cigar.   "It isn't right, is it?" he would grumble, then laugh and mumble, "Goddamn right it isn't right.   That's all I have to say.   She'll tell 'em, she will.   Won't she?"

Pat Mills
        She did and she told them often.   No day went by when I didn't hear her shout with her voice getting sharp and clear, "Tables are for glasses, not asses," from her table, cigarette in one hand, cup of coffee in front of   her.   She was little, but tough.   Frank was quiet, sweet and loved to "rub" against me in the center storage area.   He was never out of line, however, just enjoyed closeness, I think.   I never felt uncomfortable with either of them.   They were ALWAYS together, which helped.

Wallace
        And they were always frail.   Frank didn't complain, but Minnie gave constant reports on her diverticulitis.

Pete Marnane ('55, former chief lifeguard)

The ice cream they sold was in the form of a Mello Roles.   Never before and not since have I ever encountered Mello Rolls, it was a treat apparently unique to the Concession.   Their wooden tables did have marble tops.   Finally, while no one ever accused Frank Hall of being generous, he did treat the life guards to a free Mello Role at the end of each season and on very rare occasions, offer them a free cup of coffee on the coldest day of the summer.

Wallace

In the summer of '60 I set a short story in the Pavilion with Min and Frank as characters.   I sent it to my English prof at Duke, the soon-to-be-famous, young novelist Reynolds Price.   He didn't believe the character.   I wrote back, "The sketch of Minnie is of a real person and most of the phrases are from her mouth, including the one you asked about.   She is still alive although her enlarged liver bothers her very much.   She now has a lump growing in her side.   The doctor told her it is a memento of the operation this winter [for diverticulitis], but I strongly suspect it is much more than that."

Wallace

Summer paradise would be living at the beach with quick access to the action and views enjoyed by only the privileged and affluent few.   In the summer of 1959 it happened.   I wrote to a professor at Duke, "At last I am established in a home again, having found a rundown cottage and a pair of friends to share the rent.   The place is like two rectangular boxes pressed into the side of a hill, one on top of the other, but the resulting scarcity of back windows is compensated for by the panoramic view of the harbor and Long Island Sound."   The house was a cottage next to the stairs that led to the Pavilion, the owner a Mr. Kahn.   My roommates were Dave Schweers who worked as the Yacht Club's launch boy and the Pavilion's chief lifeguard Pete Marnane.   Mr. Kahn commissioned us to catch blue crabs on several occasions, then taught us to boil them with wine and herbs.   We became hosts for planned and unplanned parties and midnight swims at high tide.   The water, the weather, and the vistas, however, were the cottage's best gifts.

The beach, of course, was more than social life and swimming and sailing.   A hundred years before our time oystermen and clammers made a good living out of Hempstead Harbor.   Betty Sprague's grandfather was one of them.   By our time the oysters had disappeared along with the commercial harvesters and fishermen, but there were enough clams, crabs, and fish to keep kids busy.   Dave Schweers, Jeremy Hurd ('59) and I often went clamming at low tide off the beach near Tilley's boat house.   In the sandy bottom where the water at low tide reached only to our chests or necks, we could do something like the twist till our toes touched the upturned ridge of a hardshell clam.   We had heard the law forbid selling them, but the law was nowhere to be read or seen.   We took our buckets into town and began knocking on doors. $1.25 a dozen.

After I became a lifeguard several Pavilion regulars who had grown up in Germany saw that lifeguards occasionally went spearfishing in the rock groynes along the waterfront and caught blackfish or eels. Henry and Erika Salloch (son Roger, '60) promised to buy all the eels I could spear for them. Henry smoked them. Our spears were home made. Take an old pool cue, put a trident spear tip on the front and a loop of inner tube on the back and you had a spear good enough for the eels who stared out of the black rocks or lay on the sandy bottoms in the seaweed.

From John Broderick:

How 'bout fishing for snappers on a hot summer day down in Glenwood Landing by the warm water generated from the LILCO plant!

Yikes...we could get a bushel basket full of them with our bamboo poles and little red floats which signalled us each time one of the little critters got hooked...how good they were for us, I'm not sure...did we go home and glow in the dark after eating a bunch of them?...we will never know but we are still here so it must have been all good, eh?

I can remember proudly cleaning those little fish and wrapping some of them for the freezer to use as snacks during the long, leisurely days of our pre-work summers...how unending those days.

Barbara Thill (Schreiber)

All things must end. To have been forewarned back then that an ending was near would have been too cruel. Unthinkable. Surely as pure enjoyment never springs from a precarious perch, I gladly say that I don't remember a last day. Mercifully, it just happened when I wasn't looking. By the time my seventeenth summer began, I had through necessity fallen to the rank of fledgling wage earner. Alas, a tender petal severed from the vine of childhood, never to return. Looking back and remembering is comforting to me. That was our time. Those were our days. The Pavilion was our "Catcher in the Rye".

From Scott (Fred) Hughes [from a note on Pete Merkel's class website page that is worth posting here too.]
The harbor, the water, the views, boats--they played such a big part in so many lives. So many people have talked about them. Was it formative in some way that growing up in Wyoming or Kansas could not be?

TROUBLE IN PARADISE

How can a happy and fondly remembered communities also be full of troubled families?   Maybe the whole is greater than the sum of its parts.   Maybe a firm anchor keeps all the passengers on a rudderless boat from washing onto the rocks.   I'll leave this larger question unanswered but provide a few details that prove what Barbara Gilson once said about appearance and reality in our communities.   She said something like, if you could have taken the roof off of all the houses and looked in, you would have seen a lot of trouble.

Phoebe Burdick
   I actually believed that life as seen on "Father Knows Best", was what daily life was really about rather than how we as a family actually led our daily lives!   How naive is that?

The individual biographies in the second half of this book form a collective portrait of our generation, at least from our communities.   For many of us family troubles appear in the many mentions of divorce.   Divorce in our communities during the 40s and 50s was rare.   Family problems were not.   They were better concealed and less talked about and more embarrassing.   Peter Hodgson, who lived in Sea Cliff but graduated from Glen Cove, says, "The fact that my mother was divorced and worked in New York was the cause of a fair amount of wrinkling of brows.   They'd say, 'How's your mother, dear?'"

In those days before widespread recreational drug use and abuse, alcohol was firmly established as the number one drug problem.   Our parents had not yet become teenagers in 1919 when voters made Prohibition the 18th Amendment to the US Constitution.   They were in their early 20s when thirsty and Depression weary voters repealed Prohibition.   Many embraced alcohol with all the enthusiasm and experimentation of youth.   For both their generation and ours, of course, Hollywood made smoking and drinking an essential part of being adult.   You were still a kid until you could smoke, drink, and drive—often all three at once.

John Broderick looks back from his present home on the West Coast where wine is often the most popular social drink, and describes the place alcohol claimed among the families he knew on Long Island.   "I recall almost every parent I knew in my childhood drank liquor in one form or another...I can't recall ever seeing a glass of wine in the mix during our formative years.   My father, very successful financially, was a heavy consumer of alcohol...he went to work every day in NYC and was one of the financial editors on *The Wall Street Journal*.   He departed Glen Head on the 6:20 am train every day and returned on whatever last train was available to either Port Washington or Glen Head.   He did so for 30 years and never missed a beat.   My mother enjoyed a couple Martinis many nights.

They were not abusive and both were very successful--she as an RN and he in the Wall Street world of finance. Nevertheless, booze was a good sized part of their recreational bag of tricks as it was with virtually all of my friends' parents. Most handled it responsibly but a number overdid to one degree or another. Of course the movies did a lot to glamorize both alcohol and tobacco consumption in those years.

"I think it has something to do with the hard scrapple background from which most of our parents emerged. You know, as the words to a Ray Stevens Ballad from those days opined, "86 proof anesthetic helps you make it to the top, where the smiles are all synthetic and the ulcers never stop."

Where did many of us find life most lively—Glen Head's bar, the Knotty Pine, and Doug Andrews signed my yearbook, "Please stay sober and I'll see you in the Knotty Pine." He did, but note the "stay sober" preceding the rendezvous. Maybe he had learned from suffering life with his alcoholic father that sober and good times were not a contradiction. By the time his daughter Cyndy was born in the late 70s Doug had given up both drinking and smoking, but not having a good time.

Many more families than we imagined, even when we were drinking ourselves, let alcohol corrode their lives. Sea Cliff and probably our other communities had incorrigible drunks. "Doc Loftus" sometimes lay sprawled across the path in a vacant lot we crossed on the way to school. Pat Mills remembers one of them. "We called Doc Loftus as you refer to him "Old Man Loftus," and I used to watch him stagger down 10th avenue from my bedroom window. He used to talk to himself in his drunken stupor and one time relieved himself on a nearby tree. Needless to say, I was scared to death of him! ' A few houses down 12th Avenue from our house we often heard the drunken shouting and cursing of the Boerzets whose son was said to be "shell shocked," an excuse for his drinking but not for his parents.

One classmate wrote, "We all had skeletons in our closets Wallace. My dad was an alcoholic, so all my friends' dads were also. That way you never had to worry about going to each other's homes. All our homes were the same. It seemed like we all would protect each other's bubble we lived in."

An athlete who graduated a few years after us and whose sister was popular with members of our class wrote, "My mother was a drunk who stayed in her room drinking gin and eating scallions--don't know if you knew that--so we never had anything in the way of family life."

A multi-talented member of our class writes about the circumstances that put her to work early in her school years, "that made early employment mandatory - Dad was a machinist and had a shop in the garage . He also had a drinking problem. When he had work he was earning money but spent everything that came in and often had to borrow from relatives.   I was sensitive to this dire situation.   Also about my surroundings. There was a family of indigents living near the park at the end of Roslyn Avenue.   I often saw them mother, father and son.   All alcoholics and it was such a tragic situation to my way of thinking and knowing that Dad had a drinking problem I believe I was fearful that we might end up like that family.   I simply had to earn money of my own and felt an urgency to become independent. But it was not all bad.   We were well housed and fed and clothed and I really should not complain.   We were probably not unlike many and better off than a lot of my fellow students.   However, it was a sobering upbringing to me."

Pat Mills' early years in Sea Cliff were an idyll of family life, even if they scraped to make ends meet.   But that idyll would not last long.   "I do not remember having the luxury of 'store bought' toys or clothes.   My mother made most of my clothes, including bathing suits that fell apart with rigorous children play, and hand me downs from well meaning friends and older sisters.   I do remember evenings, however, where our family stood around the piano and sang the old songs. I still know the words and melody to most all of those we sang.   We (the children) were never left out of New Year's Eve celebrations with my parents and a few friends and uncles and aunts.   My father insisted we all have some pickled herring at midnight, a German tradition we dreaded but were told should insure health and wealth. We could never seem to hide ourselves well enough to avoid it. (I have been granted both in my later years.   Thanks, Dad!)   It seemed midnight would take forever to occur.   We would go out on the porch and bang pots and pans, welcoming in another year.   One year, I even got to play "Old Lag Sine" on my saxophone.   I felt very important, and was delighted in the applause of my family.   I also recall one year my father cooked a "goose" and it was not as delicious as he'd hoped.   We were ever and always the 'children' and our lives, though simple, seemed full and happy."

"The happiness of childhood was to fade rapidly, as my parents became more dependent on alcohol.   They were proud, quiet people, therefore would never accept help or assistance in any way from outsiders everything sort of became dark and dreary in our home, which ultimately ended in unhappiness, death and ultimately abandonment of responsibility by my father and mother."

"My mother met an early death at age 51; my father then assigned my sister Janet, age 16 to my brother and his wife in California.   I was assigned to my sister Lois (age 22) and her husband, Bill. They had two children at this time.   As much as I've tried to justify this action, it has taken me close to fifty years to recognize it clearly as the abandonment it was.   We weren't given a choice, our parents were not reliable in providing us with a secure future, and even death, though final, is a form of abandonment.   Not allowing a child to grieve and understand the death, and placing a twelve-year-old in a totally changed environment is not an acceptable solution.   This is of course, a personal opinion, which has unfortunately caused sadness and many unanswered questions throughout my own adult life."

For many of us adults outside the family gave shelter, mentored us, set examples, or just supervised.

Prom Chaperones, '56?. Front: Mrs. Sprague (?), Mrs. Weeks, ??, Madeline Bolitho, Emma Kaufman, ??; back row: Mr. Sprague (?), ??, Arthur Kaufman, Mr. Weeks (?), Ed Bolitho, ??

WHO ARE WE?

The 51 years after graduation transformed us from raw material to distinct adults, with decades of living that further separated us from each other with wives, husbands, children, partners, or years living alone.

We made choices, including some for which no name existed when we set out from school—soldiers, sailors, Marines, and airmen as well as conscientious objectors and anti-war protestors; hunters and vegans; evangelicals and atheists; big city residents and rural recluses.   About half of us learned on the job and worked our way into the careers we wanted.   Others continued education at small colleges and large universities across the country and in Europe.   We have been or are teachers, psychologists, business owners, nurses, scientists, housewives and house husbands, salesmen, stock brokers, casino card dealers, scrap metal salvagers, professors, writers, explosives experts, engineers, civil rights workers, horse trainers, lawyers, spies, writers, editors, boat captains, and artists. Some feel passionately committed to liberal politics, others to conservative values, and still others are Libertarian or avoid politics entirely.   One in ten eventually moved to Florida, one in twenty to the West Coast, several to places abroad that we could not have named on a map in 1957.   Some have been married three or more times, some not at all, some have same sex partners, and some have celebrated durable marriages of more than 40 years. Our lives have included painful struggles with cancer and other ills, joys and pleasures of family and friends, public honors, material and spiritual rewards, death before 30, and at least two suicides.

One of the built-in contradictions of human society is that as social animals almost everyone wants to be part of a society, large or small, but as thinking and imagining beings, each of us also wants to be recognized as a unique individual.   Our creation as human beings, whatever the source, has made individuality much more important to us than for bees, ants, termites, caribou, or even a pod of whales or herd of elephants, or pride of lions.

Allan Schwartz, who has distinguished himself as a clinical psychologist and scholar told us at our reunion that the challenge of our school years was creating an identity.   "As we moved from elementary to junior and senior high school, we faced the task of integrating the increasingly numerous dimensions of being that were emerging for us: child, sibling, student, athlete and, if only part time, worker.   It could also be said that we now also had to begin integrating Work and Love.   The great thing about the community and the school itself is that it supported this task.   I did some statistical work for Stanley Wolf, the district's School Psychologist even as I sought to free myself from my parents confining control, emulated my older sister's achievements as an honor society member and yearbook editor, played first singles on our tennis team.   Erikson labeled success at this task the achievement of Identity, and failure as Role Confusion."

Each of us started life as a wrinkled crying infant with the world nothing but noise and blur, and give or take a little hair, eye color and birthmarks, we all looked alike. By the time we entered grade school we were well on the way to defining ourselves as distinct individuals. For the next twelve years the process continued. In life's difficult passages we desperately wished we could just be like everyone else. The consolation was the finding and binding to a few close friends. When almost half of us came together for a 51st reunion I watched and listened to people who, in most cases, I had already talked to at length by phone or e mail or both, I was struck and moved by how distinctly individual everyone had become. The differences were there in school too, but we had not paid sufficient attention. Nor had we as individuals been seasoned and well tested. Now, much nearer our end than our beginning, we are very distinct individuals, not only physically but inside, deep inside.

Before the Reunion several people told me in various ways how important our class, the school, and those years in Sea Cliff, Glen Head, and Glenwood have always been to them, although no one could quite say why, no matter how much probing I did or how I framed the question or what I hoped might be clever little leverage questions that would pry someone loose and reveal profound insights. After the Reunion several class members wrote even stronger words about how much this gathering and our collective memory meant to them.

From Judy Brown:
Richie Loftus was instrumental in the start of the lifelong friendship between Jane and myself. We were walking out of the playground after school one day (7th or 8th grade) and he ran by and threw a ripped up math test in one of the hoods of our coats. We decided to go home and put the pieces back together and see what grade he received. We were just casual friends before that but that cemented the friendship and the rest is history.

From my old letters: July 9, 1955. Letter from my mother, Emma Kaufman, to me in South Dakota includes this news:

"From what we hear Richie and Duffy received a suspended sentence. The cops are dispersing the boys on the corner again. It sure is a shame as they don't know where to spend these hot evenings."

"Goldick [Howard, '56] is at the pavilion again, and Twink [Duncan Leckie, '56] is going to summer school, Edith, Pete Lawlor ['56]and Jack Whearty are working in the new Cosy, Jimmie Whearty ['56] is working at Rogers."

We have no idea where our past words and actions still speak and unfold in the minds of friends and strangers. We have said good-bye, moved on through space, aboard a time train that has no fixed stations, although, unless we harbor among us one or more immortals, this train has a terminal. Meanwhile, during the trip something we said is heard again and again, something we did replays over and over. In our dreams we still blow that old horn or play baseball in Clifton Park or handball on the playground, or we hurry down the Sea Cliff school corridors looking for our classroom or a bathroom. People who study dreams say there is nothing accidental about the fact that for five or six or seven decades most of our dreams continue to be about the places we grew up and in them we are often the adolescents we were in those places.

Between Sea Cliff and Glen Cove's three or four streets of shops lay the alien territories of The Orchard's Italian neighborhood and "Back Road Hill's" [Glen Cove Ave.] black neighborhood. Many of us from Sea Cliff walked to adjoining Glen Cove to go to the Saturday movies, buy model airplanes, dolls, or something else the few shops in Sea Cliff didn't offer. Crossing those territories meant becoming the lonely stranger, exposing ourselves to the unpredictable whims of people not like us.

From Betty Sprague
Jane, Judy and I used to go to the record store in Glen Cove to buy 45s after we got our paychecks (Dobkin's starting pay was 35 cents/hour). It seems like we were always being chased down "Back Road Hill" by the black kids throwing stones at us. Now the hard part was how to get home. Shore Road, the Orchard and railroad tracks with its associated undesirables, or back up the "Hill"? Both Dorie and I had nightmares about being chased, and I used to dream about missing the "last bus" and being stranded in Glen Cove.

Almost everyone I've talked to has told me how often he or she has thought of or told stories about someone else in the class. That is why, I believe, that 51 years after most of us scribbled hasty good-byes in each other's yearbooks, we came together in the class reunion effort by e mail, by phone, and for a weekend, and we still felt like a class, a miniature society.

Maybe the few who really have disappeared from phone books, street directories, and the Internet have put it all behind them, but I doubt it. They can run but they can't hide. In many ways we have always been with each other.

FOOTNOTE: Several people have asked me why I decided to write this record. *Who really cares?* They ask. *What good is it?* Answers came from unexpected places. For a long time I could find no information on Lee Berroyer, our feisty, blunt, funny, curly haired, blonde, and fierce little classmate. Late in compiling this record someone sent an important clue, the name of her first husband, Ralph Palacios. Using this I found their oldest son Mike, a former Army Ranger, living in Florida. Lee died in 1997, and for reasons I explain in Lee's biography, Mike and his brother and sister knew almost nothing of Lee's early years. I pulled together a few quotes, information from our documents, and old pictures and sent them to Mike. I put him in touch with a few other people in the class who knew Lee well. Mike replied, "I also spoke with my brother the other day and he too was as equally excited regarding your contact and subsequent pictures of our mother. Words cannot describe the joy you have given me, my brother and sister."

In a way it is no exaggeration to say we have given them a lost piece of their lives. That's happened for many in our class too. Sometimes the lost piece was an important memory. Sometimes it was a best friend who had been lost for decades. All the answers together have something to do with the conclusion of an e mail Berkeley Andrews distributed, a story about two kids' ball teams. It concludes with these words, "So many seemingly trivial interactions between two people present us with a choice: Do we pass along a little spark of love and humanity or do we pass up those opportunities and leave the world a little bit colder in the process?" In school the sparks of love and humanity and the bonds between us far outweighed the rivalries, grudges, jealousies, and cruel tricks. When I began talking to people about the reunion and collecting our stories, I found nothing spectacular and earth shaking, but I found a great deal of humanity, and in the reunion and this follow up I found an opportunity to pass it along.

"At first sight, joy seems to be connected with being different. When you receive a compliment or win an award, you experience the joy of not being the same as others. You are faster, smarter, more beautiful, and it is that difference that brings you joy. But such joy is very temporary. True joy is hidden where we are the same as other people: fragile and mortal. It is the joy of belonging to the human race. It is the joy of being with others as a friend, a companion, a fellow traveler." Henri Nouwen

----

Work, Love and School at Sea Cliff

Notes from Allan Schwartz for the Sept. 12, 2008 Reunion Evening.

My comments this evening begin with Freud's comment. It is his delightfully jargon-free response to the question [I paraphrase here], "What's it all about, Sigmund?'" His answer: Love and Work. I begin with work.

It was Erik Erikson, the self-named European immigrant to the United States, a love-child born of parents of different nationalities who never married, who provided the best exegesis after Shakespeare of the ages of man. Erikson, translating what he observed in the culture of the Lakota Sioux, saw that, as we mature, we face a series of developmental challenges that are linked to the roles of our culture. These roles, often usefully regarded as vocations, are preceded by three challenges that are less strongly, or perhaps only differently, tethered to contemporary features of our social environment. [That is, there were no computer programmers in 1808.]

The earliest of these three challenges is developing a feeling of Trust, trust that the environment – initially exclusively human and later more complexly dimensioned – will provide what we need to survive and thrive. The alternative outcome is a Basic Mistrust of the OK*ness* of the world we live in. This initial challenge is followed by our moving from a place of profound dependence to one of increasing Autonomy. The price we pay for retreating from or less successfully mastering this challenge and becoming autonomous is to suffer from a sense of Shame and feelings of Self-Doubt. The last of these pre-kindergarten challenges is developing a capacity to take Initiative on our own behalf, the downside here being burdened by feelings of Guilt.

Piaget, speaking of pre-kindergarten and early primary school youngsters, was on target when he noted, "Play is the child's work." But then comes work, and school, and our experience at Sea Cliff. For all of us, this means at least 12th grade if not all of senior high. It means junior and senior high for a smaller number, and for a still smaller number, K through 12 or some good chunk of that. In reviewing the biographical material that Wallace had collected and forwarded to me, I was impressed at the variety of vocations represented within our class. In his book, *Childhood and Society*, Erikson articulated in the western 20th century idiom what many much older cultures had grasped: the task of every society is to prepare the next generation to assume the responsibilities that allows the society to exist. Failure to do so dooms the society to extinction. To the extent that as a culture we have come to depend upon formal primary and secondary schooling to do this, Sea Cliff can claim to have done that wonderfully well for the Class of 1957. Said with greater balance, the environment that was the school did contain what we needed to survive and thrive, and we brought that basic trust in the OKness of the environment that supported our taking from it what we needed and wanted. In the earliest years of this formal education it was a question of our working at our work, being industrious, mastering the material set before us. Failure to do so meant we would feel less than, inferior. Per Erikson's antinomy, Industry versus Inferiority.

As we moved from elementary to junior and senior high school, we faced the task of integrating the increasingly numerous dimensions of being that were emerging for us: child, sibling, student, athlete and, if only part time, worker. It could also be said that we now also had to begin integrating Work and Love. The great thing about the community and the school itself is that it supported this task. I did some statistical work for Stanley Wolf, the district's School Psychologist even as I sought to free myself from my parents confining control, emulated my older sister's achievements as an honor society member and yearbook editor, played first singles on our tennis team. Erikson labeled success at this task the achievement of Identity, and failure as Role Confusion.

The loving component of our dual development became increasingly significant as we concluded our years at Sea Cliff High School. The challenge now was allowing and achieving Intimacy in our relationships with others. The cost of not doing so was Isolation from others. In this task I had the considerable assistance of Nancy Horton, a now deceased member of the Class of 1958, who, to my good fortune, decided she wanted me for a boyfriend. It would be only some years later that I began to understand the reciprocity of the passion that could inform such relationships, but Sea Cliff High School, the town of Sea Cliff, and the somewhat larger community that fed our school were the place I started that journey. But prior to Nancy taking me in hand, I recall playing Frank Gilbreth, the father in Christopher Sergel's play based on the memoir of the Gilbreth family, *Cheaper by the Dozen*. Eileen McNamara, Mrs. Mac, directed. During the dress rehearsal, in a scene where I, as Frank, was telling Lillian, my wife, how special she was to me and how much I cared for her, I found myself becoming choked up with feeling. I confess that, regrettably, I found that experience so frightening that I never said a word about it to Mrs. Mac and – I think partly in consequence – never allowed myself to get near that feeling during the performance. Worse, and despite the opportunity that my relationship with Nancy afforded me, I think it was some years before I ever did so in my life. Mrs. Mac: Many in the cast knew what a treasure she was and worshiped her accordingly. I only wish that I had.

HOT TOPICS OF THE DEBATE SCENE

Several class members have circulated as e mails lists of songs, sayings, customs, and vocabulary that seem typical of the 1950s. These are easy to find, and I don't reprint them here. But, I do include a list that reminds us of several important issues being decided in our school years and just after. Consider the national high school debate topics for a few of our years in school and just beyond. Debate topics are always proposed in the affirmative—that X or Y should do something.

- 1951 – Resolved: That the American people should reject the welfare state.
- 1955 – Resolved: That the federal government should initiate a policy of free trade among nations friendly to the United States.
- 1957 – Resolved: That the federal government should sustain the prices of major agricultural products at not less than 90% of parity.
- 1959 – Resolved: That the United States should adapt the essential features of the British system of education.
- 1961 – Resolved: That the United Nations should be significantly strengthened.
- 1962 – Resolved: That the federal government should equalize educational opportunity by means of grants to the states for public elementary and secondary education.
- 1964 – Resolved: That Social Security benefits should be extended to include complete medical care.

This last topic reminds us that during our high school years and just afterward a great change began to happen in the role of government in people's personal lives and in the powers of the national government. The debate over the powers and reach of government is as old as the Constitution and continues to be at the center of the political divide today. Immediately behind those hot topics lay The Great Depression and World War II. Those experiences led to decisions in the 50s and 60s that changed the nation for the rest of our lives. We were present, whether we were interested or not. End of discussion--I'm not fool enough to divert this history to political debate or to make it a platform for anyone's position.

SPORTS FANS AND SPORTS STARS

Let Pete Rose from the Class of '59 introduce this section. Many of us have probably read his by-line in major sports and outdoors magazine. Pete played baseball and basketball at Sea Cliff, playing varsity when only a sophomore. He went on to play baseball at the University of North Carolina, and from there to Special Forces. For the rest of his life Pete roamed the country and the world writing. He's still a passionate sports fan and outdoorsman and makes his home in Boise, Idaho.

From Pete Rose

Maroon and White,

Fight, Fight, Fight

At Sea Cliff High it was school and home work, blasting car radios with the new rock and roll, hanging out at the Youth Center, Sombrero and Pavilion, and the big game. Athletic excitement picks up when a class has an extraordinary crop of athletes. This was so with the Class of '59. Bob Johnston and Bob Lucas were among the best in Nassau County on the basketball court and soccer field, and Johnston was an incredible baseball pitcher. Mike Stanton, and Nik Epanchin were other notables, and a strong junior class headed by Bob Myles and Richard Roe contributed to outstanding results in soccer, basketball and baseball.

But, perhaps, unusual home playing sites, and the atmosphere and color they provided, most set Sea Cliff apart from others. Baseball, soccer and track and field took place not at the normal ho-hum field behind the school but at Clifton Park, a beautiful green grass village park ringed with hardwood trees. Clifton's airy, aesthetic feel was the opposite of the "cracker box" gym where basketball was played. Walls hemmed in the small court beneath the elevated spectator section. Cheerleaders in maroon velvet outfits and white gloves whipped students into a frenzy above Lucas's one-handers and Johnston's hook shots.

Despite its small size, Sea Cliff players often won national attention. In 1954 classes were stopped and students led to the court to watch the tryout of Bob Johnston's older brother Ron before a Kansas University scout. Ron averaged 27 points a game, second in the league behind Jim Brown's 40 for Manhasset. Brown became one of the country's most famous college and pro football players. Ron, perhaps Sea Cliff's best all-time athlete, went on to play with Wilt Chamberlain on Kansas University's outstanding teams.

An aside on Bob or Porky not becoming a major leaguer. He had the most talent of anyone I played with, probably including the University of North Carolina, where we had a good team with players who went on to the pros. I had to drag him out to play summer ball. I recall getting him down to the field at Glen Cove and a bunch of scouts drooling behind the backstop at his stuff. He had a very good "smoking" fastball that "hopped" and curve that "dropped off the table." It was all I could do to catch his pitches--I was an all-county catcher my senior year, so had done some catching, but third base was my true position. Bob was signed by the Dodgers and played some minor league ball. He had the ability but not the attitude to make the majors, in my opinion. And of course he went on to college and grad school and became a principal and later a college registrar and admissions director. He in a way was similar to Ferg Norton, an All-American third baseman at Carolina, who could have signed for $50,000 with the Red Sox (big money those days), but wanted to be a pilot, and I am sure, became one. White guys with unusual athletic talent but bright enough to become professionals in jobs that took educated skills. There is a reason so many of the pro athletes we see today are black...not taking away from their superb physical

Bob Johnston jumps, by Nik Epanchin

abilities, but I believe many like Porky and Ferg who are white, and could have been pros, took different, more intellectual paths...with perhaps an eye--consciously or subconsciously--on the long run.

Pete mentions the cracker box of a gym we played in, and as he suggests, that gym's size brought all spectators almost into the action. In the world of competition we had to try harder and winning was sweeter. The old saw holds that losing builds character. So does being small—playground for practice and track meets, a public park for playing field, soccer and baseball sharing the same turf.

Our facilities outside matched the gym's modesty. The four lane cinder track around the playground made no more than a one eighth of a mile. Track practice, handball, basketball, volleyball, and jumping rope mixed everyone up before school, at recess and after school. Everything happened there from K-12: the popular team sports, the pickup games, the handball matches, grade schoolers on jungle gyms and swings. Even Clifton Park a few blocks away where we played baseball and soccer was smaller than most school practice fields and doubled as a community park.

We also knew were unusual because we had no football team. Legend always said that football had been stopped when a principal's son was killed while playing. True or not, it became part of every generation's sports lore and part of our sense of school character. We were underdogs.

Few athletes excel in all sports, but many of us who liked sports tried them all, organized or not. I had been in Sea Cliff only a few weeks before I was swimming, playing baseball in Prospect Park, handball on the playground, and tackle football with Allan Gleichmann's boy-girl team, the "Back Yard Terrors". His sister Sandy starred on the team and our one opposing team, whose name I have forgotten, included Faith LaJoy and at least one of her brothers. Others rowed boats or sailed dinghies and most of us had roller skates with steel wheels and steel platforms that clamped onto the soles of our shoes.

Evy Piat by Fred Feingold

Dave Schweers and I found an old bed spring with the metal lathe attached to the frame by short springs. We dug a hole in the sand of a vacant lot above the 18 Trails and used it as a trampoline. Our version of car racing was to nail skates to the bottom of a long board, nail an upright orange crate on the front and put a stick across it for handlebars. Gravity and local hills did the rest.

A few people in class played three or even four sports, but only boys like Bob Johnston, Bob Lucas and Mike Stanton starred in all sports they tried. For the girls, whose performances I admit I don't remember so well, the stars were Lois Delgado, Sandy Gleichmann, Diane Djivre and Betty Sprague. Typical of our time, the yearbook puts "Sports" in number one position after the pages of senior faces and lower class homeroom groups, then devotes twelve pages to boys' sports.   The next two pages are girls—cheerleaders whose purpose, of course, was to cheer for boys' teams.   Next followed one page for Girls' Athletic Association and Girls' Officials Club.   Then four pages of their teams and play.

By our senior year most of us were down to two or three sports or just one.   The lessons in what we could not do were lessons in crushed hopes, sometimes accompanied by bruised muscles and broken bones.   I learned I could not compete in the pole vault with John Storojev or Dave Schweers when I crashed through the bar and fell on the pole and broke a rib.   Sometimes the lessons were comical.   I tried playing catcher in baseball but I wore thick glasses and had 20-400 vision.   When the batter popped a ball almost straight up, I would tear off my mask and with it would go my glasses.   I would stand there staring up into blank space from which I hoped to spot the ball descending.   Spectators would yell out, "Behind you, behind you, turn around."   Or "To your left" or "To your right."   My waking nightmare in those instants was that I would suddenly and too late see the ball descending toward my nose.

Several people who no one thought of as athletes did well in sports no one paid much attention to.   Allan Schwartz, the once chubby grade schooler and always scholarly sports statistician, played a fine game of tennis.   So did Carolyn Berthoud the shy English violinist and Ted Vladmiroff who would later come close to winning a Nobel Prize in chemistry.   Allan Schwartz would go on to Columbia, take up fencing, and captain the university's team.   Fred Hughes, whose closest school encounter with sports was as a basketball manager, later in life became a marathoner.

Most of us remember Nik Epanchin in sports as the school's finest miler and a star in cross country.   Here is how he remembers his struggle to find his place in the sports world.

Finding A Sport: From Nik Epanchin

When I finally caught up with my age group at SCHS (in 9th grade), I went out for soccer and warmed the bench, I tried out for basketball but was cut rather early in the training season, I then tried out for baseball.   In baseball, the only position I tried for was left field because Serge told me it was the easiest. As it turned out, though I could hit reasonably, I had no arm for throwing and I was a disaster at catching flys. So Mr. Henderson told me he had to cut me but would I be willing to be a manager and keep the game records. I thanked him but declined.

The following year, again I played soccer and again warmed the bench.   Towards the end of the season, Mr. Schiffer suggested I try out track and, if someone could sponsor a cross-country team, try it out in the following fall.   So in the spring I tried out for track.   I think both Messrs Ross and Thompson gave me a try.   I wasn't much at jumping, throwing or sprinting, so they said I should run the mile. Bob Sweet ('56) was the starting miler. I think he ran it in the 5:20-30 range. I don't remember the training we received. I think it was minimal. I ran my first competitive mile in Roslyn or Manhasset coming in last in 6:42 (that time was scribed in my mind). I improved somewhat by the end of the season and Mr. Thompson said he'd sponsor a cross-country team in the fall.

As a junior, I ran cross-country along with Bob Sweet, Dave Schweers, Soren Hansen and others (sophomores Mike Levine, Michael Meilitonov, Alex Terentief. and Doug Hoyt). We did okay, nothing to brag about, and as luck would have it, I was number one. In the spring I did track again, running the mile (Bob Sweet didn't bother to do track because, as he had told me, he wouldn't be number one). My results weren't sterling but I held my own – I probably got close but I don't think I broke 5 minutes. (By the way the '56 yearbook track write-up said "... such regulars as Devon Leckie, Kurt Kundler and Dave Schweers should strengthen the team considerably".)

As a senior, cross-country was really fun. I found my form and did quite well, winning all the dual meets as well as the North Shore Championships and Sectional (Class C for all small public schools in Nassau and Suffolk Counties). I got a 3rd in the NY State meet for Class B schools (again small enrolment schools). My successes attracted several college coaches, Colgate for one. It even stirred the attention of Lois Delgado who became my girlfriend (more correctly I became her boyfriend) for about a month before real jocks like Porky took over.

In the winter we (Buster, Dave and I) joined the new wrestling team. In the spring I did track and again came through rather well. I really disappointed myself in the Sectional meet where, though I set the SCHS record, I was 4th overall and missed out going to the state finals. I held the North Shore Championship mile record for about 5 years and the SCHS/North Shore HS record for about 25 years. I got word it was broken when my family and I were in Gabon in the mid 80s. I had meant to send the new record holder congratulations from Africa, but somehow never did. (By the way, the SCHS record I broke was set in 1936 by Lou Boudreau, and I beat his time by only several hundredths of a second which to this day has made me suspicious of Mr. Thompson's clock work.)

Obviously, my running greatly helped me get into Colgate on a full scholarship – which was substantially trimmed when in my junior year, as result of many afternoon science labs, I declined to run.

I started running again in the mid 70s, at first marathons then all sort of races from 10k to marathons and triathlons. As a Masters (over 40 years old) and to Nancy's and the kids' chagrin, I ran almost every weekend and was considered one of the top San Francisco Bay

Area runners. My best marathon time was 2:35 in Oakland, CA in 1981. I did a lot of running in many of the countries I visited both for business and pleasure. I coached a Gabonese team for the Mt Cameroon ascent & descent. I haven't run competitively since 1996 with my last race in Johannesburg, South Africa. Since then I have continued to bike but not very much at all since 2003 or so.

Rereading the above indicates that indeed my high school sport activities have given me much pleasure and, as Africans would say, "Fatigue Cadeau", i.e. getting tired and worn out for nothing.

Nik Epanchin after Cameroon
Marathon

Athletic records

Nik Epanchin sent the following record of our last two track seasons. Watch the winning times, heights and distances and you can see the improvement from year to year.

4/13/56 – vs Locust Valley

100 yard dash: John Storojev tie for 3rd

440 yard run (quarter mile) – Bob Clarke 1st 0:59

880 yard run (half mile) – Soren Hansen 1st 2:27, Tim Klenk 2nd

mile – Nik Epanchin 1st 5:06

high jump - Bob Lucas & Bob Clarke tie for 1st 4'-10"

broad jump – Dave Schweers 2nd, Bob Lucas 3rd

shot put – Tom Wolf 2nd, Serge Yonov 3rd

discus – Serge Yonov 1st 92 ft, Tom Wolf 2nd, John Storojev 3rd

On 4/18/56 – vs Island Trees

440 yd (quarter mile) – Bob Clarke 1st 0:59

880 yd run (half mile)– Soren Hansen 2nd, Tim Klenk 3rd

mile – Nik Epanchin 1st 5:01

high jump - Bob Lucas & Bob Clarke tie for 1st 5'

broad jump – Dave Schweers 2nd

shot put– Serge Yonov 1st 36'-3", Tom Wolf 2nd, Fred Gallo 3rd

discus – John Storojev 1st 101'-7", Serge Yonov 2nd, Tom Wolf 3rd

On 4/20/56 – vs Bethpage

440 yd run (quarter mile)– Bob Clarke 2nd

180 yd low hurdles – John Storojev 1st 0:24

high jump - Bob Clarke tie for 2nd

shot put– Tom Wolf 2nd

mile – Nik Epanchin 1st 5:07

On 5/2/56 – vs Farmingdale

100 yd dash– Soren Hansen 1st 11.1

220 yd dash– Soren Hansen 2nd

120 yd low hurdles – Jon Storojev 2nd, Bob Lucas 3rd

Al Behrmann on school track (Photo: Fred Feingold)

440 yd run (quarter mile) – Bob Clarke 2nd

880 yd run (half mile)– Tim Klenk 3rd

mile – Nik Epanchin 1st 4:57

high jump - Bob Lucas 2nd, Bob Clarke 3rd

pole vault – Dave Schweers 2nd

shot put– Serge Yonov 1st 39'-3½", Tom Wolf 2nd, Fred Gallo 3rd

discus – John Storojev 1st 100'-7½", Serge Yonov 2nd, Tom Wolf 3rd

On 5/9/56 – vs Westbury

220 yd dash – Soren Hansen 3rd

180 yd low hurdles – Jon Storojev 2nd

mile – Nik Epanchin 1st 5:05

pole vault – Dave Schweers 2nd

Soren Hansen, 1957, by Fred Feingold

high jump - Bob Lucas tie for 1st 5'

On 4/10/57 – vs Carle Place

100 – Soren Hansen 2nd

220 yd dash– Soren Hansen 3rd

180 yd low hurdles – John Storojev 2nd, Bob Lucas 3rd

440 yd run (quarter mile) – Bob Clarke 3rd

880 yd run (half mile) – Mike Stanton 1st 2:18

mile – Nik Epanchin 1st 4:59

high jump – Mike Stanton 1st 5'-3", Bob Lucas 2nd

shot put– Serge Yonov 2nd, Tom Wolf 3rd

discus – Serge Yonov 2nd

On 4/12/57 – vs Island Trees

100 yd dash– Soren Hansen 3rd

220 yd dash– John Storojev 3rd

120 yd low hurdles – Jon Storojev 1st 14.9

440 yd run (quarter mile) – Mike Stanton 1st 0:55.6

mile – Nik Epanchin 1st 4:45

high jump – Mike Stanton 1st 6'-½", Bob Lucas 3rd

shot put – Serge Yonov 1st 43' 2", Tom Wolf 2nd

On 4/16/57 – vs Locust Valley

100 yd dash – Soren Hansen 3rd

220 yd dash – John Storojev 2nd

440 yd run (quarter mile) – Mike Stanton 1st 0:56, Bob Clarke 2nd

mile – Nik Epanchin 1st 4:43.5

high jump – Mike Stanton 1st 5'-7", Bob Lucas tie for 2nd

broad jump – Soren Hansen 3rd

shot put – Serge Yonov 1st 43' 6½", Bob Lucas 2nd, Tom Wolf 3rd

discus – Tom Wolf 1st 105'-6", Serge Yonov 2nd

On 4/18/57 – vs Oyster Bay

100 yd dash– Soren Hansen 3rd

440 yd run (quarter mile) – Bob Clarke 1st 0:58.9

180 yd low hurdles – John Storojev 3rd

mile – Nik Epanchin 1st 4:52

high jump – Bob Lucas tie for 2nd

shot put– Serge Yonov 1st 42' 6½", Tom Wolf 3rd

discus – Tom Wolf 2nd

Tom Wolfe, 1957, by Fred Feingold

On 4/25/57 – vs Manhasset

100 yd dash – Soren Hansen 2nd

120 yd low hurdles – John Storojev 1st 14.7

440 yd run (quarter mile) – Mike Stanton 1st 55.3, Bob Clarke 3rd

880 yd run (half mile) – Al Berhman 3rd

mile – Nik Epanchi 1st 4:44

high jump – Mile Stanton 1st 5'-11"

pole vault – Dave Schweers 2nd

shot – Bob Lucas 1st 39'-10". Serge Yonov 2nd, Tom Wolf 3rd

discus – Tom Wolf 1st 97'-10½", Serge Yonov 3rd

On 5/1/57 – vs Manhasset

100 yd dash– Soren Hansen 2nd

220 yd dash – John Storojev tie for 3rd

180 low hurdles – John Storojev 2nd

440 yd run (quarter mile– Bob Clarke 1st 0:57

880 yd run (half mile) – Nik Epanchin 1st 2:08.6

high jump – Mike Stanton 1st 5'-4"

broad jump – Soren Hansen 3rd

pole vault – Dave Schweers 2nd

shot put– Serge Yonov 2nd, Bob Lucas 3rd

discus – Tom Wolf 1st 103'-8", Serge Yonov 3rd

On 5/4/57 – Port Washington Invitational

440 yd run (quarter mile) – Mike Stanton 4th

mile – Nik Epanchin 2nd

high jump – Mike Stanton 2nd

Mike Stanton (Photo: Fred Feingold)

On 5/8/57 – vs Manhasset

100 yard dash – Soren Hansen 2nd

220 yd dash – Mike Stanton 1st 24:.2, John Storojev 3rd

120 low hurdles – John Storojev 1st 14.2, Bob Lucas 3rd

440 yd run (quarter mile)– Bob Clarke 3rd

mile – Nik Epanchi 1st 4:44.5

high jump – Mile Stanton 1st 5'-9", Bob Lucas 3rd

pole vault – Dave Schweers 3rd

shot put – Serge Yonov 1st 42', Tom Wolf 3rd

On 5/15/57 – North Shore Championships (Section 2)

mile – Nik Epanchin 1st 4:34.8

high jump – Mike Stanton 6 way tie for 1st

GIRLS AND BOYS: THE AGONY AND ECSTASY

Hello, young lovers
Whoever you are
I hope your troubles are few.
All my good wishes go with you tonight
I've been in love like you.

(From "The King And I," 1951)

Anne Carder, Tom Federline, Odette Butelli, Mike Stanton
Photo by Fred Feingold

Some of us did, some of us didn't—know what to do about girls or know what to do about boys. Somewhere between 6th grade and the first year of high school most of us found ourselves caught between a rock and a soft place. The soft place was the ecstasy of the love and mating that evolution has scheduled to begin at that time. The rock was that stern demand by civilization that we begin the process civilly and the social norms or our time that dictated we wait for marriage and that the earliest time for marriage was after graduation. These were days when divorce was rare and divorcees often shunned or at least avoided. A girl who became pregnant before marriage usually found herself and her lover shamed or otherwise pressured into marriage. Parents who would support abortion did so with the greatest secrecy. Couples who could afford an abortion or even know how to find one, were even rarer. Few parents ever told their children about the physiology of sex. In college I met the daughter of a famous Ph.D. chemist whose parents had sheltered her so well she believed the accidental rubbing of buttocks with a man on a bus or train might result in pregnancy. Such were the taboos of our generation.

Why all this was so and whether it was good, bad or something else, I leave to readers and scholars. I rest my description with the obvious fact that the "Sexual Revolution" of the 1970s remained invisibly beyond the horizon of our adolescence. That revolution, of course, had already been conceived in the writing of the Beat Generation and a few banned books by writers like Henry Miller, Mickey Spillane, D.H. Lawrence, and James Joyce, but it would be another 20 years being born. During our last years in high school a novel exploded into best sellerdom by exposing the sexual secrets hiding beneath the traditional surface of a small town, not unlike Sea Cliff. Despite its absence from local libraries many of us found copies of *Peyton Place*, a book that stayed on *The New York Times* best seller list for more than a year.

Civilization, almost by definition, is the reshaping and controlling of behavior dictated by evolution to work well in the wild. Once again, I have to remind myself that this is the history of a high school class and its communities, not a treatise on how and when we should be in touch with our wild natures. I am only setting the scene—the extent to which our generation tried to distance itself from that nature and the results in our lives. For instance, maybe it's worth noting that movies, books, and magazines exposed us to romance but avoided sex. And it's a fact that many of us went after the facts of nature on our own or in small hunting parties.

No subject was a more powerful stimulus to self-education than sex. Learn we did, and we pursued it with imagination and determination unknown in school. The Sea Cliff public library—Stenson Memorial—had no banned books, but Miss Rohrback would often decide some book we wanted to check out or even remove from the shelves was "too old for you." We learned to look quietly at those art books that offered nudes. *National Geographic* almost always offered the bare breasts of women and almost naked loins of men and the bare buttocks of both in societies far away from ours in time and space, and those distances seemed to legitimate exposure that in North America would be criminally indecent. What the library didn't offer, we found in other places. Sears and Roebuck catalogs offered large underwear sections with pictures and descriptions whose circumstantial evidence revealed important facts about the nature and variety of human anatomy. Boys often speculated on whether this or that girl's breasts were real, and once Bobby H took a few fellow baseball players home while his mother was away to show us her "falsies."

From an article by Barbara Thill (Schreiber, '54)
> *Seems funny now how the boys were so obsessed with bras in those days and the maidens thought athletic underware to be mysterious. Today's TV commercials offer a thirty-second Ph.D. on everything we spent ages trying to figure out.*

At Boy Scout camp and at Boys State at least two or three boys claimed to know everything about sex, and a boy in the Class of '55 would often show his proof—a condom carried in the change or driver's license compartment of his wallet.   Once a half dozen boys abandoned a hockey game on Scudder's Pond to gather around a newly arrived skater who had found in the reeds at the edge of the pond a pornographic comic book.   Having read through the book, the finder then worried about what he would tell the priest at his next confession—sure that he must confess his reading or accept damnation.   I admired his courage as much as I welcomed the comic's bawdy facts.

No objects or literature, of course, substituted for the real thing.   One classmate knew where his father kept the nude photos of his mother.   Boys hid among the trees on the "18 Trails" hoping to see immigrants or Russian girls swimming topless.   At the Pavilion the rows of wooden lockers back to back and side by side were riddled with popped out knot holes and even holes drilled in strategic places so that boys might see actual girls and women.

I have been describing the behavior of boys because I was one.   Girls have not volunteered much about the level of their own curiosity and how they dealt with it, but I do remember evidence that they had an abiding interest in forbidden knowledge.   During our senior year, for instance, a list posted at the intersection of the main hallways upstairs caused a great sensation.   On it appeared the names of every boy in the class followed by a number. Nik Epanchin appeared at the very top.   I spare those who appeared lower down since a few days after the list caused hot and on-going speculation, a boy connected by party line to a girls' conversation discovered that a group of girls had ranked each boy by imaging themselves in bed with him.

No matter what experience or knowledge a boy or girl had, most of us became victims of nature's demand that members of the opposite sex exhibit their assets.   Society and its institutions, of course, set the boundaries for how and when those assets could be placed on exhibit.   Short skirts had gone out with prohibition, and the mini-skirt had to wait for the Beatles' era of the mid '60s.   At the beach only city boys and Europeans wore tank type bathing suits, and girl's bathing suits.   Joan Imperiali caused a stir when she transferred to Sea Cliff from a Boston area school and thought little of wearing a "see through" blouse that revealed faint images of the slip or bra underneath.   For all of us, clothes became important for what they revealed or didn't reveal—both of the body and the character.   Even more important was the body itself.   Boys didn't want to be fat or 97 pound weaklings mocked by the Charles Atlas ads.   Nobody wanted to wear glasses or have pimples.   When Mr. Matthews read Dorothy Parker's lines, "Men don't make passes at girls who wear glasses," many of us took it at face value, including boys.   I know, my own glasses were responding to my increasing myopia by morphing into the bottoms of Coke bottles.   And I had pimples.   I was sure no girl would ever accept an invitation to a dance, and I waited with hope for the Sadie Hawkins' dances where the world was turned upside down and girls issued invitations to boys.

Girls worried as much or more than boys about their appearance. One of the girls in our class says, "Being heavy all my young life was hard when my first name was . . . rimed with Fat. Going into freshman and sophomore years heavy does not make one very popular either. With boys or the cute girls whose families had more money so they had all the best clothes, etc. There were many of us who did not fit in with the popular crowd and that was fine. We formed our own crowd and had as much fun. I entered my junior year at 5' 5" and 107 lbs and was still called fat by some of the boys as they passed me. How thin could one get I thought?"

Those who were naturally endowed often became the brunt of efforts to pull them down a peg—sometimes because they flaunted their assets, sometimes out of sheer jealousy. Girls once pushed Margie Repucci, who had the full lips and big breasts and dark eyes that ignited many boys, out onto the gym floor in her underwear, knowing a class of boys was waiting in the bleachers for their turn to use the gym. Boys started mocking one of their big and well built peers, "Mr. Universe." The reverse of bringing others down was often emphasizing one's own normality by teasing those who were fat or skinny or very short or in some other way physically unattractive. The adolescent ideal, then and today, seems to have been to be normal, with the ideal being to be a more attractive normal than other normals.

As I began this chapter by saying, some did and some didn't—know how to be outstandingly normal. Peter Hodgson, a Sea Cliff resident older than us, says, "Johnny Bellafato, Charlie Amrhein, and Jimmy Green, these guys were gods to me. They seemed to know about everything to do with girls and things." I envied boys like Doug Andrews and Brud Neice who were easy going and self-confident and seemed to make girls feel enough at ease enough for an occasional hug or even a casual kiss. Jane Allen recalls, "I was able to ride a bike [when she first moved to Sea Cliff and lived on level land], roller skate and play with Judy, Brud Niece, Dougie Andrews and others on the lawn of the old Sea Cliff Methodist Church. We also played ring-o-leave-e-o behind the public library on Sea Cliff Avenue. By the age of 11 I caught a few kisses behind the library from Brud and Doug Andrews."

Brud, Doug, Barbara, Lois, Cherry, Faith, Photo: Fred Feingold

Pat Mills' first kiss came not from one of the easy going boys but one of the wilder ones. "Richie Loftus was my first love, and took me to my first movie, put his arm around me and all. I remember watching TV with him and he even gave me my first kiss (on the cheek). Must have been in the fifth grade or so. I was in love with David Bostrom for a while, probably out on the playground before Richie Loftus (4th grade?...no way)."

Maybe Lois Delgado and Cherry Campbell were their equivalents among the girls—Lois voted "most popular" and Cherry "Flirt." Dancing is one of the surest signs of comfort with the opposite sex, and did any boy not want to be able to Lindy like Bob Clarke? Getting a boy's or girl's ring and "going steady" meant you were one of those who pre-qualified for a permanent mate.

I never gave or enjoyed the offer of a ring, but that didn't stop me from thinking somebody might like me well enough to go steady with me. But geez, those damn pimples. And the glasses. And I never developed any grace with a basketball that would put me out there on the floor scoring. I wasn't fast enough to run sprints or long legged enough for distance and probably never got over 6 ft pole vaulting. I tried to learn a dance faster than the fox trot, but even my fox trot looked more like the moose trot. All my male display talents seemed severely limited, and brains didn't count for much or so it seemed.

I was both blessed and cursed by having had a memorable first kiss. My first kiss and thus first desperate infatuation with the promises of the flesh and all the comfort of female attention and sympathy was Tina Hallberg. At the bottom of Winding Way or Altamont Ave. one snowy evening as the sled we sat on came to a stop in a snowbank, she, sitting in front of me, turned her head around and leaned backward with two red lips brightened under the streetlamp and we kissed. I hope everyone's first was as memorable. A few months later, for reasons I no longer remember, Tina was spending time with someone else. Three years later she had the kindness to write in my yearbook, "Don't forget the fun we had going together when we were freshmen." I didn't, I haven't. I spent the next three years hoping I'd have someone to "go together" with. (Not a bad ideal for life—*going together*. I think of a few notable examples of couples who met in school and continued—Pete Muttee and Carole Brown, John Maloney and Anna Makowski, Betty Gelling and Frank Wood.)

Sometimes one of the people who seemed to have it all became a torment for an admirer who felt he or she had so little the gap between them was too great to cross. Even in elementary school Fred Feingold knocked his head on real or imagined barriers. "One major reason I never dated anyone from our class was that in those days in Sea Cliff one did not cross over the line. I remember my very first week in Sea Cliff playing tag in front of the Methodist Church (now Museum) and being told, and worse; believing, that I could not enter because I did not go to that church. Of course now I realize that it was just a tactic for the other kids to escape, but I, from birth, had been brainwashed by my mother. Lois Delgado was off limits although I did pursue her in the fifth grade. Did our mutual shin kicking episodes lead to her developing leukemia? I get sick dizzy thinking of the possibility. This adoration led to the breaking of small glass pane in her house with a slingshot stone. Someone was with me, but I dare not identify him. Her dad was very nice about it.   I was too poor and embarrassed to ever come up with the $0.89 for a new piece of glass.   She did once ride on my handlebars in the cemetery next to the school after a game of ring a leveo.   Once someone called her a Guinea.   I corrected him and stated that this was incorrect, Lois was a Spic.   She thought that was wonderful.   Then of course there was the terrible problem of The Upper Classman, or worse; The College Man.   I get a pain in the pit of my stomach, and my arms go numb even now remembering the hopelessness."

Dave Schweers' yearbook entry says "fond of romances and Harry James."   Harry James, the trumpet player, was not the object of romance but few people believed as strongly as Dave Schweers in the benefits of knowing and romancing the opposite sex. Most boys admit to an interest in girls only in adolescence, and for many that is when the agony and, occasionally, the ecstasy begin.

Dave recalls that his "first 'girlfriend,' like many others, probably didn't even know I had a thing for her.   Were in kindergarten in Glen Head.   (Yes I started letching really early.)   It was Genie (Jeannie) Sassamen.   She lived on the other side of town, but by the first grade I used to walk to her house just to run around with her.   She was a wild free spirit even then.   My affection showed itself to me in a bizarre manner.   I used to dream that I had died and was laying in some form of casket and she would come near me and ...... whatever she did was always obscure, but it felt nice.   I don't know if anything really happened but I dreamed of her a lot."

"I remember that one of our favorite school yard games was to pretend to tie several girls to a tree and run around them screaming like Indians, waving sticks like tomahawks, and threatening to scalp them.   The girls, and Jeannie especially, initiated this routine enthusiastically although I am not sure what they got out of it except the concept that whatever happened to them wasn't their fault because they were tied up.   That theme repeated through my life, especially with the Catholic girls I pursued.

"Somewhere in 2nd or 3rd grade I became aware of a beautiful, aloof young girl with a strange accent (the accent of money and position).   She had a tall, angular friend named Helen Johnson who guarded her viciously against the attempts to get near her.   Her name was Anita Hamilton and I dreamed of her for several years.   I only dreamed.   I was so shy it hurt."

"I am not sure she ever realized how infatuated I was.   She should have known because I did all the right things.   She took ballet lessons in the Norway Hall in Glen Head by the railroad station.   To show my interest, I and a friend used to peak in the door and watch them in their tutu's then run away.   On snowy days we used to throw snowballs in the door and run.   Some time during that period she went away for a while, I think to France.   As a class project we had to write letters to her.   I wrote how I sadly waited for her to get off the bus every day, even in the rain, and I missed her terribly. I remember there being some adult discussion about the purpleness of my prose, and I think they never sent my letter."

"The high point of this imagined relationship was the night that I came from a Cub Scout meeting in full dress to watch her (and Helen) perform in a ballet at school. When she had danced her part, she came into the back of the auditorium to watch the rest of the performance. I was there roaming around in my uniform feeling dashing. I mumbled hello and stared."

"The next time I saw Anita was around 9th grade when Glen Head students moved to Sea Cliff High. It was the beginning of the year and we were all wandering around the gymnasium for some reason. I saw her looking as cool as ever, and I thought maybe I still have a chance. I went over and said hello and she was courteous as ever, and then I found out she wasn't staying, she was going to school wherever the kids of rich influential people go. She was definitely incredibly beautiful and I have never really forgotten her. I was heartbroken, but then there was Pat Walters, Nancy Hawkins, Carole Hincula and the real love of my life, Elizabeth Morse whose features are permanently etched in to my brain."

Elizabeth "Bizzy" Morse was one girl whose looks and wit made several boys feel that way. Fred Feingold again, was one of those boys. "I felt loss when Bizzy moved from Sea Cliff to Harwinton, Connecticut. Although I was old enough to know better, I used to stand on the old hotel site over the harbor and wonder if I could see that far. I guess being brought up during WW II influenced my acceptance of the inevitability of loss. As our junior prom approached I thought that I could dress up my own selfish desires as an act of caring and have Bizzy come with me. I think that I beat out Dave Schweers by about two minutes in inviting Bizzy. I was astounded and terrified when she actually accepted. What could I do? I could not dance, make proper conversation or anything. It was an agonizing, awkward, stressful evening. I was unable to draw even half a breath before, during, or after. Poor Bizzy. Some time later, to make it up to her when she was in NYC I took her to dinner and to see "Diabolique." I was all prettied up, so under control and poised, that, after I so elegantly ushered her into one of those long chassis, jump seat equipped taxicabs; I sat on the floor. That early evening we went to the elegant apartment of her grandmother who was dying. The place was dimmed and there were various spirits gliding about in silence. This was a household in which medical care was not invoked. I did not discuss this belief system with Bizzy".

"A few years later, I heard indirectly that Bizzy was a music major at the University of Indiana. Perhaps as early as her second year she took her tuition money, went on to The Southwest where she practiced skydiving and perhaps piloting. I later heard that she was driving a van for harpists."

I have found a few entries in a journal I kept in the mid 1950s that name the objects of my hopes and affections.

Jan. 28, 1955. Dougie & Cherry are asking me if I like Judy. I've been calling and thinking about Carol Hincula.

February 7. Betty and Ceil may be getting a bad reputation from their association with Happy.

Saturday February 12. Went to the Valentine's Dance at the Youth Center. Danced with Ceil most of the night. I think I like her.

Sunday Ceil doesn't seem to like me, but I can't tell.

Monday. I'm not sure about Ceil. Saw her at the drugstore.

June 18, 1955. Spied on the girls swimming in the dark at Tilley's.

I suspect I was not the only one who made important decisions by letting romantic fantasy overpower reason. I blame Guy T. Pinkard who took four of us in his biology class to his hometown of Milltown, Alabama for Easter vacation, 1955. The nominal reason for the trip was for members of our biology club to meet members of the Milltown high school club which had joined us in forming the National High School Biology Exchange Club. Horseshoe crabs for prickly pear cactuses was not the only thing the clubs would exchange.

Figure 1Guy T Pinkard's father's store in Milltown, AL.   Photo by Nik Epanchin

I was president of our club and fell madly in love with the president of their club—the cherry lipped, big eyed, blonde girl who had been elected president of her club—Linda Welch.   We had arrived in Milltown on April 9.

My journal notes how quickly I fell:

12th - we went to Cheaha Park w/ Pinkard & Milltown students.

14th - went to party at Wayne's [Milltown student] where I made out with Linda Welch

I visited her at her home and met her mother.   We sat on the swing of their porch and held hands and kissed and imagined.   Her mother in the bedroom on the other side of the wall was also imagining, I'm sure.   The rest of that spring of the next year we wrote many letters in the kind of innocent pink passion of teenagers who expected much but knew little.   Not knowing anything about caste and class in the South, I called her "my southern belle."   The belles, of course, were something akin to debutantes, not girls from a poor millworker's family.   She responded, "Kisses for calling me a Southern Belle, the first time I was ever called that."   Later she wrote, If two hearts, two kisses make one love, I'm sure it does with two very strong arms out in a swing under the stars added with them, and a Yankee and a Southern Belle together."

The summer of '55, when I had finished work in South Dakota on an archeological project, I hitched to Milltown and spent a week or two in presidential smooching and hand holding.   Her mother, a woman with no husband and a mill worker, had to leave us alone during the day, but always left us with a bucket of peas to shell.   Later that year she concluded a letter with these words, "Well, again I'll say it has been nice, & if I see you again tomorrow—or if I never see you again—there will always be a spot in my heart for you alone."

Words like that are a siren call to a lonely, insecure teenage boy.   With Linda and future bliss in mind, I decided to apply to colleges between New York and Alabama.   I was sure I could never pass in the Ivy League schools of the north and looked for a B level college with a big English department, scholarship money and a soccer team.   Duke took me, but even before the acceptance letter came, my romance had evaporated.

I never saw her again, but one of the Milltown boys replied to a letter from our class secretary, Kay Parks.   Those letters led to marriage.   (See Kay's page.)   Fifty-five years later I found Linda living one mile from the porch swing

Footnote: Fifty-five years after seeing Linda for the last time, my research on Dr. Pinkard's life led me to web sites about Alabama, and I found Linda living in a house a mile from the porch swing we sat on.   After raising three girls she divorced and became a nurse.   She is still nursing.   She also owns her own 70 acre farm and tends a few head of cattle.

NEW LIVES: THE FIRST YEARS AFTER GRADUATION

In contemplating where we thought our lives would lead after graduation, Ted Vladimiroff went through the 1957 yearbook and categorized our announced dreams and ambitions, and perhaps a few lightly tossed off ideas, about what we foresaw in our adult lives.

Ted's notes:

For the women there still were: 8 teachers, 14 secretaries, 5 nurses, and 5 airline hostesses. Two of the women were interested in art as a career (I remember Helen [Basilevsky] was always drawing something). Then there was one each, model, actress, engineer, physical therapist, CPA, writer, literature, and reporter.
The men were mostly interested in the military (10) and engineering (9). Not always clear if the military was meant to be a career or just a service obligation. Only three were interested in teaching. Two wanted to be pilots. Then there was one each, pharmacist, chef, TV producer, musician, lawyer and MD.
The biggest overlap between men (6) and woman (10) was in business careers, but probably not the same type of business.

Immediately after graduation some members of the class disappeared. They wanted to leave behind their families and lives that had often been made miserable by alcohol, drugs, abuse, or some other plague over which their only control was departure.

Among the many letters from the past 50 years I found a short story in which a girl puts a boy's gloom in perspective. The whole story is not worth reading, but this particular passage describes her family. Few of us knew her parents. Most of us knew her. Here is how she describes her family.

"At least you were supposed to be born. Somebody wanted you. I was an accident. Mama didn't want me and Daddy didn't have anything to do with it. No, he had to act like a father to somebody else's kid. And that wasn't the first time. Nobody wanted Joe either. Mama and Daddy never wanted us. What do you think made Daddy start drinking. He was making money and getting along fine until Mama had Joe and me. And did Mama care? No. No. She had him too scared to get a divorce. She's ruined his life for him ever since they were married. And he lets her do it because he still loves her. He's a thin, little, tired man and wouldn't hurt anyone, not even when they hurt him, but Mama doesn't care. One time the doctor came to look at burns on Daddy's arm that had become infected. When the doctor asked him how he got it, Daddy said it didn't

matter. But the doctor said it did and Daddy broke down crying and said, 'She hit me, she hit me with a hot iron!' then he ran into the kitchen and put his head on the table and cried like a baby. I ruined everybody's life because I'm not supposed to be here. Mama and Daddy fight, Joe ran away, and now I sit here and make you sad telling you all this. Oh, hell!" She started crying quietly with her face in her hands.

I like happy endings so I should note that the girl seized graduation to put as many miles as possible between her and her family. She began a career, married, enjoyed a long life and full family, and still does.

Our math teacher and track and cross-country coach, Don Thompson kept a record of where most of us went. They are lists of where each of us went after high school and for each of us he lists our rank in the class academic standings. His son Norm recently found these mimeographed sheets with his father's notes and sent them to me. He said that in his father's papers these were the only record of a class and its post-graduation whereabouts.

I have cut off the class standings. One reason I do not post the rankings is because in many cases they do not reflect the person's real character or achievement. I leave it to you to decide what to make, if anything, of Don Thompson's division of futures into "4 Year Colleges," then two other lists which include "Teachers Colleges" and "Schools of Nursing".

We know from recent studies, for instance, that both academic and athletic achievement can be highly influenced by whether a person is the oldest or youngest in the class. For instance, someone who is 11 months younger than the older class members, is often disadvantaged in athletics and the older class members advantaged because physical development is so rapid until about 18 or 20. The same is true of academic potential. For skills in reading, writing, and math and even the coordination required for penmanship, a difference of 11 or 12 months can mean the youngest are significantly behind the oldest. They often struggle. Feel stupid. A teacher might reinforce that self-image.

I'm a rank amateur in child development and psychology, so I won't carry on. I will make only a few notes as food for thought.

It's interesting to compare the rank in the class and the record of life achievements. For instance among those who ranked 80th or below in our class of 110 we have fighter pilots, decorated high ranking military officers, multi-millionaire business people, accomplished fiction writers, bank presidents, Silicon Valley millionaires, and corporate executives at the Fortune 500 level. Several of the people who did not appear on Thompson's list because they went from school directly to work also had rewarding or notable lives in business, theater, education and pursuing family and personal interests.

The top 15 or so seem to have generally achieved as expected--successful careers, near Nobel Prize achievers, notable people in their professional ranks. I know enough of their personal lives, however, to tell you that at least half had very serious personal problems, including suicide.

SEA CLIFF HIGH SCHOOL

Class of '57

Schools of Nursing

Student	School
Ahearn, Ruth	St. Joseph's Hospital
Brown, Judith	Un. of Conn. Sch. Nursing
DeVeuve, Valerie	St. Luke's Hosp.
Gerroir, Dorothy	Community Hosp. Glen Cove

Armed Services.

LeFebvre, James	Navy
Hughes, Fred	Air Force
Platt, Robert	Air Force
Soper, Robert	

Business Schools

Wignes, Karen	Brown's Bus. School
Sydow, Cathy	" " "
Henninger, Maria	Berkeley

SEA CLIFF HIGH SCHOOL

CLASS OF '57

Teachers Colleges.

Student	College	Ran
Burdick, Phoebe	Plattsburgh	
Brown, Carole	Genesseo	
Gelling, Bette	Buffalo	
Meier, Walter	Buffalo	
Reppucci, Margie	Oswego	
Schweers, Dave	Potsdam	
Vaccaro, Michelina	Genesseo	
Pascucci, Ann	Plattsburgh (?)	

Junior Colleges

Frost, Susan	Green Mountain Jr.Coll
Hallberg, Christine	Dean Junior College
Snayd, Ceil	?

Technical Institutes.

Burns, Fred	Mohawk Valley Tech. Inst.
Hincula, Carole	Agr. & Tech. Inst. Alfred
Ferris, Barbara	Grace Institute
LaPierre, Joanne	Labratory Inst. for Merchandising
Muttee, Peter	Delhi
Norminton, Lola	Farmingdale Agr.
McAdams, Edward	Mohawk Valley (?)
Santonastasi, Ronald	Farmingdale (?)

Other

Klein, Richard	Acad. of Aeronautics
Moffat, Carol	Barbizon Sch. Mod.
LaJoy, Faith	Beautician School
Stack, Richard	Hofstra (Night School)
Schmersal, George	Nyack Missionary Coll.
Neice, Ed	N.Y.Community Coll.

SEA CLIFF HIGH SCHOOL

CLASS OF '57

4 Year Colleges.

Student	College	Rank i
Allen, Jane	Boston University	
Andrews, Douglas	Un. of Wyoming	
Berthoud, Caroline	Beechlawn Tut. Coll. England	
Broderick, John	Ithaca	
Campbell, Cherry	Un. of Miami	
Clark, Robert	St. Lawrence	
Delgado, Lois	Wheaton (or Marymount)	
Djivre, Diana	Syracuse Un.	
Elton, Douglas	Lehigh	
Epanchin, Nick	~~North Carolina State~~ COLGATE 340 -	
Feingold, Fred	~~Georgetown~~ ? COLUMBIA	
Freedman, Sandra	Emerson	
Gallo, Fred	Cornell	
Gilson, Barbara	Smith	
Gleichman, Sandra	Cooper Union	
Greenfield, Rosalie	Syracuse	
Hansen, Soren	Cornell	
Johnston, Robert	~~Un. of Kansas~~	
Kaufman, Wallace	~~Middlebury or~~ Duke	
Klenk, Tim	Wheaton	
Lucas, Robert	Colgate	
Malkin, Linda	C.W.Post	
Maloney, John	St. John's	
McKinley, James	Syracuse Un. Sch.Forestry	
Olsen, Judith	Augustana, So. Dakota	
Samuelson, Nancy	Augustana, So. Dakota	
Schwartz, Allan	~~Cornell (or~~ Columbia)	
Sessler, Jane	Cornell	
Sprague, Betty	Alfred	
Storojev, John	Emerson	
Swanson, Peter	Adelphi	
Vladimiroff, Ted	Stevens Inst. of Tech.	
Wolf, Thompson	Lafayette *let out*	
Yonov, Serge	Colorado School of Mines *Dropped end to Leo work*	
Stanton, Mike	Un. of Florida *left*	

(Where Mr. Thompson has a question mark for Ceil Snayd, should be Georgetown Visitation.)

Friendships don't dissolve very quickly. Many members of the class who were leaving for college and the military stayed in touch by mail and phone. Those who continued to live and work on Long Island remained friends and have continued to see each other for more than fifty years. Some of those friendships are noted in the individual biographies later in this history. When I talked to each member, of course, they could remember only rare conversations and events of the late 50s and early 60s. The fullest record is in a few news clippings and in a few extensive exchanges of letters by members who went off to college.

A few people took to college as a family tradition—of course, they were going to go—like father, mother, even grandparents. It was the natural next step in education and entering a career. Most of us did not have parents who went to college. Several people, including me, had parents who had not finished high school. Many who did not go to college or professional education in the 50s and 60s went to school after their children were in high school or had graduated. Once again, we were a pivotal generation, a generation that went to college in unprecedented numbers, reflecting a more affluent country and higher expectations.

I'm now glad I kept old letters, and I am very grateful to a several class members who have kept old letters and who have given me permission to include some of their correspondence, even if the writer must remain anonymous.

When Barbara Gilson looked over the letter selections below, she thought of the TV series about advertising people of the 50s and 60s, Mad Men. Her comment makes a good introduction.

"The 1960s ad people were Korea. It's 1960 in the beginning, the same span as the letters, and the times were about to change radically, but we certainly didn't seem to know it. The path through college and beyond feels well worn -- dating and mating, sports, deciding what to be and do, going to "the city" and Greenwich Village. Perhaps those are historical universals. I was a bit surprised by how many spoke about getting engaged and so young, but of course, at Smith it was almost a requirement that one be engaged by junior year. However, except for a couple of animadversions on the sexual morals of the younger generation, no one seems to have any suspicion that revolution was on the way -- civil rights, sexual, gender and so on. Also your collection comes entirely from middle and upper middle class young'uns. Probably the guys who worked in the garage or construction and the young ladies heading for the phone company had different concerns."

In the letters that follow I have preserved most of the spelling, punctuation, date formats, paragraphing, and grammar.   Most were written by hand and often used shortcuts, but interestingly they are nothing like today's texting on cell phones—as U cn C fm R contents.

From a letter sent by Don Rockwell ('56) Sept 21, 1957.
Don had been dating Jane Allen.   He started college in Cornell and for his sophomore year he transferred to MIT in Boston while Jane had chosen a junior college there.   (See her bio.)

"I went down to say hello to Jane last night, but she had a date.   So here I was in a girl's dorm all alone.   Jane said that the people were so friendly that they would come up and introduce themselves.   I was there for an hour and a half.   But I finally convinced the girl who was signing people out to go to the movies with me.   Her name is Joan and we had a great time.   We saw Band of Angels and Silk Stockings."

"By the way, why isn't life just a game?"

From Allan Schwartz, October, 1957.   Allan Schwartz is settling into Columbia University.   Before he graduates he will become captain of the fencing team.   In his freshman year he writes, "My sports career, as mentioned, is still in a state of suspended animation.   Though I've never fenced before, I still have hopes of having latent talent."

"It's really amazing, New York is probably the best place in the world for nighttime entertainment and I haven't been out of the University yet.   I'm inclined to think I'll get the picture on the other side when I write Diane [Djivre] and Ro [Greenfield] [Both Ro and Diane were at Syracuse.]"

November 3, 1957.   Ian Ronald ('55) answered a note I had sent with a book.   He had belatedly enrolled in Albany State Teachers College.   "I got myself snowed into coming to Albany State," he wrote, but he liked his courses and professors.   He noted, "I have yet to find a girl to compare with Sussannnnne who incidentally is now going with of all people—Ken Cox.   How does that grab you?   I didn't know whether to laugh or cry when I heard it."

(I had started Duke where Ed Gauld, Ian's classmate, was playing varsity soccer. At Sea Cliff Ian had been a passionate follower of all sports and a meticulous keeper of statistics.)
"I wish I could see him play.   Say hello to him for me the next time you see him and ask him if he's getting much.   How many goals has he scored so far?   North Shore soccer team is, I believe, still undefeated.   The football team is 3-2, the last loss to Manhasset by one point.   I was home last weekend and saw them beat Roslyn.   Myles is impressive."

"I saw Nick about three weeks ago.   He looked pretty good but missed dear old Jane.   Lucas, I understand, is having troubles.   Nick or NIK won a couple of meets.   Moose leaves tomorrow for six months of Marine life. How do you suppose our friend Marjorie is making out—literally and figuratively."

Another classmate wrote about recent news as we began new lives at work and in college and university:

So Bobby Clark[e] has taken up with a nurse, eh. How did that interesting situation come about? Somehow I never thought of Bob as the type to go for older women. Could this mean that he and Allyson are completely pfffft? Also, I couldn't possibly have heard you right when you said Lukie was majoring in philosophy. My lord that is the switch of the ages. I keep seeing him in sort of a Socratic getup and bare feet wandering around the Agora. Perhaps Betty may have a touch of Xanthippe in her makeup, but the move still seems a little drastic. Good,old gum-chewing, one-of-the-boys Lukie.

From a series of letters to and from Anonymous
Forget Gloria Steinem and Betty Friedan--they were come-latelies, lightweights and academic voyeurs compared to some of the women in our class. Here are excerpts from a correspondence that went on quite regularly in the first six years after we left Sea Cliff.

Sept 26, 1957
Don't you worry your pretty little head about falling in love either. Knowing you it'll be either some little blonde chick who doesn't know her head from a hole in the ground, or dominating, strange type who'll crush you under her strident personality. In the meantime, what's wrong with good old sex? Write as soon as you've got Duke under your grimy thumb and have made all the girls shouldn't take more than 2 days.

October 2, 1957
What I meant by advising you to stick to "good old sex" was that there seems to be no point in cluttering up your life with any grand passion during your term of preparing to be head of World Dictators Inc. but neither is there any future in squatting in the lab with your microscope from year end to year end. Remember, you've got the honor of the aggressive Sea Cliff Male to uphold. Your getting smashed doesn't worry me at all. Since we sharpened our claws on each other for nigh unto four years, I imagine you're poised enough for anything short of nuclear attack.

Oct. 13, 1957

Dear Buster,
Really now, I think it very bad tempered of you to go popping off about women like a

discontented volcano.   If women hold all the trumps, it's because the men have unwittingly given them away.   In the beginning, because men were physically more powerful, woman had to be pretty clever to survive with her individuality (and a few other things) intact.   So one high card that women really hold is the need of men for them, (such as your pal with the illustrated bunk).   Anyhow, I don't recall your ever getting the short end of the stick, so why the moral indignation.   It couldn't be your altruistic love of justice, could it?

Oct. 22, 1957
Foo yourself!   It won't do you the least bit of good to try and blame nature for the subordination of the males.   It's all their own fault for underestimating their enemy.   I can see it all way back in the primitive ages—some sere old Pithecanthropus Erectus saying to his son "Well it's like this about women, son, they are a lot of fun but they don't have any brains.   You might say they're just naturally the weaker sex.   If they show any sign of being sassy, just club 'em and that'll hold 'em for good.   Of course your mother isn't like that.   Wonderful woman, wonderful.   Which reminds me she told me . . . I mean we'd better be getting on home; it's pretty near supper."

"Okay pop.   Gee, you sure know a lot about women!"

And so by sticking obstinately to the idea that because a woman was weaker physically she was also weaker mentally men handed over all sorts of weapons, unwittingly.   Foolishly they allowed themselves to develop scruples about physically maltreating their women and lost even the use of muscular supremacy.   If you've looked into the law books of the U.S. you'll have noticed that women have been gradually working towards the same rights as men have and they have also kept their privileges.   (Need I enumerate—alimony, no draft etc.)   The laugh may be on youse guys but don't blame nature.

10/31/57
Dear Buster,
What in the world did poor old Freud ever data you that you've got it in for him so? Anyway this letter is proof that women can learn something from men.   When I read all your neatly typewritten epistles I decided to give the infernal machine a chance and am finding it a lot easier to compose.   From here on, personal type, hand written letters go out the window and cold, clear, businesslike logic comes in the door.

I don't by any means wish that man had'nt [sic] relinquished his physical dominance over women.   Black and blue are not colors in which I fancy myself.   I do say that that for him it was a mistake since it took away his only innate superiority.   And because he does have a rather prevalent need of women at frequent intervals he's down one before the game even begins.

I agree that even if you did know all the weapons that man has given away and I were to tell you about them, you still wouldn't be back in the pre-Freudistoric days; but it wouldn't be because of "damned old nature"; it would be because of damned old you.   You can't fling off your civilization like a pair of dirty pants.   You may prove to yourself logically that there's no reason why you shouldn't make women slaves again and immure you wife in purdah (poor soul) but there are several reasons why you won't.   First there are laws against that sort of thing and I doubt that you would fly directly in the face of the penal system.   Second your reason would tell you that physical might is not a sensible basis for human relationship.   Thirdly you probably wouldn't want a king-slave relationship in your little home out in Suburbia.   You'd much prefer some babe whom you believe to be slightly below you mentally but smart enough so you could expound your Olympian ideas to her and receive her appreciative coos.   I suppose you could fight the whole thing if you wanted to devote your entire life to it but it would be a pretty hollow career.

Nov. 11, 1957
I agree with you (I'll have to stop doing that, or it'll go to your head) that women do have the edge, but I see no prospect of a War Between the Sexes.   All we need is enough of the right kind of men and women, so that the question of superiority on the basis of sex will cease to have importance.   Whether this ever comes about is another story.

Nov. 18, 1957
My roommate and I just took a joint poll, to keep things interesting, on what we would take in life if we could have only six things nothing else.   It came out as expected, in this order, food, shelter, clothing; sex; cigarettes; and liquor.   It just shows how materialistic one can be underneath all the fol-de rol of civilization.

Dec. 3, 1957
Well, Peyton Place is rather the fashion up here at the moment.   However, since I read it last year after giving it to my mother for Christmas, I'm constantly being approached by furtive undergraduates, requesting me to point out the "good" parts.   My roommate just finished it lately.

As for Jung, all I know about him is that he was originally a follower of Freud but soon disagreed and branched out to form his own school of psychoanalysis.   In general, while I'm not a blind disciple of Siggy's,[Sigmond Freud] I think he had more on the ball and is twice as much fun as Jung.

May I point out that without wine and women there would be no humankind to be plagued, besotted and infatuated?

Dec. 11, 1957
Now then, what's all this querulousness about women for mmmmm?   Ordinarily, I would

say no, that wine and allied potables are not necessary to the furtherance of the human race. But taking a look at Today's Man, especially the college variety, I'm not even sure that the grain and the grape will do any good. Let's face it, the average specimen is a pretty sorry lot. Maybe that's why they're doing away with him. I don't think they'll eliminate him completely, tho because women will always need diversion at times. How would you like to be pampered, spoiled, catered to, fed chocolates and spend every day on a chaise lounge? It just might come to that. O well.

"Men give more damns about women, than they do about anything else." [says it is from her new book, Why Not Stop Kidding Yourself]

February 11, 1958
Bring Love in the Western World home with you spring vacation; I'd like to take at look at it and find out what else is wrong with us all.
"Your psyche about to go bust?
Try a little lust."

Feb. 24, 1958
If you're ever looking for a libidinous movie; calculated to drive youth to a life of wild debauchery, drop in on And God Created Woman, THAT French import sporting the charms of Brigitte Bardot. I'll say this for it, it certainly shows BB at her best.

Dec. 5 1958 [from WK to her]
All the girls are going wild in psychology since we have now embarked quite uninhibitedly upon sex drive with a very sophisticated prof. (Experiments, optional). The phenomenon is probably similar to the one you mentioned last October in connection with a popular sociology course.

February 19, 1958. **Ed Bolitho**, Sr. led Boy Scout Troop 43 that met at the Youth Center and included many boys in our class. "Mr. B" was a small, wiry man who could outdo all of us in chin-ups and situps. He expected us to pursue Scouting goals hard and to play hard. What kids ever appreciate the sacrifices adults make for them? He kept us within bounds without tying us down, and we responded by trying to be what he wanted for us. He worked for Amperex Electronic Corp., and devoted much of his spare time to Scouts, his wife Madeline devoting her time to Girl Scouts. Here are some of his observations about our years.

"The ages between 10 and 20 are the most important. If during these years you have started on the right track, the later years will take care of themselves. The trouble is we don't have enough men, women and teachers who are interested or qualified to help teenagers. Perhaps this Sputnick mess will wake them up. Yes, I'm still in Boy Scouts. We have about forty boys in the troop . . . However there will never be another troop as far as I am concerned as good as the old gang. Someday we must have a re-union."

"I met D. Leckie ('56) the other day. He flunked English and ran out of money at the same time. He has to make the English up and expects to go back this fall."

(At Christmas 1961 "Mr. B" sent me a card with a note.) "Wally give some consideration to journalism—we need young people to stand up and express their thoughts on world conditions and to find ways and means of living peacefully together. Our generation hasn't done too well and it's up to you and the other young people to straighten things out—or there won't be a world to worry about."

Our Troop 43 never did have that reunion, but for many of us, Ed Bolitho remained a reminder of what we could do if we believed in ourselves.

Emma Kaufman, Troop Mother, presents pen and pencil set to Scoutmaster Bolitho. On right: Pete Birmingham, Pete Marnane. John Behrmann. Early 50s.

11/8/58 [from Wallace to Nik Epanchin]
(I had started my sophomore year at Duke with a new roommate, a tall lanky science major from Ohio who was glad to go hiking in the Duke Forest with me. We brought back a corn snake or puff adder for a pet and kept him in a burlap bag in our closet when he slept.)

We had a 3 foot puff adder in the room, which I may have told you about. Although we robbed some specimens from the zo labs, we couldn't find any bullfrog small enough for him to eat seeing as he always does it with the characteristic single swallow. The first toad we fed him, he brought all the way back up a foot of gullet and deposited him on the floor in our after consumption – still alive.   That toad he re-swallowed and enjoyed, but others were not nearly so palatable.

When I get a chance, I am going to drop Clarkie a letter, but for now have settled for a postcard.   If you get a chance drop Min [Min Hall who ran the concession at the Pavilion with her brother Frank] a card at 4 Hill St. Glen Cove.   She gets a big thrill from it, here it. She's probably working for nothing in the taxi office again, while Frank sits home telling himself stories about ass hole and clam chowder.   Tell Clarke [John] and Lukie.   I said hello.   How's Clarke doing with Joan?

----

from Nik Epanchin to Wallace 11/12/58
I made myself another one of those vows, this time it is to answer letters promptly. I don't know how long this good intention will last.

The soccer team here piled up a 3-5-1 record.   It's high light was losing to Penn State 2-1 and tying Army 1-1.   It lost too many "rinky dink" schools.   Lucas got about 3 to 4 goals and was very inconsistent.   His last game was against Syracuse where he scored two and where we won 4-1.   Clarke [John] has been playing goal, since our #1 goalie was hurt (5-10 stitches in his right hand).   They tell me he has been really good, but he has never been written up in the paper (not that it proves anything).   We did have 2 really good sophs who sort of kept the team in the scoring columns.

My season was over with Oct. 31st when we lost to Army and Syracuse very badly. I got a stitch and ran one of my worst races (I still managed to be 2nd for Colgate).   The coach asked me if I wished to go to the IC4-A's .   But declined, I don't think I'm good enough to make the extra work worth the while.   It meant be staying out for an extra 2 ½ weeks and working my balls off.

Last Saturday, the state X-country meet was held here, and Cyril Yonov and John Kozzusko [lifeguard at the Pavilion, from Glen Cove] came up.   They both ran this year but didn't accomplish anything great (didn't make the state).   I introduced John to the track coach who seemed interested until John told him his grades were very poor in English and Soc. St.   He (the coach) already knew Cyril.

My brother, Alex ['60] was elected Veep of the Junior Class.

I started all sorts of extracurricular activities.   As to get in the Junior Honorary and get some good recommendations later.   I joined the Russian studies club and the National

Service society APO.   I'm soliciting for blood giving fund and will give some myself.

I will definitely not run winter track, I'm up to 158 already.   Chem isn't as bad as I thought it to be, I had a B going. . . .

How close are you to 4.0 this year?   I plan to take zoology and psychology next year and dropped physics, which bores me.

Teddy Vladimiroff finished 2nd in his class last year at Stevens.   I'll see you sometime,

write again,

11/14/58 [from a classmate in northern New York]

. . .   My roommate this year is the combination Andy Panda & Dumbo – not too smart but pleasant and good for a few laughs.

I'm still going strong with O----.   I think I'm going to lose that $20 soon (2 yrs) – who knows --   [I had bet him $20 he would be engaged that year.]   She's coming home for Thanksgiving.   Really [?] is a lot better – before, she didn't think her parents were coming home until Xmas time.

So I'm happy – as you can imagine.   I hear quite often from her, and I write a lot, so I'm able to keep pretty close tabs on her.   I just wonder if I'm getting the whole story – at least I have Ben [Bess?] on the lookout for me.

The last three days I've started to work out.   I have also started another attempt to stop smoking.   It will probably be as unsuccessful as all of my other attempts.

I saw Judy Engers the other weekend down in Oneonta.   I also saw Peggy Gremlesbacker, and Barbara something or other, who goes to the State teachers College there.   Judy goes to Hartwick, a small school in Oneonta.

My activities have broadened a great deal this year.   Saints [singing group] take a lot of time, but I'm considering dropping it.   I get so bored with certain activities after a while.   I especially get tired of certain people – so many are such hypocrites.

Nothing of note has happened this year.   My marks are about the same – I'm taking Spanish, and the improvement I have made is gratifying.   Someday I'd like to go to Mexico or somewhere and see if I could really learn to speak it fluently.

11/20/58   [Buster to this friend]

Dear ---,

It won't be with any great displeasure that I accept your $20, but I'll also take pleasure in seeing you walk up the aisle.   Big ear to ear grin with eyes so wide they could hold all the barf at the reception's aftermath.   When you ask me to the church part I promise I'll behave.   When Thanksgiving comes around you'll be able to let go of those "close tabs" and embrace her in a close hug.

What are you working out on?   Not yourself?   Wrestling?

I got a postcard from Serge [Yonov] three or four days ago.   His most emphatic statement – "this is a lousy school." [Serge had been at Colorado School of Mines]   Nik says he also saw Judy Engers.   The Barbara you mentioned, is MacGeorge &   used to go with a guy down here – recent Dear John.   My mother writes [from her new home in a Florida trailer park]– she's on the shuffleboard team.   Florida & the people agree with her almost unimaginably.   Billy [my brother, '56] is getting married the 13th.   Artie [my brother Billy's twin] is still floating around on a cloud of fatherhood, but has come down long enough to buy a new car ('55 Chevy).   I lent him $300 for it &   instead of paying me back, he's going to buy a vehicle for me next year.   I'll register and insure it here [in NC] for a total cost of no more than $100.

Alex Terentiev ['58] is not doing as well as he thought he was two months ago. . . . he has decided against majoring in physics.

Will you be singing in anything.   If you drop the Saints?—besides the shower. Don't give up music altogether.

The girl situation here isn't too bad, but I take it easy since money and time are running short. . . . when you come back from Thanksgiving, drop me a line and let me know what's what with everybody.   I haven't had a letter from Sea Cliff for almost 2 months. . . . I may take you up on the offer of a bed in your cellar bed.   If I come up when you're home, however.   I'll probably stay at my cousin's, aunt's, or some such relative.

Dec 1, 1958 [from same friend on college stationary]

Well you didn't miss too much over the [Thanksgiving] weekend.   I hardly saw any one over the vacation so I didn't pick up too much dirt.   Nik was around, Lukie was as always, over at Betty's.   We doubled Sat night.   We went into Greenwich Village and had a frustrating time.   It was freezing out at all the places my brother recommended we couldn't get seats.   In addition to this Lukie was never satisfied with other joints we came upon.   So we ended up having one beer apiece – boy I was a little annoyed, but we had a lot of fun!

All the "dirt" I got was from Betty.   Jane Allen is getting married in June.   It's about time they made it legal.   Diana is in love with this guy at Syracuse, and she appears to be living with him.   Then he said the only time she spends in her room is to sleep.   Beanie Greenfield has made a hit at B.U.   They think she looks like Liz Taylor.   She must be wearing some padding!   I saw Bev and Joanne for a second Thanksgiving, but they had little to say.   Mickey is in love with some guy.

Little was going on at home.   Everything is just about as usual.   I stopped in at Ray's to get a little local color.   There was enough of it.   If they weren't drinking Coke you'd think the place was the center of a Roman Orgy!!   Kids have really changed from our day, I am afraid.   As you probably realize the reason why I didn't get around as much as usual was because I spent most of my time with O-----.   Well I've got to get into a fraternity – I'm going to get pinned – I just wonder what repercussions will occur at home when they find out.   It ought to be interesting.

Well, I'm sorry I couldn't supply you with any more data (Lynda Lloyd is pregnant).   Maybe Nik can take over where I left off.

Lukie isn't going out for basketball.   He has a D, but all his other marks are A's & B's .   So he's really not doing too badly.   He made his letter in Soccer.

12/5/58 [reply from Buster]

Glad to hear Lukie is still with Betty as long as it makes him happy & Colgate doesn't lose him.

Since you were with O---- in the Village I can see why you had a good time—especially if Lukie was navigating.   I have great expectations for you & twenty of your dollars.   Beanie [Elaine Greenfield, '58] makes such a hit because she is all natural.

When you are home next, relay some witty but congratulatory remark to Mickey [Vaccaro] for me—better yet send me her address and I'll try to mail her a card.   Same for Joanne [LaPierre?], your fiancé, and your sibling.

Are you still working out – or is it out working?   On what, where or on whom?   Barbara [Gilson] wrote one of her usual hilarious letters & and a reply is next on my agenda.

Nik Epanchin to Buster Dec. 8, 1958

What a surprising Thanksgiving I had.   Wed nite I picked up ------ at the S.C. Jr. High School where the Youth Center had a variety show.   I didn't get to see Ellen but Sheila Hickey was terrific, she had a cat dance act and she just WAS TERRIFIC.   . . . .

Friday Lois [Delgado] called and asked me to come and see her, so I did and we played cards at her neighbor's house and afterwards (2:00 PM or so) we went for a little party of our own.

1/9/59 (after Christmas vacation Nik Epanchin summarizes)

I saw a few of the guys – Kozuzcko, --- raves about his Gail . . . ; Goolie (Eddie Gauld, '55) same old Ed, Cadiz [Dave, '54] is building an ice boat at Cornell and is flunking out at the same time; Feingold broke up with Glenda Boyd and sort of went nuts; Terentieff [Alex, '58] is the same . . . "Ajax". . . . Brud [Neice] is now a member of the Fire Dept. I didn't see Clarke but his brother said he spent all his time with Oonah. Funny thing happened 1 or 2 weeks before Thanks., I walked in this bar and saw this beautiful babe in high black socks, pink short shorts, black tight sweater and surrounded by a ton of hungry Colgaters. As I approached closer (to take a look) I realized John Clarke was sitting with her and it was Joan Fameleti.

I saw a [lot] of people this vacation, most of whom left me pretty cold. I'll start with the "Rooskiz"

1. Storojev . . . is the same, he still owns Emerson, his sister is turning out to be quite a girl.
Serge says: there is college, harder than C.S.M.[Colorado School of Mines]; there are no better or harder profs than at Mines; there are no better guys nor any better dates than there; (he said something about loving some airline hostess. Cyril is a very nice guy, but doesn't know where he'll go next year.

2. Teddy V. is 2nd at Stevens (in his class), plays soccer, is active in his fraternity, loosened up greatly and is extremely pleasant guy.
3. Basil [Alfarief, '56] is a bright light in Boston Society (that's all I know).
Liz Daniloff was going with Kenny . . .

Pete M. [Marnane, '55] was working very hard both physically and mentally, and toward the end of the vacations came down with pneumonia.

John K. & Gail seemed to have gone separate ways, but toward the end of the vacations they were back together.

Allyson [Rose, '58] seems extremely happy, and by the way I had Xmas dinner with her at her place and a very enjoyable evening.

Clarke said he really likes Oonah and told Allyson he was going to get engaged. He works the vacations delivering liquor.

Diane D[jivre] is enjoying Syracuse immensely, especially the physics department. She is now engaged to a member of the physics faculty there (a young one with a PhD).

Barbara G[ilson] looks rather sharp when she gives everyone a treat and wears a dress instead of dungarees and engineer boots (I see her at the Pine).

Joan is her usual . . . . She is going to go to school to be an air hostess.

My personal vacation was rather dull -- more and more I dislike Sea Cliff -- I took out Allyson . And this Canadian girl . . .

One of the main events was a lecture by my father (to me alone). He definitely wants me to follow up on science with the reasoning "that the worst that can happen to me is that I'll never use science. . . . "

from a letter from Bob Clarke 19 January 1959

I don't know about you but I'm really beat. I have already had two exams. Both too hard to even discuss! My marks are none too good this term –

Oh, I saw Allyson over Christmas. She really has changed. – you wouldn't know her. She has broken up with Walt, thank God and seems to be having a wonderful time at school. We talked over "old times" and had a few good laughs.

You'll never guess what! I'm 19 – I really feel older! This is the first time I've ever had that feeling. It must be my all too typical sophomoric attitude. I'm just too typical anyhow.

You should have seen Nik's haircut. He looked like a convict. Really a scream! He seems to be doing better this year in school. Maybe the opposite of Sampson? He expects a 3.0 – if everything goes well, but I guess you must know what's going on.

Johnny and Gail had a few tough times at the beginning of the vacation but I guess Gail got tired of staying at home nights so they made up. Johnny, of course, now feels that he has finally mastered her and that his worries are over – Oh well, maybe they are, but I wouldn't bet on it.

I saw little of Lukie. He was status quo, as usual. He's just a little tooooo status quo for me! Betty is, as usual, straggling along.

Kenny Kay [manager of the pavilion where we worked as lifeguards] isn't working but he looked fit when I saw him. In fact he looked fatter. I don't know how he could do it on Katherine's cooking.

All in all I had a pretty wonderful vacation. I almost got engaged but somehow or other I snuck out of it. I think, maybe, it might have been my mother's influence and the anticipation of Oonah's father's reaction.

from Nik Epanchin 3/4/59

Well I got my jollies to carry me through for another month. It all happened as a result of my strife for happiness. About four months ago I joined the service fraternity APR (a national one). This weekend day, or rather, we were put in charge of the punch for the faculty and chaperones at the Winter party dance. Since no one volunteered for the job I was kind enough to go through with it. I started by drinking at all the fraternity bars at the dance and got to feel good. As I tended the faculty bar I noticed this girl sitting all alone and looking miserable – I made a move. I ended up convincing her that she should drop her date and go out with me. . .   She was a high school senior from Buffalo, not bad looking . . . . The only drawback was. She was sort of a hypochondriac, but who gave a damn? I met her date the following day, and he was pretty happy that I relieved him of her . . .

About a week before you wrote your last letter I got the idea I should keep track of dreams (my own and other peoples). I have a terrific repression mechanism, I hardly ever remember dreaming anything.

. . .

My own changing standards of relation with life on more or less as follows: there is a definite switch from the previous attitude of trying to be a good guy (the sort of guy people say. "I'm proud to know him because he's great." And nothing more), to someone who knows what life is all about.   I tend to shit on myself , except things or responsibilities that I don't care for, sort of be able to discipline myself. Whenever I want to. This is not physical discipline, which would be asinine or a move to become a monk, but just neutral.

I really would like to feel that I'm doing things and living the way I do only because I want it.

from a letter by Nik Epanchin May 1, 1959

Before going to Syracuse we had a track meet where we edged out U. of Conn. 74-68. I won the 2 mile in 10:13. This was one of the events of the party weekend and explains how I met Betty Sprague. She is her usual. She also pointed out to me Judy Brown's fiancé who threw and won the javelin for U.Conn. I introduced myself to him and he seem a very "nice" guy. (take it for what it's worth). Margie Repucci was also here . . . Clarke [John, '55] said Jeanne Familetti had exams and couldn't come, he still had another date.

A few days before I talked to Lucas, who didn't qualify for pilot training. He flunked a test similar to College Boards and a spacial relations one too. At this time nothing seems to interest him very much, his preference is psychology in which he plans to major. It is not an easy department by any means. He's going to work at the school again.

I wrote Toddy [friend of Barbara Gilson's at Smith] very long ago and never heard from her. I also wrote a miserable letter to Allyson- she never answered either. That letter was miserable in that it didn't say anything.

I'll be out the 2nd of June and will work the 3rd at SCMP [Sea Cliff Municipal Pavilion].

Some of us faced the larger choices of life—marriage and career—with high expectations, others with anxiety and one classmate with distaste verging on scorn and a preference for at least parts of what would become known in the 1970s as an "alternate life style".

Anonymous, Feb. 2, 1959
The rash of engagements depresses me just because they are engagements. I can think of nothing more tedious than flinging oneself into the kind of compact this is and is and which usually ends, I believe, in a thing so disastrous as marriage. It's rather horrifying too, to see the way people go into it, clamping on the chains themselves with gleeful abandon, pledging themselves to spend the rest of their lives picking up someone's pajamas, as well as that old "love, honor, and obey". It's not quite so bad for a man, because even if he does have to pay some extra bills, he gets a all around domestic servant (although probably not as competent a one as he'd get from an employment agency, but for a woman, it turns her from a human being into a brood mare. In a word—UGH.

Hide your id, kid,

Or they'll make you wish you did;
Those weaponless ones who for recreation
Prefer the grimy safety of cold stagnation.
For if they learn and say they forbade it,
That's it buddy, man, you've had it!
As for those whose way, is the icer
That's all right, but id-iocy is nicer.

Feb 13, 1959
I don't have anything against bringing children into the world except for the fuss and bother the whole drawn out process entails it slightly ridiculous, somehow, to see people living for their children, determined that they shall excel that parents, before the parents themselves have had a chance to realize their potential.   There are certainly more than enough people in the world as it is, and I've often thought that people have children because they have no confidence in the meliorating progress of their own character and lives.

Face it kid,
The id can't be hid
Completely
It will come to light,
by day, by night.
Or Beatly.
Try and shed it in booze or by hypnosis,
and it will pop up in fetish or psychosis.
So comfort it, tend it,
Buy it and spend it,
And at the end of each day.
You'll be able to say,
"I'm interesting if not happy."

May 20, 1959
Did you notice the ads that have been appearing lately for Lady Chatterley's unexpurgated Lover.   It may be that this is a crack in the wall of Great American Puritanism.   While we're on the topic of banned books.   Have you ever read any Henry Miller?   That man lived.   I have to say that for him.

Tonight we're having the classics picnic in annual route for the slippered pantaloons who take Greek and Latin.   I didn't go last year, so I'm not quite sure whether I should wear a toga.

Righteous is not right, she said,
no more, indeed, then deftly, dead.

For when we are young we are righteous.
Not to mention fighteous.
And as for the "unclean"
at last, what does it mean,
except that one is not.
As one would be seen.
And what ideal can ever be.
Except for the those who will not see.
The real.
Because they feel.
And want the lie of.
The ideal. So it is, though, who can know,
the final blooming, horror show.

Reply from Buster12/6/60
By this time I hope the psychiatrist and you have been able to recapture the organization of
your mind.   You always said that you had no problems and that you were completely
rational and here you are going off the trolley track before me who admits being a slave to
the irrational.   I'm not trying to draw up a program of "sanity thru irrationality," only
scientists and philosophers can attempt that.

News Clippings from the 60s
[thanks to Betty Gelling Wood and others who have sent items] [consider reducing the
space between paras throughout this section]

Record-Pilot July 13, 1961
Glen Head Girl Is Guest Editor
Miss Priscilla Bowden of High Farms Rd., Glen head, who graduated from
Radcliffe College this June, has just finished working for a month as a Guest Editor In
Chief of Mademoiselle Magazine in New York.

Ms. Bowden was one of 20 girls chosen from more than 800 students, who served on
Mademoiselle's 1960 to 61 College Board.   She has written the "Memo From The Editor"
column.

Although not a newcomer to New York, Ms. Bowden was introduced to "new aspects of
the city."   She met producer Joshua Logan at a tea in his apartment and later previewed his
new movie "Fanny" at a showing arranged especially for the Guest Editors.   She also
modeled in Mademoiselle's fashion show at the Commodore Hotel.   Ms. Bowden, a
former member of the Record Pilot's staff, is planning to continue her career with

Mademoiselle. She has joined the staff of the College And Career department to work on future College Board Contests.

[no date]

Miss M. Vaccaro becomes bride

Sea Cliff. Michelina Ann Vaccaro, daughter of Mr. and Mrs. Nicholas Vaccaro of this village,became the bride of Richard Alfred Bonneau of Pawtucket, R.I., on June 23 at a 10 AM the optional mass ceremony in St. Boniface Martyr R.C. Church of Sea Cliff.

The bride is a graduate of Post College, where she received both her bachelor's degree of arts and masters degree of library science. She is employed by the Eastern Massachusetts regional library system as a regional young adults services librarian. Her husband, the son of Mr. and Mrs. Charles Bonneau, is a graduate of the University of California at Berkeley. He is employed by the George Meade Co. in Bedford, Mass.

After a Canadian honeymoon, the couple will live in Natick, Mass.

May 3, 1962

Miss Bennett and Mr. Hall Are Married

Miss Blanche Bennett, daughter of Mr. and Mrs. John Andrews Bennett, of Hillside Avenue., Glenwood Landing, was married on April 28 to Mr. Arthur H. Hall Jr., son of Mr. and Mrs. Arthur H. Hall Sr. of 9 Harriet Ct. Sea Cliff.

The ceremony was performed by Rev. Boston of Glenwood Landing Presbyterian Church, at 12 noon. The bride was given in marriage by her father.

The bride wore a long gallon with chapel train of tissue silk, long sleeves, and a pearl crown with butterfly veil. She carried a bouquet of gardenias.

Mr. James Tolmie acted as best man for the bridegroom; Mr. John Broderick and Mr. Paul St. Andre were ushers.

A reception was held at the holiday house, Glen Cove.

After a wedding trip to upstate New York, the couple will live at 7 Harriet Court, Sea Cliff.

June 14, 1962

Airman 3/c Walter G. Meier Jr., son of Mr. and Mrs. W.G. Meier, Salem Way, Glen Head has completed basic training at Lackland Air Force Base, San Antonio, Texas. He will be stationed at Goodfellow A.F.B. , San Angelo, Texas where he will receive technical training in Air Force Intelligence. He was previously employed by Powers Chemco, Glen Cove.

August 3, 1961.

Fred T. Burns, 21, the son of Mr. and Mrs. Fred J. Burns, of 37 Sylvia St., Glenwood Landing, returned last Tuesday from Frankfurt Germany where he was stationed for two years with the US Army.

August 17, 1961

Miss Gildersleeve Is Engaged

Mr. and Mrs. W.A. Gildersleeve of 3 Winding Way in Sea Cliff announce the engagement of their daughter, Joan Ellen to Mr. Peter George Madson, son of the Rev. and Mrs. G. Ralph Madson of Tampa, Florida.

The bride to be is a graduate of North Shore high school, studied A.I B. at Hofstra College, and is presently employed by the Franklin National Bank of Sea Cliff.

Her fiancé is a graduate of Oglethorpe College and is currently studying for the ministry at the General Theological Seminary in New York City. No date has been set for the wedding.

August 24, 1961

Ms. Ruth Ahearn of Sea Cliff Weds Mr. Loeber of Locust Valley

Ms. Ruth Christine Ahearn, daughter of Mr. and Mrs. James F. Ahearn of 85 Lafayette Ave., Sea Cliff became the bride of Mr. Gerald G. Loeber, son of Mr. and Mrs. Frank Famalette Of Bayville Rd., Locust Valley on Saturday, August 19 in St. Boniface martyr Church, Sea Cliff.

The Rev. John V. Tunny performed the ceremony.

The bride wore a white poiedesoie silk gown and carried a missal.

Matron of honor was Mrs. William Duffy, sister of the bride. Mrs. Duffy is a resident of Wilkes-Barre, Pennsylvania. She wore a white pique dress and carried a basket of garden flowers.

Bridesmaids included Ms. Ann Ahearn of Sea Cliff, Mrs. John Green of Glen Head , and Miss Margaret Rich of Sea Cliff.

Best man was Mr. Frank Famalette, stepfather of the bridegroom.

Ushers included Mr. Ralph Longo of Sea Cliff, Mr. John Green of Glen Head, and Mr. Gilbert Halpin of Brookhaven.

A reception followed the ceremony, at the home of the bride.

Mrs. Loeber is a graduate of Sea Cliff High School and St. Joseph's Hospital School Of Nursing, Yonkers.   The bridegroom graduated from St. John's Prep, and the University of Rhode Island.   He saw service with the US Army.   He is currently Dir. Of Athletics in the Syosset school district.

Sept. 21, 1961

Miss Mary Ann Kearney is wed Sunday to Mr. Ned McAdams

Ms. Mary Ann Kearney, daughter of Mr. and Mrs. James G. Kearney of old Brookville, was married on Saturday, September 16, two Mr. Ned McAdams, son of Mr. and Mrs. Al McAdams of Glenwood Landing.   The Rev. Mario Costa performed the ceremony in St. Patrick's Church and Rev. Sahey, S.J. said the Mass and bestowed the Apostle Blessing.

The bride wore a floor-length white taffeta gallon, trimmed with Alencon lace.   Her fingertip veil of illusion net was attached to a matching headpiece with a tear of pearl on her forehead.   She carried white orchids and stephanotis.

Mrs. Ellen Smith, sister of the bride, was maid of honor.   Her gown was of gold taffeta, and she carried rust mums.   The other attendants were Ann, Cecilia and Rosemary Duffy, Mrs. Anna McAdams and Miss Maureen O'Brien.   All were attired in sea green taffeta and carried white mums.

Mr. Jean McAdams, brother of the groom, acted as best man.   Ushers were Brian O'Toole, Fred Burns, Alfred Brown, William Lindsay and Robert Fitzgerald.

A reception was held at the Nassau country club with music by Ted Larson's Orchestra. After a wedding trip to the Poconos, Mr. and Mrs. McAdams will live on Sylvia St., Glenwood Landing.

[no date]

Engaged To Dentist

Mr. and Mrs. Mervyn Freedman of Sea Cliff have announced the forthcoming marriage of their daughter, Sandra Irene, a speech therapist, Dr. Jerome H. Oppenheim of Babylon, a dentist.

The wedding will take place July 22 in the Roslyn Country Club. The newlyweds will honeymoon in the Canadian Rockies and on the West Coast.

Miss Freedman is a graduate of Emerson College. She is with the national County vocational board at the Westbury School for retarded children.

The dentist, the son of Mrs. Bessie Oppenheim and the late Abraham Oppenheim, studied at the University College of New York University and graduated from its College of dentistry. He is currently on the staff of the good Samaritan Hospital, West Islip. He is an Army veteran.

The couple will reside in Babylon.

Newlyweds Head West

Sandra Irene Freedman of Sea Cliff, and Dr. Jerome H. Oppenheim of Babylon left for Lake Louise, Canada, and the Seattle world's fair. Following their marriage in the Roslyn Country Club.

The bride, it a graduate of Emerson College, is a speech therapist for retarded children in the Westbury School For Special Services. She is the daughter of Mr. and Mrs. Mervyn Freedman.

Dr. Oppenheim, a dentist on the staff of good Samaritan Hospital, holds degrees from New York University and its school of dentistry. He is the son of Mrs. Bessie Oppenheim and the late Abraham Oppenheim.

February 14, 1963

[from Glenwood Landing column in Record & Pilot, by Lillie Mackay]

Dear folks:

I find myself feeling annoyed as do many others who live in Glenwood, to realize that some people who receive their mail and Glen head, (although the post office is in Glenwood) seem not to know that they actually live in Glenwood Landing. Look at a map; if you live in Glenwood, say so.

Judy Olsen of Huron St., daughter of Dr. and Mrs. Raymond A. Olsen, will be married in June, to Ronald Christian of Newark, Ill., son of Mr. and Mrs. Forrest Christian.

Where In This Face

(my riff on Thomas Randolph's 17th Century"Upon His Portrait")

The years have made us what we are now,
when every wrinkle tells us where the plow
of time has furrowed; when shorter we grow
and time moves faster and our feet more slow;
Age seals its final freckles on the face.
Look in the mirror now—where's here a trace
in all we are, of Who we were?
The memory's clear, the image is a blur.
Did these dry lips take that first welcome kiss?
Look-- cheeks or hair—did he or she love this?
Who are you? we ask each other when
we meet. Please give yourself a name and then
memory restores your face again.
But face present or face past—which lies
when even those we loved wear time's disguise?
Is this a riddle for the mind or eyes?
What shall we believe—mirror or mind?
One of them is blind.
(WK)

WHO WE WERE AND WHO WE BECAME
The Class Of 1957: One by One

Caveat Lector—Reader Beware

The classmate we voted "Wittiest" and "Most Versatile," Barbara Gilson, asked me about this history, "What do you intend to do about fact checking?" Barbara has been an editor and writer for over 40 years, and she started fact checking life with a keen eye even before she could read. When she engages her sometimes biting wit to check a fact in print or in life, she often does it with the same force I've felt when body checked in a hockey game. In response to her question and to avoid being checked too sternly, here's a word about the facts in this history and those that are not in this history.

A good writer will verify important facts from at least two sources, and many publishing houses, magazines and newspapers have fact checkers to maintain the credibility of their content. I have arranged for one other person, already accused of being overextended by his wife, to do limited fact checking. Let him remain anonymous so no one can blame him for inaccuracies. In addition, I have spent many hours checking facts, often digging into public records, requesting military records, and scouring the Internet. However, I am not a publisher, and this is not a commercial venture. So I say to you, *caveat lector* (which I believe would be the Latin for 'reader beware'—let someone fact check that). What I report in these biographies is what you have told me about yourselves and about each other. You sent some of this material to me when I requested information. More comes from old letters, and at least half from our phone conversations when you talked and I used my Betty French typing skills to record what you said.

The best reporting tries to avoid unnamed sources and also quotations without a named speaker or writer. Where I quote "a classmate" or "friend" I omit the name because the source has asked to be unnamed. Maybe I should have pushed people harder to let me use their names, but I decided instead to ask you to trust me when I promise that I have made up nothing. What I have made, despite all attempts not to, are mistakes. The mistakes may be of two serious kinds—facts and judgment. Apologies in advance. I have never been known for my great sensitivity to others' sensitivities. As for wrong facts . . . well, you can't fire me. Sending corrections is weak consolation, but I will accept them humbly and without protest. That is a great personal sacrifice, because as most of my friends will tell you, or as you already know, I am not a humble person by nature. Only shy. I'll illustrate the big difference. Humble boys assumed they were not worth dancing with. Shy boys were afraid to invite girls to a dance. I was always ready to dance, but I either waited for a Betty Sprague, Judy Brown, or Lois Delgado to tell me who might accept my invitation, or I waited for a Sadie Hawkins dance, those exceptions to the

1950s prescription for boy-girl roles.

How do I know the facts in this history are not entirely accurate? In this case because I deliberately commit the sin of omission. Maybe it's not a sin but a virtue. This history deliberately emphasizes the positive. Some of you have told me the negatives about yourselves, your families, and each other, then said, "Don't print that." I haven't. (I should also add that most people spoke well of others and saved the negatives for themselves, and without saying, "Don't print that.") I have other reasons for emphasizing the positive. First, and perhaps most frivolous, most of us like stories with a happy endings. Happy endings are useful. Call them multivitamins for the soul. At our age all kinds of vitamins are important and all pharmacies offer special "over 50" or "senior" supplements.

More importantly, we deserve the positive emphasis, and we have earned it, and it reflects the general truth--our mutual story has been positive. I do mention hardships, failings, and a few crimes, but with very few exceptions, even the victims and the perpetrators overcame their problems.

THEY ARE GONE: REST IN PEACE

Douglas Dudda Andrews

Nancy Baker, Sister of Mercy

Helen Basilevsky

Lee Berroyer

Al Behrmann

Lois Delgado

Faith LaJoy

John Maloney

Bob "Lukie" Lucas

Edwin "Brud" Neice

Arlene Maass

Richard "Knox" Norwich

Doug Ransweiler

Evelyn "Evy" Piat

Margie Repucci

Nancy Samuelson

George Schmersal

Serge Yonov

WE STILL LOOK BACK AND LOOK AHEAD

Our 1957 yearbook began its student pages with its "Seniors" being allotted 22 pages, about 50 words each accompanied by one studio head shot. We are again seniors, and in this yearbook each person gets one or two pages and two pictures, if we have the information. 50 words and one picture was far too little for 18 year olds and the present allocation still can't begin to summarize some 70 years of living. That too is part of my excuse for trying to distill from existing information those facts that suggest something essential about the person.

In some cases considerable research produced too little. In others, my notes and files occupy several pages but important facts are missing. For some lives I have the facts, but the source has said, "This is off the record." And for many people I have a lot of interesting stories which are far too full, notes for individual books. From both men and women I have hundreds of pages of letters that either the writer or I have decided are too revealing or embarrassing to use.

We are not so old that we can't still buy green bananas, but time is no longer endless, so I have not circulated several drafts and incorporated what might have been new material and different points of view. I am also leery of books written by committees. So once again, I ask your tolerance, understanding and forgiveness for those biographies that may seem inaccurate, shallow, or insensitive. And with that I stop groveling and apologizing and get on with biography.

Ruth Ahearn

With Marjorie Maple, Sept. 2008

Was she ever the "timid, tall and gawky" teenager she once thought herself? Underlying her physical and quiet personal grace (the way many saw her then and see her now) "Ruthie" has always been invisibly rugged. Ruth was the fifth of seven Ahearn children in their modest house near the high school. She had "a very Irish Catholic rearing." She was an enthusiastic athlete under Miss Maple's tutelage and a horseback rider—and a fighter. "I had to be a fighter. I had two brothers." That training stood her in good stead when she confronted a local bully who enjoyed teasing and picking on other kids. "In 6th grade at St. Boniface I decked Wuzzy [Albert] Britt."

Sea Cliff life was good for Ruth. "My dearest memories were the summers we spent barefoot, walking through the village, voting for 'Miss Reingold' at the deli and walking down that long wooden staircase to the pavilion where we could meet and just live the life of Reilly." She came to Sea Cliff High in our junior hear when she "was asked to leave St. Dominic's HS in Oyster Bay for unruly behavior." She was ready for a change. "I really enjoyed tasting public school after 10 years of Catholic schooling." She thought of herself as an average student who "loved sports and music and BOYS." She would often be at her good friend Joanne La Pierre's house listening to Johnny Mathis and other crooners in Joanne's room decked out in Doris Day posters.

Ruth graduated at age 17 and entered training to be a practical nurse, expecting to spend her life as a wife and mother. She took a job with a local oncologist, married at 21, had given birth to two sons and a daughter by age 26, and spent almost twenty years bringing up the children before she divorced. She then returned to school at Friends Academy for the sciences she did not take at Sea Cliff and which she needed to go on in nursing. While her oldest son was studying at Johns Hopkins University, Ruth entered SUNY Farmingdale to become a Registered Nurse. They both graduated in 1983. As a nurse Ruth received

Critical Care certification in 1992. In 2000 she qualified as a nurse practitioner. Today she works for the Department of Medicine at North Shore University Hospital where she has been employed for 25 years in work she loves only less than her three children and six grandchildren ages two to seventeen "who are pure joy and secure, for me, silly moments of wonder."

Her children she describes as the "best magic in life that has ever happened to me, and they continue to velvetize my life. In each of their lives, strength has surfaced out of adversity (re: divorced parents when they were teenagers.) Their work and play ethos and their deep sense of family and tradition are awesome for me to watch, and be a part of."

Ruth says she is still climbing—psychologist Maslow's "Ladder" which begins with satisfying physical needs, ascends through safety from fear, to belonging and love, then to being everything one is capable of." She appears to have her hand firmly on the top rung. Along the way she also beat two bouts of lung cancer and climbed Mt. Sinai at age 40, "[I am] still breathing and smiling and happy to be alive."

Ruth Loeber
11 Franklin Avenue
Glen Cove, NY 11542
rloeber@optonline.net

Ruth 2008 Reunion

Jane Allen

Photo by Nik Epanchin

She sang, she danced, she acted, she skated, she played a sport in every season, and she had a preference for brainy boys—Cornell engineering student Don Rockwell (Class of '56) and Nik Epanchin. Jane's mother was an accomplished pianist and artist living with her husband in Greenwich Village when Jane was born. They moved soon after her birth to a cheap row house rental in Roslyn Heights where her younger brother Todd ('59) was born. In second grade they moved to her mother's native Sea Cliff to be with Jane's grandfather on Porter Place. "My transition to Sea Cliff was a horrible experience at the tender age of eight," Jane remembers, but she soon made good friends.

When younger brother Todd began delivering Newsday Jane also began to work, helping him especially in rain and snow. "I climbed what seemed like a million steps to get that paper onto the doorsill or into a mail slot." Two months before she would be legally eligible at 16 she landed a job in Sea Cliff's teen social center—Dobkins Pharmacy. "Working in Dobkins was the "in" place to work." Starting pay: $0.35 an hour. But, "That was where everything seemed to be happening except now in retrospect people only sat on stools, nursing a coke or whatever (you had to buy something or you got thrown out) and just talked. Such gossip went on in there. I bought my first lipstick there. I used to run up a tab every week and sometimes ended up owing them money."

Jane hit a version of the glass ceiling as soon as she contemplated college. Her parents felt they had to dedicate their limited resources for college to her brother "since my brother needed to get a job and support a family and I, a girl, would be supported by a husband." She could choose two years away at college until they had to send Todd, or live at home and attend 4 years on Long Island. "I could not wait to get out of small town Sea Cliff." She spent two happy years at junior college in Boston and has never regretted the choice although it took another 26 years to complete her bachelor's at night school while working full time and raising 4 children while becoming a single parent.

Jane married in September 1959 and went with her husband to Florida while he attended two years at the University of Miami. "I was having babies," Jane says. They arrived in

'60, '61, '65, '70, and Jane became a stay-at-home mom.   After a few years in Brooklyn and Queens, they bought a house in Westbury.   After divorce in 1972 Jane found herself a single mom with children from 2 to 12.   She started working with the Medical Society of the State of NY doing data entry on early computers.   "There was a room full of machinery and you keyed everything in."   She also began weekend data entry for Nassau Hospital on the 4-11 shift and she started studying again for her BA.   With her degree she began working in the Cleft Palate and Cranio Facial Center at North Shore Hospital in Manhasset.   Across the street from her lived Bill Hall.   "I had known him forever."   He was recently divorced.   Soon he was married to Jane.

One day at work a woman came in with a baby adopted from Russia and born with severely cleft palate.   The woman showed the baby's doctors a video of the girl in a bleak Moscow orphanage's crib, standing up and bouncing around with her crib mate, a baby boy.   "Don't you know anyone who wants to adopt him?" the woman asked.   Jane took a copy of the video home.   Bill had never had children and had not wanted any, but "as time went by he said 'It kind of would have been nice to have one."   He was not prepared for what he saw—a baby boy with the roof of his mouth split open from his lip to his throat.   Then he was ready.   Jane asked herself, "Do I want to do this again?   I was a grandmother already three times over.   I said sure."

Jane scheduled the boy's first surgeries even before they left for Russia.   There, in 1991, even she was not prepared for reality despite having two suitcases full of bribe goods and two more full of specialized baby supplies for both their new son and the orphanage.   When they first saw him in Moscow's Number 2 Orphanage, she noticed his slightly bowed legs, his snow white hair, then opened the baby's shirt to change his clothes and, and seeing the deformed rib case, said, "Oh my god he's got rickets."   The records showed that his mother may also have afflicted him with fetal alcohol syndrome.   The adoption became official on Christmas Day (which is still not an official holiday in Russia) 1992.

They do everything together.   With Andrew's main operations behind them and Bill's mother turning 100 in 1999 and living in Oklahoma, the family moved to the quiet town of Glenpool about fifteen miles south of Tulsa.   Although before the move she says, "I couldn't imagine anyone in their right mind moving to Oklahoma," she found the town was "like Sea Cliff without the water."   Andrew is a straight A student in his senior year.   He plays trombone in the marching band, loves cooking and is fascinated by paleontology.   Jane and Bill have never regretted their decision nor has their new son Andrew.   "The day they brought him into the orphanage he just flew to Bill.   Bill absolutely dotes on this child."

Jane now works full time in the school's special ed programs, having started in elementary school and now working with the same students in middle school.   She recently went to Russia with a woman who adopted a baby from the same Number 2 Orphanage where she found Andrew.   She also sits on Board of Directors of Around the World Adoption Agency.

Jane Allen
13650 S. Maple St,
Glenpool, OK 74033-3228
918-291-2175
janehall2595@sbcglobal.net

Berkeley Andrews, Jr

Although the writer for Berk's 1957 yearbook profile made the droll entry "Future ambition is college, then retirement," Berkeley didn't choose the easy road. "Big Jim" Fraley, the Sewanhaka High coach who ran the Sea Cliff Youth Center with his wife convinced Berkeley to try Kansas State University. He did, for two years. "My father thought it was a good idea I join the Marine Corps." He graduated from the notoriously tough Parris Island training camp with top honors and a gold medal for being highest man of the 300 in his camp. He was in the Honor Guard on the White House steps in January 1961 when Eisenhower departed and John F. Kennedy entered his last home. His duties also included security at the presidential retreat, Camp David.

The Marines was not the first time Berk's father felt he should be in the military. In 8th or 9th grade Berk decided to enliven a pending assembly and attract some attention. He rolled up a length of photo film in a sheet of paper, and soon a roil of acrid black smoke drifted down the aisles. He was out of Sea Cliff school and his father sent him to the famous Fork Union Military Academy in Virginia. His parents divorced and Berkeley lived with his father in Westbury, went to school there and worked in his father's White Fortress Restaurants. For 11th and 12th grades he returned to live with his mother, work as a delivery boy for Dobkins Pharmacy, and graduate with our class.

He returned to Long Island from the Marines and used his muscle as a concrete worker for Union 66. He used his puckish charm to woo Karen Ebbets (Class of '61) whose mother had a friend in Sea Cliff who had "heard tales of that famous Berkeley Andrews." Karen's father "suggested I get a real job," Berkeley says. "I did knock on some real doors in NYC and I gotten a hint that NCR was hiring some sales people. They said, "Yes, we are hiring, young man." I took the aptitude test and passed it and they hired me." And Karen married him.

Meanwhile Berk's good friend Richie Roe ('59) had married Grace Kelly's niece in Philadelphia and become a stock broker. Berkeley had been best man at Richie's wedding and soon "He would call us every Sunday night in Sea Cliff and say, 'Berkeley you have got to come to Philadelphia and become a stockbroker.'" Berkeley did both, underpinning his career with six months at the New York Institute of Finance, and later two years at the Wharton School of Finance part time. After several years with W.E. Hutton Berkeley went to Pasadena as a portfolio manager for Providence Investment Counsel.

Twenty years later as he retired Karen said, "Berkeley, you're retired now and we're going to move to Florida." Her mother had been there already for 20 years. That's where I found him when searching for classmates missing from the reunion list. The web site for a recumbent bicycling club listed him a member. In Pasadena he served as commodore of the Catalina Island Yacht Club and considers himself at present "temporarily boatless" but never far from a good book or Karen, his wife for 44 years.

Berkeley Andrews
4723 Storkwood Ln. #A 4723
Boynton Beach, Fl. 33436
berkeleyandrews@gmail.com

Douglas Andrews

Photo by Cyndy Andrews

Doug, or "Dudda," wasn't satisfied with life unless it was lively.   Most of us saw that in his passion for hot cars, parties, and flirting.   He seemed very much at ease with girls and they were at ease with him because he was big but gentle, witty but kind.   From an adolescent boy's view he was successful, as several classmates testify.

Jane Allen: When I first moved to Sea Cliff I was lucky enough to live on a street of somewhat level ground.   I was able to ride a bike then, roller skate and play with Judy, Brud Niece, Dougie Andrews and others on the lawn of the old Sea Cliff Methodist Church.   We also played ring-o-leave-e-o behind the public library on Sea Cliff Avenue.   By the age of 11 I caught a few kisses behind the library from Brud and Doug Andrews.

Allen Schwartz: Then there's love.   I was pretty out of it.   At a party at Doug Andrews' house,   There were Diana and Doug smooching heavily and I wondered, 'What's that all about?'

Sandy Gleichmann: Ed Neice and Doug Andrews were [my] boyfriends - they were among the gang that would get together for parties where spin the bottle and Post Office were played.   Weren't we racey?

Where did many of us find life most lively—Glen Head's bar, the Knotty Pine, and Doug signed my yearbook, "Please stay sober and I'll see you in the Knotty Pine."   He did, but note the "stay sober" preceding the rendezvous.   Maybe he had learned from suffering life with his alcoholic father that sober and good times were not a contradiction.   Doug's wife says he learned something else important at home.   His mother often had foster children, babies and toddlers.   "That's how he got so good at child rearing. Doug is a pro when it comes to kids."

Doug intended to enlist in the Navy after high school but had to give it up because of weak eyesight that disqualified him for all branches of the military. He enrolled in Spring Hill College, a small Jesuit school in Mobile, AL. Doug managed to get himself suspended from college for 6 months by staging a rousing toga party, but he returned to finish his studies. To pay expenses he worked in a pizza place and as a groundsman for the college. He also became a kind of body guard for a Jesuit professor who traveled through the region investigating Klan cross burnings.

Doug met his wife in the INA insurance company where he was working and they married in 1973 and honeymooned in Disney World. When they lived on Long Island they always kept a boat for fishing and sometimes tending lobster pots in the Sound. Both of them loved to party and travel, often spending weekends in Bermuda or Washington. His wife says, "Any time we had a buck we were on the road." Doug worked for various insurance companies until he retired in 1997 after 26 years and he was able to join his family in their chosen home near Tampa, FL.

By the time his daughter Cyndy was born in 1978 Doug had given up both drinking and smoking, but not having a good time. Even after retirement he went to work in Disney's reservation center and enjoyed the free entry into the parks and everything from the fast rides to the international exhibits. "One of my greatest joys of my Dad's life," Cyndy says, "was being near Disney. He was always kid at heart." At the parks or at home Doug's enjoyed entertainment and entertaining his family. So did his wife who says, "Cyndy has our sense of humor. Cyndy never had a chance. She is one of the funniest people I know. It's a case of nature and nurturing."

Cyndy says she has gleaned from bits of conversation that both her mom and dad were "wildcats" of a sort, but what counts most for Cyndy is that Doug was able to transform his rowdy liveliness into a gentle and secure liveliness. Cyndy says, "He was always both father and close friend. He was my Saturday morning buddy. We'd watch cartoons, and I'd get to go on all his errands with him." That counts for her daughter Tracy who calls her beloved grandfather Lunca. Cyndy says, "We call him the Baby Man." Cyndy and Tracy were living with her parents when the first symptoms of Alzheimer's struck Doug almost ten years ago. It has made no headway against his sense of humor and his love of family or their love for him. Doug was well liked in the Class of '57 but he was not among the senior superlatives, but he has obviously earned one of life's most important superlatives. Cyndy calls him, "the best father in the whole cosmos."

Douglas Andrews
1429 lakeshore Ranch Dr.Seffner fl 33584(813) 689-6072

Cyndy Andrews posted this tribute to her father on the Internet in May, 2005

The mountain of love

Most people say they have the best father in the whole world. Well ok, those of us that still use the term Daddy or papa or even Lunca say we have the best Daddy. Funny thing is that I actually do have the best father in the whole cosmos. The man is smart and funny and loving, supportive, kind, gentle, protective, everything I would want to be if I were a man but admirable qualities for any human if you ask me. He bought me my first bra and told my first boyfriend he would keep him in a box in the attic if he hurt me. Ya know normal Daddy things. But I guess not, I talk to people about my parents and always hear about how lucky I am, how other parents aren't like this. Especially when it comes to my dad, I know that I lucked out that I was blessed that this man is "my Daddy". He's in the hospital right now battling pneumonia. Trying to still be this man even through the cloud the Alzheimer has dropped over him. This blog is for Douglas Charles Andrews this most amazing man I have ever had the pleasure of knowing and loving. I hope that there are many more years to come but I sadly am a realist, so please for me anyone who reads this....call your parents today tell them how much they mean to you, how much you love them, cherish them.

Virginia Arnold

Photos by Fred Feingold

Ginny is one of the few people whose bio appears in our yearbook with not a single activity, award, or honor listed beneath her name.   Perhaps two lines from the poet Emily Dickinson apply: *The soul selects her own society / Then shuts the door.*   Perhaps by design, she was many things to many people, and she encouraged speculation.   "I never knew you too well," she wrote in my yearbook, "but you can never tell."   Then, as if nothing should be taken seriously or comes off as expected, she added "words, words, words, Love, Ginny. "

She came from an educated and affluent family, her father an editor at Ballentine Books, her younger brother David, one of the intellectual shining lights in the Class of '58.   She apparently married a man named Antea.   One story says that she and Evy Piat eloped simultaneously from the Knotty Pine.   She did live in Oyster Bay and/or Locust Valley for a while, then moved to Florida.

Nancy Baker

We were dazzled by appearances, and frankly speaking Nan's appearance was quite ordinary, her smile gentle, not showy she wore big glasses. She didn't wear the latest teen fashions.. So much for the insight of teenagers. When Nancy died in 1997 an entire cathedral filled with mourners whose ranks included bishops and Mayor Rudolph Giuliani. How did we get it so wrong in her brief and prosaic yearbook entry, "after school, it's business?"

Immediately after school Nancy entered the Mother of Mercy Novitiate in Dallas, Pennsylvania and took her vows as a Sister of Mercy in August 1960. Until 1974 she taught grade school and middle school in the Harrisburg, Pennsylvania diocese. She then moved to St. Aloysius Convent in Great Neck, New York as a member of the faculty. For the last nine years of her life she also worked in the ministry in the Diocesan Office of Rockville Centre. No public honors or awards, no prizes, no scholarly degrees or academic accolades brought her life to anyone's attention. Yet she came to be known by many thousands as an extraordinary woman, not for a few outstanding achievements, but for her selfless daily service to other people.

A eulogy written by Sister Maureen McCann sums up the Nancy Baker most of us never knew or suspected. "Our Sister Nancy Baker would not have described herself as extraordinary. But, those who have lived with her, worked wither, received her care and known her friendship, would certainly say that there was something of grandness about her presence, her simple, down-to-earth generosity and largesse of heart, her matter-of-fact, no-nonsense loving."

Our classmate Ruth Ahearn reported that she recently had lunch with Carole Brown and Joanne LaPierre and that, "They each spoke of a very humble, saintly Nancy who did great things but without any fanfare...she never spoke of her daily work." But work she did as Sister McCann noted. "I hesitate to say that she is enjoying 'eternal rest.' I have an idea there may be some creative negotiation, and, in that unconditional love which we are promised, God will create the suitable alternative."

In 1995 when the bishop chose Nancy as one of three from the diocese to meet Pope John Paul II, Nancy said, "I don't know why he picked me, but I'm glad he did." Even then Nancy was fighting the cancer that would soon take her life. Others knew. Sister McCanm said, "Nancy had a 'get on with it' attitude that drew people to her. . . .Choosing life for her was living fully and generously with and for others."

"My Friendship With Nancy Baker," by Joan Birchill Ryan

In those early years when so many Catholic children went to a Catholic school, Nancy and I became good friends at St. Boniface. We went to lunch and dinner together and spent nights at each other's home.

The Baker house was always great fun! The family included two other children. Gayle was the baby of the family and seemed like such a child to us older and more sophisticated girls. Nancy's older sister, Dolly, was someone we could admire but still have fun with. At no time was life in their house on Grove Street dull or boring.

Nancy's parents during those years opened a delicatessen—to our great delight. They began their entrepreneurial adventure in a small store which is now the St. Boniface Outreach Center. As the business grew, they moved to larger quarters on the corner of Glen Cove Avenue and Lafayette Street. Nancy's parents made a great success out of the business and were always understanding and kind when we raided the goodies.

Life was good for us then. We spent our time doing simple things that gave us so much pleasure. In those years school, the movies, birthday parties, the beach and shopping in Glen Cove filled our days. Nancy was always ready to laugh and have fun. As I think back and remember her face, I always see a smile on her mouth. Even then, I knew she had special qualities. A goodness and great gentleness emanated from her.

We graduated from elementary school and on to different high schools. We didn't see as much of each other after that, but we did stay friends and talked every once in a while. She never talked to me about wanting to become a nun in the Catholic Church, but I was not surprised when she did.

After high school she entered the Convent of the Sisters of Mercy in Pennsylvania. We talked only occasionally until she was transferred to the Office of the Diocese of Rockville Center. Then we began to talk more frequently. I would always ask her what her job was over there. She would always say that she just helped some people out and handled some things for the Bishop.

We connected at the St. Boniface Reunion and had a great time. Meeting so many of our classmates was such fun and on one enjoyed the evening more than Nancy. As happens so often, promises were made to get together and see each other, but sadly it never happened. Then one morning, my long time friend Joanne La Pierre called and asked if I knew Nancy had passed. I was stunned but so grateful to learn that I hadn't missed the funeral.

I immediately rushed over to the Great Neck Catholic Church. As I arrived there, I realized the area was around the church was crowded with cars. After I parked, I rushed up the stairs, opened the large doors and saw that people had packed the church. Never before or since have I seen such a large gathering to celebrate someone's life. As the mass proceeded, the funeral cortege entered with so many of the Church's hierarchy that I was mesmerized. AT one point I could easily see some twenty-five priests around the altar. The eulogies were many and all sang her praises while pronouncing great gratitude for her work and for having known her.

After expressing my condolences toher family before their trip to the Motherhouse of the Mercy Order in Pennsylvania, I drove away realizing how fortunate I had been to have Nancy share some of her life with me. This was a gentle soul who thought only of others by dedicating her life to helping people. Never did she need or want to receive any accolades or praises. Her whole life was spent doing all she could in every way for everyone.

She possessed so many wonderful qualities and accomplished so much in her short life onthis earth. Since that day, when I think of Nancy baker, I thank God that I knew her and feel so lucky that she was in my life.

R I P

Helen Basilevsky

Russia's loss of a great general in two generations became Sea Cliff's gain of a fine art student and New York City's gain of a fine art teacher.   Helen's grandfather Baron Wrangel became commander for the Caucasus region of the White Army in its fight against the Red Army after the Bolshevik Revolution of 1917.   (His non-Russian name comes from his German ancestry.)   He won a reputation in the territory he controlled as a fair and progressive administrator, but he soon lost half his army.   In 1920 he left Russia and became the leader of the White Russian resistance abroad.

The Nightingale-Bamford private school for girls in New York prides itself in encouraging "creativity, independence, and self-reliance, as well as intellectual discipline."   Helen had those qualities and began teaching art at the school after she finished Pratt Institute in New York City.   Sea Cliff art teacher Dorothy O'Knefski had encouraged Helen to study at Pratt where she majored in graphic arts.   Her good friend Peggy Costello ('58) remembers when Helen entered school and they took art together in grade school: "Helen had just arrived in Sea Cliff and her beautifully developed artwork dumbfounded us poor yokels and delighted the teachers."

Her strong academic record, her own graphic talent, her cultural sensitivities and her fluent Russian earned her a place as guide in 1963 on the first exhibition of American graphics to tour parts of the Soviet Union, including Armenia and Kazakhstan.   Her curiosity about culture and art and history kept her traveling around the world throughout her life.   In Egypt she worked with archeologist Kent Weeks, discoverer of a lost tomb of the Pharaohs, KV-5.   She traveled up the wilds of the Amazon River and helped create art exhibitions in Japan.   She also traveled throughout Europe, the Middle East, North Africa, Nepal, India, Turkey and Latin America.   In the Turks and Caicos Islands of the Caribbean she lived for months in a tent on the beach of an uninhabited atoll where she helped develop the membership resort of Pine Cay which keeps over 600 of its 800 acres wild.

Her ability to make friends created for her a worldwide network for her long summer vacations, allowing her to travel the globe on her modest income from teaching and art. She loved teaching and devoted her entire career to the girls at Nightingale-Bamford. She became head of the school's art department, and she became as popular with students as Kitty Strohe and Dorothy O'Knefski had been with Sea Cliff students. Her younger brother Peter says, "She never married but she considered her students members of her family, and she maintained close touch with many of them after graduation." After she died on July 31, 1998 of breast cancer, the school named a gallery in her honor.

Helen also practiced what she taught and exhibited her work in graphics and mixed media in several one-woman shows. She brought to her painting and sculptural assemblages of natural objects her great love of nature and her joy in the world's variety.

R I P

Helen on Senior Trip, photo Fred Feingold

Albert Behrmann

"Ace" grew up in a modest home on 16th Avenue as one of the four Behrmann boys, sons of a hard working craftsman immigrant from Germany and a Pennsylvania mother. Al excelled at math and enjoyed his shop classes with Mr. Driscoll. An intense perfectionist at everything, his younger brother Doug recalls that Al would wash dishes, then lay them in rinse water so hot that Doug and brother Ron had to fish them out with wooden spoons.

He left Sea Cliff to major in engineering at Fordham University. A runner in high school, Al became a rower at Fordham, putting in many hours on the East River with his eight man team on the East River even in mid winter. After two years at Fordham Al left to join the Carpenter's Union as his brothers had done.

One evening in 1961 Al's cousin Francie Blum brought her friend Barbara Ann Sleva to Long Island for a blind date with Al that led to marriage. Barbara gave birth to their daughter Beverly Ann in 1963 and to Michael Albert in 1966. Al had already started work on the New York Pavilion and its 250 ft high towers for the 1964 World's Fair. When the Fair was opened in 1964 Al and Barbara used his free pass to wander around the Fair soaking up the world's sights and sounds that so much interested him throughout his life.

In 1966, the year his son Michael Albert was born, AT&T (NY Bell) recruited Al. He became a systems analyst and troubleshooter in the field, often working under high stress conditions to analyze and fix difficult problems. Al remained active throughout his career in the Communications Workers of America labor union and rose to be a shop steward. When the union staged a long strike against the phone company in the 1970s, Al went to

North Shore Country Club and supported the family by caddying.

He and Barbara had taken up residence first in Sea Cliff, then moved to Port Washington, and finally East Northport.   Al loved being outdoors, especially with his kids and played baseball and football and kickball with them and other kids in the street or took them to Gilgo Park on the south shore in the summers.   Although he was a quiet man, he and Barbara became known and appreciated for their annual Christmas Eve open house attended by many old friends and neighbors.   Although Al did not drink or smoke, his daughter Beverly remembers the abundance of food, drink and smokers, and says that she looked forward to the visits from "Uncle Larry" and "Uncle Richie," the latter being our classmate Richard Stack.

He practiced the carpentry his father taught him on his own house and passed on his skills to son Michael and daughter Beverly, building furniture with her. As everyone who worked with Al had learned, she too learned that he "was such a perfectionist."   Beverly too would become a professional carpenter for a while before she went on to administrative work in Marlboro College in Vermont.   Michael, who resembles Al and has his perfectionist bent, would earn a degree in geology but turn his talent to custom framing for artworks.

When Al and Barbara divorced in 1982 Beverly was already 19, but son Michael stayed with Al.   When his mother became seriously ill and homebound with diabetes, Al and his brother Doug would spend long hours playing cards and talking to her.   He also remarried in 1991 and moved to Pennsylvania with his wife Diane.   In April of that year after a seizure doctors found a brain tumor.   Diane and Beverly took care of him in the following months.   Despite the efforts of Harmon University Cancer Research Hospital, the tumor advanced steadily before Al died on February 15, 1992 at age 53.   His mother, 93, survives him and continues her own struggles.

In death Al returned to Long Island and Sea Cliff where the Whitting twins conducted his funeral and his many friends and family came to say good-bye to the man who throughout life they knew by no better name than Ace.

R I P

Blanche Bennett

Roey went from school into the secretarial career she planned, working as an executive secretary in Glen Cove for five years.   She has spent most of her life close to Glenwood Landing where she grew up and where she lives today.   Her childhood was filled with bicycling, rollerskating, kids games, and the beach.   Her relatives were scattered in Maryland, Virginia and Michigan and the family often used summers for visiting.

During high school she got her first business experience when worked as a salesgirl in W.T. Grant's in Glen Cove.   Business was also her favorite subject in school, her favorite teachers being Mrs. French and Mrs. Zipperian.   After graduation she began working as a secretary at Powers Chemco.   She started dating Artie Hall when he returned and from the Navy in 1960.   They married in 1962 and their son Artie Hall III was born that year. Wendy Marie was born in 1963 and John Andrew in 1968 completed the family.

She and Artie had three children, and while the kids were growing up, Roey worked part time at the Swan Club, then part time as a secretary.   In 1978 she began working as executive secretary in Glen Head and moved on to the North Shore Schools office in 1991 where Artie also worked as head custodian.   After ten years as the principal's secretary in Sea Cliff she retired in 2006.

Today Roey and Artie continue to live in Glenwood near their three children and eight grandchildren, all still on Long Island. They divide their time now between Long Island and their lake home in the Poconos.

 Blanche Hall
PO Box 99
 30 Hillside Ave
Glenwood Landing, NY 11547
roey1234@optonline.net

Loretta Berroyer

Loretta was small, scrappy, competitive, and good humored.   Like most of her family, she was blunt and, if you will pardon a bit of euphemism, plain spoken.   In school Cherry Campbell counted herself among Lee's many friends, and gladly so.   "I could count on her to lift me up when I was down." Joan Imperiali, also a cheerleader, says, "I thought she was a good athlete. She was little bit of a tom boy and friendly."   Ted Rydzewski who dated her at times remembers, "She was a nice person.   We did weird things down at the Youth Center.   We'd go down to Tilleys Beach and used to go skinny dipping. "

After graduation Lee began to date Ralph Palacios, somewhat older than us, with an air of worldly knowledge and something of a relaxed Desi Arnez Latin charm.   Many of us knew him from long evenings loitering on the wooden stairs to Tilley's beach or nights at the Knotty Pine.   Ralph had been born in Venezuela but left with his grandmother after his father, part of the presidential guard, was killed in a coup when Romulo Gallegos, the novelist-president was overthrown in 1949.   Ralph became a US citizen and served in the Korean War.   Lee's parents were not happy when she married Ralph and never accepted him or allowed him into their house.   In their first years of marriage Lee and Ralph found themselves in financial trouble, often staying with friends.   While still on Long Island, their first son, Michael, was born in '65 and Richard (Rick) in '67.   They had moved to West Palm Beach, Florida and Ralph was managing a restaurant when Lee gave birth to Krissy in '69.   The children, unfortunately had little time to know their father and live a normal family life.

Mike remembers that their father used to take them golfing or to the beach because he worked evenings, and Lee was probably working a regular day shift.   Mike says, "He didn't want us to play football or baseball. He wanted us to be individuals and play tennis or golf or swim."
Ralph would speak and sing in Spanish to the kids and wanted them to speak Spanish. Mike says Lee learned some Spanish, but mainly "all the wrong words."   Lee kept the kids focused on academics.   "She was very strict with us about grades," Mike says, "and that

was something she wasn't going to back off on. One of her dreams was to have all three of her kids graduate."

On December 7, 1972 Lee was doing a normal day's work in an office when she got a call that Ralph had dropped dead suddenly while crossing a street. He had been felled by an unsuspected brain aneurism. His death struck Lee hard. Instantly fate had turned her into a mother with little education and three pre-teen children. She went back to work. She also remarried quickly and perhaps hastily and would soon be battling alcohol as well as grief. Her son Mike says his father's death brought unimaginable changes to his mother's once sunny temperament. "When I was growing up she didn't have time to be happy." She seemed to age quickly. Lee was always a fighter, however, and as faithful to her children as she had been to her friends when she was our classmate. "She was extremely stubborn," Mike says. She did not give up. She worked as a receptionist, then became office manager of a real estate firm and eventually earned her sales license.

In 1985 she separated from both her second husband and alcohol. That year she drove up to Georgia for Mike's graduation from Army Ranger school, a beaming and proud mother whose son was as tough as she was. Mike feels he owes a lot of his own character to Lee. "She could adapt to any situation or any environment and survive. Whenever things were going down in the army I knew I could call her, and she would pick me up."

Her toughness would soon face its final challenge. In 1988 she learned she had breast cancer. She didn't tell the kids but came to visit Mike for several months where he was stationed in Washington state, then spent another six months with Krissy in California. She said she just wanted to reconnect with her family. Mike found out a couple of years later that she was in chemotherapy and taking radiation treatments. Nevertheless, she maintained her sense of humor and began a large hat collection to cover her missing hair. One of the hats was signed by the Miami Dolphins. Her other hobby was bluegrass music. In '94 the year Mike's son was born his sister called and said Lee was slipping fast. Krissy brought her three children and Mike brought his son so she would be with family again. Lee died on April 13, 1994.

All three of her children found success, although Mike says, "All three of us did it the hard way." Mike went to Army after high school. His sister Krissy became an Army medic, then a nurse. Their younger brother Rick "was the free spirit, the surfer, got his dive master's license and taught scuba." Rick too then joined the Army and became a medic and served Afghanistan and Iraq. Krissy and Mike finished their undergraduate degrees and Rick is studying at NC State University. Krissy, says Mike, "is the patron saint of all of us." Besides being a nurse, she is the mother of five children.

"Wherever she is," Mike says, "I think she's looking down on us and smiling."

Lee's son, who would welcome any memories of his parents that our classmates might have, is
Michael Palacios
7861 Compass Drive
Orlando, FL 32810
mplegal@hotmail.com

R I P

Caroline Berthoud

Photos by Fred Feingold

Caroline and with her sister Lucy and brother Richard and their parents arrived in America aboard the maiden voyage of the Caronia on 21 September 1950. Her father had been part of the pre-war League of Nations and had come to New York with former colleagues for the beginning of the UN where he would head the English translation section. Caroline's mother (born Jocelyn Waller) descended from Irish and English gentry, but Caroline slipped comfortably into public school life in Sea Cliff. That year when we were given a form asking if we wanted to learn a musical instrument Caroline began her life's career. "I put a tick on a piece of paper saying I wanted to learn the violin." By the end of year the other would-be violinists, including this writer, had given up. Her father arranged private lessons with professional violinist and Juliard graduate Dorothy Kesner of Oyster Bay. (Kesner had studied under the famous Hungarian violinist and teacher Leopold Auer, and so does talent pass through time and space.)

Betty Gelling might have written the first original composition for Caroline but when she presented it to her in Sue Frost's dining room one day, Caroline said she could not play music that had no bars, only notes on the staff because she needed the bars for the proper tempo.

Caroline excelled in most subjects and says, "My greatest trouble after leaving school was to decide what field to go into—some know, some have to decide." She returned to England to take qualifying exams that would be necessary if she decided to continue her education there. When she returned to England she found that her American education had made her an idealist. "I thought we would all go out and make it in the world. I had been out of school only two years when my younger sister Lucy said, 'Caroline you've been out in the world and what have you've done?'" Except for English history, Caroline says, "I found when I got to England I found I had much better general knowledge. Lots of people here leave school without really knowing anything."

With the English exams behind her, she left to visit her French-Swiss relatives in the beautiful city of Lausanne on Lake Geneva.   There she studied   French at Lausanne University and took violin lessons at Lausanne Conservatoire.   An inspiring teacher helped her decide that her future lay with the instrument she had chosen in 5th grade.   She returned to London to study at the Royal Academy of Music for the next four years.   But "Why not go abroad for a bit?" she thought as soon as she finished.

For the next two years she played with the Kunstmaand Orchestra that later would become the Amsterdam Philharmonic and even later the Dutch Philharmonic Orchestra.   When she returned to England to play with the Bournemouth Symphony Orchestra, she married fellow violinist John Thorgilson, and they adopted two children.   Caroline gave up her orchestra contract to be with the children, but continued to freelance for both the Bournemouth orchestra and its affiliated chamber orchestra, commitments that kept her playing almost full time.   She and her husband divorced ten years after adopting their children, and Caroline continued playing.   Her daughter Kate went into social work and her son Oliver into acting.

As the millennium approached Caroline says, "I wound down my playing."   In our search for classmates, we found Caroline listed as a guest violinist with the Isle of Wight Symphony Orchestra.   Unfortunately, three years ago she was pulling ivy off a wall of her 19th century Dorset cottage, slipped on the wet footing, fell backward and broke her right arm badly, tearing the muscle from the bone.   That put an end to her playing.   She doesn't know if she can ever play again but says, "Maybe I've had enough."   She does listen to music, but not orchestral music. "If someone puts some on I'm straight back at work." She stays busy fixing her cottage, babysitting for her daughter, and traveling to visit family and friends and foreign venues.

"I never regretted taking up music," she says, "as I always loved it and the camaraderie of orchestral life," but it had many disadvantages, including "lowish pay, unsocial hours which were difficult raising children, and orchestral politics."   The unique reward of a career in orchestral music was "the fundamental experience of everyone doing their best to make a harmonious whole—which doesn't always occur in the outside world."

(Caroline lives in England.   Address available to classmates by request.)

John Broderick

"I was kind of a vagabond drifting through different schools." His parents nudged him into St. Dominics. "I got kicked out at the end of my second year." Glen Head residents had a choice of public high schools, and John chose Sea Cliff where his neighbor Fred Burns went. Because the academic courses at St. Dominics had given him extra credits toward graduation "I kinda went to school in absentia. I never really buckled down and did the things I needed for college entrance." Civics teacher Jean Tibbets told Peter Muttee's mother Bobbie that Pete and John were going to flunk history and not going to graduate. Mrs. Muttee replied, "I'm going to take these two guys and lock them up in a room with the text book." And she did. John says, "I always called her 'mom' after that."

Although John drifted through several schools, he was very much a part of Glenwood and Glen Head. While his own father left every morning at 6:30 for his job as financial editor of *The Wall Street Journal,* and often came home on the last train, John had "a lot of alternate dads who were very important to me. Richie Smith's dad, a foreman at Sand and Gravel had huge arms and played ball, and he included Richie and myself in everything." For spending money John did what many boys did and caddied at local golf courses.

Nonchalant as he was about studying, John did go to Long Island University and took his bachelor's degree in psychology. He also "met this gal at CW Post and next thing you know we had one in the oven and I thought boy oh boy this is good, and I thought I better go into the Air force officers' program." That took him to Vietnam where he flew as a radar controller underneath one of those flying saucer domes atop an AWACS plane. They flew off the coast directing fighter and bomber pilots and returning each night to Saigon with alternate weeks in a small town in Taiwan. "It was in the upper 1% of all things you could do over there." He appreciated the fact that others were closer to the tragedy of war. That included his friend Kevin Walsh of Glen Head whom he met by chance on a street in Saigon. Kevin was a Marine captain leading search and destroy missions.   John also remembers, "walking out to Tansanut air base in the mornings to get our orders for the day and these Huey helicopter guys would be coming in with the body bags and they would just throw them on the floor like bags of mail."

After service John found himself in Sacramento and fell in love with the West Coast.   He built a career in food sales but at 52 he retooled his professional life and worked until 2007 in real estate publishing.   Meanwhile he had been divorced in '76 and at the 25th class reunion in 1982 Carole and Pete Muttee re-introduced him to Barb Schmidts from the Class of '60.   "Once we got together it was like old times."   John set up a meeting one rainy night at Goerlich's with Barb's daughter Debbie.   Debbie looked at him skeptically and asked, "What are you going to be like one of these bums my mother hangs out with." The evening ended with rapport.   Barb moved to the Washington and in 1990 they married.

Retirement doesn't appeal to him.   "I'm not a woodworker, I don't play golf, I love Barb dearly, but I don't need to see her 24/7 and I like to be out in the fray."

John Broderick
11104 122nd Lane NE, Apt. 100
Kirkland, WA 98033
John.b1990@yahoo.com

Carole Brown

Photo by Fred Feingold   Photo Nik Epanchin

In 1957 future teacher Carole Brown and Pete Muttee were going steady and they still are after 46 years of marriage. The one exception came after a "big fight" on the senior trip that led to separate dates for the senior prom. Carole went with Serge Yonov and Pete with underclasswoman Brook Nichols. Two proms later, however, Pete and Carol joined John Broderick and Barbara Schmidts at the 1959 prom. Carole, meanwhile, had become ATT's contestant for Miss New York State and the company presented her at the Westbury Music Fair.

Carole's family had moved to Glenwood Landing from Massachusetts and the first friend she made in the new community was Peter Merkel. She still has "The Little Book About God" in which bears Peter's inscription, "Happy Birthday, Carole. For the first eight years of school she attended St. Boniface.

In Carole's last year at St. Boniface she never told her parents about the tests being given for Catholic high schools until the tests were over. When her mother asked her why she hadn't taken them, she said, "I've had it with the nuns, Mom." She remembers some fine teachers among them, but she was more impressed by the tough ones. The infamous Wuzzy Britt once broke a statue, and when no one would tell, Sister Ursula began whacking every student's knuckles, breaking her ruler but moving on without stopping. Another time when she had forgotten her beanie head cover for church, a nun took one belonging to Gertrude Whalen and slapped it on Carole's head. She came home with head lice.

When she came to Sea Cliff School she decided "I wasn't going to go to college. I had absolutely no interest in any more books." However in the last part of the junior year when she heard so many talking about college, she says, "I thought 'Oh boy I'm getting left out.' In the fall of '57 she and Mickie Vaccaro left for Geneseo State Teacher's College, the alma mater of Sea Cliff's 7th grade teacher Miss Alice Daldry. By October she and Mickie were so homesick, they came home unannounced. Carole told her mother she wasn't going back. "Oh yes, you are," her mother told her. After three years, however, she did come home to go to work for the telephone company and finish her degree at Nassau Community College.

She and Pete would soon be married. Twice. "I was married in '62 and I married the same guy in '63." Pete had finished his Army service in early '62 and they decided to elope. "We had never done anything really bad," Carole says. "We looked in the phone book and found Chief Justice Adler in Yonkers. We walked into his house and he asked if we had any witnesses and we said no and he called his wife out of the kitchen." They returned to their separate homes with their parents and said nothing. The next year Pete asked Carole's father if he could marry her. Her father said yes, and soon Pete and Carole said yes again.

Their son Robert arrived in '64, then brothers Peter and Eric, and finally daughter K in '69. Carole left her job with the telephone company but soon had three or four children in her home day care operation. When her own children were in school she took a job with the North Shore Day School, teaching pre-schoolers. She continued until 1989 when she again began her own home day care and nursery school. "If you were to ask me today if I were to be a teacher, I'd say no way. Parents. Parents have too much say in the school system." Too many parents, she feels, blame the teacher for their children's failings. Discipline is difficult. "The word respect isn't even in our vocabulary anymore."

Carole and Pete have lived their lives in the Muttee family house where Pete grew up . While Pete volunteered as a Boy Scout leader, Carole served as a Girl Scout leader. She also volunteered as a driver for senior citizens. When she and Pete are not traveling, they walk twice a day, go to the library. Six days a week Carole goes to the gym in Glen Cove.

One year she suggested to Pete that they think of something different for Christmas. On Christmas day she opened her present, a package of Raccola cough drops. She said she didn't have a cold. Pete said, no they were from Switzerland and he had arranged a hiking tour in the Swiss Alps. They went to and hiked five mountains in five days.

Carole has never been deterred by age from trying something new. At forty she learned downhill skiing. At 55 she decided she would learn to ride horses. She learned to ride English saddle and took up barrel racing. For a while she owned two horses. She still rides, but carefully since she a spell of back trouble revealed that a fall from a horse some years ago had broken the wing tip off one vertebra. "Who knows what I will do for my 70th?"

Carole Muttee
57 Clinton St.
Sea Cliff, NY 11579   cmuttee@verizon.net

Judy Brown

Photo by Nik Epanchin

Judy and Jane Allen used to go to the Methodist Church "while the service was going on we used to read the wedding service to each other. We weren't doing it because we wanted to get married. We were romantic and the words were pretty. That's what put a little spark of spirituality in me." That spark has warmed others as Judy went into nursing after graduating from the University of Connecticut. She took out sixteen years for her family and returned to nursing in 1980, serving in the life and death environment of Intensive Care Units for many years, most of them in New Hampshire where she still lives and works.

Judy's family moved to Sea Cliff when her father finished service in the US Navy after WWII and immediately fell into the rhythms and culture of village life—play, school, church, the beach and skating on Scudders' Pond. "Walking to school from home. I got lost my first day and went right instead of left. We didn't have to worry about predators at that point." Miss Laura Smith in 5th grade infected her with the urge to travel with stories of trips and places and what she had seen. In 6th grade she was in that half of the class that had the sometimes formidable, sometimes zany ex-Marine Robert Allen who could mimic Victor Borge's vocal punctuation routine or suddenly announce, "Spit ball fight time." Lunch was often bologna on white bread topped with catsup. In 7th grade "Richie Loftus brought Jane and I together when he ripped up his math paper and stuffed it in one of our hoods and we were so mad we went home and pieced it together."

In high school she worked in Dobkins Pharmacy as one of the trio—Betty, Jane and Judy—who almost always greeted restless or lonely boys with a warm smile and willing ear. They were more therapeutic than most bartenders. Judy, however, bears a permanent Dobkins scar, the result of climbing on the counter to change the clock and having a pot of coffee water overturn on her foot.

When she left Sea Cliff for the University of Connecticut, "I was a little scared because I'd never gone away and was going to have a roommate. My father said you're not to get pregnant." She graduated with a nursing degree and also married in 1961, divorced in '79 and remarried Dr. Fred Brown who died in 1995.

While continuing her nursing career , she has also found time to live in Canada for a while and to travel to Paris, Venice, Galapagos, and make fifteen trips to Alaska.

Judy is now working in a nursing home with rehabilitation, but says, "I don't want it to happen to me. I try to take good care of myself. I'm extremely healthy." Over the years I've become very spiritual and come to believe the best way I can live my life is o be very present for people to be kind and thoughtful. Every day is a new day. I look forward to every single day. I woke up today and thought 'great I'm going to pick blueberries." She may not admit it, but she has probably achieved one of her most important goals, "Maybe be a blessing to somebody."

Judy Brown
PO Box 652
Newburg, NH 03225-0652
judybrown@tds.net

Judy (left) with Lee Berroyer

Phoebe Burdick

Phoebe with the girls, 2008

"Feeb" replied to our request for information by apologizing that her story offered no "earth shattering" events. But what's to regret about a life that has been fulfilling in family and friends?

Phoebe went from Sea Cliff north to SUNY Plattsburgh starting as a home economics major before switching to the profession she had her mind on in high school—nursing. She worked in Helena Rubinstein's cosmetics production facility in Greenvale for 3.5 years then went on to attend nursing school at SUNY Farmingdale. Once Phoebe began serious nursing studies, she realized the practical benefit of her mother's insistence that she take Latin. Of course, like most of Mr. Matthews' students, she learned well under his discipline and his passionate love of the subject. Her two years of this language that many students assume useless "was a godsend" in understanding the terminology in anatomy and physiology and has continued to be her guide in learning new words.

Before finishing nursing school she married Fred Klein, a Suffolk County police officer. She and Fred soon had three children in close succession, and each has grown to be a successful adult. Phoebe's greatest regret in life was coming "s-o-o close" to a B.S. in nursing, but her daughter Elizabeth became an RN and works in pharmaceutical research. Fred Jr. owns his own electric business, and Suzanne is a Florida court reporter. When the girls were younger, Phoebe volunteered as a Scout leader.

When Fred retired as a detective/sergeant in intelligence work in 1985 they moved to Sebastian Florida a mile south of Cape Kennedy. Phoebe says, "Being married to a police detective did gradually turn me into more of a cynic and I no longer trust many lawyers, doctors and priests." It did not shake her trust in family or the value of helping others. Phoebe has also worked for several years with the board of elections in Florida, including the 2000 election with its famous hanging chads. "We were all made to feel like nincompoops here in Florida with all the negative publicity we received."

Phoebe remains close to her daughters, helping one daughter with an autistic child who requires considerable attention.   Together with her daughter Phoebe learned Applied Behavior Analysis and worked with her teaching her grandson the highly repetitive lessons of social skills, emotion control, and even the basics of dressing.   Nevertheless, Phoebe says, "I absolutely love being a grandma-it's so much easier (not to mention more fun) than being a Mom!!!"

Phoebe was an athlete in school but afterward limited herself to family ski trips.   She and Fred have traveled abroad every year since his retirement, creating a wide network of friends through his membership in the International Police Association whose members often host each other in their home countries.

Phoebe Klein
4103 Limerick Court
Sebastian, FL
frognphez@aol.com

Fred Burns

When Fred's parents sent him from his native Glenwood to St. Boniface with its teaching nuns and discipline, he pleaded with them to be allowed to go to Glenwood elementary. The cloakroom that divided the boys' from the girls' classrooms was the one place where students could let loose though even that the nuns often raided. The cloakroom was also the solitary punishment cell where miscreants served time. (See Mary Ann Vanek's bio.) In retrospect Fred says, "It was a great education."

Transferring to Sea Cliff in 9th grade offered great freedom. Fred's favorite teachers were the easy-going Coach Ray Conlin and the relaxed John Henderson in social studies who would sit on his desk, tie held in place with a paper clip. The tall, elderly and craggy Dorothy Comfort who taught Spanish was a mixture—stern disciplinarian who would give him detention, then give him and others a ride home because their bus had departed.

As soon as he had his driver's license Fred acquired the first of his three high school cars, the most famous being his yellow Ford convertible. He ran his own transportation service, driving Carole Brown and Nancy Samuelson to school every morning. After school and weekends he often worked at the elite at Piping Rock Country Club as a uniformed doorman and later in the office. As doorman Fred often worked debutante parties ushering in the kids from wealthy families in their cummerbunds and formal wear to dance to the music of Lester Lanin's Band of Reknown. Brian O'Toole ('58) worked there as a busboy and would often sneak out champagne for other employees. After working all night parties, Fred sometimes found himself in assistant principal A. Stanley Goodwin's office being lectured on the destructive effects of such work.

Fred didn't go to the Air Force as his yearbook note predicted, but to Mohawk Valley Technical Institute in Utica, NY with Ned McAdams. The two year school emphasized hands-on education and field trips to business and industry. Fred soon decided he would join the Army. "I told my parents I quit college and I joined the army and they flipped out." He spent the next three years mostly in Germany. When he returned home he took a job with New York Telephone. He also accepted a blind date arranged by Charlie

Davies ('58) girlfriend. He and Pat Barry married in 1964. Their son Michael was born in '65 and daughter Laurie in '68.

For some 32 years Fred worked for New York Telephone as it reshaped itself under several different names before becoming the present day Verizon. He started as a technician, then took on a variety of jobs and challenges, including teaching courses throughout the Bell system and becoming a supervisor for New York City and Long Island with a large staff. His last post was was Director of Technical Services where he worked with government committees to establish the uniform technical standards that allow the many service providers, cell phones and high speed Internet connections to work compatibly.

When his wife Pat died in 1996 he also retired. Except he did not retire. He was given the advice, "Retire and you don't have any money problems you do what you want to do." He sold his home in Nesconset and moved to a condo in East Hampton and became a New York State Park Ranger on Montauk Point during the summers. "This is probably the most interesting job I have had," he says, "outside all the time in a great environment on the east end of Long Island."

For the winters Fred enjoys his condo in Ft. Lauderdale, Florida. He is also an enthusiastic traveler. He cruised Russia's Volga River and watched as Russia's revamped military paraded its might in celebration of their victory over Nazi Germany. He was interested to find that university students he talked to knew little of Soviet times. "It seems like a block in their minds." In November 2008 he visited Beijing, Xiang, and Shanghai in China.

Fred Burns
514 Pantigo Rd
East Hampton NY 11937
351 NE 19th Place
Ft Lauderdale, Fl 33305
Fripper@aol.com

Cherry Campbell

1944 was a bad year for Cherry—her parents divorced and she contracted a case of measles that would leave her handicapped for life. Cherry's mother, fortunately, was good at calculating the odds in more ways than one. Cherry's mom knew the odds were against them, especially in that era. But she was also an odds calculator at racetracks for Totalizator, calculating and posting the numbers on the statistics boards. She decided to send Cherry to St. Paul's Girs School in Baltimore where she boarded during the week, spending weekends with her mom or relatives.

After Cherry had been in boarding school for 4 years, her mother married colleague Arthur Ulrich who was in charge of all Totalizator racetracks in NY. They moved to Glen Head and in her freshman year she started at Sea Cliff. That was also the year she discovered how bad her handicap was. "I was trying to learn French and I could hardly understand my own language." The measles had left her with a 57 decibel loss in her right ear. Her mother talked with our long and lanky and thoughtful counselor Alfred Johnstone, and he arranged for Cherry to sit in the front of every classroom. And to improve the odds of her success in and out of school, "My mom sent me to lip reading school because I wouldn't wear a hearing aid."

Cherry, of course, became very much a part of our school's social life although she says, "I never smoked and I never drank." Her mother enforced those conditions. "Boy was she strict. She was strict and hard." As a result Cherry often found herself operating as what we now call "designated driver." Her freshman and sophomore years she went out regularly with Butchie Kundler "best looking" in the Class of '56. She hung out with Lois Delgado, Nancy Samuelson, Lee Berroyer, Brud Neice, and Pete Lawler ('56). John Murray became her buddy. "I could always cry on his shoulder."

From high school Cherry went to the University of Miami, intending to be an airline stewardess, although her mother wanted her to be a concert pianist and had bought her a baby grand. Her college plans were cut short when her mom, who had transferred to New Orleans with her stepfather, became seriously ill and Cherry joined them. Her mother was allergic to the airborn petrochemicals from Louisiana refineries. The company transferred them to Clearwater, Florida in 1962. Cherry was working in a local bank when girlfriends from Michigan came to visit. One weekend she sent them to a local liquor store to buy a case of 7 Up for a party and the salesman said their host said, "You're friend doesn't know what she's talking about. She needs a 6 pack." When they returned with the 6 pack and told Cherry the story, Cherry got in car, went to store and demanded to know, "Where is the idiot who told my friends I didn't know what I was talking about?" She dressed him down and forgot about him. A few weeks later she accepted a blind date with a friend's brother—the same salesman, who was also Pinellas County deputy sheriff Gary L. Stevenson. "I fell head over heels." They were married in '64. Gary decided he had better go to college and Cherry agreed to continue working. He got his bachelors and was two years into law school when Cherry became pregnant.

Gary took a job running a friend's car dealership in Texas. They eventually bought their own dealership. Meanwhile their son, Gary L. Stevenson II was growing up and became a member of the school tennis team. Cherry, a tennis mom, was driving on afternoon when she misheard something another mom said from the rear of the van and the kids began to laugh at her.

Embarrassing her son was something she would not willfully do. At age 52 she started wearing a hearing aid. She hadn't told anyone and when her son in the next room passed wind and she remarked on it, he said, "You couldn't have smelled that." She replied, "I heard it." It was the first new sound she heard with her aid.

When Cherry's mom, living in Clearwater, Florida, began to develop senile dementia, she knew she had to be there. She and Gary moved back to Florida. Her mother's decline was a six year ordeal. "It was one of the hardest things we ever had to deal with..I don't wish it on anyone or their family. Meanwhile they bought a house on the Rainbow River in Dunnellon and started a used car lot that is run by their son, Gary L. Stevenson III.

Cherry's greatest joy, besides children and a grandchild, is the Rainbow River that runs cool and crystal clear year round beside their backyard. Everybody in the family scuba dives but Cherry sticks with her snorkel, swimming, pontoon boating, and kayaking. She'll never know what odds her mother gave her, but she has clearly beaten them.

Cherry D. Stevenson
18691 SW 109th PlDunnellon, FL 34432-4553

Edward Capobianco

Photo by Dr. V N Epanchin

The little shy Italian guy we sometimes called Meatball or Meat would become as adventurous and innovative as his father. Ed's father Michael, an immigrant at 13 from Italy found his niche in working with metal—first silver, then his own radiator business and scrap salvage. He once bought for $100 the 240 foot shell of Submarine 51 that sank in LI Sound off Block Island in 1925. He intended to put it on display but safety concerns stymied that plan and he cut it up by Hempstead Harbor and sold it for scrap. Ed's sister Gail says, "He wasn't afraid to try anything."

In high school Ed hung out at Freddie's Service Station and liked to contemplate the uses and value of the wrecked cars in junk yards. When Ed left high school and went to working for one of the zanier and more daring local experts—Don Deeks the "tree man." While doing tree work Ed earned himself a place in *Ripley's Believe It Or Not* when he cut down a large old elm and found growing inside of it, an 18 inch sapling.

Ed's experience in scrap metals and mechanics led him into the scrap metal business. His expertise in the uses, values and markets for scrap took him into places and projects few people think much about, but which are vital to the way the world works and which require both a practical mind and a good imagination. We tend to think of progress as building and assembling. A great deal of such progress cannot begin until someone does the un-building and hauling away of the old. Call it un-building because wrecking doesn't begin to describe the kinds of skills and knowledge that led Ed to become an expert on disassembling a whole power plant on Gardiner's Island and employing helicopters to lift outmoded air-conditioning units off of high rise buildings in Manhattan.

Ed has lived his entire life on Long Island.

Ed CapobiancoPO box 362
Peconic, NY 11958631 734-7246

Gail Capobianco

Gail with Lynn Maker in then and now

Gail was number eleven of her parents' traditional Italian family, her brother Ed number twelve, and her sister Deb the last of thirteen.   Her father had emigrated from Italy at 13 and found his wife in Glen Cove's Italian community.   His early profession was silversmith, but he soon had his own business on Glen Cove Avenue, Sea Cliff Radiator Works.   For his family he bought them a house on the upper end of Sea Cliff Avenue next to Dr. Marsden's home and office.

Gail found most of her entertainment outside of school rather than inside.   In grade school she was a regular at the Saturday matinees in Glen Cove.   In high school she became one of the group Ginny Parks calls the "Four Musketeers"—Ginny, Gail, Annette Caselli, and Fred Burns.   They went where whim took them.   A short trip to Manhasset by car ended up as train ride and a day's adventure in New York.   Another day, playing hooky, "We ended up in NYC watching a TV game show when she realized they were part of the audience being occasionally scanned by the cameras and projected onto millions of screens, including some in Sea Cliff.

In her sophomore year she was working in Grants in Glen Cove and had started going steady with a Glen Cove boy, Lynn Maker.   When the great storm of 1954 enveloped Hempstead Harbor, Gail and Lynn walked out of her house into the storm headed for his place in Glen Cove.   "Let it rain, let it rain, let it rain," but Gail and Lynn had each other and were amazed but unphased by "items and clothes floating out of the lockers at the Sea Cliff Yacht Club into the water and water almost to the top of Hempstead Harbor Yacht Club."   Three years later Lynn went into military service and Gail went her own way.   "I guess I really broke his heart but he never forgot me."   True.   A song would come on and he would think of her.   He was sure she had gotten married and in fact she did.

Although she had passed exams for college entrance, Gail went to work for Columbia

Ribbon and Carbon.   On a blind date at a USO dance she met airman Alfred Schramm and they married in January 1959.   Almost immediately she found herself pregnant.   She enrolled in parenting classes and found herself practicing on dolls alongside her former business teacher, Betty French.   Gail's son was born late that year and a daughter two years later, and shortly thereafter a son.   "You have your three and then you say wait a minute."   She and Alfred separated and Gail found herself a single mother of three young children.   She began to work as a teacher's aide in special education.   "You bring home $80 every two weeks.   That was hard."   She took the kids and moved to Florida where her mother had begun to spend the winters and where younger sister lived in Lakeworth.   She took a job at the West Palm Beach County office.   After a short reuniting with Alfred, they divorced in '74.   She came close to marrying again but never did.

In September 2005 her friend Ruthie Furst attended a class reunion at her Glen Cove alma mater and met classmate Lynn Maker who asked if she had kept up with Gail.   He was surprised to hear Gail had never remarried and asked for her phone number.   Ruthie hesitated, but when she gave it to him two months later he made the call.   "It was love all over again.   He had never forgotten me all those years.   I saw him for the first time in over 50 years Thanksgiving 2005, then Christmas....and eventually he moved to Florida."   They vacationed in the Virgin Islands on St. Thomas and St. John's in March 2006.   "It was wonderful we were together.   He couldn't believe it and I couldn't either."

In February 2007 doctors diagnosed Lynn's lung problems as inoperable and incurable lung cancer.   That fall they drove through the Catskill Mountains where he once lived and visited some of his children, then stayed a few days with Gail's family in Sea Cliff.   The photo above was taken in Memorial Park.   With her steady boyfriend back at her side, she had a memorable time visiting beaches and parks and reminiscing with Annette Caselli.

Lynn entered hospice on Thanksgiving of that year and the next day he died.   "We had been together just two years, and although the time was short, I was so glad to have the unexpected happiness in my life once again."

The years went by and never knew
That each one brought me nearer you;
Their path was narrow and apart
And yet it led me to your heart –
(lines by Sara Teasdale)

Gail Capobianco
6011 Alhambra Court
New Port Richey, FL 60453
Gcapra37@verizon.net

Annette Caselli

Like several other members of our class, Annette arrived in America as a grade schooler surrounded by strangers making unintelligible noises that would become her new language. The only help for foreign students then was de facto immersion, and like the others Annette had become part of the class in less than a year. Her experience makes her a skeptic about today's preference for bilingual education. Learning English, she says, "wasn't that hard. I had wonderful wonderful teachers, and they stayed after school to help me. I had kids that wanted to help me, and they did, they taught me everything. I learned. They even drove me home from school, but that was before people got sued."

Soon the memories of the war and its guns and the bombs that fell around her in France, the Nazis and the American soldiers on whom her family had depended for life soon faded. How completely she put that time behind her may be reflected in her description of life in high school. "I didn't really appreciate what life is. I thought it would go for ever and ever."

"I was busy being Americanized. I wanted to be like everybody else." We thought she was. She thought she was, but to be like everybody else did not that we wanted to become carbon copies. As Annette puts it, "the meaning of life was to be accepted and have fun." She became close friends with Gail Capobianco and Angelica Izzo. Since graduation, "We kind of floated in and out of each other's lives."

She was also good friends with Margie Repucci who would babysit for Annette's great Dane. If any of her friends was dedicated to having fun, it was Faith LaJoy. She and Annette reconnected toward the end of Faith's life as Faith was dying of cancer.

Annette still loves her native language though she finds little opportunity to speak French, except to her dog. "If can grab someone who speaks French I will." More importantly, life has come to mean much more than being accepted and having fun. "I think if you are lucky and you have children, that's part of it into infinity. I think the good that you do, that's important.   Each day—the birds on the trees, the flowers that grow.   To me that's the meaning of life."

Annette Caselli Capobianco
9 Elliott Pl.
Glen Cove, NY 11542
bijougirl104@yahoo.com

Patricia Cavanaugh

Pat's yearbook entry concluded, "What's next?"   In September 1957 with Marlene Lynn, Faith LaJoy and Pat Bangert at her side as bridesmaids in St. Boniface Church, she married the man who is still her husband, Walter Alexander.

Pat and Walt had four children, and until 1974 Pat stayed home to safely into adolescence. For the next thirteen years she worked for Estee' Lauder.   Pat received top marks on her work review every year, but one year "I destroyed my back one day at work."   She didn't apply for disability support but quit to support her younger daughter who was expecting her first child.   Three years later her daughter added a second charge to Pat's care.   Pat grew up with a firm sense of what she thought a good family should be, and she welcomed her new role.   "That was much better than any job in the world."

In 1995 her husband Walt retired from the Long Island Lighting Company after 39 years of service.   Walt had developed emphysema and they moved to the dry, hot climate of Las Vegas/Henderson, Nevada.   In 2005 they tried a couple of years in Waterloo, NY but the cold aggravated Walt's condition and they returned to Nevada.   Their 4 children, 2 girls and 2 boys, and their 7 grandchildren live on Long Island, and she considers each of their births and lives as a major event in hers.

Pat's school years were not the best in her life, but she prefers to remember in this book, the best of it.   "If there was any special person in my school life, it was Douglas Elton.   In Glenwood Landing School, 1952-53 we had to attend dance lessons after school.   Douglas would always pick me to dance even though I was the fat one.   I would never have attended those classes if not for him always choosing me, because no one else did.   He was the perfect gentleman who kept me from running home crying. If I think back on anyone I remember in my school years to thank, it is Douglas Elton.   So thank you, 55 years later.   I am really sorry I didn't thank you years ago for being so nice."

Pat Alexander
waljmadre@yahoo.com   waljmadre@embarqmail.com

Robert Clarke

Both photos by Nik Epanchin

Bob was always good for a laugh, and the laugh was always a good laugh. Sometimes he ould get it without saying a word, as when he a male visitors to the female theatrical boarding house in the senior play—enter Bob wearing a Bermuda short suit with knee socks and carrying the kitten. The flip side of his kind of humor is human warmth. An essential quality of a "best dancer" is being able to read another human being. Both contribute to being a good teacher and counselor, the leading roles Bob has played since leaving college.

In 1957 he had his choice of Georgetown, Colgate, and St. Lawrence. "I didn't want to follow brother's footsteps [to Colgate], and Georgetown seemed very oppressive," so he chose St. Lawrence "at the end of the world, where the temperature goes down to about -40 below zero." But this was the same Bob Clarke who didn't hesitate when track coach Don Thompson said. "You know Rob we have to have someone in the hurdles and you gotta run the hurdles." He said he didn't know how to jump, but he ran and he won.

When he left college he was engaged to his future wife Una whom he had met when fellow lifeguard Pete Marnane ('55) introduced them. Once engaged, "I needed to get a real job." He took a job near Syracuse teaching social studies and Married Una in June. Bob was then in the career his grandfather had followed and his mother had tried and rejected and his sister would follow for life. Bob's father ran a printing business. After a year upstate Bob and Una moved to West Hampton where he continued to teach social studies for five years. He found teaching to be a "tough business. I was half way through a lesson one day and I thought, another 25 yrs of this?" Soon he went into guidance in the same district. "I enjoyed that immensely. The interesting thing about counseling is that it is very multi-tasking." Unlike teaching or a being a psychologist who deals all day with troubles, "it's really kind of joyous helping kids to get to their goals." Bob became District Direct of Guidance.

He and Una had four children and they soon found themselves with three in college at one time. Bob says he had loved shop in junior high, and his father-in-law was a wonderful carpenter who helped him develop his woodworking techniques. "When the children were in college I started a carpentry business, just myself. I'd be up till 11 o'clock at night making coffee tables, headboards, mantel pieces."

Bob decide to take early retirement in 1995 and soon found himself again with hurdles he didn't know how to jump. He got a real estate license but found success depended on getting people he knew to help him find listings. "I have a real aversion to being beholden to people for helping." He and Una were also getting divorced, and he found himself in the hardest year of his life, living in a rented place, having nothing to do. "I was amazed I never got depressed. Part of our ego gets tied up in our work, especially for men, and I've known a number of people who retired and ended up having to go to shrinks."

Bob and Una divorced, and she died suddenly at 57 when an infection in her foot went into bloodstream and killed her as she was dressing to go out with friends. Bob decided he should go back to work. A friend in Florida spotted an ad for a counselor in a private school and Bob moved to Florida and worked for another five years before he was finally ready to leave education. He stays very busy with carpentry, remodeling, children and grandchildren. His grandson Danny recently did several pictures of "grandfathers" Rob and his partner. "Happy situation for me and very fulfilling." Bob and his partner run a small real estate business "which keeps us busy and off the streets."

Robert Clarke
1215 Satona St.
Coral Gable, FL 33146
robclarke33146@yahoo.com

Sarah Colgan

The Colgans moved to Sea Cliff from Franklin Square in 1944, into a small but bigger-than-before house on DuBois Ave.   Sally started first grade at St. Boniface and is grateful for the quality of the teaching by the Sisters of Mercy.   She also remembers how her classmate Ruth Ahearn responded to the class bully Wuzzy Britt by decking him.   Her older brother Billy went on to Shamanade, the Catholic high school, and Sally came to Sea Cliff as a freshman.

Sally says she was and still is very shy and her opportunities to develop ties in the class were limited by her mother who demanded she come home right after school.   "My mother was very controlling."   More important, she says, "Sports was my life saver.   "It gave me something to do other than studying and sticking around the house."   She particularly appreciated Miss Maple's approach—"she let you do your own thing.   She was there to tell you to try this or that."   She also loved bookkeeping and band where she played bass clarinet.   Sally had always been a sports fan, and when she would see the soccer team passing her house on its way to a game in Clifton Park, she would often follow. Shy Sally didn't know then that she had been noticed and noted by a Glen Cover player ten years older than her.

After graduation she began work in a small Glen Cove printing shop doing bookkeeping and typing.   Brother Billy commandeered the family car and her mom took her to work and picked her up.   She had tried Driver Ed with Miss Tibbets, but the manual shift stymied her.   "Miss Tibbets hated to get in the car with me."   At the print shop and later at Helena Rubinstein's she saved her money, and in 1963 enrolled in Ryder College in Lawrencevill, NJ.   Meanwhile she continued to follow local sports.

One afternoon a soccer player came over to talk to her.   He was Dan McKinney, the Glen

Cover player who had noticed her before.   He was working at a Glen Cove grocery and they started dating and going to movies when he got off work.   In 1964 they married. Dan taught Sally to drive and they bought a VW bug that took her 180,000 miles before she gave it up with a broken axle and regrets.   She and Dan had moved to Coppaigue and had been making the long commute to their jobs in Nassau.

Their son Daniel was born in 65, Charlie in 67 and Sally in 68.   Sally stayed home while the kids were growing, but her husband, "a workaholic" was hospitalized for two weeks with what doctors first thought was heart trouble, but that turned out to be fatigue from overwork.   Sally took charge.   "I said we're moving."   And even without jobs in sight, they moved to Roanoke, Virginia where Dan had been born and where they had honeymooned.   Soon Dan had a job in a supermarket, Sally in the main office of the 7-11 chain.   When one of the boys got into trouble in the public school, they moved all three to a nearby Catholic school where Sally knew discipline would be stronger.   The kids all graduated and went to college and have professional careers.

In the late 80s Sally accepted the offer to work with a firm that was computerizing their bookkeeping in their catalog and marketing business.   Health problems sidelined her in '93 and her husband Dan died the next year.   Sally went back to work part time while she decided what she wanted to do.   One day her daughter, now a physician's assistant, called from New Hampshire and suggested she move up there.   "I had decided it's retirement time.   I said sure, when do you want me to come?"

For the last few years she has been an increasingly busy and happy baby sitter for first one, then two, and in 2008 three grandchildren.   Although she suffers from chronic obstructive pulmonary disease she says, "I love to walk except in the ice and when the wind chill is below 0."   The cold is hard on her at times but she says, "I refuse to move south.   I'm not leaving my kids."

Sally McKinney
23 Gould Ave. Apt 2
Meredith, NH   03253
SS287@metrocast.net (daughter)

Lois Delgado

Photo by Fred Feingold   Photo from Woody Delgado

"I went to see Lois Delgado at Roswell Park Cancer Hospital just before she died of leukemia.   She had married and had a young daughter at the time.   She fought valiantly and underwent experimental treatments, but to no avail.   She was my best friend in school and I still miss her."   Diana Djivre

Many in the class remember Lois in that way.   Lois was not voted "most popular" because she was good looking or because her family was affluent and had a swimming pool.   As Phoebe Burdick wrote, "What a beautiful person she was, both inside and out."

Betty Sprague says she does not remember who attended Lois' sweet 16 party, " just that she had a hot-dog eating contest and I won - I LOVE hot dogs, especially Nathan's. "

That truth shows in how Fred Feingold remembers her.   Once someone called her a Guinea, and, I corrected him and said, that this was incorrect, Lois was a Spic.   She thought that was wonderful.   Such a nice person. Such a delightful life ahead."

Dave Schweers remembers her as honest and tough.   "I really noticed her [Bizzy Morse] was when someone had put a tack on Peter Muttee's seat in class. Dorothy Comfort made a big issue out of it, and we were all surprised when Bizzy and Lois Delgado confessed. Girls weren't supposed to do that kind of thing. I was impressed. I used to ride my bicycle at Lois and Bizzy in an attempt to get their attention.   They used to step aside, grab my handlebars and flip me off the bike."   In her sophomore or junior year Lois took her turn on the popular rope swing hung from a red oak on the "18 Trails" near Tilley's beach.   She fell and her back and ribs, after which several friends started calling her "Amazon."

Pete Marnane ('55) remembers that he "met Lois at the Pavilion one summer in high school and began dating and continued through my freshman year in college.   Lois was one of the liveliest and enthusiastic individuals I ever met.   She always had something good to say about most everyone. She had a special charm about her that just made you smile each time you saw her. Her parents were reasonably strict but fair with Lois and her brother Woody and it always seemed that her mother was more relaxed when we double dated with Jay Siegel and his date *de jour*. That fact spoke volumes about her confidence in Jay but not much for me. I can clearly remember a photo of Lois on my desk at school during my freshman year. It was a picture of her in the family swimming pool and it reminded me that first semester that I would be seeing her at Christmas."

When Lois would come back to the playground after school, she usually brought with her the loyal family collie Gage. She also often baby sat for her brother Woody, 6 years younger, who remembers well how "full of life" she was, "Always had a big smile on her face." He also remembers she occasionally snuck into house a boyfriend, Porky Johnston being one. Woody (Ralph) was in his first year at Windham College in Vermont when doctors diagnosed Lois' illness as leukemia, but his parents did not tell him until he came home in May of '65. With his parents he drove to Buffalo in June and they were with her, her husband, and their almost two year old daughter Elizabeth when she lost the battle.

Lois majored in history at Wheaton College (then for women only) and played softball and swam on the swimming team. She also sang with the Wheatones and in the annual college musical, *Vodvil*. She married Brown University's star hockey player Frederick Rodney Dashnaw in the Methodist Church in Sea Cliff in 1963. After a honeymoon in Aspen, Colorado, both took teaching positions in Buffalo, NY.

R I P

Photo by Fred Feingold

Valerie DeVeuve

Val did not feel a lot of self-confidence in Sea Cliff, she says, but she was certainly confident enough to play the French horn, and when Dr. Shulman advised her to go to college instead of nursing school, she chose nursing school.   After graduating from St. Luke's Hospital School of Nursing, NYC, in Sept. 1960 she didn't do nursing the traditional way.   She spent a year working at Massachusetts General Hospital's intensive care unit, then she and another nurse decided to be traveling nurses.   "We pooled our money and bought a used VW Bug and headed south."   They worked in New Orleans, San Francisco then in Pennsylvania where they both met their husbands.

Valerie married Fraser Lyle in August 1963.   While Fraser worked on his MBA at The Wharton School Valerie continued nursing, moving from staff nurse, to head nurse, supervisor, then instructor.   When Fraser took a job on Wall Street they moved to New Jersey where their first child was born in 1966 and a second in 1968 and a third in 1972, two sons, then a daughter.   Val had stopped nursing to raise the children but she joined the local First Aid Squad, then became an Emergency Medical Technician and continued on the squad for 26 years.   She also substituted as a school nurse.

In 1988 doctors diagnosed Fraser as having multiple sclerosis.   He tried to continue working, but the aggressive disease sidelined him within a year, ending a career as a successful portfolio manager who "would hate to see the greed that has engulfed the financial community of late."   Valerie and health aides cared for him at home until he died on Christmas Eve 1995.

Seven years later Valerie married a man from her church, Bob Kent.   Bob graduated from Princeton in 1957 and Harvard Law in 1960 and had 4 children and 9 grandchildren.   With Valerie's 3 children and 6 grandchildren they suddenly had a family of twenty-two.   She and Bob traveled to Scotland when they married in 2002 and continue to travel far and wide, dog sledding in Aspen, Colorado, touring Russia, south to Australia's Ayers Rock and New Zealand, floating the canals in Venice and seeing the ruins of Pompeii.

Valerie, however, still works occasionally for the Visiting Nurse Association and as a community care nurse.   "My expertise is in geriatrics, and my standing joke is that I'm almost as old as my patients!"   When Val learned about the 2008 reunion, she pulled out her 1957 yearbook "and read a lot of the written comments from classmates, and many mentioned my hair color and [French] horn playing."   She refused to play the French Horn for the reunion, but her hair is still that notable soft red.

Valerie and Bob Kent
23 Wyckoff Way
Chester, NJ 07930
vkent1@comcast.net

Diana Djivre

Diana left Sea Cliff as valedictorian and "most likely to succeed." Four years later she left Syracuse University with Magna Cum Laude attached to her degree in physics. However, she writes that the unexpected death of her husband, Dr. Jack Leitner, in 1967 "left me with two small daughters, a mortgage, and only a BS in Physics." It's often noted about the world in general that the greatest resource is not oil or money but human intelligence and spirit. So with Diana, earning a masters in computer science by 1972.

She was working on her Ph.D. when she met Binghamton, NY allergist Dr. Robert Weiss, a widower with two small boys. "It was more important to help heal these two families than to continue in a graduate program (available only at Syracuse over 70 miles away). We were the 'Brady Bunch', but with only 4 kids, one dog, and no housekeeper."

Diana also applied herself to managing her husband's medical practice. She computerized it, took over the management of insurance claims, set up and invested pension funds, and managed the office staff. The goal was not just improving the business but liberating her husband to pursue medicine and nothing but medicine, a rarity for many doctors.

Despite the changes in her life, several threads begin in Sea Cliff. She won the Dr. Andrew Lawrence Service Award her junior year and she has continued community service with volunteer work for the League of Women Voters, Brandeis University National Women's Committee, Hadassah, and Temple Israel Sisterhood. She started tennis in Sea Cliff and "it has brought me joy, happiness, and many friends." She was chosen for the All State Music Festival and the yearbook called her "the second Paderewski. She remembers the pieces she learned over 50 years ago and is grateful for "the time and effort my father put in helping me practice and drill all those years ago."

.

Fifteen years ago she and her husband Bob started collecting contemporary art glass near their vacation home at Mount Snow, Vermont. Their collection now includes museum quality pieces and works with the Art Alliance for Contemporary Glass. The girl who had a "passionate dislike for making speeches" now gives presentations in her home on art glass.

Diana Weiss   dweiss2589@aol.com
Summer Address: Winter Address:
11 Campbell Road Court   8 Bermuda Lake Drive
Binghamton, NY 13905   Palm Beach Florida 33418

Photo by Fred Feingold

Douglas Elton

Photo by Fred Feingold   Photo by Nik Epanchin

When Doug took dancing lessons in grade school, he says, "I never really learned to dance. I was more terrified than enjoyified." Although our yearbook describes him as "very reserved," he did not give up on dancing or on much else in life, though he took a few detours. Doug came to Sea Cliff from Glenwood Landing school and soon became known as both a math whiz, a reliable center fielder, and a master bowler. "My favorite teacher was Donald Thompson. Math was hard but he was very encouraging to stick with it." Tim Klenk, no sloucher himself, once said he owed his math success to Doug.

Doug began Lehigh University as an engineering major but switched to accounting. "I didn't see much excitement in accounting and I went into the Navy for 4 years as a payroll clerk." That is not an entirely adequate description for two years on a sub-chasing carrier, then another two years on a destroyer, or even for packing a .45 caliber pistol when he had to pick up large cash payrolls twice a month, although " they had told us if anyone comes around to rob you, put up your hands." At sea during the Cuban Missile Crisis the calls to general quarters made Doug realize in such a situation self-preservation might require shooting first, but in everyday life he has little use for guns and says, "I love to watch nature but not shoot at it."

Doug married another payroll clerk, a California woman, who had their first child shortly after being discharged. To this daughter they added a son before their divorce. Doug had decided to stick with math and accounting and went back to college at nights, working for Safeway during the days. "For stocking shelves I am a neat, orderly person and everything faces the right way and in orderly lines and that's not the way you stock shelves." He excelled at the cash register where his math and his memory for sale prices made him stand out.

In 1969, a single man again, he listened when a friend in Oregon said, "You're good at math and working with people. You could have a good career in real estate." And so he has—moving to Oregon and later Vancouver, Washington. He also went to Arthur

Murray's dance school and danced his way into a marriage that has now passed its 35th year. Their three girls have now finished college. That too fulfilled one of Doug's ambitions. "It made me feel good because I never finished."

Doug says he is retired but still goes to work each day to train a younger partner. The business, he says, "has all gone Internet and high tech and we've lost some of the personal relationship." It's that appreciation of the personal that made Doug the unknown idol of many girls in our class. Cherry Campbell says, "He was an absolute, adorable huggy bear. He was a gentleman. He was sweet. He was thoughtful. Everyone of the mothers [in a local mother's group] wanted her daughter to date Dougie." He won a special thank you from a grade school dance partner who said, "He was the perfect gentleman who kept me from running home crying." (See Pat Cavanaugh's bio.)

Douglas Elton
2501 NW 117th St
Vancouver, WA 98685
dougelton@hotmail.com

Photo by Fred Feingold

Nicolas Vladimir Epanchin

Photo by Nancy Epanchin

In 1995 Nik and his wife Nancy came to spend a week or two with me when I was living and working in Kazakhstan. One evening as we sat at the table in my closet sized kitchen having tea with a local friend. Nik related how his maternal grandfather, a general, fought with the White army in the Russian civil war and had been one of the last officers getting on the boats when the Red army came into the Black Sea port of Sevastopol. My friend laughed and said his grandfather had been one of the first red army officers to enter Sevastopol. "Well, your grandfather won," Nik said. My friend replied, "No. Your grandfather won. You are an American."

Nik's family arrived when he was twelve bringing with them only seven or eight trunks and planning to stop in Sea Cliff only briefly before moving on to Cleveland. They stayed and moved into an abandoned store front next to the boat builder on lower Sea Cliff Avenue. To learn English the school started Nik in 3rd grade where he towered a head above other students. His parents also called Newsday and secured a paper route for him. "I hated Thursdays that summer of 1951 when I was 12. On Thursdays, Newsday, Nassau County's suburban paper, was extra thick and heavy with the weekly advertising insert." He also had one of the steepest routes in town.

Maybe biking those hills with a one speed, balloon tired bike was the build-up for Nik's outstanding performance as a long distance runner in high school. Nik continued running marathons long after he had graduated from Columbia with a degree in engineering. He spent several years with Boeing in Montana and the Dakotas installing Minuteman missiles. He went into the Army for 3 years, serving at the Cold Regions Research and Engineering Laboratory, Hanover, NH and also qualifying for his pilot's license and becoming a single engine, land and sea flight instructor.

After a few short jobs in civilian life Nik spent more than thirty years with Bechtel in its

Mining and Metals Division and developed expertise in both the economics and reduction of metal ores. His work took him to France, the Philippines, South Africa, Gabon, Australia, Russia, Sweden, Brazil, Chile, Argentina, Peru and Canada among others. He and his wife Nancy, a registered nurse from Minnesota, have lived in France, South Africa, Gabon and Brazil. Their children Tatiana, born in France, and Peter, the first Epanchin ever born in the US, are both married. Tatiana is a charter school principle in Oakland while Peter is a PhD candidate at UC Davis. During Nik's 4 years in Gabon, as an economic adviser on budgeting, he led a cross country team running up a volcano in nearby Cameroon, but with instilling fiscal responsibility in the treasury of the corrupt regime of Omar Bongo he reports that he had "no or very minor success".

When Nik retired he and Nancy decided to move from San Rafael near San Francisco to their cabin four hours up the coast to get away from urban and suburban life, although they also rented an apartment in Berkeley.

Nik continues to apply his knowledge of budgets and engineering to volunteer work in his community, work that ranges from his homeowners' association to the renovation of the local lighthouse. He serves as an EMT with the local volunteer fire department as well as with the regional ambulance service. He has also immersed himself in the study of geology, enjoying the West Coast's varied displays. He and Nancy have traveled widely—Tunisia, Sicily and Malta in 2007, polar bear watching in northern Canada in 2008.

Nik Epanchin
2550 Dana St, Apt 7B
Berkeley, CA 94704
and
15721 Forest View Road
Manchester, CA 95459
vagabs@wildblue.net

Marilyn Fehr

When a flood in the Glen Cove low lands found its way into Marilyn's apartment and wiped out many of albums albums, memorabilia and her yearbook, she cleaned out the mess and went on with her life. No big deal—she had five children, a busy husband, and little time to spare for the past. It wasn't very far past in any case. As she grew older and the children began leaving home, she had more time to think about "life's unanswered questions," and the fact that some of the answers seemed to lie in the past and the people and events that remained so strong. "The memories are always there. Seems like there was never any closure."

She asked around Sea Cliff where she might find a '57 yearbook but found nothing. Then her youngest son Mark suggested he browse the web with her computer. When they found our class albums and our web site, "It was like a new door opening up," she says.

The yearbook she lost says, "Where there's Cappi and Ginny, you'll find Marilyn." It also noted her interest in stock car racing and someone named Tommy. Now Marilyn remembers only that he was Tommy Greenrose "from Glen Head or Glen Cove." The yearbook did not mention the more important boy in her life, Ronnie Jeacomo who was bussed into school from Locust Valley and who was in the class of '59 before he dropped out to work at the Record and Pilot and then become a partner with his brothers in Preferred Sand and Gravel.

Marilyn began school in Glen Cove but when the family lost their home, they went to live on the edge of Harlem with an aunt and uncle. Then, as now, the city public schools were loud, overcrowded, run down, and did little educating. When the Fehr's bought a house on Cromwell Place in Sea Cliff Marilyn should have entered 9th grade with the Class of '56, but she was too far behind. She says that of course, she was angry that she could be made to repeat a grade as if she had failed, but "It was for my own good that I stayed back because I began picking up what I should have learned in Manhattan." If going from Glen Cove to Manhattan was a shock, the transfer from city to Sea Cliff was a change of worlds. "I was used to all these rowdy people being around. So I just took a back seat and watched."

After graduation her father sent her to business school, and when she decided that was not for her, he found her a job at Luyster Motors. "My father did everything," she says, but even her father could not beat fate. When the beaches opened on Memorial Day in the summer of '58 her 18 year old brother Bobby and two friends took a homemade boat out into the harbor. On the wake of a big boat the homemade boat flipped and Bobby was struck on the head and drowned. At his funeral Marilyn was surprised and moved to meet one of the most formidable teachers of her time at Sea Cliff, Dorothea Comfort.

The next June Marilyn married Ronnie Jeacoma in St. Boniface Church. A month later she was pregnant. "This was when life started coming in. I had answers for everything except for life." Life didn't give her much time to look for answers. A second child came a year later and soon she had five. When a friend took her to Inwood on the border with Queens. "I just fell in love with it. It was just like Sea Cliff. It broke my heart when I saw it." Marilyn liked the schools and the family stayed there till they had graduated.

When the youngest entered pre-kindergarten, Marilyn went back to work. She started nursing school and began work as a nurse's aide in St. John's Nursing Home. She was working with Alzheimer's patients and loved it. After 8 years she left St. John's and began work at with the mentally impaired at Dix Hills, then with the vocational training program VOCES. She also worked as a residential counselor in a group home for a few years, then as manager in another house until she retired. But soon she was wondering, "What the heck do people retire for?" She went back to work in Oceanside.

Working with the mentally impaired and Alzheimer's victims, Marilyn says, "It should have been depressing, but I learned if you are going to be in this business you can't take on the personal side and say you can't leave me. You just have to love them and have respect for them. I couldn't go back to work if I felt sorry for them. I just needed to be there to help them."
Looking back over the decades of work with family and in nursing, she says, "The things that I have done over the years and the kind of work that I've done over the years required giving a lot of myself. I don't know if I would have picked it. There were heartaches, there was sorrow. As I look back it was good."

During her marriage she also found that she and Ronny were "drifting apart" and they divorced but remained close, so close that they came back together. He died in 2002, survived by his identical twin brother Ray who would soon accompany Marilyn to her granddaughter's wedding.

Marilyn says her heart is still in Sea Cliff, still in the house that her father put so much work into.   Meanwhile she lives in Massapequa.   When she's not at work, she works out in the gym, bowls, and no matter what the weather is, every day she and friends walk a few miles. Classmates who watch Channel 21's marketing programs might see her now and then answering the phones.   It's her moment of fame, she says, and she has enjoyed meeting performing artists and writers.

Marilyn is still engaged in looking for the answers to life, the ones that "didn't come when I needed them.   Now there's something there for me [to find]."   Finding old friends from Sea Cliff has helped. She says, "The older I get the things that would have almost destroyed me, I'd let it go and move on. I don't get stuck in it.   I've grown a little bit."

Marilyn Fehr
221 Oakley Ave., Apt 159
Massapequa, NY 11758
gymnmarilyn@gmail.com

Frederick Feingold

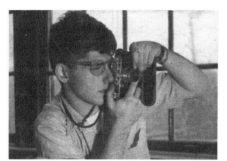 

Photos by Nik Epanchin

Few remember Frank W. Eller, and he does not appear in the faculty section of our yearbook, but Fred calls him, "The teacher we should have had. If that guy had stayed in my life, it would have gone in a different direction." Fred might have become a scientist, but he became and is what Dr. Eller was—an innovative teacher who insists students live what they learn.

At the end of 5th grade Fred entered our class to find himself in a different culture. "I came from a very protected school in New York City, Hunter [College Elementary] experimental school . . . I tried to impress everyone walking around with a 500 page book. I used to walk around with a big eight inch knife I said was for paring apples. . . . I remember having to pinch my leg till I drew blood when I heard Carolyn Berthoud speaking English English."

Despite having reading problems, Fred did well in school although he regrets not seizing all the opportunities. "Donald Matthews, for my 13th birthday went out and got a collection of great books and I never opened one of them. To this day I feel absolutely horrible about it." One day Fred noticed by accident that Mr. Matthews had left a Harvard recommendation form lying around uncompleted. "My mother got the idea that I was a child genius and should go to Harvard." When she took him there for early admissions Fred looked at the students and knew, "I couldn't fit in here." He was also in love with Glenda Boyd ('59), and so he chose Columbia University to be nearby.

He hated it. "I grew up in a family with a European orientation, and I thought when you went to college all the book stuff ended and you wandered around learned from the master." He changed from a biology major to psychology, "because I would like to find out about the human mind. The psych they taught at Columbia you could learn in 6 days." He wanted to study the psychology of reading but was directed to a host of other courses so he abandoned the psych major and took whatever he wanted until, with all his classmates qualified to graduate and Fred without the right constellation of courses, "Kindly old dean

Alexander who valued a liberal education and who had probably intentionally thrown my file behind the file cabinet, said, 'Well Mr. Feingold, could you take something so we can give you a degree?'"

Fred took an exam to be a New York City public school teacher. "There were 6 people sitting in a semi-circle who interviewed me." They asked how he would teach writing. His answer, "I wouldn't have them write, I'd have them read." Fred did not get certified but he had begun working as a volunteer in Bellevue Hospital's psychiatric ward for children and in "Higher Horizons" which recruited college grads to teach in inner city schools.

Fred started full time teaching at a special school for gifted students on Sands Point, hoping to soon go to Harlem to teach. He was, he says, "completely innocent" and fortunate that an experienced teacher from Roslyn sent him on to teach at Brentwood, a "under blue collar community" on Long Island. Because the superintendent and principals gave teachers great autonomy, Fred found "it was heaven." Until the state insisted he go back to college to take education courses to be certified.

"I gave my entire library of school books to Glenwood and went to New York City and took the substitutes exam and I floated around for 26 years." Then a friend in the system walked him through the necessary forms for a Permanent Substitute License. "I am very proud that during my whole career I took about 8 education credits."

Meanwhile Glenda Boyd had gone her own way at Bryn Mawr, and the woman with whom Fred had fell madly in love at Columbia had married. Fred then made a decision that he describes as "Absolute complete disaster." When he and his new wife moved to Machias, Maine close to Canada, she hated it. They lived simply in a small house. Fred was making a living cutting oak firewood and substitute teaching. During their 5 years in Maine their two children, Judah and Miriam were born. They moved to the booming and fashionable Austin, Texas. Eleven months later they were divorced. "I read all the books n how to have a civilized divorce. The judge sleeps through the whole thing." Fred lost custody and his ex-wife took the children to Amherst, MA.

Fred recently moved to the Berkshires where his living is filled with the 19 kayaks he uses for kayaking instruction and his life is filled with a relationship that is "just magnificent."

Fred Feingold
100 Laurel Street
Lee, Massachusetts 01238 PO Box 13   (mail to) 242 Anthony Ave, Apt D-7
                                            Hillsdale, NY 12529
                                    ffeingo2@hotmail.com ffeingo2@excite.com

Barbara Ferris

Barb began her secretarial career has come full circle. She left school and began work across the harbor with the US Navy at Sands Point. She found herself in the division that trained Navy pilots using the famous Link Trainer. Its inventor Edwin Link was one of two men who founded Harbor Branch Oceanographic Institute in Florida where Barb worked as an employee and now as a volunteer in the Biomedical Marine Research Division (searching for cancer cures from the sea). She was Volunteer of the Month in April 2003. In between Sands Point and Harbor Branch she was a principal's secretary at a Vero Beach, FL elementary school.

Vero Beach was not new to Barb since her grandparents had started visiting the town in the 1950s, and in 1962 her grandparents, parents, brother, Barb and husband Walt Mills adopted Vero Beach as their permanent home.

Barb continues the church activities that began at St. Luke's in Sea Cliff. During high school she taught Sunday school which provided the 2nd grade angels for the Christmas pageant. St. Luke's Rev. Frank Lambert, the former Navy Chaplain, married Barbara and Walt in 1960. Their first child, David, was born the next year. Son Paul was born in 1969. She now spends a lot of time with a 12 year old grandson who started fighting lymphoma cancer at age 8 and reports he is doing well.

In Florida for many years she has applied her musical talents to playing the hand bells in the hand bell choir. Her music began in Glenwood Landing elementary where she played snare drums and timpani, something she continued in the Sea Cliff High band. She also plays piano and organ, but only for her own enjoyment.

For 35 years Barb and Walt have traveled in their RV across the country and into Canada, but they have come to love the North Carolina mountains around Maggie Valley and now spend their summers there.

Barbara Mills
1845 Sixth St
Vero Beach, FL 32962
bwmills@bellsouth.net

Sandra Freedman

Either Sandi changed 180 degrees after graduating or we were far off in her yearbook bio that said her motto was "Better late than never."   In fact, Newsday in 1949 featured her in an article reporting that she and Joanne LaPierre had raised $12 for the March of Dimes selling pinwheels, Lemonade, cake and sandwiches.   Sandi impressed one of the strongest class skeptics with her powers of event organization and management when she threw a party in the 1950s.   Dave Schweers says, "She threw a party in our Soph or junior year after some event. It was the only good party I ever went to."   She says she still loves a good party, and she has spent and continues to spend much of her time organizing meetings, courses, and parties for other people.

In high school she thought the car that would best fit her festive spirit would be "a little red MG."   (Most of us had a car preference that fit our self image.)   Earn the money, her father, a tire dealer, told her.   Neighbors offered Sandi many babysitting jobs, but, "Being my father's 'princess,' however. . . .he would pay me not to babysit. I would take the money from him, but would often go and babysit as well."   When she finally had enough money to go car shopping, her father said, "No daughter of mine is going to drive around in a tiny car and possibly get killed as result."   She remembers one of those rare moments when his faced turned red with anger.   He sent her to his best friend in Port Washington to help.   " I was desperate to have a car, so gave his friend all my saved babysitting money and wound up with a huge boat-like YELLOW BUICK--as ugly as could be!"

In high school Sandi dated the popular Angelo Davino ('56) a champion bowler who may have sported, at one time, the only mustache in school.   She also had romantic interests in the South as a result of spending many vacations and summers visiting an aunt and uncle in August, GA.   Boys who pursued her but did not enthuse her, often found themselves assigned to Sandi's "poor mother" for entertainment.   She might have gone to the

University of Georgia except, "My parents . . . insisted that I "get some culture" first." So it was that she left Sea Cliff not for the south but for Boston College.

When she left high school she intended to have a career in speech and hearing therapy. She finished college in three years with a second major in English and returned to Sea Cliff. She began work for the Board of Cooperative Education Services for $5,900 a year. At a party in February 1962 she met a young dentist from Bay Shore, Jerry Oppenheim. Three months later they were engaged, and three months after that they married. Despite having a nice home on Great South Bay, Sandy private practice had begun to bore Jerry. When they and their three high school age children moved to Cleveland. During their sixteen years there Sandi went into public relations and management of non-profit agencies. She formed a merchants' association, a tutoring program, community housing programs, and storefront renovations. She also became the alumni director for Lake Erie College, Cleveland-Marshall College of Law, and Cuyahoga Community College and its three campuses. Along the way she won many awards, including the 1994 "Outstanding Leadership Award" from the Congress of Ohio for her accomplishments as executive director of community development.

When the boys had left home and finished college, Jerry wanted to move to a warmer climate with retirement amenities. They moved to Sun City West, Arizona, but Sandi was not ready to stop work. She took a job in Phoenix in a program that created new options for juvenile offenders.

Now, in what she calls retirement, she continues to organize tours and events around the theme of tea and her collection of rare tea wares. Her much praised 2003 Afternoon Tea honoring family members of those deployed in the Middle East was attended by 150 wives, mothers, teenage children, and other relatives of service men and women. "I will always remember how grateful these ladies were that someone cared enough to treat them to a day they'd always remember, and had never experienced before: one of kindness, caring, and remembrance of their loved ones far away. While they were sent away with many gifts, my gift--of giving--made all the hard work & effort worthwhile."

Sandi Oppenheim
15806 W Sentinel Drive
Sun City West, AZ 85375-6679
 tealadyaz@cox.net or Oppy5@aol.com

Susan Frost

Sue has dual citizenship—Vermont and Sea Cliff.   She grew up in Sea Cliff only because her grandfather was a country doctor in Worcester, VT who made many house calls during the great flu epidemic of 1917-18 that killed hundreds of thousands of Americans, including him.   That started the family moving.   Her mother attended Columbia Presbyterian School of Nursing and met Sue's father in the city.   But Sue went back to Green Mountain College in Poultney, VT for higher education.

Sue grew in a close family with younger brother Peter and older sister Gail.   Sue's father was a draftsman who later became an architect.   He was also a master gardener, sailor, and registered bee keeper.   Their home was on 17th Ave. near the long flight of wooden steps that led to a little scrap of beach next to Newell's Dock, about halfway between the Pavilion and Rum Point where Prospect Ave. reached the beach.   She grew strong swimming and playing outside and in with neighborhood kids who included Al Behrmann and brothers.   She stays strong swimming in Vermont.

When   Sue's college roommate married a Vermonter and introduced Sue to a friend up there, Sue was back in New York beginning to work with the airline industry.   Sue, who left school intent on becoming a stewardess and traveling far and wide, found herself office-bound in American Airlines, working with special accounts and living in Jackson Heights.   She remained friends with her roommate's husband after short marriage ended, and he brought a load of friends with him to camp in Sue's apartment while they visited the 1964 World's Fair. "Bodies were sacked out on the carpet everywhere," Sue recalls, and one of them was this fellow Ralph she had met at her roommate's. She started flying to Vermont and he began visiting New York and in a year they married.

When she married her husband Ralph, she put her business skills to work in a printing company that they owned and operated for 30 years in Rutland, Vermont. Sue also devoted her time to raising three children, two of whom have graduated from college.   She left the printing business in 1996 when her husband died.   Her father, who had moved from South Carolina to Vermont and across the street from Sue, also died in 1996 at age 88.   Her mother died in 2001 at age 87. Sue has a busy life of volunteer work, home maintenance, and travel. She helps run her church's office, visits shut-ins and the hospitalized, and is an almost daily assistant to a blind friend. She has also sung in the church choir for 25 years. She now counts four grandchildren.

Sue swims every morning, sometimes starting at 7:30, and she tends to her Vermont property where she does everything from mowing and pruning to snow and ice removal. Her steady companions are her daring duo of dogs, a young schipperke and an aging shepherd. As a member of the Folksmarch, a Syracuse group dedicated to 5 to 10 kilometer walks, yearly camping trips, and other tours. Sue has been to all but three states in the US, as well as Italy, Scotland, England, Austria, Germany, and Holland, fulfilling one of the motives for her intended career as a stewardess.

Despite her long residence in Vermont, Sue has never really left her neighborhood. She recently visited her 17th Avenue neighbor Mrs. Behrmann. Sue's own father died five months after her husband in 1996 and her mom died in December 2000. She regularly gets together with neighbors and schoolmates Janet Smith and Norwegian immigrant Karin Espeland.

Sue Smith
300 Flory Heights,
Center Rutland, VT 05736
susmvt@aol.com

_____

Fred Gallo

Fred Gallo had the talent, brains and personality that should have left clear tracks through time, but so far no one in the class and none of the sources we've tried reveal any record. Fred's family moved into Sea Cliff's new subdivision on the former Eihler Estate lands north of Shore Road, but he quickly became part of our class. His passion was biology, and he left school intent on becoming a medical doctor.

Fred attended Cornell University, but other Sea Cliff students do not know what he did after graduation. No one has been able to supply information on Fred's life after Cornell.

—

_____

Betty Gelling

"We just wanted to do something worthwhile," Betty says of a girls' club she joined shortly after moving in 1952 from Baldwin to the big white stucco house on Prospect Avenue with its expansive view over the harbor.   With Sue Frost, Caroline Berthoud, Sandi Freedman and other girls Betty became part of a club that met in each other's homes, enjoyed their mother's refreshments, and collected weekly dues which they used to help poor people. Mrs. Durbin the school nurse might recommend someone and the girls would go to Glen Cove to buy a present or clothes.

On a bright summer day two years after her arrival in Sea Cliff her father, an executive with Kerr Steamship, shopped in the Nelson and Rhinas hardware store when a fatal heart attack felled him while Betty was at the Yacht Club for a regatta.   A few days later she received a sympathy note from a teacher and, "I saw a totally different side of Miss Kittelburger." She and her sister and mother were already rooted in Sea Cliff and her mother would continue to live in the house for some 50 years and today her sister lives there.

She also participated in that very close group from the Gospel Chapel called Young People that gathered in the home of Ralph and Natalie Howell.   In that group she became good friends with Jinny Wood and then with Jinny's big brother Frank ('55).   She and Frank were married in the Gospel Chapel in 1959 with Ducky Frances ('55) singing at their wedding.   Frank had graduated from Syracuse School of Forestry and Betty had finished two years at SUNY Buffalo studying the education of exceptional children.   Frank would soon begin his obligatory 3 years in the Army, so Betty left school and they began the life of a military couple.

Frank entered flight school in Alabama, then they were posted to Ft. Knox where they found our classmate Tim Klenk, who was also Frank's cousin and who had received his pilot's license before leaving high school.   Betty gave birth to their first son before

Frank's discharge in 1963. After that Frank used his training in forestry and industrial engineering in a series of jobs in New York, New Hampshire, Pennsylvania and finally in Connecticut where Frank finished his 40 years with US Envelope. They also had two more children and Frank had picked up an MBA.

In 1988, "sick of bosses," they decided to open their own business and bought a Mailboxes, Etc. store (Later UPS Store). Making boxes, packing, and lifting from early morning till evening was new work for Betty. "I was numb the first year," she says, but she enjoyed the customer contact and the detective work of tracers and claims. Frank liked engineering new containers. In the holiday season sometimes they found themselves eating supper after midnight, but they were satisfied to be their own bosses and "We both have always loved office supplies and retail stuff." In 2005, after working together, they sold the store and retired together.

Betty and Frank have moved thirteen times in 50 years (once every 3.8 years), and each time she has carefully packed and moved boxes of notebooks, clippings, programs, and other memorabilia of our class history. For our reunion she became the most important source of personal documents and clippings that inform our new digital and written records. "I guess I realized eventually there would be a reunion and some of it would be of interest." That's more than foresight. It reflects how important high school and community were in her life. Throughout their lives she and Frank have often found their common experience in Sea Cliff provided touchstones for their understanding of life.

Betty Wood
31 Glendale Rd
Enfield, CT 06082

————————————————

Dorothy Gerroir

Our yearbook said she intended to take a degree as a registered nurse, then marry a millionaire. We have no word of progress on either ambition.

She used to date Pete Merkel and she attended the Senior Prom with Tom Wolf. Other than those few facts, we know nothing.

Our last information is that she became

Mrs. Dorothy Benson
4345 Smith St.
Flushing, NY 11351

Bette Gildersleeve

"I made it in spite of them," Bet says of the strep throat and rheumatic fever that put her in bed at age nine and kept her there for the next four years. Rheumatic fever rarely strikes in the US today, but until the 1960s or 70s too often it struck children from six to fifteen, usually two to four weeks after a bout of strep throat or scarlet fever. The runaway Streptococcus bacteria in her body swelled her joints and enlarged her heart dangerously. "I had to use a box at the end of the bed to keep my feet straight."

During those years she seldom saw other kids except her older sister Edith ('55) and her younger sister Joan ('59) and her best friend Linda Malkin. She took up crocheting, knitting, drawing and painting and working with plastic carvings. Featured in a *Newsday* article saying ""Bets has everything to make her happy—everything that is except her health and a few pen pals." The article quotes her mother, "Every day she waits for the click of the mailbox and her face drops so when I tell her there's nothing for her." After the *Newsday* article people from all over wrote, sending stamps and coins.

Unknown to the rest of us Bette kept up with her studies through tutoring, first by Miss Ely, then by 6th grade teacher Robert Allen, and next a private tutor. Finally she was allowed to start 7th grade for half of every day, but to her dismay, sports were forbidden. The legacy of her years of seclusion, she says, was a permanent shyness. Art with Miss Strohe and singing became her refuge and she says, "I adored the music teacher Mr. Sterling." Miss Strohe inspired her with a desire to go into design. Unfortunately, she said, "I was dope and got married." Nevertheless she says, "It was a wonderful marriage and we had [our son] Bill."

Her husband was classmate Bob Platt who "was kind of a loner too." Bob was a buddy of Pete Merkel's, and Bob and Betty, Pete and Dottie Gerroir often double dated. For the first eight years of marriage Bob was in the Air Force and they lived wherever he was stationed, from Alaska to Florida. Their son Bill was born in 1960.

When her parents moved to Florida she and Bob also made their home there in Port Charlotte. "It was like Sea Cliff, small and nice in those days." Bette worked in a pharmacy, then as a secretary for an electrician, and finally for Dollar General, working her way to manager of the local store.

She and Bob were divorced in 1979 and she married Douglas Lynch in 1981. He was a native of Canada who had been in the Army and whose parents had also moved to Florida. He died in 2002 and Bette moved to her own villa in a senior living community. She also enjoys having her son Bill, owner of his own surveying company and father of her grandson. Although she enjoys her friends in the community and spends much of her days visiting, she says, "I have never really gotten over the shyness. I have my circle of friends who understand how weird I am. I never feel like I really fit." Port Charlotte has grown far larger and busier than the Sea Cliff like town it was when she settled there, and she remembers home on Winding Way and says, "I'd give anything in the world to be back home."

Bette Lynch
2285 Aaron StPort Charlotte, FL 33952_____

Barbara Gilson

Photo by Fred Feingold

Photo by Nancy Epanchin

The 1957 senior superlative "wittiest" in applied to Barbara's incisive humor, meaning her humor often seemed delivered by incisors. In conversation and correspondence Barbara taught me the meaning of many useful words, among them repartee and badinage (swift witty back and forth). Wittiest also applied in the much older sense of living by one's wits and having the brain power to make it possible.

"In my house growing up, you were expected to be fast on your feet, intellectually and physically; if you weren't, you got clobbered. In one sense I believe that discipline and agility were advantageous. I couldn't have moved through the world as I wanted to and have without a good degree of toughness. Most of the time, nice guys do finish last, and nice girls even farther behind."

"For most of my youth, I required an ongoing supply of adrenalin, generated by raising hell and daily histrionics. It took getting a little older to calm down."

As a kid I spent some summers on a working dairy farm, and while I loved it there, it was all too apparent that it was a pretty Hobbesian life for the people whose full-time business it was. Getting up a 4 AM in the midst of a Massachusetts winter to milk 40 cows, cooking massive meals on a wood stove, getting that stove started in the frigid mornings, it being the only heat in the rambling house, using chamber pots, keeping up the vegetable garden, bringing in the hay -- all this was far from idyllic. The owners of the farm had very little time for anything but the farm; they aged early, and the usual form of amusement was to go down to the Eagles Lodge and get a load on. And this was a relatively modern farm -- it had milking machines and vets with up-to-date equipment. I can only imagine what the work was like before technology.

In the summer of 1961 she and Ceil Snayd were renters in Sea Cliff's cheapest lodgings, the venerable Artists' Colony, a ramshackle two story dormitory that once housed performers acting in the adjacent Summer Theater. By November of 1961 she and Ceil had begun to move up, renting a private home and both leaving their jobs at Howard Johnson, Barbara moving on to the Parkway Grill on Jericho Turnpike.   I was in graduate school in England, beginning to publish a few things, and Barbara asked, "Is this literary racket really on the level?"   She would soon be in the racket herself, for life.

First, she married Robert "Moon" Sawicki, starting out in a quiet civil ceremony with Farrell Sheridan and Joan Imperiali as witnesses.   The wedding, however, was soon "surrounded by such an uproar and rending of garments from our respective families that I felt a little like the eye of a hurricane."   They had given parents less than a week's notice. Moon's sister "still doesn't approve of me since she doesn't drink, smoke or go out with boys."

She once thought of going into law, but she had always wanted to write.   She found that "publishing let me earn a living in a world that was all about my principal interests."   She started at Doubleday Book Clubs in 1966.   In 1978 she moved to McGraw-Hill Latinoamericana as Senior Sponsoring Editor in the Spanish-language university division. That job took her and her son Blake to Bogota, Colombia.   "It was a bit like living in a preserved 18th-century enclave. Drugs had not gotten to prominence, and life in Bogota was formal and refined in many ways, particularly language."

She followed Colombia with twelve years at Simon & Schuster as Executive Editor for Trade Education and Reference.   In 1996 she returned to McGraw-Hill as Publisher for Trade Education.   A brief clip of her riotous 2006 retirement party and the applause for her song and dance number indicates the high regard of her co-workers.   "My management style," she says, "is to dump as much they can take on staff and let them run with the ball."

She now spends her time writing and traveling on several continents, or walking and jogging and horseback riding in Manhattan where she makes her home on the heights which Washington once abandoned.   Son Blake finished college, lived and worked in Japan and has returned to New York to teach and enter law school.   Barbara, still wittiest, says that her 1990 knee replacement "gave me back a full-spectrum life, and I hope will see me through a grumpy but active senescence."

Barbara Gilson
565 W 169th St   Apt 5D
New York, NY 10032-3911
bfcg13@hotmail.com

———————————————

Sandra Gleichmann

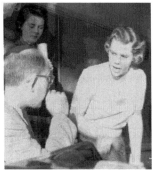

(photo Fred Feingold)

(Photo by Nik Epanchin)

Our yearbook calls her "female Rembrandt," but more modestly she says, "I'm going to be known as the Grandma Moses of Palm Beach." She's a grandma. She lives in Palm Beach. She paints Palm Beach. She has her own gallery. And what Sandy has set out to do in life, she has always done. She learned how to compete and fight in her own backyard. Her older brother Alan put her on his ad hoc tackle football team full of boys and she became one of the Backyard Terrors. "As I developed into a pistol-packing Black Bart and Tomboy, I often invited boys, Berkley Andrews for one, to join me in the garage loft where we'd put on gloves and go into the boxing ring that had been installed. I was a pretty tough gal." Fifty-some years later at our class reunion she quipped, "Berkeley Andews was the guy I really beat and maybe that's why he's not here." Berkeley, of course, went on to graduate with honors from the US Marine Corps camp at Parris Island.

Learning and earning stayed at the center of her life. The Gleichmann family had a small income, and as soon as she could, Sandy began to earn money babysitting. At school she earned a free lunch washing dishes in the cafeteria. As soon as she mastered typing and shorthand with Miss French, Mrs. Phillip Huntington, who lived on Littleworth Lane and who served as President of the American Pewter Society hired Sandy as her social secretary. She also learned on the job. "Mrs. Huntington defined charm as the curiosity to show genuine interest in others by engaging them in conversation. That lesson served well years later when writing memoirs became a passion."

She grew to appreciate the city's opportunities on trips with her parents, school trips to museums, and Eileen McNamara's theater trip to see "Long Days Journey Into Night." "I became intrigued by the dynamics of Manhattan that beat with a pulse that quickened me on many levels. I knew early on that I was destined for 'The City' after graduation."

After school she used her secretarial skills to become assistant to the art buyer at Grey Advertising "where the most extraordinary array of art and photographic portfolios passed before my eyes." That income allowed her to attend Cooper Union art classes at night. After a year with Chanel, she became the art buyer at *Redbook Magazine* which brought her in contact with the work of Richard Avedon, Eric Sloane, Andy Warhol and Henri Cartier-Bresson. "It was a feast to savor and inspire."

In 1961 she decided to move with her parents, brother and sister Diane to Florida, knowing she would avoid the cold she disliked and hoping to find a job that used her own talents as an artist. The owner of McCarthy's Deli warned her, "you'll be back . . . no one leaves Sea Cliff and stays in Florida. "She's still there, and she found what she wanted. She went from advertising design and past up at the Ft. Lauderdale *News and Sun Sentinel* to their first editorial artist, drawing section covers, hurricane maps, and cartoons.

In 1964 she married local businessman and widower David Robinson Thompson, and they soon added two children along side his two grown sons. Sandy stayed at home raising the boys and doing freelance design work. She also became a golfer and, with Dave, played some of the world's great courses in the British Isles. "When we decided to marry I vowed to perform two creative efforts inspired by the beautiful tropical paradise: to one day write a memoir to record his early life experiences and also to perform in some art medium to capture the great beauty of Palm Beach." She has done both, of course. *PALM BEACH FROM THE OTHER SIDE OF THE LAKE,* was published in 1992. The memoir recorded, among much more, Dave's Civil Air Patrol flying in the early years of WWII and his later service under Gen. George Patton in the Battle of the Bulge. That book led to other books, all written on the same manual Olympia typewriter she had in high school. She thanks "Betty French for her uncompromising work ethic and devotion to students. She kept it simple--when writing a letter, write as you would speak. I found that useful and was fascinated as I asked questions and recorded so many unique life passages."

When foreign travel became too arduous for Dave they settled into an apartment, and Dave began to decline into senile dementia, but not before enjoying the reward of seeing his own four sons fulfill his dream of graduating from college. During the final six years of his life Sandy became an associate in a Palm Beach art gallery where she is now co-owner. But it was a one woman show that launched her ambition to become the Grandma Moses of Palm Beach. She has always done what she set out to do, but she says, "I credit God firmly and gratefully for the many blessings that have been mine. I believe that we are all watched over by a loving God who knows the path each life will take. . . . I have always felt God's presence.

I feel blessed far beyond my deserving."

Sandra Gleichmann Thompson608 Cypress Key Dr.Atlantis, FL 33462

pbartiststhompson@yahoo.com

Rosalie Greenfield

(2008 photo Nik Epanchin)

The long list of activities that precedes Ro's biography notes in our 1957 yearbook suggest she was part of almost everything in school from four sports and Riding Club to editing and writing for the Pioneer so singing and performing in the senior play.   She didn't always feel that way, however.   "My parents wanted us to go to school at the Brookville School but we couldn't get in."   No Jews admitted.   And in that era Jews were still officially and unofficially banned from many social clubs, country clubs and other organizations.   When those forms of discrimination were generally accepted, even teachers sometimes showed their biases.   Rosalie, however, also found ready defenders in the class and says that her boyfriend Jimmy O'Donnell as well as Brud Neice were among them.   Jimmy would not repeat what he heard, but he "would come over and my mother or father would see a black eye and he would say he got into a fight.   I almost didn't want to know about it. Part of me would make believe it didn't exist."

The Greenfields had chosen to live in Greenvale because it was a quiet place and Ro's father, an inventor and industrial designer, had a heart condition and her mother was frequently ill.   She and her sister "Beanie" (Elaine, Class of '58) "had these anxieties about losing our parents."   Nevertheless, Ro became very much a popular member of our class, in school and out.   We voted her "most enthusiastic" for the energy and optimism she showed.

Rosalie left Sea Cliff intending to be a teacher or reporter.   She became both.   In college she switched her major from theater to film and found work with Broadcast Music, Inc in New York, then entered the American Musical Theater Writers Workshop.   She began writing musicals and libretti, and she married one of the Theater's conductors.   The marriage lasted less than two years.   With a master's   in education from Columbia she started teaching in New Rochelle High School.   From '65-7 she was at Edgmont High in Scarsdale, then at Herrick's in Williston Park on Long Island.

In 1969 she left education to become a reporter for *Home Furnishings Daily*, reporting on fashion and business in the home furnishing market.   Then and now, Rosalie says, "Politics is a pretty big part of my life," and so she moved from fashions to political research at WNBC TV.   However, "At 34 or 35 I was getting a little bit over the hill and thought it was too late to have a career in television."   She enrolled in Columbia to work on her doctorate.   "I decided I had to study anthropology, and then communications theory.   Finally, my advisor said, 'wait a minute, stop, you'll never finish.'   I never felt I had done enough."   She received her doctorate in education with a thesis on married couples and their movie going preferences and habits.   The interconnection between film and personal behavior continued to occupy her as she became an instructor in media studies at Penn State's Abington College campus.   She also published work on media violence and its impact on children.

Meanwhile Rosalie had fallen in love with a man she interviewed for an article.   Stanley Matzkin flown 59 missions in a P-47 Thunderbolt in WWII, participating in the Normandy invasion and winning a Purple Heart.   "He was a real hero," Rosalie says.   "He read everything, but he cried at the ballet."   Her sister Elaine says, "he was one of the really good people, and the world needs more like him.   . . . . He was more than an Uncle to my children. In many ways he represented the 'good father' to them."   He was also a noted philanthropist and a founder of the Forman Day School in Elkins Park, PA.   In November 2003 doctors told Elaine and Stanley that he was terminally ill and they had no remedies.   Three days later he died.

Rosalie has lost none of her enthusiasm for life.   She is on the board of Directors of the Jewish Social Policy Action Network, still very active in politics, and she has returned to writing lyrics for musicals.

Rosalie Greenfield Matzkin
1201 Walnut St   Apt 3D
Philadelphia, PA 19103
rgmatzkin@comcast.net

_____

Palmina Grella

Other classmates report that Pam, now Pam Lalondi, lives in Glen Cove and that she did not want to take part in the reunion or this record.

_____

Lorraine Grote

From the '57 yearbook: "Lorraine . . . impish young miss." Lorraine left Sea Cliff immediately after graduation and she has returned a few times. We can supply the basic public details that are public record. Lorraine Grote lived in the old wooden apartment building that Richard Norwich lived in next to Fransisco's little corner store at the top of Prospect Ave. After high school she married Ronald Thorsen from Glenwood Landing. He was a graduate of Glen Cove. Shortly after marriage they moved to California. She lives happily in California and has a strong interest in theatre.

Lorraine Thorsen

Arthur Hall

Artie Hall grew up in Sea Cliff and during high school he worked with his father in construction and also at Big Ben's Supermarket in Glen Cove.   His family did not travel often and Artie spent his free time and vacations in typical Sea Cliff activities—sledding, going to the beach, and hanging out at the Youth Center.   He is one of many in our class to note with special gratitude the time and care "Mom and Pop Fraley" donated to keeping the Youth Center open and in the good graces of the community.   Artie played soccer for two years.   He says, "All the kids were good to be around and as I look back now I wish I wasn't such a hothead, oh well."   He rates "Pop" Driscoll as his best teacher and Ed Nelson as the worst.

Our last two years of high school required split sessions to accommodate the growing student population, and the schedule didn't suit Artie.   "So I joined the Navy with Bob Engle and Paul St. Andre."   His tour of duty took him to the amphibian force and the Underwater Demolition Team Eleven, which later became a part of the famous SEAL program.   Artie served aboard the USS Virgo in the Pacific, touring the Far East.   He was awarded the rank of Petty Officer and served with the fleet training group evaluating ships on their engineering readiness.

When he returned to Sea Cliff in 1960 he went to work with his father for a while before beginning a series of other jobs before settling in at Grumman Aerospace in facilities operations.   Over 27 years he worked his way up and had become a construction manager before Grumman merged with Northrup and offered him a buy-out.

Not ready to retire, Artie worked for a while in real estate sales, then took a position on the North Shore High custodial staff and became head custodian.   Returning to school, so to speak, he says he found the kids the same as we were, but much greater parental involvement "makes the job harder."

For the past eleven years Artie and Roey have enjoyed a second home in Pennsylvania's Poconos Mountains on a large lake with four islands, and Artie is President of the homeowners' association.   They and their kids and grandchildren enjoy their pontoon boat, kayaks, and swimming docks in the summer and nearby skiing and snowboarding nearby.

Artie Hall
PO Box 99
Glenwood Landing, NY 11547
roey1234@optonline.net

Christine Sonja Hallberg

Tina much preferred enjoying life outside of school to the routines inside. So it was that she looks back with gratitude toward Mrs. French who "was always so good to me even when I used to cut classes in the spring time and go to the Russian deli to get loaves of hot bread. Pete [Muttee] used to wear army pants and put Pepsi in the pockets. And we used to go down and swing on the ropes on the 18 Trails." (The 18 Trails was the heavily wooded bluff above the shore between Tilley's boat house and Shore Road.) She was such an avid ice skater that she once skated so long and late on a bitterly cold night that she could not untie her skates and had to walk home in them.

As the '57 yearbook went to press it noted "future plans lead her to an office or the altar." Easter vacation changed that. "I was up at Cozy Corner . . . and everyone was talking about going to college, and I was so insecure and unsure of myself, I didn't want to go away from home. But I was getting so jealous that I decided I wanted to go to college."

Mrs. McCormack, the new guidance counselor, told her she was very late to apply but with her help Tina found a place in a junior college. Her surprised father asked, "Where am I going to get the money?" Her very pleased mother said, "Don't worry about it."

Two years later while working for the athletic department at C.W. Post College she took advantage of free courses for employees. She also met her husband, baseball and football standout Joe Stone. In August 1960 he reported to the Giants football camp to train with greats like Rosie Greer and Sam Hough, but he returned to Long Island, married Tina and took a teaching and coaching job at East Meadow. From there he went to coaching at Post, then to Comack as a biology teacher, and finally to Windsor, Vermont where they saw a better environment for their children. After 11 years of marriage their hopes crashed when Joe took his own life. Tina learned later that his family had a four generation history of suicides.

In the hard years that followed she focused intensely on her children. "I was so afraid after losing someone so close that I might lose one of them, and I wanted to be there for them." She and Joe had both become Jehovah's Witnesses, and Tina found support from her friends and remarried. Tragedy, however, struck again when her daughter died in 1996. Tina also continued to suffer bouts of pneumonia. Then in her new house she fell down stairs, landed on one heel, drove the lower leg bones into the knee and shattered it into 40 pieces.

She now has a new knee and her old determination to carry on. That means continuing her active life in religion and raising her granddaughter, now almost 17, the owner of a mini-horse and an aspiring poet.

Tina remembers her own struggles with writing poetry for Norman Ross: "It's tadum and then reverse, not even Keats could write much worse." She believed she couldn't write poetry. But today she writes and recently penned a poem about the cutting of an ancient apple tree for a new Jehovah's Witness hall.

Christine Pollock
PO Box 802   Chester, VT 05413
cspchester@yahoo.com _____

Soren Hansen

Photo by Fred Feingold

NOTE: First person passages from Soren are mixed with my notes which are in parentheses and based on material sent by Soren.

Most of my classmates knew that I came to the United States as an eight-year old from Denmark on the *MS Falstria* in February 1948. I could only say, "shut the door" because that was the extent of my father's good intention to teach us English before we left. But first he had to take a nap after dinner. That's when he taught us to "shut the door."

My father was in the Danish diplomatic service. He previously managed a Danish chocolate factory before applying, I think on a lark, to become Industrial Attaché at the Danish Embassy near Wall Street in New York City. He applied for a two-year contract, which the Danish government kept extending.

I started school in Glenwood Landing, after having only had one-and-a-half-years' schooling in Denmark. There I made fast friends with Richie Smith for the rest of our grade school years. He and I were both good at math and tried to outdo each other. I also remember sitting on Miss Stevenson's lap to learn the colors in English. And then, seemingly magically, I spoke fluent English at the end of that summer.

(Soren's parents liked Glenwood school so much that when they rented a house on Glen Cove's Morgan's Island for two years, the Hansen kids walked the three miles to and from the bus to Glenwood Landing. Sea Cliff classmate Sandy Gleichmann would describe him as "serious, shy and quiet," but he was also adventurous. When Richie Smith came to visit him in Glen Cove, they and other eleven year olds ventured onto the Morgan Estate recently vacated by the Russian UN delegation and entered by an open basement window. At the height of the Cold War the Russian presence in Glen Cove and the diplomatic immunity with which their vehicles flaunted the law caused bitterness and controversy.

Like most local kids, he "had been warned not to talk to any of the Russian men, walking in pairs in black suits around the Island, because they were armed. The children knew, because their parents told them, that the men were instructed to shoot their comrade, should either one attempt to defect. Subsequently, a Catholic order of nuns rented the mansion. The children were again told by their parents not to talk to these black-clad women walking around the Island in pairs, this time because the nuns were not allowed to talk to anyone.")

After Denmark renewed my father's contract several times, my family moved to Sea Cliff, first in a rented Victorian house, complete with a moose head in the entrance foyer. When my father realized that we might stay in the United States for a longer time, we purchased a new house on Woodridge Lane. We moved in when I was in eighth grade at Glenwood Landing.

That year I determined to become a civil engineer. For reasons I can no longer remember, I wanted to build large dams in Latin America. That led to taking Spanish for three years with Mrs. Comfort. I never did go to Latin America, nor ever spoke Spanish.

While attending high school I often walked to school with Serge Yonov and Fred Gallo, both of whom lived close by. I ran Cross Country in the fall and track in the spring, both coached by Mr. Thompson. Those four years went by quickly. "Studious, serious, shy and quiet" is how Sandy Gleichmann describes him.

(Soren, along with Fred Gallo and Jane Sessler, left Sea Cliff for Cornell University whose costs, even in that time were so high that his father sent Soren's brothers and sisters to boarding school in Denmark to prepare for higher education there.)

(At Cornell Soren paid for his education by working in the University Library and on overseas engineering projects. These projects included spending twenty-four months in Greenland on four separate contracts to help build the Distant Early Warning (DEW) Line, near the Arctic Circle, and the Ballistic Missile Early Warning System (BMEWS) in Thule. During those trips he was privileged to stand on the place near Thule where a person can see three glaciers calving.

Before finishing my degree I succumbed to the lure of New York City and chose to do a reverse commute to work in New Rochelle from an apartment on East 36th Street in New York. In the apartment upstairs, I met my wife-to-be, Mary Jane Hekker, who persuaded me to return to Cornell where I graduated in 1966 with a Badhelor's and Master's degrees in civil and environmental engineering. In Ithaca we started attending the religiously liberal Unitarian-Universalist (UU) church and have continued that affiliation.

(After graduation Soren moved his family to Watertown, NY on the St. Lawrence Seaway where he intended to stay two years because it offered "the exact kind of field experience I

wanted.
I thought it was a wonderful place to raise children.")

Our original intention was only to spend two years there for the exact kind of field experience I wanted. But then the "intriguing" offer occurred - the officers of the company told me they wanted to consider me as a future candidate for the presidency of the company! That never happened because I got caught on the wrong side of the major stockholder, I worked there for eight years, the last position as Head of the Engineering Department.

In 1977 I joined Republic Steel in Youngstown, Ohio, and a year later the company transferred me to its corporate headquarters in Cleveland, Ohio as Manager of Project Planning and Control during an exciting time when we invested a billion dollars in three-year running averages on corporate projects. I also introduced computer applications to the engineering department. I founded my own regional engineering consultancy in 1987 with a focus on computer graphics. That continued for twenty years until my retirement.

For the past fifteen years, I've developed an abiding interest in Indo-European pre-history, while researching and spending a lot of time writing a book about this topic.

Mary Jane and I enjoy visiting our two children, Maia and Kai, and three grandchildren. Mary Jane encouraged me to speak Danish to our children and they in turn encouraged me to speak Danish to their children. Every two years we travel to Denmark to visit my Danish family and to enjoy the straw-thatched house I own jointly with my sisters and brother.

Soren Hansen31320 Marvis DriveBay Village, OH 44140soren@en.com

_____

Maria Louise Henninger

,

We have not a shred of material for Maria. She left intending to study business, become a secretary and a housewife—if we believe our '57 yearbook. Marie H was only child, mother housekeeper for   German immigrant. Her mother spoke no English. One classmate says Maria may have returned to Germany.

We also have a report that she had become Mrs. Maria Eliuk at the following address:

Maria Eliuk
215 S. 19th St.
Deer Park, NY 11729

Geraldine Rita Herman

On snowy mornings in the 1950s Joy set out as usual to walk to school from her home on Club Road near Glen Cove Avenue.. She often walked with neighbors Allyson and Pete Rose, Susan Loftus, and Rose Martone. Another neighbor would come by in her car—Miss Maple the PE teacher—roll down her window and quip "*walking is good exercise for you.*" On the most bitter days Miss Maple might stop and tell them to hop in. Today Miss Maple lives in the same house and neighbors often see her out walking for exercise, past the school and to Shore Road and back. Joy sees Miss Maple on the bus to Atlantic City, New Jersey where they both enjoy the exercise of pulling the levers on slot machines.

Joy came to Sea Cliff from Bayonne, New Jersey. He father worked as an electrician, her mother at Columbia Carbon and Ribbon in Glen Cove. She entered school in Miss Shelland's kindergarten class but soon returned to New Jersey. For fifth grade her family was back on Long Island and Joy was attending St. Boniface. In 7th grade she transferred to Sea Cliff School. The family's Club Road house was recently torn down and rebuilt by one of Joy's sons.

In high school she enjoyed the relatively unstructured atmosphere of homeroom and home economics. Among her best friends were Lorraine Grote, Faith LaJoy, Jimmy LeFebvre, Brud Neice, Pat Cavanaugh—"all hell raisers." She also fell in love with Sonny Palumbo, a graduate of Glen Cove High in 1954 who took over the family butcher shop. While he was working she enjoyed the freedom of his convertible, one time packing Jimmy, Faith, Lorraine and a few others into it—"a lot more than I should have"-- to spend the day carousing at Jones Beach. "We had a ball. I always had a ball."

When Joy graduated Sonny was already in the Army. They married in October 1957 and took up residence at the base in southern Germany's beautiful Bavarian region. Sonny was then working as a mechanic, but having had his own butcher shop, the US Army decided to make him a cook.

The first of their two sons was born in 1963, the second in 1965. Joy became a "baseball mom," proud that her pitching son was scouted by the Phillies but decided he wanted to stay near home. The other was her home run hitter.

When the boys were grown Joy got bored at home and went back into the insurance business where she had had a brief experience before becoming a mother. "Always hated math when I was in high school, and here I was in a job that I had to use math all the time." She did well and stayed with it for 26 years until two knee replacements, then a serious auto accident laid her up. The painful recovery from the accident kept her away from the reunion.

She is still recovering and suffers from continuing pain of nerve damage. But she says "I'm not giving into aches and pains." She still gets called to fill in for someone absent from the insurance agency, and two or three times a month she visits relatives in New Jersey and the casinos. Against the slot machines, she says, "I have a system. I'm holding my own." As she has done with life in general.

Joy Herman Palumbo
30 Third St.
Glen Cove, NY 11542
Jsonjoy303@aol.com

_____

Carole Hincula

Photos by Fred Feingold

Carole and her husband live in Boynton Beach, FL from November to May, then in Pawling, New York.

Last known contact information:
Carole Hincula Clarkson
46 Fernwood Dr.
Pawling, NY 12564
CRFenwood@aol.com

Frederick Scott Hughes

"Waddya gonna do with an English major?" is a question many parents asked college students in our day and today."   Fred's father didn't have to ask that question until Fred had almost flunked engineering drawing at Clemson University and asked if he abandon his slide rule for Chaucer, Shakespear and Faulkner.   What did he do with his English major?   First, he received straight As in ROTC and became a commander in the Persian Rifles and led them as they marched in the Cherry Blossom Parade.   He also became student body treasurer.   He also became student body treasurer and played tenor sax with a combo called The Naturals.   He joined the Army in April 1963 as a 2nd Lieutenant and was assigned to Military Police.

At Fort Bragg he chose the MP service "because MPs did not have to do a lot of marching." After 3 years in Germany and interim duty back home, Fred went to the famous Demilitarized Zone (DMZ) between North and South Korea to serve as a Panmunjom security officer.   In Vietnam he became an advisor to a Vietnamese MP battalion, returning to DC in 1972.   In '75 he married.   He adopted his wife's daughter and two of their own followed.   The Army sent him to Central Michigan University where he earned a masters in Management and Supervision.   In 1984 Fred finished 21 years of military service and retired as a Lt. Colonel.   Among his honors and awards he has the Legion of Merit, two Bronze Stars, and three Army Meritorious Service medals.

The next year Fred began working with GTE Government Systems from '84-'91 as a systems security engineer in a project to modernize the US Military Command and Control System.

During this same time Fred's personal life began to spin out of control.   "In February of 1986, I entered the program of recovery from alcohol addiction through Alcoholics Anonymous, and through individual and group therapy.   I am thankful and humbled to say that, through the grace of God and these programs,   I have not had a drink of alcohol or any other mind-altering drugs in the more that 24 years since then.   This transition to sobriety is probably the single most transformative experience in my life, leading to many blessings and vastly enhancing and improving my quality of life, and, especially, the depth and quality of my relationships.   May it continue ODAT."

His marriage ended in divorce in '89, and he set about rebuilding his professional life and his body.   In the early 90s he began working on a masters in counseling psychology.   In '95 he added that degree to his others.   He also had to earn his wife Linda.   Fred, a marathon runner, had been pursuing for some time, but, "She didn't want to have anything to do with me."   Then she said, "I do."

The closest Fred got to sports in high school was being a manager on the basketball team and someone wrote in his yearbook profile, "breathing really rates with Fred".   Of course, he had developed extra lung capacity playing trumpet in band and orchestra.   In the early 90s Fred gave up golf.   Fred had begun to run long distance competitions before marriage. He ran two marathons in 1997, finishing the second in under 4 hours the day after his 58th birthday. During a final training run for the 1998 Boston Marathon a car hit him.

That ended his marathons, but he still did 10Ks for several years until he quit entirely after 2000 and scaled back to daily walks.   He is also playing golf again.

In late April of 2009 Scott found out he had prostate cancer.   He says, "I chose to have a prostatectomy done with a robotic surgical system called the Davinci robot (check it out at www.davincisurgery.com), which was done on August 17th at the Boston Medical Center, the teaching hospital of Boston University."   As of March 2010 he was doing well and cancer-free.

 Despite his accomplishments in the Army and business, Fred is most satisfied with his work as a counselor where he saw hope enter and improve people's lives.   Fred's now enjoying retirement with Linda and playing golf again.   He looks back on what he did with a degree in English.   He did not plan or anticipate his "tri-partite career" and says, "Life just kind of happened.   There was no grand plan."

Scott Hughes
(Nov. - May.) 1530 Maseno Drive
Venice, FL 34292(Jun. - Oct.)   28 Voyagers Lane
Ashland, MA 01721scolinmax@comcast.net

Joan Imperiali

Photo by Fred Feingold   Photo by Nik Epanchin

Joan appeared at the beginning of our freshman year from the distant planet of Brocton, Massachusetts speaking that strange language wherein people 'paaahked the caah' when they went to a "paaahty."   And for boys with hormones boiling there she sat with her warm freckled smile, dark eyes, and flouncy skirts, innocent of the havoc she was wreaking on academic concentration by wearing a gauzy see-through blouse.   Her father had just been transferred from New England to New York City to become a Howard Johnsons vice president in their food processing operations, and her mother, Joan says, "just happened onto Sea Cliff, what a lucky break."   They rented an unheated summer cottage near the beach from Mrs. Tilley before finding bigger rental offered by a former Miss Rheingold where they stayed while their home on Littleworth Lane was being built.

While at least the boys in the class thought she had come from some wonderful planet, Joan says, "I loved New York and Sea Cliff from the moment I stepped in it. I thought it was so much more sophisticated."   In her senior year Joan would recall her first Sea Cliff summer and swimming off the bulkhead at Tilley's beach: "That summer at Tilley's was one of the best of my life."

After graduation Joan's work at Helena Rubinstein would introduce her to the world of computing and a vision of the future.   Rubinstein's, she says, "had a computer that was the size of a very big room."

In her spare time, like many in our class she often visited the Knotty Pine in Glen Head. "One night Barbara [Gilson] and I were at the Knotty Pine and there he was. He had just come out of the army. I went home and the next morning I told my mother, 'I think I met someone I might marry."   He was Charlie Mouquin ('53), big brother of Chloe ('58). During their engagement Charlie started work with Howard Johnson's food processing operations in Queens.   They married in 1960, took an apartment in Sea Cliff for a year before buying a white brick house at the corner of Prospect and Carpenter just above Winding Way's steep twist to Shore Road.

While the lived there Joan gave birth to their daughter Stephanie in '66 before he was transferred to Hingham, MA where daughter Jennifer was born in '69. Joan was more than pleased when he was transferred again, this time in the mid '70s to Miami. A former member of Science Club, she became an avid shell collector. In 1977, however, the company transferred Charlie back to Massachusetts where they spent the next 31 years in Medfield. Joan had stayed home to care for the girls until Jennifer was nine. Then she began working in the schools with special needs students. One summer "I took a temporary job with Raytheon [the big defense contractor] where they had one of the early office computers. It was a revelation. I could see that this would really change everything." That included her career. She found a job with New England Library Network (NELINET) developing their on line interlibrary loan system. "I could see a computer would allow me to do things I could never do before." She began to write and produce their newsletter, "and when Pagemaker [a publication design and layout program] came out I had even more fun." She eventually became assistant to the executive director and began marketing their on-line reference service to New England university librarians. It was a job that kept her constantly in the car driving to every college, large and small, in the region demonstrating NELINET's services. However, she was traveling from early morning till late at night and as the century turned she realized, "I have to stop this before I have an accident."

She immediately suffered from "a little bit of retirement shock" and returned to working with special needs students in the schools. Two years later she and Charlie were ready for complete retirement. They are both avid golfers and Charlie had started visiting home shows to gather information. Someone said, "What you need is Tennessee." In the northeast corner of the state's Appalachian region they found their home in Loudan south of Knoxville and not far from Asheville, NC. Making friends, Joan says, was easy since "everyone is from some place else. We have a social life like we never had back home.. No matter what you like to do, there is a group here that does it." Joan belongs to the Great Books Club, plays lots of golf, and does a lot of hiking. She's also enthusiastically getting her new laptop up to speed.

Joan Imperiali Mouquin
201 Oohleeno Trace
Loudan, TN 37774
mouquinj@att.net

Sue Izzo

Gail Capobianco Schramm

We called her Sue because when she came to Sea Cliff in the freshman year, people kept tripping over Angelica.   She soon said, all right, just say Sue, which was her middle name. (Yes, the yearbook also tripped up and listed her as Sue A. Izzo.)   Nevertheless she was happy at Sea Cliff as she had been at St. Patrick's in Glen Cove and in 7th and 8th grades in Glen Head after her father, a builder, finished their home on Frost Pond Rd. in Brookville. She was the oldest of four children, the last being sister Debbie born in Sue's first year at Sea Cliff.   Living in sparsely populated Brookville had limited her socializing with other kids, and once Debbie came, "As soon as I would walk up the front walk my mother would say here's your little sister, take her for her walk."

Nevertheless that same year her new friendship with Janice Painter bore interesting fruit. Janice had been talking about Angelica at home.   Into Mrs. O'Knefski's art class one day walked senior Bill Painter ('54), walked right over to Angelica and started talking.   He was a well built gymnast with intense eyes under waves of blond hair and a talented French horn player.   "I was overwhelmed," Angelica recalls.

The next year Bill and several buddies enlisted in the Air Force, and after basic he was assigned to band duty in Hawaii.   "When he was going to leave for Hawaii," Angelica says, "my mom and dad were arguing.   My mom didn't want me to go steady.   My father said, 'Leave her alone.'"   She knew he was sure Bill's three year absence would conquer her attachment and that going steady might keep other boys at bay.   Religion may also have played a part since Bill's family was Episcopals and the Izzos Catholics.   "Religion was a big divider" for parents she says.   "'You marry your own kind' I used to hear.   I understood as I got older what that meant, that the culture and the ways are the same and it's easier to get along.   That was way too late."

Her father may have been proven correct if she had not been very naïve.   She remembers a school performance of some kind where before the performance a debonair Dickie Robson in a white sports coat pulled her aside before he mounted the stage.   He told her he was going to sing a song especially for her, and he did—"A White Sports Coat And A Pink Carnation." Did it mean more than she could imagine? She would never know, but she would remember clearly.

Despite being in Hawaii's luxury, Bill "wrote every single day and I wrote back every single day." Unfortunately, five or six years after they were married, her mother, "a cleaning nut," decided to throw out boxes from the attic and the letters were lost forever. She was working in Helena Rubinstein's when Billy returned from Hawaii and they married in April '59. Their daughter Elizabeth was born in 1960 and 19 months later William Britton. Angelica would be a full time mother until the kids entered junior high. When the kids were growing they moved from their first apartment in Glen Cove to a new house on Leonard Place in Sea Cliff, then to Clearwater, Florida for a year, back to Long Island and three years later back to Florida for another year before finally the family rented part of a big farm house in Matinecock, NY. The kids finished school in Locust Valley. "Bill was extremely intelligent and he always liked to keep moving." In 1978 her father built a house for them in Bayville and that remains her part time residence.

When the kids were in junior high Angelica had started working as a secretary again. Looking back on her life, she says, "I've been very blessed all my life. There were really no hardships." When her son Britton started school he called her from the cafeteria pay phone at lunch time. Why? Because when he had been at home he knew that his dad called his mom every day at noon from work and he would do the same. However, when Angelica and a friend took their daughters to school for the first day, her friend's daughter cried, but Elizabeth turned to Angelica and said, "You can leave now." Neither ever had trouble in school or gave their parents trouble at home. Elizabeth now does marketing for a LI radiology office and Britton runs his own commercial fishing boat out of Oyster Bay.

Angelica and Bill divorced in 1992 but have remained close and get together gladly at family events and holidays. She continued to live in Bayville and work with Canon USA until 2005. She also spends a lot of time in her Boca Raton, Florida home. Her best friend there is Judy Graziosi, a 93 year old former Roslyn school piano teacher. Angelic used to be compulsively busy like her mother. With her friends in Florida, the never-ending activities in her living complex she says, "I've learned finally how to relax. I thank god every day."

Angelica Sue Painter
384 B Bayville Ave
Bayville, NY 11709
reneepainter@hotmail.com (daughter's e mail)

―――――――――――――――――

Robert Johnston

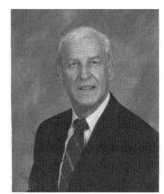

Photo by Nik Epanchin

Soccer goalie, baseball pitcher, basketball center—in many a tight game "Porky" Johnston knew how to make the difference. He used that same judgment in deciding his path through the years after high school. Sometime teammate Pete Rose (Class of '59) himself star athlete, Green Beret, then a journalist, said of Bob, "He had the most talent of anyone I played with, probably including the University of North Carolina where we had a good team with players who went on to the pros. I had to drag him out to play summer ball. I recall getting him down to the field at Glen Cove and a bunch of scouts drooling behind the backstop at his stuff. He had a very good 'smoking' fastball that 'hopped' and curve that 'dropped off the table.' It was all I could do to catch his pitches--I was an all-county catcher my senior year, so had done some catching."

Bob modestly remembers another side of sports. "I boxed Arty [Kaufman, '56] all the time and he was left handed and he knocked me down." And he deliberately avoided at least one reward. "I recall taking typing with Mrs. Zipperian and never chose to exceed 39 words a minute because 40 or more meant you were to receive an award at Moving-Up Day."

Bob did sign with the Dodgers his senior year and played with their Bluefield, West Virginia and Kokomo, Indiana teams. When he came home in the fall the only strutting he did was with a mailbag on his shoulder. In spring of '58 he reported to the Thomasville, Georgia Dodgers team, traveling the South in a bus. Then his pitching arm "started going kerfluie." He had already begun to think about the guys he knew who had a wife and kids and were spending spring and summer riding around in buses. "I said, this is not for me." He delivered mail the rest of that summer and Twink Leckie ('56) said, "Hey, I'm going to Emporia, wanna go?" Emporia State in Kansas was the university where Mr. and Mrs. Jim Fraley who ran the Youth Center had gone and where they had sent on several Sea Cliff kids.

At Emporia Bob met Sandy Pound of Wichita and married her. While she was finishing her degree in education, Bob started on his Masters in Counseling. When Sandy was ready they moved to Colorado to teach then returned to Kansas to take jobs near her hometown, Shawnee Mission. Bob finished his masters and began work as a counselor. Four years later he took a job in the financial aid office at Wichita State College. One morning he came in early and noticed the flag a half mast but knew of no news to explain it. The staffer who raised the flag said he had not been able to get it up any higher. A few hours later the nation heard the news that the plane carrying the college football team had crashed and killed all on board.

From Wichita Bob went on to take his doctorate and work at universities in Illinois, then in Texas and Nevada as head of admissions and registrar. His status in the last two positions was recognized by election as President of the Nevada Association of Collegiate Registrars and Admissions Officers and as Vice President of the same organization in Texas.

Bob and Sandy retired in Texas in 1998. Bob says he can't sit back and watch life pass by. He substitutes as an elementary teacher because he finds the opportunity at that level to help kids shape their own futures. And the kids have no politic. "There are no Democrats or Republicans there. If you pay attention to them, they love you. "

Bob had his tickets and reservations for the class reunion when he heard about the hurricane heading for Galveston. He had a feeling he ought to stay. Thousands were left homeless, and Bob volunteered to work with the Salvation Army preparing hundreds of thousands of meals. "That's what I enjoy doing---working with people and helping." He still enjoys being on the team and, when the game gets tight, he knows how to make a difference.

Johnston, Robert
251Pin Oak Drive
Brenham,Texas77833-6550
bnsjohnston@sbcglobal.net

_____

Steve Kalakoc

Photo by Nik Epanchin

Steve's father saved him from the worst and inspired him to reach for the best. Steve was 3 when the Nazis who conquered his native Ukraine took his father and family to Germany because his father was a chemical engineer. That profession probably saved the family from the worst ravages of war on the eastern front, but in the fall of 1944 the Russians were on their way to Berlin, spreading pillage, plunder, rape, vengeance and panic across Germany. In the chaos Steve's father commandeered two horses and a farm wagon in which he moved his family constantly to avoid the fighting and the Russians. They camped in fields and woods and stayed in abandoned houses until the Germans took the wagon and horses in 1945. "We then moved around the country with our worldly goods on a child's sleigh until the war ended."

They then became three among millions of refuges. They lived in a UN Relief Association camp for several years. Two or three families shared a large room, separating their space from others with blankets. Steve started to learn to read and write in a German school. When finally offered a choice of emigration, his father again saved them from the worst. "We did not want to go back to Ukraine, a Communist country. My family had had enough of Communism." He requested America. "That was his dream: to get us to America. . ... We arrived in New York late in December. Two months later my dad died of a brain tumor on my 13th birthday."

Steve and his mother moved from Glen Cove to a basement apartment in Sea Cliff at 250 8th Avenue. His mother worked as a domestic in private homes, and within 3 months Steve was delivering papers. Later he worked at Gallon and Wolfe cleaners. "With her working and me working we got by." In retrospect, yearbook had a bitter irony with the phrase in Steve's bio, "if you ever want your clothes cleaned, call him up." Work meant that Steve could not participate in the after school clubs and sports he wanted. Nevertheless, he says, "I was a happy camper in Sea Cliff because I had shelter, food and money."

He did have time to become friends with another classmate, Pat Mills, in 7th grade. When Pat moved to Bethpage romance blossomed and they married in December 1957. "In 1959 "the Army was looking at me pleasantly so I joined the Air Force." He and Pat lived off base in Germany where Steve worked with the military weather service. Gas was 11 cents a gallon and hamburger 11 cents a pound, and for Steve that meant living and traveling well. He also started night school.

After the Air Force and taking a degree in Boca Raton College in Florida, work seemed to keep bringing him back to the Mississippi River. He worked for Harris Corp., Bendix, Motorola, Siemens, and Sharp in Florida, Louisiana, Tennessee, and Illinois. He and Pat had three children. "I was living a typical American dream: a home, mortgage, children and the good life." Then their 17 year marriage ended in divorce.

A year later he married his present wife, Heidi, herself an immigrant from Germany. He took his MBA from Western Illinois and began working for Siemens, often travelling in Europe and making good use of his Polish, German, Russian and Ukrainian. In the last years of his professional life Steve bought a farm in Tennessee. He had never raised crops or livestock, but he had always wanted to. Fourteen years ago he retired to the farm with his cows, horses, chickens, raspberries, blueberries, apples and pears. "I got it out of my system." By the time this story is published he expects they will be living in a home in Hendersonville, TN, about 15mi north of Nashville.

Steve feels he has gotten what his father wanted him to have. "My father wanted very badly for us to live the good life. My desire was always to work, earn a living. When he passed away he left me 50 cents. . . . Having lived in Europe during and after the war, and having visited other countries, there is no country as good as America. With all of America's problems it is the best country in the world, and I am very proud to be an American."

Steve Kalakoc
280 Opossum Rd
Portland, TN
hkalakoc@nctc.com

Chester Katoski

Certain things have remained constant in Chet's life—his love of the Yankees and a few close friends. Chet and his sister grew up in Glen Head where their father ran his carpentry contracting business. In third grade he went to St. Boniface where he became close friends with Ted Rydzewski who remains a close friend. At Sea Cliff he played outfield for the baseball team and during vacations he was often playing ball with friends from Glen Cove. He also enjoyed his art classes with Ms. O'Knefski and developed his gift for pencil drawing.

After high school Chet worked a couple of years at Glen Cove's Photo Circuits. Feeling that he should serve his country, he enlisted in the US Army in 1959 and went from Ft. Dix to the hot, flat pine barrens of Ft. Bragg in North Carolina where he specialized in heavy artillery and the 8 inch mortar. After three years of service he returned to Long Island to work in Grumman aircraft assembling its famous A6A Intruder. He also wasted no time in marrying his high school sweetheart, Patricia Collins ('59).

He and Pat had their first child, a son, in '63 and a daughter in '68. After 5 years Chet left Grumman for a career with the US Postal Service, working in Roslyn. Over thirty years he saw mail handling go from a slow manual job to a highly computerized process. Pat became assistant director of human resources for the Bethpage Federal Credit Union. They also paid close attention to their children, laying down the rules that Chet feels has led to their successful lives as well as a close family relationship. Their son is superintendent of River Run golf course in Ocean Pines, MD and in charge of the homeowners association. Their daughter worked with the US Secret Service guarding the White House and president's family until an injury sidelined her.

Shortly after retirement Chet and Pat went to visit their son near Ocean City, MD and that same week they decided to buy a home in a 55 plus community nearby and only 6 miles from the ocean. Although Chet gave up playing and umpiring baseball 25 years ago, he remains a diehard Yankees fan.   He stays very busy with physical fitness training and his two teenage grandchildren who live nearby.   Pat is urging him to take up again the drawing he enjoyed in school.

Chester Katoski
5 Columbia Ave
Berlin, MD 21811
kchetski@verizon.net

Wallace Kaufman

Photo by Fred Feingold

From the first moment I envied my twin brothers who could walk when I could only crawl I have suffered from that condition of hyper ambition that soon metastasized into wanting to do anything anyone else near me could do.   Those little orange books about the lives of heroes and heroines like Davy Crockett and Clara Barton that teachers read to us in second and third grade aggravated the condition.   When I transferred from Roslyn to Sea Cliff in October of second grade, the first thing I did from the opened doorway was survey all the boys in the class, asking myself, "Which one of these kids can beat me up?"   I decided it must be that rather tough, wiry kid with the olive skin and dark eyes, Bobby Solon.   My first big defeat came that same year when I tried to jump into my brothers' 3rd grade but flunked the test for script and multiplication.   The second defeat came two years later, from Richie Loftus and not with fists but with ballots.   The young and pretty 4th grade teacher Miss Pinnney introduced us to democracy with an election. Richie beat me handily for class president.   Hyper ambition, however, is an incurable disease.

In Mr. Allen's 6th grade I decided I would become a poet.   I proudly showed him my first poem. It was about a stream and I fortunately remember only two lines: from the mountain/ like a bubbling fountain.   If I couldn't be a poet, I at least wanted to be the subject of his psychological experimentation and I was mightily insulted that he gave inkblot tests to Richie Loftus and Allan Schwartz but did not choose me.   Like any teenager afflicted with hyper ambition, I was more concerned with failures than success.   I wore Coke bottle thick glasses and had pimples.   Out of 110 senior pictures in our yearbook only Nancy Baker, Fred Feingold, and I wear glasses.   Mr. Matthews read us the Dorothy Parker poem with the lines, "Boys don't make passes/ at girls who wear glasses."   I was sure the same was true for girls and explained why no girls made passes at me.

When I played catcher on Phil Fraley's summer team every time I threw off my mask to catch a pop up, my glasses came off and I found myself staring up into a fog wondering if I could see the ball before it crashed into my face. Meanwhile teammates were yelling, "to the left, to the left." I went to the golf course after school one day when I had broken my glasses playing basketball at school. I was lucky to get a single bag to carry, but I was assigned a terrible slicer. When he sliced a ball, he would say, "Caddy, where did it go?" I never knew. He turned me in after I lost 10 balls in nine holes and told the caddy master, "Mo, this kid is blind." I also failed at basketball, baseball, broke a rib trying to pole vault, and was too stubby to run distances. My three consolations were wrestling, swimming and soccer.

With girls and romance my two consolations were that at thirteen when I crashed the sled on which Tina Hallberg and I had ridden down Hammond Avenue, she leaned back with fine red lips and kissed me. The other was that when I despaired for a senior prom date, someone convinced Joanne La Pierre to go with me. And our valedictorian Diana Djivre did accept my invitation to ride with me to Jones Beach and see Song of Norway. Or did she ask me? I dreaded asking girls out and seldom did. Hyper ambitious people also often suffer from a hyper active fear of rejection.

Because the Wah Chang tungsten refinery turned Hempstead Harbor purple, green, blue and white with its toxic brews, I was fortunate to become the recipient of one of their foundation's (Li Foundation) four year scholarships. Knowing I was not like the people I saw going to Harvard and Yale and Princeton, I applied to Duke where there was a large English department and a soccer team. I won a Marshall Scholarship to do graduate work at Oxford and made the stupid decision to follow my undergraduate degree with a thesis on William Wordsworth's poetry.

Fortunately degrees in literature don't serve ambition well, and when I did not win tenure at the University of North Carolina at Chapel Hill because they considered me a useless "generalist," I had to earn a living in some other way. All the rest is told at length in my 2001 memoir, Coming Out of the Woods. At the center of that story is my daughter Sylvan who lived with me for long stretches in a house I never finished building and which remains a museum of sloppy carpentry and experimental stone work. Professionally, suffice to say my interest in living in the woods and preserving them, led me to experimenting in environmentally sound (so I thought) land development, then into real estate appraisal, and consulting with law firms on property litigation. Then, combining my Boy Scout interest in Morse Code and electronics with my off and on work as a journalist I joined an arctic expedition of Soviet and American radio amateurs at age 50. That led to learning Russian. Combine that with my motley work experience on farms and in factories, the understanding of basic economics from real estate and I got a job running interview teams that the World Bank sent to Eastern Europe to find out what problems were facing newly liberated entrepreneurs.

I followed that with two years as resident advisor on housing and land reform in

Kazakhstan and teaching property valuation for the education division of the World Bank, training journalists in Kazakhstan, and helping new businesses in the Russian arctic. I continued to write, publishing some fiction in Redbook and Mademoiselle, articles everywhere, and several books. The last book was a guide to invasive plants co-authored with my daughter who has her Ph.D. from Rutgers in plant ecology. From 1965 – 2001 my home base was my evolving house in the forests of North Carolina. When I began to hear highway noises and planes overhead drowned out the croaking of frogs in my pond, I sold out and moved to Oregon where I continue to write (poetry too) and consult, and where I have recently begun to work in dispute mediation. Hyper ambition is a fatal disease.

Wallace Kaufman
34251 Mt. Tom Dr.
Harrisburg, OR 97446
taconia@gmail.com

Highgate Cemetery, England
Photo by Reynolds Price

Richard Klein

Photo by Fed Feingold

We have not located "Bones" although Richie, like many of us, started regular employment as a paper boy with a large route. He went on to buy several old cars. One classmate remembers "how thrifty he always was. He did not like anyone borrowing cigarettes from him and did not like to reciprocate at the Villa Sorrento when someone bought him a beer."

He is one of the few in the yearbook for whom no future plans are mentioned. A friend says he may have gone on to join the US Navy and become a flier.

Timothy Klenk

Photo by Nik Epanchin

The year Tim was 14 his mother announced she would give the family a present for her birthday—she took them all flying in a friend's plane. Tim fell in love with that freedom and its wider view of the world, and he knew he was ready for the responsibility the goes with the risk. He saved his earnings at Bohack's supermarket and at Dugan Poultry Farm and paid for flying lessons at Zahn's Airport in Amityville. By graduation he had a pilot's license to go with his Regents diploma. He intended to become an aeronautical engineer. "Don Thompson impressed me with how interesting math was when I took geometry from him."

At Wheaton College in Illinois he did receive a BA in math, but ROTC dictated he would serve in the Army after it permitted him and his wife, Anne Schuessler, a year's extension for her to get teaching credentials. Tim expected to fly in military transport, but a crisis in Berlin triggered by a Check Point Charlie guard who refused to let armed Soviets pass found Tim reassigned to Armor in a rapid troop surge in Germany. He found that the Army needed the same computerized rail car tracking that he had learned at IBM while his wife studied. He also found himself practicing law. "I was the dumbest, greenest lieutenant and they assigned me as special counsel for defendants in court martials," at a time when minor cases did not require trained lawyers on either side. "That was my night job. The first case I had was very high profile. I had to challenge the chairman of the board because of conflict of interest. It became known that I had pushed hard against this guy who later became my boss." Tim soon found himself in great demand which Army rules did not allow him to deny. After a year with a winning record, the Army decided he better be a prosecutor. "I could see how the law had such a tremendous impact on people's lives," Tim said, and that interest led him to enroll in Northwestern University School of Law in Chicago in '64.

After Tim and Anne's daughter was born, Ann was killed and his daughter critically injured in a car crash. Three years later he married Margaret Jo, a biology teacher who later became a software engineer. Tim gave her the gift of flying lessons one year and soon Jo was delivering Cessnas on her own. Last year he gave his 7 year old granddaughter her flying first flying lesson.

About the time Tim had decided to retire from class action and employment law work, he agreed to move to another Chicago law firm, Bryan Cave to mentor younger lawyers and handle pro bono work for the international firm with over 1,250 lawyers. Tim also serves as treasurer for Advocates International, a non-profit that supports over 30,000 Christian lawyers around the world who help the poor and promote the use of law to support religious freedom. http://www.advocatesinternational.org/ Often, Tim says, this requires fighting corruption in regimes that have law but where justice is often purchased.

Tim says he still occasionally plays his baritone horn at home. It also became clear, as I talked to Tim and did research, that he doesn't blow any personal horn in public.

Tim Klenk
217 S. Gables Blvd.
Wheaton, IL 60187
tim@klenks.net

Bette Kreidemaker

One day English teacher Bernie Shulman stood in front of the class to read an example of an excellent student essay that began, "I wanted only one ride on this merry-go-round." Bette, the author, shrank down in her chair, "mortified," then grateful that he did not read her name. "I was probably born shy," Bette says. She was one of the quieter members of the class and few knew her well, but those who did respected her intelligence and judgment. The first sign of good judgment came after she graduated from Glenwood Landing school and had to decide between starting 9th grade in Glen Cove, Roslyn or Sea Cliff. She first signed up for Glen Cove, but her good friend Judy Olson had chosen Sea Cliff and Bette has never been sorry that friendship tipped the scale toward the smallest school.

Like many shy people, she found team sports a good way to become part of the larger community. She played softball and soccer but particularly loved basketball, and with family and trusted friends she was far from shy. Sandi Freedman remembers high school pajama parties and says "the ones at Bette's were most memorable. " Perhaps one of those friends wrote in her bio for the yearbook, "appears reserved, but we know better." The *we* may have included the class member who recalls that she learned to play Spin the Bottle at a party at Bette's. Whether these two observations had any connection in the historian's mind, the note does not say. Bette says her father was "pretty strict. If I had a party, he was there."

Her steady boyfriend in school was soccer, basketball, and baseball player Richard "Knox" Norwich. They married in May of 1959, and instead of the secretarial profession she had envisioned she had twins, Judy and Bill in 1960 and son Gerard in 1961, and finally Carol in 1967. They were her full time job while Richard worked for the New York Transit Authority. They lived on Maple Avenue between the firehouse and St. Boniface, and Sea Cliff was changing rapidly. They decided they wanted to get off of Long Island where the kids would have a rural environment, and they moved to Monroe, NY about 70 miles north of the city, and far enough out of town that the kids weren't on the streets. They found plenty to do at home, the boys "always taking the car apart and putting it together."

After Richard and Bette divorced in 1985 she went to work for Troll Communications, a children's book publisher. She was Troll's production coordinator, making sure all the supplies and processes came together to meet book club and publishing schedules. She worked for them until 2004 when Scholastic bought the company.

Her daughter Judy has become a malpractice attorney on Long Island, Gerard is a cell biology researcher at UC San Diego, and Bill is a mechanical engineer with the Long Island Railroad. Bette has turned her house into a mother-daughter house, with her quarters upstairs and her daughter Carol and son-in-law and their children ages 3-9 downstairs. It's a noisy house, but she enjoys being with her family. She also still has a bit of Sea Cliff with her—a set of Cutco knives that she bought from John Maloney when he was a kitchenware salesman.

Bette Norwich
458 Old Dutch Hollow Rd
Monroe, NY 10950

Faith LaJoy

Photo by Nik Epanchin

I first ran into Faith, literally, playing tackle football when Sandy Gleichmann's brother Allen organized a team called the Backyard Terrors. Faith and at least one other LaJoy, a brother, played on the opposing team. They were tough, bold, competitive, and fair. That's the way Faith remained. Add compassion and a love of humor.

Faith married Charlie Hanson from Glenwood Landing who attended Roslyn High, then went on to work with Long Island Lighting Company. He proposed to her on the same night that his friend Walt Alexander proposed to Pat Cavanaugh, although neither man knew it until they met later in the evening. Charlie shared Faith's zest for good times and they traveled widely in the US. Faith also became Godmother to Pat and Walt Alexander's first child. In fact, they drove Pat to the hospital. "Charlie nearly fell down the flight of stairs, ran over curbs, etc getting us there." For many the two families lived on the same street in Central Islip. Their children remain good friends.

Annette Caselli (Capobianco) rediscovered Faith when a friend married a young woman who had that "Same kind half cocked smile." The woman was Faith's niece Mary Lou. Annette found Faith to be the same tough and compassionate person she had been in high school. "She had come to a nice point in her life," Annette says. She had the same quick sharp but never nasty wit. She donated a lot of time to the soup kitchen. "That's kind of who Faith was. She was always interested and interesting." When Faith found out she had lung cancer and very little time, Annette saw that she met this challenge as she met others in life. "She was tough, she was tough, yes. That's how she faced cancer. She would give that little grin and she hung in and she didn't complain." She also never stopped smoking. She never gave up being herself. That's the way she played the game of life.

R I P

Joanne La Pierre

Looking over Joanne's shoulder as she poses in her prom dress, that's me.   In one of those selfless acts of kindness that a shy person remembers throughout life, Joanne agreed to go to the Senior Prom with me.   If we had had a senior superlative for worst dancer, I deserved it, and perhaps Joanne deserved *most charitable*.   I did not know, however, that I was stepping on the toes of one of the few foreign citizens in our class.

"Canadians have a lot of difficulty giving up their Canadian citizenship," she says.   She is still a legal citizen of Canada where many relatives live.   Jo was born in Halifax, Nova Scotia to a family from Grand Desert.   No, not the Vegas casino but that coastal town settled by French Acadians centuries back, and whose present population is 332.   In the late 1940s her father's search for work landed him a job with Long Island Lighting Company.   They bought the modest Altamont Ave. house in Sea Cliff where she lives today.

Jo attended St. Boniface until the 8th grade and quickly made friends for a lifetime. Several girls her age lived nearby and they became a phalanx walking to school until graduation.   As others have noted, their route often brought them in contact with the notorious bad boy "Wuzzy" Britt and they found safety in numbers.   Making the transfer to Sea Cliff High, for Joanne meant even more friends.   For an only child friends substituted for siblings.   "I was an only child and all of a sudden I had all these wonderful new friends—Judy Olsen, Sandi Freedman, Mickie Vaccaro."   Ruth Ahearn remembers, "We would sit up in her bedroom and listen to Johnny Mathis music for hours."   Pat Walter remembers that Joanne's mother made "this incredible chocolate fudge" when they had sleepovers in Joanne's room whose walls were covered with Doris Day posters. Joanne and Pat would soon be following similar careers.

In the fall of '57 Joanne went to New York's Laboratory Institute of Merchandising for 2 years.   She began working in photography styling, coordinating, backgrounds and making model selections for commercial photographers.   She freelanced at that work for several years before she became a children's casting director—scouting talent and preparing her subjects for commercial photography.   Again, her work and life in New York City expanded her circle of friends.   As she does today with friends from St. Boniface, she also gets together regularly with friends she made in the city.

In 1982 Joanne married art director Russell Valdes.   Five years later when cancer claimed her mother, she inherited the house on Altamont Ave.   By that time she and Russell had become faithful watchers of "This Old House" on PBS.   Russell taught himself remodeling and undertook the renovation and expansion of the house himself.

In 1990 Joanne's interest in style and antiques led her to open a shop in Sea Cliff with her old friend Joan Ryan.   When she had begun working in New York, she and a roommate went to an antiques show at the armory on 34th and Park "and that was it."   She ran the shop until 1993.   "I didn't make a lot of money but I had a lot of fun."

Russell passed away in 1998, and Joanne has stayed on in the family house.   Of course, she has close friends in the neighborhood.   Three days a week she baby sits for a neighbor's three pre-teen children.   She also spends a lot of time reading, traveling, visiting friends and family, and going to antique shows.   Of the antiques, she says, "It's in my blood."   Today, however, she has a firm rule—acquire something, get rid of something else.   The one in, one out rule, does not apply to friends.   The reunion plan included no music or dancing, but if it had, I would have gladly returned her familiar smile with, "Shall we dance?"

Joanne La Pierre
58 Altamont Ave.
Sea Cliff, NY 11579-1402

Rita Laszewicki

The '57 yearbook says "future ambition is to do a lot of traveling," but the kind of traveling that meant she put off for almost 50 years. The traveling she did do was on horseback, leaning left and right, kicking up dust and racing through a course metal barrels. The summer following graduation Lasz was part of Marlene Lynn's wedding, then a few weeks later she married Robert McDonough of Glen Cove. His father had a stable and soon Rita and Robert were on the barrel racing circuit on Long Island and in upstate rodeos. Crashing into one of the metal barrels and coming near ruining a leg didn't stop her. When her children became old enough, they also began riding.

She always had a desire for distinct transportation, and while other kids in school were engaged in sports or cheerleading and twirling, she left the twirling squad and started work at Lord and Taylor's, taking the bus from St. Boniface's corner after school and on weekends. Meanwhile her friends were having a good time at Cozy Corner. She says she thought of them and "I used to eat my heart out." But she knew why she was working and in the senior year she got what she was after—a red '49 Ford convertible.

Rita and Robert also occasionally rode motorcycles. Their first child, born in January 1960, would grow up to become a motorcycle policeman. Their second son was born in December of the same year, and a daughter a few years later. Robert drove a tractor trailer before working in the post office. Rita worked in the administrative office of the St. Christopher's children's home in Sea Cliff, then for Helm Industries. Robert, unfortunately, died in 1984.

When Rita remarried to Glen Harvey in 2006 she began traveling—in her own style, of course. She and her husband drove a rented truck full of her son's possessions to his home in Lolo, Montana, driving headlong into a South Dakota blizzard that stranded them for two days. They also took on the Arkansas River in Colorado on a rafting trip that she says "was like a death wish." They both came out whole, but only after her husband pulled in their guide who had been washed overboard.

Although her son lives in Montana, her two daughters are still on the Island and daughter

Kim lives in a house behind hers in Glen Cove.   Rita enjoys her two granddaughters. She has one granddaughter in college in Oswego, a grandson who is a policeman, and a grandson in the Air Force who saw service in Afghanistan.   She continues to be a close friend of her kindergarten classmate Pat Tenke.   She misses horseback riding, but she says, "Having grandchildren is the most wonderful thing."

Rita Harvey
21 Collins Rd.
Glen Cove, NY 11542
516 671 5637

James Le Febvre

In 1957 Jimmy (or Red or Big Jim) "had no idea" where life would take him, but he had descended from French Canadians and Blackfoot Indians and he wasn't going to sit still, especially when life at home "was not so good." He was already thinking the US Navy might take him somewhere interesting. He was right. After a summer as a graduate he entered the US Navy in September. Jim worked as a fire control technician training the big guns on whatever the computer ordered. The computer he worked for was a 6 x 6 x 5 foot high apparatus deep in the ship.

"These were the worst years of the Cold War, and I saw an awful lot of it," Jim says. As tensions mounted between the Soviet Union and the US over missile bases in Cuba in 1962, Jim found himself "playing cat and mouse with Russian submarines." He didn't get tired of seeing the world wherever the submarine destroyer USS Damato carried him. It took him to exotic foreign ports in the Mediterranean and Saudi Arabia, though in Arabia "all we could do was ride camels." On a destroyer with about 350 enlisted men and officers Jim found himself in a community "where everybody kind of got to know everybody else." He still considers service in the Navy one of the two best decisions in his life.

The other great decision he made when on home for a week's leave. "I wasn't interested in women 'till I went in the Navy," Jim says. To satisfy that new interest, Danny Pawul suggested a double date, and he hooked up Jim with Linda Lisberg ('59). After two dates Jim spent considerable time with her parents and started a regular correspondence. They married when he left the service. Their daughter was born in '66 and their son in '72.

After leaving the service in October 1962, Jim went to work for Photocircuits, then for Grumman for six years, beginning with the lunar module. When NASA cut spending after Apollo 15 Jim switched to work on the F-14 Tomcat flight instrumentation work. With a big layoff at Grumman, Jim returned to Photocircuits and spent 35 in motor division. He eventually moved to the highly secret drafting department making glass prints. In June 2000 he took early retirement. Meanwhile Linda had been working with Genovese Drugs, retailer. She worked there till '93 when a woman ran a red light on an overpass and slammed into her car as she came off an exit ramp. She found herself on disability for the next 15 years.

For Jim retirement, in part, meant making airplanes again, but this time highly detailed model fighter jets, some taking 3 months to complete. He also takes his woodwork to craft shows, and plays golf, but quit hunting in the late 1980s.
We suspect there is much more to the life of a classmate described by another as a "hell raiser". He also offered, in my own yearbook, to teach me the "all the fundamentals" of drinking at Jones Beach. However, what you read above are "the details of my exciting life," he assures us. There always was more to Big Jim Le Febvre than met the eye.

James A. Le Febvre
45 Waverly Place
Farmingdale, NY 11735

Linda Lloyd

One of Linda's best friends in school says, "She married soon after graduating and after I moved to Florida I recall returning to Long Island and looking her up. She had married and had two children and was living in an apartment in Glen Cove and planning to move to Oklahoma. I had the feeling as though she had gotten herself in a trap as many do when they marry so soon out of high school and have children and become so burdened that they cannot without huge and impossible effort get out. I never heard from her." No one else in the class has either.

Linda had been secretary of the senior class, active in many sports and clubs, and she had many close friends. Why a person who everyone agreed had great promise and who several considered a very good friend has disappeared remains a mystery.

Robert Lucas

We saw Bob's talents in the ease with which he solved math problems, cleared a high bar, and rose up with power and grace from among crowd of basketball players to score a crucial point. I don't remember that I ever saw him discouraged or frustrated for more than a moment. If I did, the event was lost in his every day competence and his frequent triumphs. He and Nik Epanchin both left Sea Cliff on a Regional War Memorial Scholarship for Colgate. (The award was made on the basis of both academic and athletic achievement.) If a high school class can be said to have heroes, Bob Lucas would qualify.

No one gets to be that good without being driven by inner forces. The passion to achieve, of course, he expressed in his dedication to practice instead of just playing. Allan Schwartz who lived close to Bob often went to his house in our junior and senior years and fed him balls as Bob worked on improving his one-hand set shot from the left wing. "Bob and I," Allan remembers, "also played some stickball behind Doug's [Hoyt] home, using a window screen placed on a box as a strike target."

Bob's other inner forces remained largely invisible, even to his family. In his sister Patty's mind he was "a happy person other than he was quiet and very shy." He was quiet. He was shy. The yearbook says, "We thought he was shy." Even of his academic achievement it says "a quiet brain in math." He caused no trouble for teachers or coaches. He was always ready to help a classmate or a teammate. Even in the rough and tumble world of sports and its heartbreaking defeats, Bob rarely lost his temper and never seemed discouraged for long.

Bob roomed for his first year in Colgate University with Nik Epanchin and both were recruited for the Phi Delta Theta fraternity by John Clarke ('55). John says the fraternity was "three quarter jock" and heavy on parties. Nik declined to join but Bob did. Nevertheless, John Clarke says that Bob, "Stayed in his bunker. A very too-himself kind of guy."

Bob stood out as an achiever in both sports (lacrosse, soccer, and basketball) and academics. He was selected to the psychology honorary Psi Chi and was a Regional War Memorial Scholar. He also participated in the AFROTC Drill Team. Yet among the forces that drove him were demons that would prove fatal.

Bob went on active duty in the Air Force in January 1962 as a 2nd Lt. and by '63 he was flying the big C-130 Hercules out of Travis AFB in California and then out of New Zealand in support of Operation Deep Freeze in Antarctica. In January of 1966 Bob's unit began flying the long crossings to Vietnam, first with the Hercules, then with the C-141 Starlifter. Bob received a number of decorations, including Antarctica Service Medal, Outstanding Unit Award and National Defense Service Medal.

Toward the end of his service the symptoms that would later plague him as bi-polar disorder began to appear. If such decisive burdens spring from earlier ones, the precursors may have been gathering since childhood. Bob was five when his father died and his mother moved with Bob and his three year old sister Patty to a modest cottage on Ransom Ave. Mrs. Lucas worked full time for a coal and lumber company in Glen Cove. His sister Patty says, "He had difficulty because he wasn't 'social social'." And he was serious, maybe too serious. "He had a difficult time talking nonsense to people," Patty says, and she used to think it was because of his high intelligence. Most in the class liked Bob, but he had few, if any, very close friends with whom he studied, hung out, partied. His mother died while he was a senior at Colgate, and both he and Patty accepted an invitation to live with the family of Bob's Colgate roommate in Pittsburg. There he met Mary Schoffer whom he married. They had two children, Karen and William Lucas. William is in art design and Karen married an Air Force Captain who flew the same transport planes that her father flew.

Lithium treatments seemed to help Bob's condition, but not enough. Some of his fate may have been in his genes. Patty said he had an uncle and a grandfather who had committed suicide. Bob's troubles grew despite the lithium. His marriage was troubled. He went to live with Patty in Florida for a year. He became an outpatient with the VA. He died in 1985. Bob played hard, studied hard, worked hard. For reasons we will never know, he met a challenge he could not overcome.

R I P

Marlene Lynn

Lyn left high school and in July 1957 married Bobby Baldwin from Glenwood Landing and Roslyn High School. Then soon had the first of their four boys while living in St. James in Suffolk County.

Lyn devoted herself to raising the boys and maintaining their home while Bobby sold plumbing and heating equipment. In 1971 Lyn began working as a nurse's aide in a local nursing home. The state had not yet begun to impose very specific regulations on what a nursing home could require of an aide, and the work was often heavy and hard. "Nurse's aids did everything before the state stepped in and limited what they could do," Lyn says.

Building on more than ten years' experience, she went to school to learn medical coding and then entered the business world as our '57 yearbook said she would. Until Bobby retired in 1996 Lyn worked in medical billing. By that time one son had bought a large property in Hopkinsville in western Kentucky and they moved nearby.

Today she is "Just enjoying not working." But she also became an avid reader twenty years ago. She remembers with some irony her time in Norman Ross's English class. *The old Man and the Sea* drove me nuts. That was not a good experience. I threw my education away. I was too busy having fun." However, at least two classmates who remember her well, appreciate all the fun they had in those years, and Lyn's contribution to it, in and out of school. For one of her friends who had serious problems at home, Lyn and others were a safe and understanding haven where laughter also healed. That friend remembers finding Lyn again years later through Classmates.com and says, "It was the best day of my life when she contacted me."

If Lyn had the chance to take Dr. Ross's class again, she says she would do it. "Maybe the light bulb just went on," she says about her interest in reading. Being in Kentucky, she finds Civil War history interesting and also reads a lot of biography and some fiction.

Marlene Baldwin
Box 252
1440 Beeker Rd,
Pembroke, KY 42266
marbo@hopkinsville.net

Arlene Maas

At times the obvious blinded us to the important. In our yearbook's pages of seniors many biographical notes are sparse—a few pleasant comments, no club affiliations, as if this is someone who was run of the mill. Take Arlene Jeannette Maass. "Glee Club 1" is her only school activity. The bio says, "Quiet miss with a pleasant personality . . . friendly toward everyone . . . snobby, conceited people don't set right with her . . . just loves a good time . . . after graduation any kind of work will suit this gal."

We missed her real character. I can tell you what I think we missed in Arlene by telling you about her husband. Arlene married Kerry Weber, two years older than her. I remember him from grade school as a tough, wiry guy. I never knew him well, but I remembered him well because he beat the crap out of me one day when, for reasons now forgotten, we got into a fight in Prospect Park over something to do with a ball game. Kerry remained a tough guy with a good business head who built a successful business in heavy construction, driving tons of steel bulkheads along the shorelines of Long Island. He was obviously a tough guy with a soft heart who saw in Arlene a strength most of us missed.

Arlene's good friend Bette Gildersleeve also saw that quiet strength. She was the right person for Kerry, Bette says and their marriage worked out well. "Arlene was my very best friend through high school." She was very, very kind, very giving. If you had a problem, you could talk to Arlene and you felt better. She was there for you."

Arlene and Kerry and had two children and four grand children before she died. "Arlene's life was her family and our home," One Sunday, Kerry remembers, he took Arlene out to buy for her the BMW she always wanted. The dealership was closed, so they went to the Buick dealer across the street and he found himself buying a "new fancy Buick" that she liked but disappointed him greatly. They always used his Chevy work car for their Maine vacations together. Kerry had a chance to sell the Buick a year later. "Arlie was heartbroken." Kerry conspired with a friend to fill the void. One Sunday when they were out driving, Kerry drove past a Lincoln-Mercury dealership where his friend worked and asked Arlene if she wanted to stop in, say hello, and look around. She decided she liked the Mercury Cougar in the front window. "We'll take it," Kerry told his friend. This became Arlene's favorite, and perhaps for that reason she refused to drive it farther than Roslyn Bridge or Rt. 25A. "Those were her boundaries," Kerry said. Her daughter-in-law whom she grew as close to as a daughter, became her shopping companion as Arlene made her regular forays to find clothes for her kids that would hold up to their active lives.

When Arlene was diagnosed with breast cancer in the late 1980s, they sought out the best doctors they could find. The cancer seemed to go into remission for 2 years and they celebrated what they thought was a victory. Then X rays found spots in her lungs. Again they went to the specialist, including Dr. Atkins in New York City where Kerry says, "It cost me $500 to walk through the door." They knew they had a serious fight and grim prospects. Kerry's life was driving heavy machinery and installing hundreds of tons of sheet steel bulkheads in difficult environments, but when it came to family tragedy, he says, "Arlie was so much braver than I was. They showed us the X rays and her lungs looked like snow."

Arlene asked the doctor, "How much time do I have?" The answer was four to six months. Kerry took her to Virginia for her birthday. The cancer was already crippling her and she apologized constantly for holding him back as they visited special places.

I asked Kerry what he was going to do in retirement, go fishing? No, "I got 36 fishing poles but I haven't wet a line in 26 years." He has a hunting license and a good selection of shotguns and rifles, and used to go to Maine to hunt. That's finished too. "I don't have any interest in killing anything," he says. "We got a family of raccoons that comes around and we feed them." Arlene is gone but Kerry says, "I'm still angry." And it's clear that Arlene left with him not only a good family, but a deeper appreciation of life itself.

R I P

Linda Malkin

"Did you get picked last for everything?" Linda's daughter, an accomplished athlete, asked her diminutive mother. "Yeah, how did you know," was Linda's reply. Such was the fate of most small people in competitive teams which dominated the sports of our school and community. Yet the yearbook credits her with two years of softball and soccer and four years of volleyball, suggesting that she is not a person deterred by an assigned status, that participation is more important than stardom.

For a career, however, she chose teaching where size was irrelevant and desire to do the job is the foundation. Two of Linda's uncles and aunts were taught in tough districts of New York City, and she credits them with her ambition to teach. Although she married in her senior year at Hofstra University, she graduated in 1962 with a degree in elementary education. Her husband was Richard Suss whom she had met at a kids' coed camp two years earlier. Her first year she taught at Deer Park, LI.

"I loved teaching—absolutely wonderful," Linda says, but she also loved becoming a mother and left teaching for the birth of her son Andrew in 1963. The family moved to Wayne, New Jersey where she gave birth to her daughter Jilliane in 1968. Wayne was a developing bedroom community for New York City, and Linda found life there "kind of ordinary" but very happy. She "had a wonderful time being a mom and playing tennis and being part of a newly developing community." She and several other couples made their own contribution to the town's development by joining a successful effort to establish a branch of the Patterson Temple in Wayne.

After both her parents and her husband's moved to Florida, Linda and Richard followed in 1976. They had been vacationing in Florida twice a year and found both the weather and the abundance of community activity appealing. Why not do year round those things they enjoyed on vacations? Besides, they would live a few miles from the beach and in Sea

Cliff summers she had spent most of her days at the Pavilion.

As the kids grew up Linda decided to return to work. Richard worked in the high pressure world of exporting, and Linda decided she wanted "a no brainer" so they would not both return home tired and stressed. She spent ten years as a receptionist with Macy's frozen food service before moving to a real estate office where she continues to work.

Meanwhile she has accumulated two grandchildren who live close by and a fourteen year old grandson in Atlanta. She enjoys going to her granddaughter's soccer games and cheerleading sessions, something she and Richard enjoyed on many weekends when their children were growing up. We're reliving it again."

Linda Suss
8276 Nw 14th CtPompano Beach, FL 33071
954 752 9474
pvfrsuss@bellsouth.net

Linda, top right. Bottom, Jane Allen, Judy Brown
Top: Betty Sprague, Ceil Snayd

John Maloney

John left high school intent on a profession and a dream. The dream was not to become another James Dean, whose voice and gestures John had learned well. The profession we had noted in the yearbook—pharmacy. He enrolled in St. John's University to study pharmacy, but his senior year at Sea Cliff he had become interested in trotting horses. "I've always had a love of horses, animals in general," John says, but trotters also offered the sport of the race and "a certain amount of pageantry". Not far from Sea Cliff the biggest names in training turned out the best trotters at the world's largest harness track—Roosevelt Raceway. "I had to go over there and beg. These low end trainers will hire you." They did. Beginning as a 'hot walker,' John began to learn both pharmacy and trotting, and he studied hard enough at Roosevelt to become an assistant to the "master horseman" Howard Beissinger and began working on his trainer's license. But harness racing, for John, was always about love, not money.

For money he took a job selling baby food to Long Island stores for Beechnut . He also chose to join the National Guard for a three year stint as a tank driver with the 142nd Armor. After 6 months of active duty he began selling business forms. And he married Anna Makowski ('58). In 1964 they had a daughter.

John and Anna vacationed in Farmington, New Hampshire in 1969. Ten miles away in Rochester was a trotting track, and in Maine trotters could run in a new fair every week. They moved to New Hampshire in 1974. "We came up here with nothing going for us and Anna got a job running a paint distributing company. I was pursuing my horse racing career. Unfortunately there's no money in harness racing up here. The best year I had I actually broke even." John worked as a part time truck driver for the paint distributor. Two years later the owner needed a salesman. "I said I'd give it a shot, and it worked out very well." Meanwhile John's daughter also took an interest in harness racing. "It was a nice family affair sort of thing. We'd go up to the fairs and she had a ball."

The horse breeding business that John tried, turned out to be a "disaster." He bet a lot on a colt he had bred from a sire that had been the fastest three role trotter in the country.   The colt died mysteriously.   Another broodmare failed to produce, and John abandoned the project, but not horses.   When the Humane Society called and said they had an abused racehorse, John adopted and nurtured it and 20 years later it continues to graze in his pasture.

John's experience with the paint company gave him an idea for his own company, Wood Finishing Supplies where he produced lacquers and peripheral products.   He built it up successfully.   "Briefly in 1990 I flirted with the idea of putting up a new building and expanding, but if I had expanded at that point [in the recession] I would have gone down with them [others who failed].   That was my lesson in not being too greedy."   He sold the business to a big distributor.   "If it wasn't for my wife, I probably wouldn't have made it, because I don't like the bookkeeping thing," John says.   He retired on Jan. 1, 2008.   His daughter and son-in-law live a few houses away her parents, and John and Anna were proud to have a granddaughter who is a ballerina, actress, and member of the National Honor Society.

"We all think we could have been better in our lives if we'd done it differently . . . I've done all the things I wanted to do in life.   I wanted to be a successful horse trainer, and I think I was.   And I wanted to own my own business. "

John and Anna traveled to the places they considered beautiful and intriguing.   They cruised to Alaska and around Florida.   They began exploring northeastern Maine and Canada and John wanted to visit the Allagash Wilderness in Maine.   Their favorite place, however, was Bermuda and its dolphins.   John, the animal lover said of the picture above, "The dolphin is smiling because of all the money he makes from the dumb tourists."

IN MEMORIAM:
John knew he had liver cancer in 2005.   He continued to cherish his family and his life with them. In the last months he left the hospital and rehab to be with his family, who cared for him at home to the end. It's worth remembering what John told me when I talked to him while writing the class history. I also follow those words with a few lines that seem appropriate to John's spirit. John accepted life's failures and challenges.   "You're faced with yourself and you say 'this is it, boy' and there's no turning back and you have to deal with it.   That's when you really grow."
"We all think we could have been better in our lives if we'd done it differently . . . I've done all the things I wanted to do in life. I wanted to be a successful horse trainer, and I think I was. And I wanted to own my own business."LATE OCTOBER Listen, the damp leaves on the walks are blowing With a ghost of sound; Is it a fog or is it a rain dripping From the low trees to the ground? If I had gone before, I could have remembered Lilacs and green aftern-noons of May;I chose to wait, I chose to hear from autumn Whatever she has to say.
(by Sara Teasdale)

RIP

John Maloney
395 Chestnut Hill Rd
Farmington, N H 03835
woodfin@metrocast.net

John and granddaughter Adele

Ned McAdams

Photo by Nik Epanchin

Unlike Ned's one high school sport, bowling, one way to identify success is to note who is standing when the others have been bowled over. When the 2007-8 banking and credit crisis laid low the famous names and revered CEOs who were supposedly worth $100 million salaries, Ned McAdams, the quiet boy who had only three lines in the class yearbook, was still smiling and his bank was still standing and thriving.

Banking was in Ned's family.   His aunt had once been vice president of an independent community bank, First National Bank of Glen Cove where Ned was born before his family moved to Glenwood Landing.   After two years at Mohawk Valley Community College Ned went into commercial banking, starting in the First National Bank of Glen Head (now 1st National Bank of Long Island).   Its motto was, "Where everybody knows your name." He rose to President and CEO by age 34, then the youngest bank president on Long Island. In 1978 Long Island University recognized him with its Distinguished Alumni Award in Finance.   Ned went on to become chairman of the board of three different commercial banks on Long Island before he retired in May 2008.

In the late 90s when mergers and megabanking seemed the wave of the future and no new bank had started on Long Island in 9 years, Ned and a small group of local investors founded the American Community Bank in Glen Cove where he was born. It's business plan emphasized the same friendly community banking as Glen Head's bank were he started.   "We're going to know our customers, and they're going to know us," Ned said as the bank prepared to open in 2000 in the Little Italy of Long Island Business Improvement District.   The bank soon became a solid small bank with a second branch in Commack. It remains profitable lending mostly to small businesses and growing from $30 million in assets in 2002 to over $90 million in assets and continuing to be profitable while others are failing.

The 1957 yearbook called Ned "quiet and pleasant," which he still is, but his record speaks loud and clear.

Ned McAdams
5 Allen Dr
Locust Valley, NY 11560
Ejul50@hotmail.com
e.mcadams@att.net

Also: 347 South Ocean Blvd, Apt. 309
Palm Beach, FL 33480

James McKinley

When "Big Jim" was little Jim and eight years old his family moved to Sea Cliff and he began to hang out with Frank Haggerty. He also hung out with the LaJoy and Hallberg kids. One day Frank suggested they might make a few pennies or nickels boxing and took Jim up to the loft of a neighborhood garage. "When I stepped into the ring I met Sandy Gleichmann. In thirty seconds I was gone." Whether or not Sandy Gleichmann had any influence, Jim didn't have a girlfriend in school and didn't go to either prom. Jim came back strong as a soccer fullback famous for his big foot. He also came back strong after his father's sudden death from a heart attack when Jim was 14. That left Jim the oldest man in the family, with four younger brothers, the baby only four years old. His mom began waiting tables at North Shore Country Club on weekends and working for Vulpis coal and ice delivery during the week. (Mr. Vulpis was a familiar sight in Sea Cliff carrying big blocks of ice on his shoulder pad to fill the still existing ice boxes, or burlap bags of coal for the furnaces in so many cellars.)

Jim's father had been a commuter to a city business, leaving at 7:15 in the morning, returning at 7 in the evening. "That's why I decided I was never going to be a commuter," Jim says. After graduation he went to Syracuse University because it had an Air Force ROTC and "I thought I'd give flying a try." He went into forestry products at Syracuse because of his love of wood and the creativity offered by laminated beam engineering. Jim also began to make up for the lack of romance in high school. In his junior year he dropped out for a semester of "girls and playing around" knowing he had better drop out "before they kicked me out." Because he graduated a semester late, in January '62 he began five months of carrying mail for Sea Cliff postmaster Jack Durancy.

After his initial year of pilot training Jim found himself in the big day room where on a big board were two lists. One offered all the planes and their locations around the world; the other listed each new pilot and his grade in flight school. The top men made their picks first, almost always the fighter planes in the best locations. Jim chose a fighter on the Air Force Base at West Hampton on Long Island. Now one of the military elite, Jim also enjoyed more romance and his yellow Corvette convertible.

When he arrived in Vietnam in 1966, however, the Air Force put him in a slow and low flying Cessna spotter plane and sent him out north of Saigon into the Iron Triangle to pick out targets. "Withering fire is a totally inappropriate term" Jim says for what he experienced, often flying at treetop level. "One day I went down to take a peak under the trees to see what they were doing and three fellows came out and pointed a long tube up at me." Suddenly he was seeing orange flames and hearing the snap snap of bullets flying by. After 416 combat missions and one year he left Vietnam with seventeen Air Medals and a Distinguished Flying Cross.

He returned to base on Long Island, then went to Portsmouth, New Hampshire to fly the controversial swing-wing, fighter-bomber the F-111s, known to some in Congress as the *flying Edsel*. "All Air Force guys end up in Texas," Jim says, and he was there in 1971 when he met a young woman he married. In '73 he attended Air Command and Staff College and rose to be Major McKinley. He also earned his Masters in Political Science from Alabama's Auburn University in 1974. Progressive assignments took him Alabama and then to Omaha and the Joint Strategic Target and Planning Staff where he specialized in planning US defenses against Soviet air power. From there he went to the US base in Iceland which was then the lynchpin for intercepting Soviet sea and air power. He returned to the US and again became a single man.

While serving in the joint command in Norfolk, Virginia, a friend of a friend arranged for him to meet a woman in the cafeteria. Jim married Irene in 1984 and they moved to his final posting in Portsmouth, NH where he developed military exercise and readiness programs and did war planning. In 1989, with twenty-seven years of service behind him, Jim decided he didn't want to leave New Hampshire and retired. That is he went to work flying commuter planes for Northwest Airlink. When the company went bankrupt in 1995, Jim retired from work and flying. "I'm a great believer in the law of averages." He had logged over 9,000 hours of flight time or nearly four and a half years of working time above the earth. "I am very happy to report that I have achieved the ultimate milestone in a jet fighter pilot's life--my number of take-offs equals my number of landings. Jim's mother is proud, and while Jim has quit flying, at 94 she is still driving around Sea Cliff.

Jim now chairs the Finance Commission of St. Michael's Church and serves as president of the Old Mill Homeowners' Association, both in South Berwick, Maine. Jim and his wife Irene live an active life skiing and snowshoeing near their retirement home in Maine. "My objective is 100 rounds of golf, 20 days skiing and 30 to 35 days boating."

Jim McKinley
23 Quarry Dr.
South Berwick, Maine, 03908   jandimckinley@comcast.net

Walter George Meier II

Wally Meier didn't take to college at first and joined the US Air Force where he may have found the talents he would develop the rest of his life. In the service he began to play banjo in a folk group and eventually played in 22 countries. By 1962 he was ready to finish college and become a teacher, but with a more definite focus than he had when he first started college. He took his bachelor's degree from SUNY at Buffalo and went immediately into teaching art. Once he began in Weedsport, NY he was there for good, and the record shows that "good" is more than a matter of time.

As soon as he arrived in Weedsport, some 20 miles west of Syracuse, he started the Community Theatre program and introduced musical theatre in the high school. Challenged with limited budgets and grand ambitions and eager students, Wally developed low cost "one-set-fits-all" designs for musicals. His special love has been Musical Theatre International and its programs for the Broadway Junior Collection. He also became the sponsor of a magic teaching program in the middle school and still performs magic shows for the schools.

Free from his daily teaching routines, he now volunteers in the schools, producing and designing the annual musical theater productions. He also serves as a design consultant for Music Theater International, and pursues his own course as a kinetic artist. He has also been active in Boy Scouts, having been an Eagle Scout himself, and he has designed many Scout emblems and insignias.

Wally was elected one of the three honorary members of the Weedsport Performing Arts Hall of Fame.

All the world's a stage,
And all the men and women merely players:
They have their exits and their entrances;

And one man in his time plays many parts,
(from Shakespear's "As You Like It")

Wally Meier
PO Box 186
Weedsport, NY 13166
wmeier@baldcom.net

Peter Merkel

Photo by Fred Feingold

Of the lanky kid with spiky blond crew cut and the coins jingling in his pocket or zipping around Scudder's pond reaching for a puck, our yearbook concluded that he would become "either an engineer or a hobo." About hobo he says, "I failed to make the grade." But looking back on his professional life he also concludes that he became both, if the number of places he has lived and the number of jobs he has done can qualify as a kind of professional hoboism.

He wandered even in school, one year playing hooky almost a third of the time he estimates. His attitude toward school may have been influenced by something he learned later in life—that he was mildly dyslexic—able to read but "I just couldn't sit down and write things." He gives English teacher Bernie Shulman credit for recognizing that what he could not put in writing, he could speak. After an oral presentation Shulman said, "Merkel, I don't understand why you're not getting As in this class. Nobody ever said anything like that to me before. Usually people said the opposite, 'Why can't you spell cat?'"

If he couldn't spell, he could shoot. "My big brother Ed gave me a new Red Ryder when I was about ten. I loved that BB gun and had years of fun with it (most of it safe fun). The scouts and NRA literature showed me the correct way to handle rifles, and when I started hunting with firearms I had good safe skills. I taught all four of my sons shooting and handling guns. Two are very good small game hunters and one is an awesome marksman. I just got my nine year old grandson a small BB rifle for his birthday. Before he could go out with his dad he had to read and explain all the safety rules and how handle a rifle correctly. I was told today that he passed the test and did very well with his first target practice."

When he graduated Pete didn't have the money for college so he tried unsuccessfully to get into the Electricians' Union but he didn't have the necessary contacts.   He went to work in Jakobson's Ship Yard repairing and building tugboats.   His on-the-job training included machining as well as risky work on high structures, both of which would become surprisingly useful later.   By 1961 when other classmates were graduating from college, Pete enrolled in the University of Kansas because it had a good engineering school, and, "I happened to be enamored with these cowboy novels I was reading by Will James."

He graduated in '65 with already recruited by the   CIA recruited because of his communications skills and knowledge of antenna design, and also because his work experience in machining, driving and running a boat.   After intense training in which he was one of the top students in lock picking, the Agency assigned him to Greece.   "It turns out I had a knack for breaking and entering."   There he used his skills in electronics and machining building antennas and becoming an operative in the targeting program that helped the US listen in on embassies, ambassadors, and code rooms as he traveled to other countries in Europe and Africa.   Most of that work stopped after a few years when his station chief called him in and told him the Soviets had put him on their watch list.   "If we don't keep you in low profile for a while they'll probably kill you."

He returned to the States in 1969 still working with the CIA but also wondering how he might bring over a woman he had met in Greece.   Her father was on the Agency's surveillance list.   Unfortunately for the father but fortunate for Peter the man died soon of throat cancer and Pete became engaged.   He found new work with Hewlett Packard, brought his fiancé home and married her.   Work with HP again took him to other countries where he always tried to learn at least the rudiments of the local language and realized that Dorothea Comfort his Sea Cliff Spanish teacher had been right and he had been wrong when he thought learning a foreign language was useless.   Pete also found himself in Iran as Khomeini was taking power in 1979 and often flying through Beirut airport during that country's civil war when mortar shells were flying.

The first of Pete's four sons was born in 1970.   In 1989 when his wife left him and the boys to return to Greece and open a restaurant, Pete had to adjust to being a single parent.   "That's when I retired early."   This was the first of several retirements.   After the CIA Pete had returned to Kansas to get his MBA and he now combined his business training with his electronics expertise working in sales and marketing with large and small computer firms.   Among the jobs he would pursue, he formed The Merkel Guys, a home improvement company run with three of the boys.   He also began working with the Fairfax County, VA police department on surveillance and occasionally participating in search and seizure operations.

After retiring from sales and marketing with Digital Equipment, and then retiring from police work, and also from running a school computer system, Pete says, "I finally succumbed--Hell, I'm not going to retire anymore." He went into real estate work which he continues to pursue. He invites "anyone interested in good real estate deals in Athens Greece or Washington, DC" to contact him.

Peter Louis Merkel
5001 King Richard Dr
Annandale, VA 22003
fathermerk@hotmail.com
fathermerk@verizon.net

from John Storojev

I knew Peter longer than anyone else in school. I knew him from the time I was first plucked down into the good US of A from a childhood in Japan and China. My parents rented rooms at his family's home in Glen Head. It was my first exposure to America and Pete was a part of it. We eventually moved out to a Levittown-style development in Southridge, which straddled Glen Head and Glen Cove counties. The walls were so thin that you could hear everything in the house and it was very easy to put a body part through the sheetrock walls. Pete was a quiet, reclusive guy. But he transformed himself apparently because when I went to the 25[tth] Reunion (Yes, I was there!) he was this tall rather gregarious, glad-handing person. I guess he had moved into sales, of some sort, and the shy, quiet guy was no more. I wish him well.

Patricia Mills

"I love the picture we have of our second grade class because I stood tall and proud and smiled my heart out. That was before life brought me to my knees and I really enjoy seeing myself in that image." The happy years of Pat's girlhood in Sea Cliff making mud pies and playing with friends crashed suddenly with her mother's death when she was twelve and her sister Janet fifteen. Her father handed Janet over to an older brother in California and Pat to an older sister who lived with her husband in an apartment at the bottom of 12th Ave. in Sea Cliff.

Pat says of the following years in school that she was not very obvious, "I just was." But that is not how others in the class thought of her. She had made fast friends with many including Sandi Freedman. "I loved playing the piano but there was no means for lessons in my family. She lived on Cromwell Place, as I recall and whenever she had piano lessons, I would watch and go home and practice. I question who's lessons her parents were paying for. When I ate over at Sandy's, they served Hebrew National hotdogs and to me, they were the best hotdogs I ever had."

She also remembers the guys who sat on the parking lot railing on Sea Cliff Avenue. "We always had to bolster ourselves to walk by, even across the street. It was embarrassing and yet flattering at the same time." One of her admirers was Dave Schweers who says he "didn't realize she was beautiful till she started dating Steve Kalakoc." Steve was the only boy she was allowed to be with. "My sister was very, very strict, and was going to make sure I didn't 'look for love in the wrong places.' In order to go out, I had all sorts of rules and regulations. Everyone and anyone was criticized for whatever reason, which made it easier to give in and do nothing. Fortunately, Steve was a friend and he admired me a lot. She somehow trusted him. I was allowed to associate with him (he was safe)."

When her sister's husband moved them to a home in Bethpage in our sophomore year, Pat found herself working hard to adjust to the new school that considered her a suspicious city stranger. She also found herself in great demand at home where her sister was "busy having babies." Pat decided to chart her own course. "I got a job in a dime store called

Neisner's (to pay my room and board, and get away from constant baby-sitting." When in March her sister said she had to move with them to California, Pat had just turned eighteen and decided to stay put. "I desperately wanted to get to college, even if it was Farmingdale Agricultural and Technical school to be a dental hygienist." She took a room and graduated, but even her boyfriend Steve failed to attend when his car broke down. "I graduated with NOBODY even there to clap for me. To this day, I clap for EVERYONE when I attend a graduation."

Pat and Steve saw marriage as a good fit for their situation. But she never did get her diploma. They moved with Steve's Air Force posting, then back on Long Island Pat worked from '61-7 as a secretary at Grumman's. Looking back she says, "It was almost the only way out for each of us from our "unhappy" (or lack of) home life. My father was not pleased I was dating a Russian, but he wouldn't have been pleased with anyone his daughter's dated." Pat and Steve adopted two children, Lisa and Steve, and after they had moved to Florida Pat gave birth to their son Greg. Four years later their seventeen-year marriage ended in divorce. Pat and the three kids returned to New York. Her former boss at Grumman, Jim Koschara, had taken on the renovation of a family chicken farm in Suffolk County and suggested she join him in that enterprise. They married a year later, adding Jim's son to her three children. They found themselves working around the clock seven days a week raising 16,500 chickens in the middle of high rise developments. In 1978 they bought 68 acres near Nellysford, Virginia where they built a house, airstrip and hangar. The airstrip caused a bitter battle in the community, and Pat said she never felt welcome there.

When the buyer of their LI farm defaulted on the mortgage, they changed plans and opened a Southern States hardware store in town to make ends meet. With two other investors they also built a six store shopping center that included their store. When they sold out in '86 Pat went to work in the Medical Photography department at UVA and Jim flew a tax service from their airstrip to Washington, ferrying executives who had second homes in the Wintergreen ski area. When the children had grown and left home Pat and Jim built a new log home on their land, but in 1995 their marriage failed. Pat's self-confidence plummeted, but again, she took charge and began climbing out of the hole. Part of it was climbing around the local mountains with a young friend. One day after a many hours of boulder hopping up Old Rag they reached the top. Pat looked around and felt sure not many fifty-five year old women had made it.

Soon Pat packed up everything in a rental truck and moved to southern California for a change of scenery and the warmer weather. She took a job as Program Assistant on a National Institute of Health study of Statins (Lipitor, Zocor, etc). Five years later she wrote, "I'm 61 years old, but feel better than when I was at 40. I somehow lost my identity (which is common for women our age) and gave it all away. . . ." But she also had thought long and hard about the course of her life from her mother's death to her divorce, and she came to understand it in new ways.   "I'm ever so grateful for the enlightenment, regardless of my age. Most people never find that in a lifetime. So... I, too, feel I have loved and lost, but... found myself in the struggle."

The story does not end with the loss, however.   After a knee replacement a few years ago Jim came to visit and talk.   They decided to remarry and on Thanksgiving 2008 in Maryville, TN where Jim had built a home for their new life, they said Thanksgiving with their four children and their grandchildren gathered around them.

Pat Koschara
1311 Apache Ct
Maryville, TN 37801
pkoschara@aol.com

Carol Ann Moffat

Carol worked in the Sea Cliff Summer Theater and wanted to be an actress. Mickie Vaccaro remembers getting to know Carol when they both worked on the senior play, Stage Door. Mickie was in charge of props. She says of Carol, "Kids gave her a hard time. She was different. She was dreamy. She had the red hair. She didn't seem like she belonged." Mickie says Carol went into modeling and changed her name.

That is the last anyone has reported of her.

John Murray

photo by Gail Capobianco Schramm

John grew up on horseback, but he would spend his life wearing out shoes. John's family lived on the Bodmen estate in Brookville where his father worked and John and his three sisters played. John and his sisters had their own horses. "It was like living out in the old West, really." And being the older brother, "I was the king of the pile. John could do no wrong."

The drawback was that he had no other kids to play with. "I couldn't wait to go to school," he says, and throughout he enjoyed the community that school meant for him. If he had it to do over again, "I'd go back to school in a minute." His best friends in school were guys who knew how to have a good time—Brud Neice, Doug Andrews, Jimmy O'Donnell ('56), Bob Johnston, and Ted Rydzewski.

A year after leaving school John was at the Knotty Pine in Glen Head with several friends when a few girls from Glen Cove came in. He danced with a girl named Jo and in 1961 he married her. That same year he left his work in a Glen Cover store and became a Glen Head mail carrier. Jo and John's daughter Barbara was born in 1968.

For 21 years John would wear out many shoes delivering mail until he switched to a "mounted route" driving the mail around Brookville until he retired in 2001. As a walking mailman John became known as the Pied Piper because of the kids who would spy him on the street and walk along with him to their homes as he dropped off their mail. He was as much at ease talking to little kids as he was talking to good friends. "If you didn't like people and kids, you might as well have quit that job."

One day in his late thirties John was at the Glenwood fire department where he volunteered and decided to join several friends who were going out to play golf. He continues to play whenever he can. "I'm no Tiger Woods," he says, but he scores in the 90s and plays with his son-in-law and grandson. He also works part time at the firehouse and is an Advanced Medical Technician. Jo has retired after 29 years of work as a medical assistant. They both enjoy having their son and their two grandsons in nearby Lindenhurst.

John R Murray
30 Post St
Glen Head, NY 11545-1809
Johngolf30@aol.com

Peter Muttee

Photo by Nik Epanchin

There was Peter Swanson, Peter Merkel, and Peter Muttee and there was trouble. Maybe Miss Comfort had made him and Pete Swanson the butt of one of her stern lectures on missing homework, but in any case "There was a little feeling of animosity" the day they decided that it would be fitting retribution to wrap a rock with leaves and stuff it up her tail pipe and rearrange her spark plug wires. This they did in broad daylight, then sat in Pete Mutte's car a few hundred feet away. They enjoyed the big bang when the engine fired, then the *puta sputa poot puta* when the engine struggled to turn the drive shaft. They survived the chewing out they got by the principal. He did not take the approach to two other teachers who were known for their discipline. "I was in Mr. Driscoll's class. I found if you did what you were supposed to do he wasn't a problem at all" He took the same approach with the matron of math, Miss Kittelberger.

Speaking of Peter and Peter, it's also worth mentioning only two boys had the panache to wear bow ties for the yearbook pictures, both named Pete—Swanson and Muttee.

Being preoccupied with such creative ventures and life outside school and Carole Brown, Pete had no idea at age 17 where he would go after high school. When school crowding brought split sessions and free afternoons, he and Bob Soper worked at the Associated supermarket by Cozy Corner to earn pocket money. In summer he scrubbed boat bottoms at the Yacht Club. The money gave him the freedom he wanted to choose his own clothes, go to the movies or take Carole out for a soda.

Pete and John Broderick made their final push for graduation together after Pete's mother locked them into a room to study for the Regents exam. Pete found John one of his first jobs, launch boy at the Yacht Club, and at our 25th reunion he reintroduced John to Barbara Schmidts, now John's wife.

In the fall of 1957 went to Delhi Agricultural and Technical Institute to study building construction. He was out in two years but the job he had that first summer dried up and he figured, "If I goof off, I'll get drafted." He volunteered. His two years with artillery survey had almost ended when President Kennedy responded to the building of the Berlin Wall by declaring a national emergency and prolonging service terms. In February '62 Pete was out and working for a surveying company on the new railroad grading near Hicksville. In '64 he became a construction coordinator at the World's Fair site in Flushing. From there he went into school construction and finally to work for Nassau County. For most of 32 years with the county he was overseeing the installation of new sewer lines. As he neared retirement in 2000, he began Sea Cliff Carpentry, a home improvement company operated with son Robert.

One day in 2003 Pete was soaping up in the shower when he felt an unusual lump in one breast. The doctor thought it was a cyst, but soon Peter's surgeon had him lying down while he removed a lump of tissue for lab work. Three days later he learned he had breast cancer. He and Carole had Thanksgiving dinner and the next day Pete was on the operating table. The surgery was soon followed by six months of chemotherapy, then thirty days of radiation. After the last five days of extra-intensive radiation he looked at himself. "It looked like I had a piece of alligator hide."

After that experience Pete says he has even less patience for postponing what he wants to do. He and Carol take their kayaks out on the harbor, walk twice a day, ski, and hunt together. They've been on river cruises on the Rhine and Danube in Europe and Windjammer cruises in the Caribbean. In 2008 they celebrated 46 years of marriage, a union as important to him today as any event in his life. Pete and Carole have traveled together, hunted together, and together planned many of the logistics of a fine 51st class reunion.

Peter A. Muttee
57 Clinton St.
Sea Cliff, NY 11579

Edwin Neice

Photo by Nik Epanchin   Photo from Glen Cove Record Pilot

Brud's family and their garage by the corner of Glen and Roslyn Avenues was a fixture of our time in Sea Cliff and Brud's roots were deep.   He grew into the community he loved. The strongest and most central civic organization in Sea Cliff has always been its volunteer fire department, and Brud rose through the ranks.   As the Class of '57 convened in the fire house for the first session of its 51st reunion, Brud's familiar face looked over the class from the gallery of former fire chiefs.

His sister Carol (Neice) Snayd wrote of him:

Brud was a true Sea Cliffite.   He lived for this mile square village.   Brud touched the lives of many people.   He served as chief of the Sea Cliff Fire Department, (his picture was on the wall where your class gathered on the first night of the 51st reunion).   He was also chief of the Sea Cliff Auxiliary Police Department.   He gave 100% to anything he did.

Brud enjoyed fishing for relaxation, locally and at Montauk Point where he vacationed almost every year with his family.

Most local residences knew Brud as manager of Frank's Beer And Soda in Glen Cove, where he worked for 38 years.   He started making deliveries while in high school.   He was also an owner of K C Gallaghers (the Old Pine Tree Bar and Grill, better known as "Mom Longo's")   That was always his passion to own a bar and he made it come true.

Brud, of course, was also dedicated to his family, his wife Peggy and his children Elain and Kenny.   Local journalist and historian Carol Griffin ('56) reported that "Kenny's receiving his pilot's license made Brud swell with pride and tears formed in his eyes the first time he saw Kenny fly."

Brud died February 18, 1997 at age 58. At a Sea Cliff Fire Department service after Brud's death, his daughter Elaine said she was very proud to have "followed in his footsteps" and become a firefighter.   Over 100 firefighters from Sea Cliff and neighboring departments attended his funeral.   At his funeral mass Father Michael Torpey of St. Boniface summed up his place in Sea Cliff saying, "Brud was a part of everyone's life."

R I P

Lola Normington

Lo-Lo was diminutive, light hearted, and liked by most in the class. Her size did not keep her away from sports (which, for girls, were run by the equally diminutive Marjorie Maple). She was close to Linda Lloyd who has also disappeared, and Sandi Freedman, who has not. Her father owned and ran the Avon Bar on Glen Cove Road. Horses were one of Lola's passions.

Richard Norwich

"Knox could shoot the eyes out of a basket in 7th, 8th and 9th grde."   That's how teammate
Bob Johnston remembers him.   And as a soccer fullback he had a booming foot.   Knox
lived with his mother and his father, a Long Island Lighting Company employee, in a
humble apartment in the old converted hotel building off Prospect Avenue which also
housed Sea Cliff's long time luminary Charlie Hix.   Knox loved being near the beach
where he was an avid fisherman and where he knew all the best places for digging
bloodworms and sandworms and softshell crabs that we used for bait.

Knox fell in love with Bette Kreidemaker during high school and they married in May
1959.   Knox worked for the New York Transit Authority in maintenance.   He and Bette
had twins, a boy and a girl, in 1960, another son in 1961 and a girl in 1967.

To give the kids a better environment, they moved to Monroe, NY about 70 miles north of
the city and Knox commuted.   He also became an avid deer hunter and a good one.   His
other pastime was building and racing go-carts.   After divorce in 1985 he continued to
work with the NYTA.

He died in March 2003.

R I P

Judith Olsen

To be a really good singer, you have to know what you are singing about and believe in it with passion. That's how our "best dancer" also became a member of one of the nation's outstanding collegiate choirs—Augustana College's A Cappella Choir that was invited to sing on several continents. Judy didn't need a guidance counselor to help her choose a college. She had inner guidance. Her Lutheran faith was strong and she applied only to Augustana in South Dakota where she majored in French and English and minored in biology.

That was the end of her romance with her high school boyfriend Oogie (Ogden) Smith ('55). He and Judy had been part of the religious group Young People coordinated by Ralph and Natalie Howell in Sea Cliff. Oogie had graduated and gone to Colorado School of Mines. South Dakota's early winter and sub-zero temperatures were new to Judy, but "After the first snowfall (in early October), I learned to focus on things other than the weather." In addition to touring the US and Europe with the choir, she co-edited the college yearbook and worked on its newspaper, and was inducted into the senior honorary society for academic and leadership achievement.

After college she roomed with two girlfriends from Augustana in suburban Minneapolis where she taught French and English at Osseo HS. One day her roommates invited friends for dinner with Judy designated as cook. One of the guests was Ron Christian, a student from Luther Seminary in St. Paul. Judy says, "I guess he liked my cooking...and still does!" The supper was in September, their wedding the next June. After Ron's graduation and ordination they moved to San Diego for his one year internship, then to his first parish in Maryland. Since 1969 they have been in Virginia where Ron started Lord of Life Lutheran Church in Fairfax. To start the church Ron had to canvass the area to find a congregation, but with Judy at his side, he has been so successful that the church has grown large and now occupies two sites.

As pastor and wife Judy says, "We live in a 'glass house' that has not always been easy."

She was careful to be sure her children led normal lives instead of trying to mold them into model kids.   Both children now have their own families. When the kids began school Judy studied to be a librarian.   "Several postgraduate degrees later, my career path eventually took me into school administration in Fairfax County Public Schools."   Judy has been librarian, supervising librarian, principal, elementary coordinator, and a cluster director. Teaching, however, she could never leave.   "It's in my DNA. Even though I was an administrator for so many years, I always taught staff development classes as often as possible."   The only level she never taught was 7th and 8th grades.

She recently retired but continues to do occasional consulting.   Meanwhile she also tasted politics when she and the kids became involved in Ron's 2002 campaign to become the Democratic nominee for the Virginia state senate.   "The whole family walked neighborhoods, made signs, did phone bank duty, and hosted meet-and-greet parties. We were totally exhausted by the last day.   We relied on the goodness of so many people to get out the vote, march in the parades, hand out campaign material, etc. It was a firsthand learning experience for us in what America is all about."   Ron lost by a narrow margin and they may try again.

Judy's zest for dancing was fired when she took after school lessons for 8th graders, lessons our other best dancer, Bob Clarke, also attended.   "Bob and I danced a lot together, so we were comfortable 'showing off' a bit. I still enjoy dancing, but now we only dance at weddings.   Ho, hum..."

Ron has also retired from the church he founded, but he and Judy continue as active members of the congregation just as she was in Our Savior's Lutheran Church in Glen Head.   "My faith has been the grounding factor in my life and I continue to be grateful for each day and the opportunities afforded me."

Judith Olson Christian
10001 Manor Place
Fairfax, VA   22032
christianjudy@msn.com

Janice Painter

Looking back Janice is thankful that in school she took typing and business courses, because she needed "a few pennies." When split sessions started, her coursework earned her a part time job with the Hawes Insurance Agency in Sea Cliff. She liked it so much she decided she should leave school and work full time, but Mrs. Hawes sat her down and said, "Janice, you can't do that. You have a mother and she's worked very hard." That was an understatement. One day when she was about eleven her father, a Painter by name and painter by profession, came home from work, went upstairs to lie down before supper and died of a heart attack. To support Janice and her older brother Bill and younger brother Gordon, her mother took a job in Marie Burke's dress shop in Locust Valley. Billy took care of Janice and Gordon.

Janice knew immediately Mrs. Hawes was right, but by 1957 she also knew she wanted to continue in the insurance business and she did. The Hawes Agency, she says, gave her excellent on-the-job training. "Everybody thinks the Hawse Agency was a little agency in Sea Cliff, but their agents were all over. I had a lot of opportunities because of them."

Janice, well trained in insurance and looking for new challenges, left Hawes to work with the Greyhound company's insurance business as an underwriter. These were the years of women's liberation movements, but Janice says, "it didn't help me at all. Insurance underwriting was a man's world." She nevertheless broke the glass ceiling in that part of the business, becoming Greyhound's first woman sales rep in the US.

She left Greyhound in 1981 as an accomplished sales person. She took up a new career selling durable medical goods. "I was a very good seller. I believed in what I sold." She stayed in that business for twelve years before retiring, or almost. By chance the Hawes Agency was about to wind up their business and Bob and Abbey asked her to come back and help.

She now lives with her brother Gordon in the new and rapidly growing Gulf shore Florida town of Spring Hill. Her mother died in 2008 at age 102 plus, in full possession of her faculties. "She never had a primary care doctor and she never took a pill," Janice said. Janice is a walker, and one day while walking she came upon "a dog tied to a tree without food and water. I kept going back to see about it and finally, I asked the owner, 'Would you mind if I walked your dog?'" She enjoyed the walking company and volunteered with the local ASPCA for whom she walks dogs and feeds them.

She would not return to Long Island or Sea Cliff, but "I tell everybody down here that I grew up in the best village in the United States."

Janice Painter
5373 Frost Rd
Spring Hill, FL 24606-1229

Kay Parks

Photo by Nancy Epanchin

Kay's grandfather emigrated from Ireland, and when he had saved enough from his job with the New York subway system, he and his wife bought a small hotel in Sea Cliff. In 1927 he and Kay's father built the house Kay grew up in on 14th Ave. Like many Americans of that time, they sensed a good investment in Long Island's growth and bought a lot farther out on the North Shore in Southold where Kay and her family would spend many vacations.

The narrow streets in the center of Sea Cliff with their houses large and small created a thick Mulligatawny soup of families and children and the Parks family was in the middle of it on 14th Avenue. With Central Park and its canopy of red oaks and tulip poplars next to the Youth Center and a few blocks from the beach and from stores, and with Central Avenue being one of the preferred sledding streets, kids had everything, including close bonds with each other. Bob Platt's family lived across the street and invited her and sister Ginny over every Tuesday night to watch the Milton Berle show on one of the first televisions in the area. "My parents just gave in and bought us a black and white Dumont tv." Her family "lived from pay check to pay check" and when they had guests coming, her mother went to the Royal Scarlet grocery on the corner of 12th and Roslyn Avenues and asked Coach Ray Conlin's father and mother, the proprietors, to sell them food on credit, and they did.

Kay's real love was roller skating, and as soon as she saw skate dancing, that was for her. "When I was 15 the only thing I wanted for Christmas was white shoe skates." She has a picture of herself with the box and the skates held high. Despite a limited family budget, her father took her to Mineola for lessons. One reason she did not date much in high school were those trips to Mineola and the Friday night Mineola Swing for skate dancers. The other reason was that on many weekends the family packed up and drove to Southold to work on the summer cottage her father was building—a project inspired by Richard Robson's family that already had a cottage there. "Another reason I didn't date," Kay says, "is because we disappeared on the weekends to go to Southold to help my brother build the house.   Besides, I liked going out with groups. The more the merrier.   Safety in numbers."   In one of those unexpected chain of events, the arrival of Guy T. Pinkard as our biology and chemistry teacher changed Kay's post-graduation plans.   Mr. Pinkard had started a biology exchange program between his old school in Milltown, Alabama and ours. He had taken four of us to Alabama in '55 to meet students there.   Our senior year, one of those students, Wayne Roberts, came to Sea Cliff.   He and Kay married in November after he had joined the Air Force.   During his service they lived at Ft. Monmouth, NJ, then Japan for eighteen months. In Japan Kay worked at the US Army hospital as secretary to the Chief of Personnel.   She was in that post when a US jet hit an Okinawan school and dozens of burn victims were brought in by chopper.   Kay and Wayne's daughter Dawn was born in Japan 18 1960, the same year they returned to America.   Three years later they were divorced.   Kay loved medical terminology and continued in her career as a transcriptionist for a variety of doctors from orthopedic docs to brain surgeons.

When her daughter graduated from high school in '78 Kay said to her, "If you don't want to go to college, I'm going to go."   She worked nights to pay her way through Florida Southern University, sharing her transcriptionist job with a friend who worked days.   Her last semester in '82 she attended Richmond College in London to study archeology and English.   She graduated Cum Laude.   Her daughter Dawn went to college later and graduated Summa Cum Laude with a double major in math and engineering.   She works with Lockheed in the Apache program, specializing in target acquisition systems.

Before that Dawn had acquired a new father.   Kay was living in a rented place in Orland and says her landlady couldn't wait to introduce her to a single neighbor who was a full time member of the Florida National Guard who ."knew that we were meant for each other."   She says she had found "a jewel."   She married George Rice in November '66 and moved into their new home between downtown and the airport, and soon to be a half hour from Disney Land. George adopted Dawn Marie.

Kay continues to work part time for two commercial real estate companies who agreed to let her have summers off to spend with George at the Parks' family cottage in Southold, Long Island.   At the cottage they enjoy swimming, rowing and paddling their two kayaks as well as reading and gardening.   Kay says she was particularly surprised and pleased when Pete and Carole Muttee asked her to spend a night with them so she could attend the reunion on her way back to Florida.   Since they had not seen each other in 50 years, "They no idea whether I was an ax murderer."

Kay Parks Rice
2617 Lando La.
Orlando, FL. 32806
Kathle5195@aol.com

Virginia Parks

Like sister Kay, Ginny formed her first close friendships in their 14ᵗʰ Avenue neighborhood and nearby, but often they were different friends than Kay's, and the sisters went quite different ways in school and afterward.   Ginny and Pat Mills spent a lot of time together in grade school and on into high school, studying together, walking around town, listening to Rock 'n Roll and classical music.   Ginny also recalls playing hooky with some of the boys.   She excelled at the clarinet and Mr. Ryder came to her home to give private lessons.   Clarinet was his instrument and he enjoyed playing with another clarinetist. Neighbors and passers-by remarked on the well played popular music flowing from the Parks house.   Ginny also took lessons in sewing from her mother and a professional.   In Mrs. Scudder home economics class she produced a pair of slacks and lined black corduroy vest so well done Mrs. Scudder did not believe it was her work.

The Marching Band often included 14th Avenue on their parade route and Ginny enjoyed seeing her mother and father and the neighbors on the porches and in their yards waving encouragement.   In general, Ginny seems to have enjoyed a festive crowd whether it was assembled for the Marching Band or to go sledding on the family toboggan when snow covered nearby Central Avenue.   She recalls the faces in the sledding groups—Richie Loftus, Eddie Capobianco, Allan Schwartz and several others.

Dobkins Pharmacy's soda fountain was a natural place for a sociable girl to work, although she says that she began without knowing how to mix sodas.   She recalls, as I do not, that the author of this piece who had spent many hours hanging out at the fountain and watching the girls mix sodas gave her instructions.

Ginny, of course, enjoyed summers at the family's Southold cottage which her father had built when she was about nine.   One year she learned to water-ski there after she bought a speedboat from Abbey Hawes and had her father tow it out to Southold.   Her social life in Sea Cliff was also often lively.   She found some satisfaction in her "mad crush" on Richie Robson when he turned to her for a party date to avoid a girl who also had a crush on him. She describes herself, Annette Caselli, Gail Capobianco, and Fred Burns as "the 4

Musketeers" in their various sojourns.   Annette's parents, she says, were quite strict, but both worked and before they came home the musketeers would slip in and "have a few drinks," which for Ginny one day became a few too many Crème de Cacaos and Fred having to dispose of the emptied bottle.   They also haunted Frank's Alibi in Hicksville for its Italian food.   She says she was also smoking two packs of cigarettes a day.

Her notably bad binge should be paired with a notably good drink.   After school Ginny's friend Cynthia Turnbull got her a job as a filing clerk at Sperry.   Cynthia, who made travel reservations at the company, also convinced her to vacation jointly in Mexico.   Over champagne on the plane Ginny met a man going to Mexico to see a teacher friend there.   When she returned to the states he called and "pestered me."   She married Clyde Schrempp, a mechanical designer, in May 1963.

With her daughter Karen on the way in 1965 Ginny gave up work and smoking.   Son James arrived in '68, Ginny used the embroidery and sewing talents she had learned in Sea Cliff and began producing Barbie Doll clothes and which became the subject of a *Newsday* article.   She also sewed and embroidered communion dresses.   Most of the work she did for her own enjoyment, but she also occasionally sold on the Island.   Clyde's work took him to Grumman, to Electric Boat in Connecticut and for most of the time to a Hicksville manufacturer of cases and containers.

Fifteen years ago Ginny and Clyde moved to North Carolina when he took early retirement and needed to wear a pacemaker.   The kids had grown up and gone out on their own and Long Island taxes had grown but would not leave.   Near Hendersonville they built their own custom home and found their community of Etowah "a little Long Island" with so many northern transplants.   In 2008 they moved to a senior community in nearby Fletcher, NC.   Ginny continued to enjoy her flower gardening and her herb growing.   Her son James became a mechanic and carpenter in Roanoke, VA. Her daughter Karen has been with the New York City police, married to another policeman.   Ginny came to love the small towns and mild climate of Carolina as well as its beaches and says, "I don't think I could ever go back to LI."   In 2008 a tumor began growing in Clyde's brain and he was buried on January 29, 2009.   They had led a quiet and uneventful life in Carolina.   "We just enjoyed our retirement years."

Virginia Parks
128 Foxtrot Path
Fox Glen
Fletcher, NC 28732-7020

Anne Pascucci

Anne knew what she could do when even teachers and guidance counselors did not. She remembers a biting remark that biology teacher Pinkard said. After graduation she saw him in a store and reminded him that he had failed her in biology. "He replied that I had 'failed' myself. How true." Nor was she happy when Dr. Shulman, later a guidance counselor, showed no support for her plans to go to college. After all she had been in one of his easier English classes and hadn't been too serious about it. But no sooner was she out of school and in college than she became serious about education. Whoever wrote in her yearbook profile that as a profession she would "sit on the boss's lap as a top notch secretary" thought wrong. Anne has been serious about it for over 50 years as a lifelong teacher. Today each of her four children, one a Ph.D, engages in teaching in some form.

"I have to say there were many reasons I loved coming from a small town like Sea Cliff," Anne says. "We had the opportunity to be able to walk to everything; the school, the library, the church, the post office, the soda fountain and the beach." In high school Anne had a lot of friends, but she was particularly close to Nancy Baker and Linda Lloyd. She and Gail Capobianco were good friends the last two years of high school. Gail says she had "a fine sense of humor and if we were talking, she always had a quick response." Anne served as a maid of honor in Gail's wedding.

Anne is grateful that she "had very dedicated teachers in college and I loved the profession from the start." Even with four children she managed to be a substitute teacher. When her last two children, twins, were born, she did stay home until they began school. Her first year out of college she taught in Glens Falls, NY before moving to East Islip where she teaches fifth grade today at John F. Kennedy Elementary School..

One career was not enough for Anne, so she also became a practical nurse and from the mid 80s until 2006, she worked in a Huntington nursing home on weekends and in the summer months. "People used to ask me which I liked better nursing or teaching. They both had to do with helping people, but, in teaching at least I get to sit down once in a while." She was 68 when she decided to go back to having only one career.

Anne Conte
26 Ramondo Lane
Smithtown, NY 11787   littleboo98@yahoo.com

Daniel Pawul

"Give him a car, a little gas and away he goes," the yearbook says, and Danny always went his own way.   He came to Sea Cliff after only two and a half years at St. Boniface because, "I was a wise ass.   I got beat up with the pointer, the ruler, the erasers.   My mother finally said, 'You gotta take a straight walk down the street to the other school.'"   Even the formidable Dorothea Comfort couldn't hold him down.   "I took detention class from her," he says.   He would sit in detention hall, often with Billy Duffy ('55) and do things "just to bust her chops."   He gave Dave Schweers a run for the money in narrowly losing the superlative, "Teachers' Trial," although he swears he does not know why he caused so many trials and tribulations.

Danny's parents had emigrated from Poland when they were teenagers, sponsored by someone in Queens, but they eventually came to Sea Cliff and opened the Quality Meats butcher shop on Glen Cove Avenue and bought a home at 41 Franklin Ave.   Danny worked for the family shop while in school, a job that knocked him out of a basketball season.   "I was forced to work in the butcher shop.   I nearly got my fingers taken off when I was cleaning the slicer machine and a young lady walked by and that year I couldn't play basketball."   A nearby doc sewed his fingertips back on his left hand and he earned his varsity letter.

After graduation Danny went to Farmingdale technical college for for drafting and math, but "A female got involved and I quit that."   For the next few years he had odd jobs, one of which was Tappen Beach lifeguard.   Basically he lived at home and says, "I didn't take any responsibility.   I goofed around, had a good time" until the US Army drafted him 1963.   "I took tests and all of a sudden the computer said I was qualified" for chemical warfare training.   The Army assigned him to Maryland's Aberdeen Proving grounds, but he often traveled around the country "escorting things that didn't exist.   One time I was in a Moon Suit for several days."   His responsibility was to rescue the researchers if anything spilled.   Beyond that, he says he signed a statement saying he would not talk about the specifics of what he did, and he still won't.   Looking back on how many in our time evaded and avoided the draft by a variety of ruses, Danny says, "I did my part. I didn't claim to be religious or married. I did my time."

The rest of his life, he says, is simple.   When he finished his two years of service, "All of a sudden I worked for UPS and 37 years later I was retired."   Danny worked in the UPS package handling operations.   He also got married in 1968 and divorced in 1971 and for consolation bought himself a Corvette convertible.   He remarried in 1973 and his daughter Diane was born that same year.   She now works in pharmaceuticals and lives in Maryland. The next year Danny gave up smoking and drinking after he found himself driving home at night with his eyes closed.   "It was too much.   I did it cold turkey."   Danny's wife died in 2004.

Since then Danny has again been going through life in his own way, accompanied only by his dog, half border collie, half pointer, and three tanks of tropical fish.   "I get up when I want to. I go to sleep when I want to.   I have my dog. I have my tropical fish."   He says he has the usual problems that come with this age, including arthritis in the joints.   "If a ten dollar bill falls on the floor I'll bend down to pick it up but I can't stand back up." Nevertheless, he enjoys doing what he wants, when he wants and being his own boss.   "I see these people shopping together and the poor guy gets browbeat.   I think I'm okay."

Daniel Pawul
2082 Stuyvesant Ave
East Meadow, NY 11554

Evelyn Piat

Evy came to our class in our senior year. Janice Painter, one of Evy's close friends, recalls that Evy's mother was a New York City school official, her father a doctor. Our yearbook says she hoped to be a model. To date, we have found very little information on her life after leaving school. Two or three friends prefer not to talk about the course of her life except to say it ended tragically.

Evie attended Glenwood Landing elementary, and some of her hardships started there. A classmate from 4th grade remembers that Evy's physical development was far ahead of others in the class and that boys began to make fun of her in unpleasant ways, and that their teacher, a man, had no control over the class and their teasing. She also went to live for a while with her father in Florida, then returned to live with her mother and attend Sea Cliff High.

She and Ron Santonastasi were close for a while and he and a few other friends tried to help when she had emotional problems that may have led to attempted suicide and had to be hospitalized. Soon after leaving school she married Artie Parsons and they lived in Glen Head. She had a daughter named Katharine. (Evy's middle name in our yearbook is 'Kathryn" but in other publications, Katharine, as is her daughter's.)

Below is her obituary from the *Glen Cove Record-Pilot*.

Evelyn Katharine Parsons
Evelyn Katharine (Piat) Parsons, of Glen Cove, died on Nov. 22, 1997. Born in NYC. Mother of Katharine. Sister of Suzanne Canetti, Eileen Haden, James and Robert Piat. Arrangements were made by the Whitting Funeral Home, Glen Head. Funeral service. Interment Roslyn Cemetery.

R I P

Robert Platt

Bob grew up in that central part of Sea Cliff that was a rich and thick mix of houses and people and that special category of people called kids.   The place had a house, activities and peers for everyone.   Across the street from Bob were his classmates Kay and Ginny Parks. At the end of the block lay Central Park, a hub of impromptu play, and across from it the Youth Center for teenagers. Boy Scout Troop 43 headed by the dynamic and well organized Ed Bolitho enrolled Bob and held its meetings at the Youth Center and its outside games in the park.   In high school Bob would play hooky with Ginny Parks and John Maloney.   The bluff by Tilley's boathouse, the "18 Trails" and its rope swing hung from the high branch of a big red oak was a favorite hideout.   Pete Merkel was another comrade.   He and Pete once scavenged a bumper for the '34 Ford owned by Pete's older brother who had left home, and they carried it across the North Shore Country Club to Glenwood Landing for installation.

Bob's father was one of Sea Cliff's craftsmen. He built the wooden bodies that were popular for the new family car of the middle and upper middle class—the station wagon. On Saturdays he would often take Bob to the beach to dig bait worms near the pumping station then out on the water to fish.   On slow days Bob would complain of boredom with no fish biting.   He says it took some growing up before, "I realized Dad was out there to relax."

After graduation Bob went into the Air Force to learn electronics.   He trained at Scott Air Force Base in Illinois, came home to marry his high school steady, Bette Gildersleeve, then had duty stations in South Dakota with the Strategic Air Command (SAC) that stood ready to retaliate against any Soviet invasion.   Bob installed radios in B-14 bombers.

Bob and Bette's son Bill was born in 1960.   Bette's father worked in the Sea Cliff post office, and after the Air Force when they returned to Sea Cliff, Bob began delivering mail. Since that job, "kind of bored the heck out of me," he began talking to an Air Force recruiter and signed up for another four years knowing he would get advanced electronics training.   After stints in Alaska and Texas, he finished his service in at McDill AFB near Tampa, Florida.

When he came out he went into the relatively new industry of cable television, beginning as an installer and rising to plant manager in his fifteen years with the company.   While living in Florida he and Bette divorced in '79 and Bob remarried, this time to Connie May Chapman, a colleague in his plant who had two children.   His company, Stork Cable TV transferred him to New Jersey and after a year to Richmond, Virginia.   When the company laid him off in the '82 recession, he and Connie formed their own company—Egan May Originals—to make custom furniture.   (Bob's middle name is Egan.)   They began by working on restoration and repair for an antique shop whose owner was a recent widow. When she decided to close the shop a few weeks later, Bob and May took it over.   "Things just took off from there," he says.   They eventually moved the company to their own home and workshop. On twelve wooded acres near Richmond they built the log house they had always wanted to retire in.   Connie, who managed much of the business detail, died of Leukemia in 2006.

In 2007 Bob married his present wife Jean, a friend from church.   Finding themselves with two homes, they sold both and they are now refurbishing a recently purchased house.   Bob stays very active in his Southern Baptist church, and in February 2009 Bob again acquired a business license and has returned to making furniture and general woodworking, back to his father's profession.

Bob Platt
12331 Natural Bark Dr.
Chesterfield, VA 23832

Colette Relation

All that divides Sea Cliff from Glen Cove is the center line of Glen Cove Avenue, and Colette's parents moved across the street so she and her sisters could go to kindergarten in Sea Cliff. They had been living in the big house connected to her grandparents' butcher shop and bar. From first to third grades she attended St. Boniface. Her father did not want the kids to go to Sea Cliff school but when they got "nits in our hair" he said, "If you get nits in your head again, you can go." When they returned home a second time with a case of the nits, they transferred to Sea Cliff school. (Some of us remember that the fear of nits, head lice, caused our parents to ban us from attending the Cove Theatre because it had the nickname "Cootie Palace.")

In school her enthusiasms lay outside the classroom. That enthusiasm made her head JV cheerleader in our sophomore and junior years. "I wasn't that great in school," she says. "I was good at gym and I was good at lunch." She often worked in the school cafeteria in her free period, then when her turn to eat came, she received a free lunch. She also worked at the St. Christopher Home for children next to the North Shore Country Club. She says she had few girlfriends and most of her friends were boys. One of her few good friends among the girls was Lee Berroyer. They drifted around town together having "a lot of fun" and spent many evenings together at the Youth Center.

In our junior year Colette and Richie Smith left school and married. Richie took a job driving a milk delivery truck. Their son Richard was born in 1956 and now lives in Roanoke, VA working as head of maintenance in the post office. Their daughter Jill born in '62 works in a home for handicapped adults. Their son Ronald born in '61 owns his own truck on Long Island doing contract pick up and delivery.

In 1963 Richie and Colette divorced but remain very good friends and occasionally visit. He lives in Delaware. "He's like my brother I never had." Colette began to work at Roman's clothing store in Huntington. In the earlyl 80s friends called and invited her to a party at their home, saying "Two guys coming from Flushing. Maybe you can hook up with one of them." One didn't show, but she did hook up with the other, Richard Cuozzo and four years later they married. Richard had never been married and had no children. Colette's three kids loved him. Colette and Richard soon had a son, Gary.

In 1987 with Gary in elementary school, Colette returned to her old job—working in the high school cafeteria and "I loved it. I could relate to the kids in the school." Richard retired from his plumbing work and began to work part time driving a school bus. Today they have nine grandchildren from 3 to 30. Colette is still close to her identical twin sisters, Marsha and Sandra and they celebrate their March birthdays with a trip every year. With her daughter she enjoys attending NASCAR races though Richard says he doesn't want to sit and watch "cars going round and round a track." With Richard Colette enjoys visiting nearby casinos at Orient Point, Yonkers, Connecticut and Atlantic City.

In 2000 Colette battled her way through colon cancer and chemotherapy. When she had breast cancer three years ago she lost her hair to chemotherapy and her grandchildren told her, "You look like Uncle Fester." (The famously bald member of the ghoulish Addams Family.) She laughed with them and said, "I hope it comes in better than when it went out. Wished for curls. It was a big joke." Colette still laughs about it. "When you got cancer, you gotta fight," she says. "I'll be here forever and ever. Only the good die young."

Colette Cuozzo
6 Eldorado Drive
E. Northport , NY 11731

Margie Repucci

"She projected something that she really wasn't," said one of her good friends. Marge matured early and with a figure that and a flirtatious friendliness that ignited fantasies in boys and won her few friends among the girls. Perhaps because of a strict home regime, Marge felt she could or should test her charms. Jim McKinley remembers that one day she came to St. Boniface wearing lipstick and scandalized the nuns, one of whom took sandpaper to her lips. Another classmate says, "Even in high school she was often the butt of vicious teasing and jokes by other girls . . . particularly in the gym locker room. She was a good-looking girl and woman, in a rather flamboyant style -- the Marilyn Monroe/Gina Lollobrigida model -- and that made her a target of resentment." And resentment led to cruelty. It started in Glenwood School where one classmate remembers stealing her falsies and flushing them down the toilet once and nailing them on a tree in the schoolyard another time. In Sea Cliff Kay Parks remembers when girls one time pushed Margie out of the locker room onto the gym floor in only her underwear when they knew the boys were waiting in the bleachers above for their turn to use the gym floor.

Margie grew up in a very traditional Italian Catholic family. Her father worked in construction and knew the hazards and pressures a girl like Margie would face. He was strict and protective. Margie never had a boyfriend during the school years. Yet a close friend says, "She absolutely adored her father." His death was one of the most devastating events in her life.

Margie left Sea Cliff and attended Oswego and New Paltz State Teachers Colleges. She married George "Gus" Hauser who had first come to Sea Cliff in summers with his parents. They had a daughter, then a son. George and a friend ran the Harlequin Restaurant in Sea Cliff for a few years. When Margie began teaching in Glenwood Elementary, one of the girls who harassed her in Glenwood had children in Margie's classroom. She went to talk to Margie and told her, "I am so sorry." Margie's reply was a friendly, "We were kids." Jim McKinley says that when "Marge was your friend, she was always your friend."

When the children were young George and Margie divorced. The following years were often hard for her, and classmates who met her around town said she seemed lonely and sometimes adrift. Another friend during these years says, "She had tremendous pride. Even when she hit bottom you would never ever have known she was depressed, which she was." She weathered the storms, met a man and moved to Florida. We know little of her life there with certainty except that she died there.

R I P

Richard Robson

Photo by Fred Feingold

Our yearbook described music, dancing, and singing as "habits [Richie] acquired during a long childhood." At least one member of our class remembers that just before he went on stage to sing, "A White Sports Coat and a Pink Carnation," he told her he would sing it for her, and he did (in case you remember that memorable performance and did not know the reason for its success). The following Christmas Eve he says, "I got in a car wreck returning from a gig in New York . . . , broke my nose, bled all over the jacket and had to throw it out."

In high school Dick proved himself a gentleman of great restraint one summer when the family vacationed in Southold. His father had inspired Kay and Ginny Parks' father to buy and build out there also. While the Robson's were renovating their own place they moved into the Parks' unfinished cottage. Dick and Kay shared adjoining rooms, but rooms divided only by the wall studs on which the sheetrock had not yet been applied. Kay says, "We were kind of prudish and we weren't touching any boys." Kay was one of several classmates who report Dick's good conduct and trustworthiness.

He left Sea Cliff High following the music, so to speak. "I was in Hempstead one day in Jan, 1958, it was cold, and as I passed by the Navy recruiter's offices, a first class Navy recruiter offered me a cup of coffee. Two days later I was in Boot Camp in Great Lakes, Ill. Just as cold, and the coffee was lousy, but I stuck with it for 28 years." When he enlisted he envisioned four years performing while fulfilling his military requirement and saving funds to study music in Potsdam, NY.

"On the second day of boot camp, I lined up with the rest of my platoon, and went by six sailors who gleefully stuck me in both arms with everything from tetnus toxoid to, well, who knows. Two other sailors were at the end of the line waving smelling salts to those who didn't make it through. I asked one of them what he was, and he responded, 'We are hospital corpsman.' Me, too. I said, and that afternoon, I changed my designator from HSMR (high school musician recruit) to HMR (hospitalman recruit)." In June '63 he also changed his social designation from single to married.

After his first four years Dick visited his best friend Doug Ransweiler who had married and was living in a NY apartment. Doug's wife's cousin, Helen Komoski from Glen Cove ('60), a nursing student, was also visiting. She had grown up two blocks from Dick, but they hadn't met. But soon they married. His medical training in the Navy would continue for many years. "From that second day in boot camp, I made sure I was on the good end of those needles." He became a Hospital Corpsman, Laboratory and Blood Bank Technician, combat Corpsman, Physician Assistant, then a commissioned officer during the Vietnam War. For thirteen years he served with the Marines and for two with the SeaBees. The Navy also paid for his bachelor's degree and then his Masters. Although he volunteered twice for Vietnam service, the Navy assigned him to "many hardship tours: Hawaii, Okinawa, Puerto Rico, Key West, North Carolina, California, Texas, New York" allowing him and Helen to visit Hong Kong, Guam, and Thailand among other places. Assigned to the lab school at the University of Virginia, Dick also held the rank of associate professor.

Dick retired after 28 years of service with the rank of Lieutenant Commander. He then worked eight years for the State of Florida, first with Health and Rehabilitative Services as a child support enforcement officer, later as General Services Manager. Dick's wife Helen now travels Central Florida as a nurse auditor for Blue Cross/ Blue Shield of Florida, recovering $1 to $2 million a year from improper insurance claims.

He and Helen live on the "Redneck Riviera" of Florida near Pensacola. Dick is a member of SERTOMA of Gulf Breeze and of the largest all male Mardi Gras *Krewe* in the Florida Panhandle, the Krewe of Lafitte. The Krewe members have built over 13 floats and its 250 some members entertain schools, senior citizens and other community groups. He also has his own Naval supplies business Gulf Breeze Marine Boat Sales, Inc. He no longer plays any instruments but he sings "around pianos at Christmas" and the music has clearly not gone out of his life.

Dick Robson
3009 Coral Strip Parkway
Gulf Breeze, Fl 3253
jrrobsonsr@bellsouth.net

from John Storojev:
I was a close friend of Richie, more so in Junior High (now called Middle School) but still good friends as SCH. He was a cool guy and knew how to make moves with the girls. We shared some crazy times. We'd exchange notes in Mr. Mathew's Latin class.
Consequently, Mathews saw me as a jerk and couldn't believe I could write as well as I did in his Lit class. He even accused me of plagiarizing! After the graduation ceremony, Richie

and I tanked up on champagne and got pretty high and somehow ended up running and shouting up and down the hills of a local golf course. My memory is rather hazy as one might imagine. Needless to say, being the neophyte drinkers that we were, we did not keep down the liquor too long. Hey, at least it was champagne and not Ripple! After school, he moved elsewhere and I never saw him again.

Theodore Rydzewski

Photo by Nik Epanchin

Ted came to Sea Cliff High from St. Boniface where the sisters kept his high spirits in check. "The sisters made you concentrate on what you were doing. Once I got to high school that went out the window." But he had learned how to learn and he had few troubles with teachers. One day when he got carried away with being "a hotshot senior" and was teasing underclassmen, "Mr. Matthews picked me up by shirt and pinned me against the blackboard and said you don't treat people that way." He still respects our former Marine English and Latin teacher. "After that I became a good little boy." Fair was fair and unfair was unfair. When Norman Ross, coaching soccer, once kicked a ball at him by surprise and caught him hard in the groin, Ted reared back and kicked the ball right back at Ross. Probably wearing his famous broad grin.

In his senior year, with the option to choose a couple of subjects of his liking, he joined one or two other boys in the Home Economics class. It wasn't the girls, he says. He decided maybe he should learn to cook. After graduation he ran deliveries to the big estates for Begatti's deli in Glen Cove. Then he and a friend decided to push up their draft selection and joined the Army. After 6 months in Georgia, he shipped out to the motor pool in Schweinfurt, Germany. The Army classified him as a mechanic "but I didn't know the first thing about mechanics." He won a transfer to the stock room. He and a few friends stayed out of the usual GI hangouts and found "off the wall places" including a dog kennel where they used to help the owners, bringing them coffee and cigarettes. In return their German friends took them around the region.

Free from the Army and working again for Begatti's, Ted accepted a blind date for the 1960's New Year's Eve Glenwood Fire Department party arranged for him by his sister-in-law Audrey Maass. On Valentine's Day 1961 he was engaged to Mary Jo and they married in 1962. Their first son Teddy was born in '64, Tommy three years later and their daughter after another three years. In 1972, after Mary Jo's father was killed in a work accident, they moved to her family house in Locust Valley. Ted left Begatti's for a job in Photocircuits that Jim LeFebvre helped him get, then he moved to Grumman Aircraft where he worked for the next 32 years, moving up from the stockroom to warehouse manager at the Green River plant. He enjoyed Grumman's well known generosity to its employees, but when Grumman merged with Northrup in 1994, Ted foresaw the reduction in management personnel and took early retirement. He retired to a job with the Town of Oyster Bay.

At Grumman's Ted worked for many years, 12 hours a day, 7 days a week and he learned another important lesson. When his kids were 6 or 7 and started playing T ball, he realized he had missed most of their early years. When they grew up he told them "When you get the chance, enjoy your kids when they're small." He says, "I think they're better parents than I was."

In 1982 a minor tendon injury while bowling almost killed him. His orthopedic doc sent him home with a crutch but soon he had phlebitis, then chest pains so bad he couldn't breathe. "They thought I was having a heart attack." The pulmonary embolism had been caused by blood clots moving to his lungs from his leg and he was in and out of the hospital for 42 days. He has also beaten prostate cancer after surgery in 2002, and with a re-do on his hip replacement he is playing golf again. He continues to work part time with the Town of Oyster Bay in the mail room and is still a member of the Locust Valley volunteer fire department that he joined 36 years ago. All three of his children have finished college and are in the middle of successful career--Tommy as a mechanical engineer, Teddy as a corporate accountant, and his daughter as national vice president of Arbonne Products. "The best investment I ever did was sending my kids to college." He's a proud father and grandfather of seven.

Ted Rydzewski
16 Ash St.
Locust Valley, NY 11560
tedjo@optonline.net

Nancy Jane Samuelson

Photos by Nik Epanchin

"You will go to college," said Oscar William Samuelson to his three daughters with unwavering resolution in his voice.   He and his wife had moved from Brooklyn's Bayridge section to Glenwood Landing a week before Pearl Harbor so that one day those words more likely would bear fruit.   And they did.   Each year C.W. Post campus of Long Island University bestows the Nancy Jane Meyer Honors Thesis Award on the outstanding thesis of the year.   That Meyer is our Nancy Jane Samuelson who also has a lounge in the honors program bearing her name.

She won no academic honors at Sea Cliff, but she won everyone's respect as a good student, an outstanding athlete, a team player on and off the court, and a font of good cheer, good humor, and personal warmth.   In addition to participating in most sports and being a cheerleader and twirler, she worked at Glen Head pharmacy after school and on weekends.

John Broderick worked with Nancy at the Glen Head Pharmacy and admired her in high school.   "I just thought Nancy was the greatest.   In high school she dated an older guy, Bob Engel, and he had gone into the Navy and when he came home everybody wanted to take a shot at him to see how tough he was. I always thought, 'that stinks' she's already going out with the older guys.   Every time I hear Frank Sinatra sing 'Nancy with the Laughing Face' I think about her."

After graduation Nancy left for Augustana College in South Dakota with Judy Olsen.   Her second year, however, she decided to attend school where the action was, in New York City.   She studied at Katherine Gibbs School and the following year began work as a secretary.   There she met a young man working in the CBS TV sports division, Stuart Meyer.   They married in 1964.   They soon moved to Long Island, first to Glen Cove, then to Locust Valley.   Their daughter Dena was born in 1969 and son Craig in 1973.   Nancy never left them any doubt that they would go to college.

Nancy also made sure her children were athletes.   Dena says her parents took her skiing when she was four.   She remembers her mom as a tennis player and a very graceful swimmer who took great pleasure in introducing them to the big waves and the undertow at Jones Beach. She can still feel herself there with the waves pushing her, then the undertow trying to pull her out to sea, Nancy holding each by the hand and everyone laughing.

Dena and Nancy grew very close. On weekends Nancy would often take her out for breakfast, then to window-shop at the mall and "just talk." And when Nancy cooked, "I'd just sit on the kitchen counter and hang out." Only later did Dena realize how important those talks were. Nancy and her sisters had taken piano lessons in Glenwood, and Nancy passed on her love of music by taking Dena to the city, just the two of them, to attend the children's concert series at Lincoln Center. They also enjoyed pop music together. Dena says, "I have fond memories of my mom and I turning up the radio really loud and belting out whatever was on the radio at that time." One of those songs was Donna Summer's "I Will Survive."

When Stuart passed his 42nd birthday he quipped to Nancy, "Ha, ha, I beat my dad." His father had died from a heart attack at age 42. The next year Stuart suffered a heart attack but survived. Nancy decided time had come for her to go to work, just in case. She became an assistant to the head of the honors program in the C.W. Post English Department. As she had been in high school, at Post Nancy again became a confidante for students. So many people in the local communities came to know and like Nancy and greet her on the street and in the stores that Stuart once asked Dena, "Who does your mom not know?" And when someone else in the family ran into an unexpected friend, he or she would say, "I did a Nancy today."

She never did finish a four year degree or have a professional career, but she became a source of inspiration and strength to many students. Like her father, she told her own children women should get a degree and have a career. Both finished LIU. Dina became a physical therapist. Craig works in sales in Chicago.
 The children had grown up and moved out of state when Nancy developed breast cancer in the mid 90s. Dena says, "She was extremely private" and she did not tell Dena or Craig. Signs of that cancer disappeared with treatment but at Christmas 1996 she was feeling sick. She had lung cancer. She died in March, 1997

Many class members were shocked and sad to hear that Nancy would not be at our reunion. Nancy wrote in my yearbook that she "hoped we'll be able to get together on vacations to talk over old times and to tell of the new." Most of us have missed that opportunity.

I will survive.Oh as long as I know how to loveI know I'll stay alive.I got all my life to liveand I got all my love to give.and I'll survive. I will survive. hey hey
(from "I Will Survive" written by Freddie Perren and Dino Fekaris)

R I P

Ronald Santonastasi

"We're nearly seventy and who needs to remember all that stuff," was Ron's initial response to being asked for information. For reasons he prefers not to elaborate, has quite thoroughly left Sea Cliff and Long Island behind but not the ambitions that started there. The short version of life he offers is, "I married a beautiful woman and lived happily ever after." His pursuit of happiness, however, deserves a larger description and has very much to do with Sea Cliff. As a kid Ron's father took him fishing on Long Island sound and he says he "never remembers not having a boat or going fishing." And he looked forward to having his own boat.

Ron gave some the impression of being a bit rough and rowdy outside of school. He dated Evy Piat our senior year, and Evy was going through what we'll describe only as a very bad time and personal crises. Dave Schweers was on a few dates with Ron and Evy and recalls, "He was just an angel and took care of her and took care of her."

The yearbook says he also was looking forward to "being a big business man with a still bigger bank account." He now has his own charter boat, and to whatever degree he satisfied the financial ambitions, he obviously had enough to create his own business.

After graduation Ron "did a little bit in Suffolk Community" and studied at San Jose State University in California. The more important education, he says, was studying for his sea captain's license and fulfilling Coast Guard qualifications to captain a 100 ton boat. That was made possible because almost 35 years ago he began to work in Silicon Valley and "got a little bit lucky." As the Roman philosopher Seneca observed 2000 years ago, "Luck is what happens when preparation meets opportunity." Jefferson had a slightly different version, "I'm a great believer in luck, and I find the harder I work, the more I have of it."

His luck began at Photocircuits in Glen Cove where he and local friends worked on the production line. One of them was John Davila, a Puerto Rican immigrant who went to

Silicon Valley and developed his own line of printed circuits. Ron became part of his effective management team along with another Sea Cliff native. Soon they had three plants turning out quality products.

Only part of Ron's luck, however, was in business. Perhaps the more important part was finding his wife Jennie, who was marketing IT software. Throughout his business life Ron says, "I pursued my ultimate game--to have my own boat, take people out and have fun. I've always been an ocean guy." He and Jennie now run their own 40 foot luxury motor yacht "The Bequia" (pronounced beck way) on Monterrey Bay, sailing out of Santa Cruz. They named the boat after the small island in the Caribbean's Grenadines that Ron and Jennie fell in love with. Jennie is the marketing director for their business, Park Place Excursions. Besides fishing, they specialize in introducing guests to the wonders of Monterey Bay National Sanctuary Reserve so well described by John Steinbeck.

Ron and Jennie live in the seaside village of Capitola. Their web site says, "The ocean is their love, and their desire to enrich others lives with the beauty of the Monterey Bay National Sanctuary Reserve is an exciting one for both of them." Sea Cliff is far behind him. "We're almost 70 years old, and what's so important about remembering that?"

Captain Ron Santonastasi
825 Balboa #103
Capitola, California 95010http://www.parkplaceexcursions.com/
captrjs@parkplaceexcursions.com

George Schmersal

George received the first 2007 e mails announcing our belated reunion.   He and his wife Caryl had attended her 50th in 2007 and looked forward to ours.   He died on October 13, 2007.

At school George had enjoyed math, his trumpet, and his blue Plymouth.   After graduation he attended a bible college in Nyack, NY where he met Caryl.   They were married ten days after graduation in her hometown of New Brighton, PA and George never returned to Sea Cliff to live.   But he said that the town of Beaver where he taught for 37 years was "not unlike Sea Cliff" with its one square mile of territory and its narrow streets. Caryl also taught school, but in New Brighton.   George and Caryl had one daughter and two sons.   For 38 years they lived in the farming community of New Sewickley Township in western Pennsylvania.   "I was born in New York City and after growing up in its suburb, it rather surprised me to end up on the fringe of Appalachia."

George began his teaching with elementary school science before he and a colleague developed a computer program.   After that he taught computer operations in second through sixth grades enthusiastically for 15 years.   He and Caryl loved to travel and took a total of 14 cruises.   In 1999 he suffered a severe heart attack with major damage.   Caryl says, "We always felt from then   on that each day was a gift from God, because I could have lost him then."   When he recovered they continued traveling.

George wrote to Pat Mills in 2001, "It seems ironic that all the ailments that afflicted my mother have followed on to me: diabetes, high blood pressure, and heart attack.   What a way to retire.   Needless to say I am living a much more relaxed life style."   Relaxation, of course, for Geroge meant traveling.   In 2006 he and Caryl took two cruises George had wanted to take for a long time, and in March 2007 they flew to Lima, Peru and cruised through the Panama Canal to Puerto Rico.   Six weeks later they flew to Venice for a Mediterranean trip and George found getting around difficult, but he did not complain. Two days after their return in May doctors started him on dialysis.   Nevertheless, George was in reasonably good health, Caryl says, until "he went to sleep the evening of the 12th, and woke up in heaven.   We had 45 wonderful years, and I miss him terribly."

George's widow Caryl Schmersal 510 Bank Street Beaver. PA 15009

R I P

Allan Schwartz

Photo by Fred Feingold

Photo by Nik Epanchin

Allan's parents lived with him and his sister Laura (Lolly) in lodgings above their pharmacy business on Sea Cliff Avenue.   When they sold the store to Dobkins, they moved to Laurel Ave.   I remember his parents as protective, but Allan was never a kid who "needed a little extra help," but when I first got to know him in third or fourth grade I thought he did. He was a chubby, short boy. Every year's physical or change in gym revealed a deep hole under one shoulder blade from a serious childhood operation. Before high school his best sport was croquet which we played on the back yard of the library that fronted 12th Avenue.   In 5th grade I roughed up a kid who called Allan "fat boy" while we were playing handball.   But Allan had already become a formidable handball player and soon went on to become the best tennis player in school and a champion fencer at Columbia University.

Metaphorically speaking our class salutatorian was always good with the parry and very judicious with the thrust because he was more interested in finding out what made people tick than in the triumphant touché.   Sixth grade teacher and psychology grad student Robert Allen first whetted Allan's interest in psychology when he administered Rorschach Ink Blot tests to several students.   Later Allan began doing statistical work with school psychologist Stanley Wolf and he decided to "pester any number of you to take Readers Digest tests."

What he didn't understand, he says, was love and intimacy.   "I went to a party at Doug Andrews' house and there were Diana and Doug smooching and I wondered, "what's that all about?'"   He soon found out with "the considerable assistance of Nancy Horton, a now deceased member of the Class of 1958, who, to my good fortune, decided she wanted me for a boyfriend."

Despite his love of psychology, Allan set out to become an engineer and chose a chemistry major to fulfill the dreams his father was unable to realize.   I had no idea I was going to spend so many years trying to make up for my father's shortcoming.   "I hated being a chem major.   I was a pretty bummed out guy.   It was when I had my third fire in chem. Lab and the entire aisle erupted in fire that I thought I needed to do something else." He took a masters in educational psychology, then a second masters from Rensselaer Polytech in natural sciences, followed by a Ph.D. from the University of Rochester in 1973. By 1981 he had become Chief of the University Health Service-Mental Health Section and later Director of the, University Counseling Center.   Since 2001 he has been the Center's Senior Staff Psychologist.   His is married to Sharon Hoffman.

Allan J. Schwartz, Ph.D.Associate Professor of Psychiatry and Senior Staff Psychologist, University Counseling CenterUSPS: University of RochesterP.O. Box 270356Rochester, NY 14627-0356aschwartz@UR.Rochester.edu

David Schweers

Photo by Nik Epanchin

"Stop the world!" We all know that phrase, but for Dave Schweers, a good, patient, understandingly critical, and tolerant friend since sixth grade, I have never been clear whether what comes next is, *I want to get off*, or *I want to get on*. We're speaking about a frame of mind, of course, since we got put on this world without a choice or a ticket and none of us gets off until our music stops. To follow Dave's path over the last 51 years is to someone who seems to be trying to shake trackers. From Sea Cliff he went to Pottsdam State Teachers College to study music but didn't take it any more seriously than most classes in high school. He returned to Sea Cliff to begin a family and work at the Yacht Club. In 1962 First Mate ('there was no second crew member') on an old lady's yacht in Florida. Back on Long Island he went to C.W. Post to finish his degree and try acting--on a stage. In January 1963 he summed up in a letter: "I'm living on Harriet Ct. [Sea Cliff] with a 4 months pregnant wife, a kitten, 4 potted plants, a houseful of Salvation Army Furniture, working as a file clerk at Republic."

He was also working on drawing and sketching and planning a landscaping business with his brother Pete, but went to Rhode Island where he worked as a diesel mechanic and lobsterman before finishing his degree in art at URI. He began teaching English. He left that career to marry one of his students, Deb Miner, and after a year they bought a small motor home and soon they were on the road. That road led to North Carolina and deep into the woods where they parked in front of the little house I had begun building myself in '74. With that as a base Dave took a job sanding floors. That Christmas Deb bought Dave a compass. "She hid all my presents out in the woods. I spent Christmas morning out in the woods trying to find my presents out in the rain." That may have prepared him for his next move.

One day after work he stopped in the old millworker's house in town where I ran an 'alternative' real estate office. In the next room he noticed a crew of guys come in joking and opening cold beers, and he went over and asked what they did. Surveyors. He thought, "They look awfully happy when they come in. Maybe I ought to try that." He started cutting line for them and he liked it. Later that year when he and Deb found themselves in Cheyenne, Wyoming, almost out of gas and out of money he looked for work in nineteen different engineering places and "I had to hoc my last 2 trumpets." Finally one company sent them to Colstrip, Montana as relief crew.

When snow closed the job they headed south to Wyoming and on the way Dave talked to his daughter, Frederika who had leukemia. She was full of her plans for the future. A couple of days later when he called, his son Edward told him Fred was in the hospital. Dave and Deb fought their way back east through miserable winter weather. They arrived in time for only the funeral. Fred left behind the story of her life and bright courage in a PBS documentary.

When I mentioned that I would be in Las Vegas to moderate a debate on the environment, Dave and Deb drove out to meet me. While they waited at a gas station for me to appear, they met a crew from a company doing seismic surveys in the oil industry. The three of us and their huge sheep dog lived in Vegas another four days while Deb collected free casino tokens in the mornings and cashed them in evenings and finally had the money for a little fur jacket. They dropped me off in Texas for a flight to Guatemala, and they began their career in seismic surveying which soon had them living in Alaska. They started as "juggies" setting out lines of sounding jug-like recording devices on Alaska's arctic tundra in winter as part of the sonic mapping of underground resources. Ten years later they moved south to Washington state, and eventually to Whidbey Island from which they both commuted to different surveying jobs.

Their preferred investment has been a larger and more complete and comfortable motor home which they plan to make their retirement home. If they can't get off the merry-go-round, they at least want to ride their own horse, and as always, live life their own way. Until the motor home becomes home, Dave continues to commute across Puget Sound on his motorcycle (which rides on a ferry, not on water), to work despite a recent heart operation and back problems that started in Sea Cliff when he was a launch boy at the Yacht Club.

From high school classes to surveying standards and governments, Dave has seen few things in the world he wouldn't change if he could. Dave's confrontations with people and systems that refuse to change have often elaborated on his senior superlative—Teacher's Trial—but he has wasted little energy charging windmills, perhaps illustrating the prayer, "Give me the courage to change what I can and the wisdom to know what I can't."

One part of the world Dave left early was contact with other class members. In 1963 he wrote to me in England, "I have no contact with mutual friends or classmates other than the few who are mailmen or gas station attendants, so I can't fill you in on homey gossip. As a matter of fact, my wife and I are not too sociable back-fence style." However, Dave was one of two or three people who sparked the idea of a 50th reunion even though he later reflected, "Why is it that I have so little desire to re-strike up friendships from school. There are a few people I would like to apologize to for being such a shallow self involved jerk, but I don't want it to be the basis for a friendship."

David Schweers
PO Box 1048
Clinton, WA 98236
driftr@whidbey.com

2009 Commuting on the Whidbey Island Ferry

Jane Sessler

Photo by Fred Feingold

Jane grew up with applied math and an appreciation for its importance. Her father, a Glenwood Landing native ran a soda distribution business out of a concrete block building next to their home. Sessler Beverages bought wholesale and sold door to door, to delis, beach concessions and mobile peddlers. As a girl Jane sat many hours in the office playing pinochle with her grandmother. Her grandmother also paid her a penny for each nail she picked up in the driveway.

Jane appreciates the difference in that era and the present. "Your parents cared about you. The family was a much bigger influence on your life than maybe it is today. My grandparents were always around. Any time I came home there was always somebody there. You were used to having adults in your life. I can remember my grandfather taking me down to the Swan Club Sunday mornings to feed the swans."

Jane was the only Sessler child, as her father had been when he grew up in the same house. She had two cousins from her maternal aunt who both died young. She feels that limited family led her to expand the sense of caring to friends. Coming to Sea Cliff in her freshman year, she says, "I don't think I ever really felt a part of Sea Cliff high school. I have a pretty thick hide and I don't think it ever really bothered me at that time." Nevertheless, her habit was "to find nice people to work with." She became good friends with Diana Djivre, Barbara Ferris, Valerie DeVeuve, Bette Kreidemaker, and Lois Delgado. She says she was not good at sports, but she enjoyed being in the intramural teams with her friends. When she went to her grandfather's funeral in 1965 she was dismayed to find Lois' wake in the next room.

Jane excelled at math although she was not always fond of Mr. Thompson. "I remember what Mr. Thompson said because he used to talk through the tests. You should be able to work under any conditions. He would talk about the track." She was one of three classmates who went on to Cornell where she studied math and also studied physics under Nobel Prize winner Hans Bethe. She graduated with a degree in economics and certified to teach math.

She knew she wanted to teach and went to work in Fairfield, CT. After four years she left to study on a National Science Foundation grant at Ohio State University where she began programming and computer work. She went to IBM in downtown Columbus and took their tests. They sent her to their offices in Bethesda, MD in 1966 to see their equipment and observe the work. "I watched people working in little cubicles doing programming and when I walked out of the place and thought 'this isn't for me.'" She returned to Long Island and began teaching math in Manhasset. She stayed there 34 years, 22 of them as chair of the department. That was a job she says she did not really want, but the principal "wasn't someone you argued with." In 1997 the Mathematical Association of America awarded her its prestigious Sliffe Award for Distinguished Mathematics Teaching. This award is most often won by teachers in private schools, specialized math and science schools and magnet schools. No one in Sea Cliff or North Shore schools ever won the award.

In 1999, a year before her retirement, a friend began to talk to her about race horses. Jane had been in the riding club in high school, ridden at camp, and her parents had always gone to the races. She and her friend bought part of a filly. When they sold her thirteen months later she had won two races and Jane had lost only $14.11 (still applying the math). They then invested in four more horses and Halfway to Heaven won ten races. Today she and two other women partners have Halfway's offspring. Except for the six weeks of the summer racing season, Jane continues to live in Manhasset where she serves on the Advisory Committee for the school budget and does some volunteer tutoring.

Jane feels parents in general no longer put in the kind of personal time with their kids that she enjoyed, but she says math is "definitely taught more for understanding now" and the top level students get a "much more intelligent education."

Jane Sessler
5 Dewey St
Manhasset, NY 11030-1815
horsehere@aol.com

Richard Smith

"I always owned a boat," Richie says about growing up in Sea Cliff, Glen Head and Glenwood. From those boats he hauled in a lot of flounders, snappers, bass, and those spiny, bony little fish we called begals. To get the information for this biography we had to wait a few days for Richie to end a two week stint as chief engineer on a tugboat operating between New Jersey and New York. He doesn't fish much anymore but when he does, it's from a tugboat.

His childhood in Glenwood, he says, "was the greatest time in my life. You played a lot of baseball. I was into sports then. I was in walking distance of school [Glenwood] and we went to school early to play." One of his closest friends was Danish immigrant Soren Hansen, and when Soren's parents moved to Glen Cove for a few years, Richie would visit and explore the Morgan Estate recently vacated by the Russians. Although he attended the Lutheran Church, he also went to the church run by Tim Klenk's father and the affiliated Young People's group run by the Howell's in Sea Cliff. Among their many activities for kids, he remembers, "They had free cake, and you didn't have a lot of money in those days."

In high school Soren says, "He [Richie] and I were both good at math and tried to outdo each other." Richie says, "It was unusual for me not to like a teacher," but he didn't get along with was Mr. Matthews, perhaps because of his air of military authority, Richie speculates.
In his freshman year he and Nancy Samuelson, also from Glenwood, "were sweethearts for a little bit." In our junior year he left school with another classmate, Colette Relation, and began married family life. John Broderick became godfather to their son Richard born in 1956.

To support the family Richie began working in the soda distributorship run by Jane Sessler's father, then drove for Keyco Trucking in Locust Valley, before settling down with Borden's Milk in the early 1960s. Because his mother took care of the children of the man who ran the Dale Carnegie schools, Richie took their night courses to improve his confidence when he had to knock on doors and try to sign up milk customers. Those early self-improvement and motivational courses, he remembers, were full of car and real estate salesmen. Despite his new self-confidence, after ten years with Borden's, "I could see the milk business was going to crap." He and Colette had had three children and divorced in 1963 but remained close. Richie married a second time and had two more children, and then married again briefly. Sociologists tell us the typical entrepreneur starts a business in his or her late 20s or early 30s, and that's when Richie went into business for himself.

He had regularly stopped in at Pace's Place bar and grill in Westbury, and when it came up for sale, he bought it. That was in the early 1970s. A few years later he bought a second bar and grill. Like most new entrepreneurs, he also found running his own business required long hours. He found himself going to work to open up at 8 in the morning, taking a nap after lunch, and going back to stay through the long, smoky, boozy hours until three or four in the morning. His oldest son Richard had turned 18 and begun working with him. When federal pressure forced New York to up its drinking age to 21 and increasingly successful trial lawyers forced insurance rates to quadruple in a year, time for change had come again.

His father was a foreman with Colonial Sand and Gravel's tugboat operation, Bronx Towing, and Richie found a job. "I learned all about tugboats real quick. I took my coastguard test and I got my chief engineer's license." He would go on to an unlimited license. Along the line Richie realized he could earn extra job security by being a cook since boats no longer carried cooks. John Broderick who visits Richie at least once a year, says, "He flat knows how to get around in a kitchen." Richie's wife, whom he met 26 years ago while bowling, agrees. He has worked from Canada to Mexico, and still works two weeks on and two weeks off. When he's not delivering sand, his boat may be bunkering (refueling) the giant ocean liners.

Richie, who rebelled under Mr. Matthews authoritarian regime, and who once quit a boat because the new captain, a former Navy Seal, wanted to rule like an admiral, says he likes tug-boating because, "Basically you're your own boss. You have to answer to the captain but he doesn't fool with you either." All good things, come to an end of course, and he says, "My license expires Feb 2011, that's when I'm going to retire." He has a large collection of action movies on CD, but "Not the kind where they catch bullets and throw 'em back." He prefers the traditional Clint Eastwood type of action. He will also indulge his passion for golf, and he has sent in his registration for the 55th reunion.

Richard Smith
706 Christopher Dr
Middletown, DE   19709

Ceil Snayd

Photo by Fred Feingold   Photo by Nik Epanchin

When Ceil came to Sea Cliff from St. Boniface she was already a part of the class.   In the summer between the two schools her older sister, a friend of Dorie Sprague ('55) had introduced her to Dorie's younger sister Betty and soon her friends included Lee Berroyer, Judy Brown and other future classmates.   Nevertheless, Ceil says, "I was definitely shy. I wouldn't raise my hand in class and I was petrified if I was called on."   Why the middle sister of five siblings should be shy, she doesn't know.   Nevertheless she enjoyed school except a few incidents, including math teacher Don Thompson telling her she was not prepared for advanced algebra.   She would go on to spend most of her working life doing math.

As the senior year rolled on she toyed with the idea of becoming an airline stewardess like her cousin, but decided not to pursue it.   With the encouragement of Barbara Wade ('56), she left the Island to attend Georgetown Visitation, a two year Catholic college for girls in Washington, DC.   By the time she arrived Barbara had departed, perhaps because of an unconsummated elopement with Art Kaufman ('56) earlier in the year when he sprung her from school and they headed for South Carolina where marriage required no waiting period.   (Both sets of parents called out the police and started a man and woman hunt, though the couple on their own reconsidered, turned around Art's nosed and decked '50 Ford with its roaring glasspaks, and returned to the island unmarried.)   Ceil studied to be a medical secretary, a career she never pursued.

When she returned to the Island in '59 she worked at Nassau Hospital in Mineola, as an accounting secretary.   As soon as she bought a car, she began picking up Dave Schweers' mother since she was a nurse at Nassau.   Ceil had always kept close ties with Barbara Gilson who married Moon (Robert) Sawicki and who were good friends with Farrell Sheridan and his younger brother Forrest.   Ceil married Forrest who worked for IBM.   In 1971 after Ceil had taken accounting courses, she and Forrest started their own company, Den-Mark Business Machines, servicing and selling and leasing office machinery.   They were also active in the national dealers' association and traveled widely.

The business went well despite large responsibilities that Ceil had to cope with. The most pleasant of the burdens, of course, were daughter Denise born in '66 and Mark born in '69. (Thus the business name.) For a while Forrest was in bed with a bad back and Ceil found herself running both the family and the entire business. Nevertheless they also found time for visits to Berkeley Andrews, sailing with him in California and skiing with him when he lived in Colorado.

In the early 80s the spread of small computers disrupted their industry. Their business and their marriage went downhill at the same time and they dissolved both. Ceil went to work as a headhunter in an employment agency. When she noticed an interesting job with an insurance company, "I sold myself to a job opening they had." The company sold commercial insurance across the country and Ceil began working in their accounting effort. She's still there, now engaged in all areas of daily management. Ceil did most of her accounting training in the World Trade Center with AON. Most of her trainers perished in the 9/11 attack.

Ceil's daughter Denise graduated from American University and volunteered to teach English in Costa Rica where Ceil visited her. After returning from Costa Rica Denise lived with Ceil for almost 10 years while she worked as a speech pathologist. Son Mark took a degree in economics and works as an investigator with Legal Aid in Port Jefferson. Ceil also stays in touch with Carole Neice who married Ceil's younger brother Joe who died in October 2006.

Ceil hopes to retire soon after almost 20 years in the insurance business. On her way home from work she occasionally goes to the gym, and until recently she was a member of a ski club that took a lot of trips. She says, "I think I gave it up but I haven't sold my skis." That club led to trips with members who were also cyclists. On her hybrid bike she has taken 5 day trips with Elder Hostel in upstate NY and in Main's Acadia National Park. She's still driven by the same curiosity and energy as the little Snayd girl who used to bike to St. Boniface and all over Brookville.

Ceil Sheridan
3761 Ferndale Drive
Wantagh, N.Y. 11793
ceilsher@optonline.net

Robert Soper

Bob grew up in the gray shingled house behind its Prospect Avenue hedge just below 16th Avenue, a quiet kind of Tom Swift boy, and one of the first in town who had a bike with what we then called English or racing tires.   In school he excelled in shop (Industrial Arts).

We have little information on Bob after he left school, but we found him in Broken Arrow, Oklahoma where we believe he worked for Phillips Petroleum.   He has not responded to mail and the listed phone no longer works.

Robert S Soper21451 E 102nd StBroken Arrow, OK 74014-3642

Betty Sprague

With Bob Lucas, Photo by Nik Epanchin

Betty has a long Sea Cliff pedigree. Her great grandfather was a mason who plastered the ceiling in the Methodist church (now town hall and museum). "Gramps" Sprague started life in 19th Century Sea Cliff as a cook for the "Oyster House" by the power plant. Next he worked at the old water company, then with his wife opened "Sprague's Fish Market" near Longo's bar. Betty's father used to drive a Bohack's delivery wagon taking fish and groceries all over Sea Cliff and up and down all the hills for 10 cents a wagon load. He started kindergarten when the school was just the front section, no gym or auditorium. He starred for the high school basketball team. He remembered the end of school days when the principal would put march music on the Victrola as students marched out the doors to go home. During the Depression her grandparents lost their house. Her grandmother worked in a pocketbook factory in Glen Cove until she was about 75. She lied about her age for years in order to keep working.

Betty inherited the family's determination and grit. Her own childhood was filled with the pursuits typical of the time—playing "bottle-tops, ringaleevio on bikes, hopscotch, paper dolls, listening to the radio. Pete Swanson's mother ran her Girl Scout troop. She did hate living two houses down from the "boys side" of the school. (Boys entered doors on one side, girls on the other.) Whenever she and her older sister Dorie tried to cross to the girl's side on a snow day they had to pass through a barrage of snowballs. Like many of us she and older sister Dorie ('55) went on foot to Glen Cove for supplies. In a day when the racial divide was particularly destructive that trip could be risky. She recalled, "Dorie and I still have nightmares about being chased up/down 'Backroad Hill' by the black kids while walking (sometimes running) to Glen Cove on Saturdays. I used to dream about missing the "last bus" and being stranded in GlenCove." Pretending she was Wonder Woman, falls outside the norms but speaks of her early determination to control her own fate and do good for others.

Richie Loftus and I gave that determination a boost from what would today be shameful bullying serious enough have us sentenced to therapy. "One day, when I was in 3rd or 4th grade," Betty recalled, "I was riding my bike on the far side of the playground (where Mike the Good Humor man plied his ice cream), and you and Ritchie Loftus (not sure if there was anyone else) stopped me, held my bike by the handlebars and wouldn't let me go. I was so upset I cried, and you finally let me go (this was when I was into paper dolls, dresses and girly stuff). Now here's how it changed my life – I vowed NEVER to let a boy pick on me or make me feel helpless again! And I didn't. From that day on, I became a tomboy – dungarees and all – and would beat up boys that picked on me (especially Reggie Burdick)."

Despite being from a multi-generational Sea Cliff family, Betty wrote a few years ago, "I hated the sun and the beach. I would wrap up in towels, sit under an umbrella, and never go in the water. I hated everything about it, sand, sun, salt water – even so far as to be allergic to it – broke out in hives and got sunburn on tops of feet. But Mom made us all go – to Bayville Beach – with all the stones in the water. One day, I was at the Pavilion – have no idea how old I was but would guess 5th or 6th grade, and decided that if everyone else could swim, so could I! With that, I dove in the water – underwater – and said "this isn't so scary". Same day started diving off the floats. This was my new "can-do" attitude that you and Richie [Loftus] had inadvertently given me. After that, you couldn't keep me away from the sun, sand and salt water!" After that she may have overdone it. "I ended up with skin cancer and they swear it is from when I was young."

During school Betty started work at Dobkins before the legal age of 14 and had to be hidden in the back room when the Health Inspector came. Although the starting pay was $0.35 per hour, she got to eat the cherries out of the cherry vanilla ice cream.

From Sea Cliff Betty went to Alfred University but could not finish because her parents had run out of funds. She began working at Glen Cove hospital and taking a few classes at Hofstra. She became a medical transcriptionist, and when the radiologist she worked for moved to Fairfax, Virginia in 1960 she went too. There she met Air Force veteran Arrol Harnage and married him in 1962. When he went to California to get a mechanic's license, she went and worked in the Englewood hospital. From there they moved to Las Vegas, back to California, and then to Phoenix. Betty did not like the hot weather but they are still there. They have a motor home, however, and have used it for frequent travel.

Their daughter became the CEO of Workshop Way, an educational organization for disadvantaged kids. Their youngest son works in computer animation, and their oldest son, "the smartest of the bunch--stocks a grocery store - go figure!" Betty's sister Dorie lives in Bayville and her younger brother Buzz in Muskegon, WI. Looking back and thinking of the kids, Betty says "I wish I had been a nurse." But today as she manages family investments, she says, "I'd love to be a stockbroker—this is fun." She also developed a passionate concern for the natural environment. "Years ago, I planned when I retired to picket nuclear power plants and go to garage sales! Well, that hasn't quite worked out." She did get involved with the movement to stop an electric utility from raising three big smokestacks, although she doesn't consider the one they did erect an effective compromise.

After working in a hospital for 22 years Betty found herself stumbling and falling over a two inch curb. She quit the hospital and doesn't regret not having to get up at 5 a.m. However, in 1994 X rays revealed kidney cancer. "The radiologist said, 'It's going to get you. They gave me five years." She also had to have gamma radiation for a brain tumor. Nevertheless, as this goes to press, Betty is in Arizona and brother Buzz came to be with her as they put their 88 year old mother in Hospice care.

Betty says, "We were so fortunate to grow up in the 50s. . . . Life was so good back then. The whole world has changed. . . I still believe the same things I believed back then . . . This country has gotten more greedy. Back then it was *do your best, make the most of things, try to make the world a better place somehow*." Maybe that is why she says, "I've made sure all my kids have been on the old cobblestone road off Laurel Ave, climbed the "rock" at Clifton park and run up and down the stairs by what used to be the old pavilion!"

Betty Harnage
1176 E. Carmen ST
Tempe, AZ 85283
480 838 9268
bharnage@mindspring.com

Richard Stack

Richard learned early that life is a gamble.   After he and his older brother Ed ('52) went to a Methodist camp one summer, Ed developed polio, and health authorities quarantined both him and.   Ed spent more than a year in the hospital and emerged with crutches, braces and a lifelong bad leg.   Ed would come back to school and prove losses are not permanent. He would win senior honor student, later an honorary doctor of law from Hartwick College, and serve as President of the Baseball Hall of Fame as well as a director of numerous businesses, charities and cultural organizations.

The 1957 yearbook note for Richard Stack said, "A business career is right up his alley." He went into business straight out of high school and a short walk down Back Road Hill from his home on Altamont Avenue—six days a week washing dishes in a luncheonette. He also went to night school at Hofstra to improve his chances in the business world.   "I was too young to go to night school," he realizes, but his courses saved him when, after three years of drowning dishes in sinks of detergent, his skin erupted in allergic reactions.

A friend who ran a gas station also repaired card reading computers for the Long Island branch of Sperry Rand Corporation.   "Go to Sperry," his friend said.   "They hire people who run these computers."   Sperry hired Richard to do the kind of basic clerical work he had started learning in school.   "I really hated it," he says, "but when I was about to leave, my boss suggested I try computers."   Richard had been good at math in high school, although a long bout of asthma in his sophomore year meant, "I barely passed by the skin of my teeth."   The asthma disappeared after high school and nothing prevented him from developing his career as he liked.   He rose in the ranks of Sperry to become   Senior Programmer Analyst.

The "Rand" in the corporate name came from Remington Rand, best known for their typewriters.   Sperry developed the famous UNIVAC computer.   But Sperry was soon to be eclipsed, and Richard's instincts were good.   He wanted to learn the IBM computer systems, and IBM would soon become America's computing standard.   Richard moved to the Harris Corporation that used IBM equipment.   There he developed his programming skills and worked for the company's director on special projects. He also honed his gambling skills, playing poker every day at lunch for 17 years and many Friday nights at friends' homes.

Around 1990 government spending cutbacks left Richard unemployed. "I had my resume out all over," he says, but he had been looking at land in a Kingman, Arizona development. He flew out on vacation and surveyed the area around the Grand Canyon. He liked the quiet, the waters of the Colorado and Lake Mojave. He didn't like the idea of commuting to New York City. And he loved to gamble.

For six months he rented a condo in Laughlin, Nevada and signed up for unemployment. "I was entitled to rehabilitation," he says, and he found that the local community college offered a six week course in card dealing. He also "found a piece of property on top of a hill overlooking the mountains" where he now lives. He turned down a job in Vegas and began to deal in one of Laughlin's ten casinos, eventually also working roulette. After a couple of years, "I got physically sick dealing with the public and people in gambling. You'd have to be brought up in the business to really like it." He saw that the people who came for short term work were always broke.

He has retired to Laughlin where he contentedly runs his own life—cleaning, cooking, doing the yard work, and and walking with a neighbor every morning. Richard, however, did not get sick of gambling. "I love to fly to Vegas every year on vacation for a week or ten days." He also plays video poker. "I've been playing so many years I'm pretty good," he says. He is cautious with his money as befits a former business manager for the Senior Play. He doesn't bet a fortune and as this biography goes to press he says he is still in the black. "It's satisfying when you win a little bit."

Stack, Richard
2915 Desert Vista Drive

Bullhead City AZ. 86429

rls@npgcable.com

Michael Stanton

Photo by Fred Feingold

For our class and our almost self-contained communities, many nearby places were as exotic as foreign countries and sometimes the people who came from them were stranger than real immigrants. So with Mike Stanton who arrived our senior year, tall, hair greased into a spiky ducktail, and a "bring it on" attitude combined with a "come to me baby" look at girls he liked. One of the girls says, "He was regarded as what young girls today refer to as a 'hottie'; many were the caps set at him."

Behind the public persona was a kid struggling to become part of something worthwhile. "The first thing I remember in life is driving across the Triboro Bridge with my parents," he says, although he does not know why that comes first. Whatever the reason it may be symbolic of his growing up which he describes as "bouncing around" among parents, step parents, grandparents and other relatives, in and out of Catholic schools, living in Greenvale, New York City, and Camp Lejeune, North Carolina. In his senior year alone, when he finally came to Sea Cliff, he lived with two foster families, was taken in for a few weeks by Mike Levine's ('58) parents, lived with a grandmother in the city, and sometimes out of his car. Yet Mike became a big contributor to the basketball, track and cross country teams. "It was a transitional year," Mike says. "I was living in more than one world and parallel existences all at the same time."

Several teachers left their mark with Mike. He welcomed Norman Ross's encouragement in track and says, "I behaved for Mr. Driscoll" our no-nonsense basketball coach and shop teacher who demanded precision in shop and on the court.

After school Mike drifted around until he headed west with a friend whose father offered a job at Lake Tahoe on the California-Nevada border. When the car broke down near the little town of Wells, Nevada Mike took a job there washing dishes in a hotel near the railroad tracks. "I was always crazy about trains so I stayed there." After seven months he gave his two weeks' notice and joined the Army in 1958. "All I did in the army was play ball. I knew I was too immature to go to college." Once again, as with Mr. Driscoll, the discipline worked well for him.   Play ball, of course, was not all he did.   He had been assigned to transportation and found himself in France, then assigned to a UN operation unloading supply planes in the Congo during one of its many bloody periods.   "I never left the airport," Mike says, "but an Italian crewman went into town and they beheaded him."

After the Army he was ready for college in Plattsburg, NY where he also played ball until he injured his Achilles tendon in 1964, "the worst year of my life."   He transferred to Fredonia State Teachers College.   After graduation he stayed on to teach English and coach cross country for a couple of years.

In 1965 he met "a farmer's daughter" Kathleen Kahm from Fredonia and they were married after in 1974.   Mike already had one son, David, and he and Kathleen added their son Michael to the family in 1976.   Asked how she tamed Mike, she joked, "With a whip, I gotta tell you."   David lives in Fredonia and works with the phone company.   Michael lives nearby and works as a debt collector.

Mike left teaching to follow his love of railroading.   He began as a brakeman on the Amtrak line out of Buffalo to Cleveland and Toledo.   Later he became a conductor to finish a 31 year career with Amtrak.   During that time he saved and began investing in real estate and began study the paperwork.   "I got a little interested in finance and I always wanted to be wealthy." In 1986 he incorporated his own mortgage company as Valmy Enterprises named for a tiny trailer park and railroad town in Nevada where he and a buddy passed through in the 60s.

Mike's mortgage company is operates by word of mouth without a website or Internet, and he knows everyone of his clients personally.   He reports he has been unscathed by the mortgage "meltdown" that began in 2007.   He also consults on property questions for senior citizens.   His other pleasures include his love of his native Fredonia area which he says is very much like "a mini California" with playgrounds, parks, a beach, a good library, and recreation summer and winter.   His greatest pleasure, however, is his family and helping raise his granddaughter, an elementary school student.   For the many classmates who did not have time to know the Mike behind the newcomer to our class, and to the many who doubted he had much of a future, he says, "The best thing to say is I'm a family. I used to be pretty wild in Sea Cliff."   And if there's any doubt left, "Tell all the kids I'm a multi-millionaire."

Michael P. Stanton
115 Central Ave.
Fredonia, NY 14063-1133

John Storojev

Photo by Fred Feingold

John Storojev arrived in Sea Cliff only because history is pock marked by the fact that if something can go wrong, it will.   Begin in 1918 in the Ural Mountain city of Ekaterinberg and Lenin's decision to murder the Czar's family and hunt down the family's closest supporters.   One of them was Father Ivan Storojev who had been priest to the royal family. Father Storojev fled to the east into China.   He would have gone farther, but while in the Russian community in Harbin, his son had appendicitis and the journey stopped.   There in Harbin, his grandson John Storojev was born in 1939 during the brutal Japanese invasion that turned much of China into a slaughter house.   During the war the Japanese commandeered John's multilingual father and the family moved to Japan, with two trips back to China where John once served as altar boy in his grandfather's church.   In 1948 the family came to the US so his father could work in the UN Secretariat as simultaneous interpreter of Chinese, Japanese, Russian and English.   John says his mother's profession became "*nag-avator*" to him and his younger sister.

After a brief time in Glen Head the family came to rest in one of Sea Cliff's older homes near Central Park.   On the track team John became a pole vaulter.   Something in the pole vaulter aspires to be above much more than a very high bar held between two posts, and it is in this sense that I suggest John has always been the pole vaulter.

He started higher education at Emerson College where he became editor-in-chief of the college paper.   After two years he decided the academic bar was not high enough and he entered New York University where he says, "I took some really hard courses and became a grind."   When he finished in 1961 he went to Johns Hopkins School for Advanced International Studies (SAIS) and found himself in classes with a young woman who had been born in Czechoslovakia--Madeline Albright.   John married a fellow graduate student, and after earning his Masters, he went to work for the policy department of Radio Free Europe and transferred to their Munich, Germany operations center.   His daughter Daria was born there while John worked in planning programs for communist Eastern

Europe. He soon felt weighed down by the bureaucracy. "You do all this research and write all this stuff and they shovel it into a big hole."

After they returned home their second daughter, Kyra, was born in 1966 while they were living again in Sea Cliff. From this point John began a series of jobs in public relations and publishing, setting the bar higher each time as he moved from McGraw Hill to John Wiley and Sons to Harcourt Brace. He learned marketing in all forms of media from personal presentations and in-store events to national radio and television. His daughters began school in Sea Cliff, finding themselves learning from some of their father's former teachers.

After his divorce in the late 1970s, John and the girls moved to San Diego where he worked with Harcourt Brace Janovich. He chafed at what he calls the company's "dictatorial approach," and was soon an entrepreneur. John told a California interviewer recently, "I was never a good organization person," he said. "I have problems with authority. When I went out on my own, it was a growth experience. I made a living selling advertising copy." However, while at Harcourt his decision to market through Scholastic publications introduced him to Scholastics space salesperson—his second wife Susan. She joined him in their own advertising and direct marketing business. Their daughter Laura was born in 1990.

John had never entirely abandoned his ambitions in art, and in the 90s he began to devote more and more time to it. Not content with two dimensional work, he took courses in sculpture. He moved from a garage studio to a separate studio devoted to his own work and complete with gallery-- Storojev Fine Arts Studio. For the past eight years he has taught art and sculpture at California Lutheran University.

About John's art, he speaks for himself on his web site: "You'll notice that I work in a wide variety of materials (metal, stone, clay, bronze, etc..) Each medium offers its own challenges and beauty, sparking my creativity and igniting my imagination. The results can be whimsical, spiritual, full of movement, such as in water or in the wind, or it can be peaceful and just beautiful to behold by itself."

In 2003 *Lifescapes Magazine* said of him, "John Storojev's works demonstrate his mastery of texture and color, combined with enjoyment of movement, light and whimsy. The result is an adventure in decorative and bold designs that enhance homes, gardens, and offices." Although John continues to raise the bar for himself, he says he has passed an important milestone, "the coming to my senses and belief in myself as an artist, with the result that at the ripe age of 70, I am having a ball and hope the Great Creator gives me time to create art that will glorify the human Spirit."

2503 Sandy Creek Dr.

West Lake Village, CA 91361
http://www.johnstorojev.com/gallery.php   john@johnstorojev.com

Additional notes from John [Very early in our reunion and book planning, John agreed to send a written memoir. As things developed, it seemed more appropriate to break it into pieces and put them in the relevant bios and chapters. Some material also appears here.]

GIRLS:
These beauties I had the "hots" for. I will name them without comment, knowing only that at that age they appeared alluring, unattainable and untouchable, though I did get a lucky kiss of two from the ones "I went out with." . So much for youthful fantasies and illusions.

Sandy Gleichmann
Judy Brown
Carol Hincula
Judy Olsen
Diane Djivre

On looking over this list, I am going to brag a little. Young as I was, I think I had good taste. All these fine attractive girls became women who lead lives of challenge, perseverance, and personal fulfillment, as far as I could tell.   I am glad to have had a boyhood "crush" on them. Let me postscript that by revealing that after SCHS, I got involved in a long-term relationship that was a classic example of blind youthful passion and obsession. It did not end well but I learned many life lessons from the experience.

TEACHERS I WOULD HAVE GLADLY DONE WITHOUT:

Without attaching too much negativity, for who can fathom at that innocent age what really was going on with each teacher? Nevertheless, this my list of teachers who could have used some remedial help, psychologically and pedagogically. I only knew Tibbits by reputation but not through class attendance. This is a very subjective list at best and is not meant to disparage these teachers, though I might exclude Kittleberger from this qualification, as she was very handy with a ruler and was a dead-shot with an eraser and chalk.

Dorothea Comfort
Guy T. Pinkard
Freda Kittleberger
Jean Tibbits

POSTSCRIPT

There's much more I could relate about my experience at SCHS. These are splotches of paint on a large canvas that is still being painted. There's no doubt high school formed an indelible impression on how I moved on in life. I was an unformed human being who carried a lot of baggage, particularly my experience in Japan during WWII. In many ways I acted out my insecurities and shadows. It is said by wiser men that one should not regret anything in life. Well, I am not there yet, so I do regret a lot of stuff then and after. But as I live longer, my understanding deepens and my compassion grows slowly but steadily. I am certain that knowingly or unknowingly, I caused others grief and consternation. For this I am truly sorry and ask for understanding. My mother is 96 now so it seems I have a slight edge on the longevity factor. I hope that the next 26 years (if I can match her) are going to be productive and fascinating. Above all, for myself and for all others, I wish good health and happiness.

Charles Peter Swanson

Charlie Swanson and Marie at Aspen

The essential Pete has changed in name only. Pete Swanson who bought a '39 Ford for $10 when he was 14 and turned it into a working hotrod is now Charlie Swanson tinkering in a garage full of Porsches, two of them his. He also sends a variety of things traveling hundreds of thousands of miles in space, part of his work as mechanical engineer designing payloads and working on Space Station apparatus.

Pete follows his father as a tinkerer with machines. During the War they lived in the Buffalo/Niagara Falls area where his father was a troubleshooter for airplanes. In 1945 his father took a job with Sperry Corporation on the Island and moved the family to an old white clapboard house fronting on the rapidly vanishing steep Tilley Place just off Prospect Avenue. "My father was always tinkering with his cars and I was right there helping him." His father was also good friends with Sandy Gleichmann's father, a machinist, and sometimes helped him with big jobs.

Pete was learning from teachers who were doing, while in the school classroom his mind was often elsewhere, and that sometimes led to trouble. He did not like the fierce Miss Comfort who taught Spanish and English, and he didn't like Spanish either. "Pete Muttee and I wrapped leaves around a rock and put it in the exhaust pipe of [Miss Comfort's] car. It blew the muffler out. We made the mistake of returning to the scene of the crime. The next day we were in Furlong's office." One could speculate interestingly on why he remembers the prank but not the punishment. He does remember one phrase he learned, since he sat next to the door, and class often began with the command, "Carlos, cierre la puerta. [Charles, close the door.]"

Pete tried Adelphi College on the Island after graduation but says, "I just hated it." He went back to the work he did on weekends during school—servicing cars, then moving into welding and mechanical work. He also became a union laborer on various jobs, earning more than many college grads. Nevertheless, he tired of routine jobs and in September '61 he enrolled in the University of Alabama which offered both the warmer climate he craved and mechanical engineering. "When I got to college I decided I'd be Charlie instead of Pete."

This time he did well in the classroom and won a fellowship to go on for his PhD, "but when I got the masters, I had enough college at that point and I bailed out."   In Melbourne, Florida he began work in structural analysis, the discipline that is still at the heart of his work.   His first subjects were large antenna systems for Harris Corp.

In 1968 he married a girl he had met at the university.   Their daughter was born in 1976. Pete says that their part of Florida had a bad drug scene with kids lying around the beach smoking pot.   His wife said, "We're not raising our daughter here."   They moved across country to Phoenix where he worked for Goodyear Aerospace on missiles.   By 1982 they were back in Huntsville, Alabama where Pete started work with the Teledyne conglomerate where he continues to work today.   His daughter graduated from the Unviersity of Alabama and went into banking and money management, taking positions in international financial crossroads like Nassau, Vienna, and Monaco.

Several years ago Pete and his wife separated and went their own ways.   Although he continues to work full time, he says, "When they retire the shuttle in 2010 I guess I'll retire."   He will continue to work on his own and other people's Porsches.   He also has found time to travel widely with his companion Marie and with a local group that makes its own travel itineraries.

Charlie Swanson
2317 Meridian St, Suite 22
Huntsville, AL 35811
fox@hiwaay.net

Catherine Sydow

Although Cathy attended grade school at St. Boniface and lived in Sea Cliff and Glenwood in those years, she did not come to Sea Cliff High until her junior year. Her parents, with a family expanding from Cathy to another five children, had to keep moving to have enough space. She was born in Brooklyn and after reaching 5th grade in St. Boniface she moved to Levittown. When she came back to Sea Cliff she found, "I kind of lost touch with the class. Everybody had grown up." And she had little time to catch up because to help her large family she took a job working at McClellan's five and dime in Glen Cove after school. She was also doing a lot of at-home babysitting but at least being the oldest child and 'big sister' was fun. "Everybody had to follow me."

On Independence Day the year of our graduation Dotty Gerroir took Cathy to South Hempstead to watch the Fireman Games in which a friend of Dottie's was participating. After the tournament Dottie and her friend introduced Cathy to fellow fireman Harry New. They married in September 1959. After graduation Cathy had started worked as a teller for First National Bank of Glen Head where she would soon be joined by classmate Ned McAdams starting his fast climb to president. In 1960, however, she became pregnant, and "They had to hide me because you weren't allowed to be in front of the customers with a pregnant belly showing. When I got too big I had to leave." Their daughter Donna arrived in '61, Christine in '63, Jeffrey in '64, and Harry in '65. They became Cathy's job for the next 12 years. Meanwhile her husband Harry left Grumman Aircraft to work with the Nassau County Police Department. Like her own parents, Cathy and Harry had to move to find needed room for a family. After a short time living in an apartment in his parents' house, they bought and fixed up a two bedroom bungalow in South Hempstead, but soon had to move to a larger house in Deer Park. They missed their friends in South Hempstead and the volunteer fire department and the community woven into its membership. They moved back, bought a bigger house, fixed it up and stayed.

Cathy found Harry's shift work easy enough to adapt to since her own father had worked rotating shifts at LILCO. They enjoyed their life together and the social events at the firehouse. They took up line dancing and square dancing. When Harry retired from 25 years with the police department, he was able to fulfill his ambition of becoming fire chief in South Hempstead, still a volunteer job. He also did occasional insurance investigations. In 1977 when Cathy had sent her youngest child to junior high, she began started work driving a small bus for a nursery school and helping tend the children during the day. By that time, she says, "I was good at being with little kids." A few years and she had had enough time with little kids and through a temp agency she found work with GMAC's insurance wing.

During those years she and Harry had been visiting her oldest brother and her father who had moved to New Bern, NC, and they liked the climate and the town. In 1990 they decided to sell their house and settle   in New Bern, Carolina's old colonial capital on the Cape Fear River near the coast. As they packed up, Harry began to feel run down. Doctors in New Bern ran many tests and finally, two days before Christmas 1990, they diagnosed him as having a rare blood and liver disease. They gave him 6 months to a year to live. He died in March. Remembering the many fire department dances and other social activities they had enjoyed together, she regrets that the retirement with her husband that she had looked forward to never really started.

Cathy stayed in New Bern because other family members had also settled there. In 2004 she began to take an active part in Republican politics and became the county treasurer. "It's probably the best thing that ever happened to me meeting all these people," she says. She is also treasurer of the GOP women's club and visiting her five grandsons and five granddaughters spread across the state.

Catherine New.
1511 Fairfax LnNew Bern, NC 28562
cnew@suddenlink.net

Michelina Vaccaro

Mickie wrote that her life "has been pretty mundane," but looking back, perhaps we should have voted her "most enthusiastic." In 1957 she thought she would become a teacher. Instead, she became a librarian. She credits that choice to the influence of our school librarian, Mrs. Eileen McNamara. "She made me think not as a little Italian girl who was going to get married and have lots of children."

Many people remember Mickie's father as one of Sea Cliff's two barbers, his shop on Sea Cliff Avenue across from Bohack's grocery. Her father had wanted to be an engineer, but during the Depression, he had to go to work and earn a living. Besides being a barber, he was also Mickie's private source of intelligence. "Dad enjoyed Jim McKinley. He really thought Jim was a terrific guy. He cut his hair for years and used to tell me everything about him. He had his favorites among the kids, especially if you were in engineering." Her father, Nicholas died in 1999, her mother Jennie in 2001.

Mickie began her college work at C.W. Post, took her master's degree from Long Island University. Along the way she met Richard Bonneau. "I took an instant dislike to him, but he ended up walking me home. That has been true for 35 years." In 1975 she gave birth to their son Nicholas. Mickie went on to advanced professional studies at Rutgers in 1976. At New Jersey's Somerset County Library in Bridgewater she developed its institutional care program to put libraries in jails. Her work there in the early 1980s became the model for the state library's Jail Services Institute and won recognition from the American Library Association only 3 years after its startup. Mickie went on to help organize and establish regulations for institutional libraries in NJ.

In 1987 she and her husband Richard took the family to Rhode Island where she worked in the Providence School library program until 2007. She immediately immersed herself in programs for inner city schools. She organized the E.W. Flynn Folktale Puppeteers and was co-organizer of the public library's Joy of Reading Program. In 1992 she brought the

Ezra Jack Keats writing grants to the school to inspire elementary school students to read and write. Her enthusiasms and commitment to improving other people's lives also took her into volunteer work in a children's hospital, onto the board of the RI League of Women Voters, and into volunteer work with Hospice of Rhode Island.

Mickie has been recognized many times for the enthusiasm and dedication that marks years of service to the cause of reading. For Mickie, a professional librarian, the most important clients are not those who regularly walk in the door of a local library, but the could-be and would-be readers wherever she can find them.

Mickie V. Bonneau
132 Scenic Dr.
Cranston, RI 02920
mchbonneau@aol.com

Mary Ann Vanek

Mary Ann on left, 2005

"I got caught in the toilet smoking so many times by Miss Kittelburger I should have a flat head."   Mary Ann looks back and sees that she and a few other girls settled into their own niche in school—the rebel niche.   "I was just full of life," she says, and her niche was how she told the world she was somebody worth noticing.   The niche was part image, part fact. The fact began even before she came to Sea Cliff from a stay at St. Boniface.   "They got tired of locking me up in the closet and I came back to Sea Cliff in 4th grade."   In high school being a rebel also meant dressing in tight skirts and wearing black leather jackets.

Her father was a Czech immigrant who worked at the A&P days and at a deli at nights, but the family had little money.   "Most of my clothes came from the Salvation Army."   She flirted with boys she found attractive or lively.   "I went for the guys with the rolled up sleeves and leather jackets," but when two guys sandwiched her between them in a movie and started fumbling she got up and called her father to come get her.   She was a tease but she also believed, "A girl should save herself for the man she loved."   Why she chose the sexy rebel way to express herself?   She says, "Who the heck knows?   If you'd have asked me ten years afterward, I might have said to get attention, and ten years after that I might have said some psychological problem.   And ten years later something else.   As you become older you become more aware of your errors in life."

When her father suggested that *he* knew the right man for her, she was sure "If your father knows someone it's got to be a nerd."   Not long after when she gladly accepted a ride from a friend she found herself sitting next to a good looking guy who she thought was a "fast cookie."   She told her father, "This pervert is going to ask me out."   He did, but he turned out to be what his friend Chet Katoski described—"a nice quiet guy".   He was also the president of a youth group and a recent Roslyn High graduate.   Mary Ann was 15.   They were engaged.   The day after she graduated she married her fiancé, Raymond Salavec. He came from a Czech immigrant family and delighted her father who had emigrated from Czechoslovakia.

Mary Ann had begun working before she was of legal age.   After school she worked at the phone company. When her first of three children came in 1959, she and Raymond agreed she would stay home and be a mother. Her third child was deaf and Mary Ann learned sign language. He's now a machinist on Long Island.

When she began working as a North Shore High 'matron' in the 1970s, monitoring halls and other spaces, she knew she had made the right decision to stay home with her children while they were growing up. Nevertheless, At North Shore she felt many of the kids' parents were both working and paid too little attention to where they were and what they were doing. She kept busy "dodging smoke bombs, rounding up rowdy kids, and "sniffing out drugs." Her own experience, she feels, allowed her to stay one guess ahead of the kids.

Eight years later Mary Ann next opened her own store, A Touch of Fantasy, in Glen Head where she sold wicker furniture. The business had been going some 8 years when doctors diagnosed Raymond with a fatal case of lung cancer. She took a big loss on the business, "but what's important--money or the man you love?" Raymond was dead within a year. For three more years, "I was in the Land of Limbo."

Then her doorbell rang and on the stoop stood an old friend of Raymond's from the Sea Cliff Fire Department, Frank Remacle. She invited him in. "When you trust somebody you have known for years, strange things happen." They moved to his place near Hot Springs Village, Arkansas. Soon "I was dying of terminable boredom and was taking to the fish and they were talking to me." They were both happy to find The Villages, a lively, new community near Ocala, Florida. Mary Ann is busy fund raising for children's charities and working with battered women. Having grown up in a time when few women would talk about the problem or leave their husbands, she says, "I have great respect for anyone who can take off and try to save themselves and their kids."

She also belongs to a Red Hat group. "We do nothing. We go out, we party, and enjoy each other's company." She enjoys country dancing and has been belly dancing. It's not for skinny women, she says. And she's proudly not skinny. "You want to make love to a woman, you need something to hold onto. At least I can bend over and put my shoes on."

Why did she have 17 Christmas trees inside her house in 2008? Because she likes parties and is still very much her own person and very much full of life and nobody is going to lock her up in a closet.

Mary Ann Salavec
170 73 SE 93rd
Yondell Circle,
The Villages, Fl 32161
tweetyismymojo@thevillages.net

Theodore Vladimiroff

Photo by Fred Feingold   Photo by Nik Epanchin

Before war broke out in Europe and before Ted and his younger brother were born, their parents danced ballet for audiences all over the world.   They lived in Paris which hosted a large number of Russians who had left before and after the Bolsheviks took power in 1917. Ted and his brother grew up with posters announcing their parents' performances covering the walls.   After the Allied Forces liberated France and the war ended, the Vladimiroffs emigrated in the summer of 1946.   After a visit to an aunt in New York, they spent their first American summer on Cape Cod.   They chose Sea Cliff as their permanent residence because it had a small but growing Russian community.   To keep food on the table his father took a factory job.   His mother became known as Sea Cliff's ballet teacher, Madame Vera.

That fall Ted started school in Sea Cliff with the Class of '58 because of his rudimentary English.   In 7th grade he joined our class.   He went on to win the senior award for the highest average in math and science, although unlike Einstein, he did not continue with the violin.   He did continue playing tennis, a sport his cousins played and which his mother thought "was kind of a social thing I could get into."   When he left Sea Cliff to study engineering at Stevens Institute of Technology he won his varsity letter in tennis.   He also switched from engineering to physics because, "I decided that I was more interested in the science behind the derivation of a formula than its application to a practical problem."

He switched again for graduate work and financed by a National Defense Graduate fellowship in Chemistry he continued at Stevens to receive his masters in '62, and his Ph.D in '67 working with the well known and highly regarded E.R. Malinowski on nuclear magnetic resonance (NMR) shifts in molecular structure.   He went on to do two years of post-doctoral research at SUNY Stony Brook.   For entertainment and relaxation Ted restored old cars and during his graduate school years his transportation was a '57 Porsche speedster.

In 1969 Ted began work at the Picatenny Arsenal as research chemist.   He would stay there 37 years until retirement in 2006. As part of his work Ted was a co-inventor of a new high explosive insensitive to impacts that was patented by the Department of Defense in 1995.

Ted stands among the well published writers in the class, with more than 40 articles in print after review by the best scientists in his field--chemistry. Quantum chemistry and its analyses of how atoms respond to molecular vibration, however, is not the kind of publication we find in airport bookstores or even on Amazon. Nor will you find The Journal of Molecular Structures or Chemical Physics in your dentist's waiting room. When John A. Pope received the Nobel Prize for his work in computational chemistry, he was standing on the shoulders of a relatively small group of pioneering chemists in that field, among them Ted Vladimiroff. The concentration of Nobel selection committees on individuals and small teams, often misrepresents the importance of larger and less organized groups in doing the fundamental science behind the winner's visibility.

Since retiring, Ted's interests have shifted to bioscience and biotechnology, especially as they might help reduce health care burdens. Ted likes to keep up on research but says, "Unfortunately science is a full time job." Another possibility occurred to him one day when he and several other people were at his brother's fishing camp. "A friend asked me what propane was and I started thinking what a profound ignorance." Ted is thinking about ways to introduce children to atoms and chemistry by way of an entertaining story that doesn't use scientific vocabulary or even mention the word chemistry.

Meanwhile he keeps fit lifting weights and working out, and mentally fit perusing the New York Times Book Review every week to choose the reading that occupies much of his free time.

Theodore Vladimiroff
281 Newton Swartswood Rd
Newton, NJ 07860-6341
tvladim@embarqmail.com

Patricia Walter

Photo by Fred Feingold

Ice skating comes as close to the freedom of flight as any self-propelled motion a human can make, and skating was Pat's favorite pastime and remains connected to her love of the outdoors and nature. It began near her home in North Shore Acres. "Behind Mrs. Little's house was a small pond. We'd call and ask "is the pond frozen yet." She was also one of the best skaters on Scudder's Pond by Rum Point.

Pat went to kindergarten in Glen Head, then to St. Bartholomew's where the strict discipline often enforced by physical punishment scared her. She remembers teachers using a pack of playing cards, fanned slightly, to wack boys' knuckles. Although she does not remember her own transgression, she says, "For some reason I found myself kneeling on the marble floor in front of Mary." In high school she enjoyed close friends like Carole Brown, Kay Parks and Joanne La Pierre whose mother made "incredible fudge" for their sleepovers. "We went to the beach, to the movies. Your normal good girl kinds of things." Her dad let her drive his MG for a while, but one day at the Pavillion several guys picked up the front wheels and leaned them up against the fence. End of MG driving for Pat.

When Pat and Carole Brown began to take confirmation classes at St. Bartholomews, her father would drop them off and pick them up two hours later. She recalls that one evening instead of walking into St. Boniface, they turned and walked down to the village social center, Dobkin's soda fountain to spend the evening chatting with whoever was there. Two hours later as they returned to ST. B's, there stood Father Gately on the sidewalk. "Carol says brightly, 'Good evening Father Gately.'" She remembers being horrified, but not the consequences.

After graduation Pat "I didn't have a clue what I wanted to do." She moved to Manhattan and attended the Laboratory Instute for Merchandising (LIM) in the heart of the fashion district to satisfy her bent for creative work. She went to work for photography studios as a stylist picking backgrounds and selecting and prepping models for magazine and mail order catalog displays. She learned how to use "paper clips and clothespins for a lot of good reasons no one sees."

Her lifelong appetite for travel was whetted when her roommate and she went on a six week tour of Europe. When she came back she went to Central Park with a group to ice skate. By that time she could do some skate dancing. On the ice she met a recently discharged Navy veteran, Richard Miller. They married in 1962 with Carole Brown Muttee as one of the bridesmaids. Pat and Richard bought a stationery store in New Hyde Park on Long Island and operated that for two years. Their first son, Richard was born in 1963.

When her dad, whom she was very close to, died at age 50 she says, "I needed to get away from New York." Richard had a brother in Charlotte, NC and when they visited him they fell in love with the location and decided to move. They both liked Charlotte for its easy access to both the coast and the mountains, and they bought a small mobile home at Surfside, SC for their coastal vacations. Richard opened a dry wall shop and became a contractor for home improvements and occasional commercial work. Their daughter Christy was born in North Carolina in 1971. In 1977 Pat started work as an administrator and teaching assistant in a local Montessori school and continued that work for twenty years until the public school system asked her to work in a pilot program that would include a Montessori school. She worked there for ten years. "I loved my job and the children kept me young at heart. I still volunteer many hours a month."

Pat had also started a little business of her own, Botanical Treasures, making unique clear glass plates with pressed flowers in them, some plates up to 18 inches in diameter. They became a best seller at the well known Stowe Botanical Gardens and she still makes some and sells occasionally at crafts exhibits.

Daughter Christie lives in Cary, NC where she was a mortgage originator, and son Richard runs All Pro Painting in Monroe, NC. Pat's husband suffered a stroke in 1997 that confined him to a wheelchair until he died in 2004. Once retired, Pat began to enjoy her freedom of movement. She went to Alaska in '06, to Peru in '07, and to Oregon's high desert and coast in '08. Always innovating, she continues to water paint and has begun to do finger print art for families, turning the family's prints into colored flowers.

Pat Miller
5134 Valley Stream Rd.
Charlotte, NC 28209
Pattwm@aol.com

Karen Wignes

Karen grew up in Glenwood Landing.   There she and Roey Bennett began a lifelong friendship.   When Karen married Daniel Reynolds of Glen Cove at Trinity Lutheran Roey was a bridesmaid.   Karen has two daughters and one son, plus three grandchildren.

In her school years Karen was a swimmer, skier, and softball slugger who played the piano for relaxation.   After graduation she worked for First National Bank in Glen Head until she moved to Florida where she has been living for many years.   Dan Reynolds passed away in '81 or '82.

We would like to include more information but in deference to her wishes, we leave the story with these few facts.

Tom Wolf

Photo by Fred Feingold

If we had voted on a superlative for "most modest," Tom Wolf might have received the label. Instead, when he came to Sea Cliff from Glenwood School, he was often most noticeable. From our freshman year on he was the tallest person in the class, unmatched until Mike Stanton, also 6'3", arrived our senior year. Tom grew up like the average Glen Head kid, delighting in the Saturday matinee movies at the Cove Theater in Glen Cove where he remembers that the manager Uncle Max always treated kids well.

Being tall had something to do with being modest. "I wasn't exactly outgoing and being tall didn't help matters too much." But that left Tom possibly freer than most to be who he was. He did not hesitate to use his size and strength in basketball and in throwing the discus and shot-put. Tom also played soccer. While the expectations aroused by his size and strength often made him feel unusual pressure, he enjoyed competition and representing Sea Cliff High. He appreciated Coach Driscoll's practical and encouraging tutelage in both mechanical drawing and on the varsity basketball team. "He was tough but fair and made sure you were learning what you were supposed to learn."

Tom's father had a surveying business in Glen Head and during the school year Tom began working in that business as a "gofer" when he was 14 and gradually took on greater responsibility. During summers, the family vacationed in New England's Berkshires and around Lake Champlain.

After Sea Cliff Tom went to C.W. Post College for three years to study business, but found himself thinking, "Why am I taking all these courses when I'm not really going to use them?" He left to work in surveying with a Mineola firm. "It wasn't a very smart decision at the time because I was so close to the end," he says, and today he thinks it was immaturity. On his lunch breaks he would often stop in a little Glen Cove restaurant where local employees ate. He noticed an interesting young bank teller also eating there, but says, "I needed help." Friends "leaked the word to her that this guy was interested." They had begun dating when the Army called.

They never asked him about his surveying or civil engineering skills. After basic at Fort Dix, NJ, they gave him a battery of tests. "I have no idea what came out the other end. They decided I would make a wonderful cook." They sent him to cooking school at Ft Lee. "I wasn't crazy about being in that class," he says and after one summer he moved into administration because "Thanks to Betty French from Sea Cliff I knew how to type and that's what got me into that slot and that's where I stayed." He was in charge of temporary duty and short timers and processing AWOLs coming through.

Tom was discharged in 1965 and had continued to see Susan the bank teller when he was home on leave. They married in 1967. Their daughter Karen was born in 1968. Tom was now working hard in the surveying business with his former Mineola firm, and he earned his license in 1976. He returned to Glen Head to work with his father, and they eventually moved the office to Sea Cliff. Tom was able to continue the family tradition of summer vacations in northern New York. He also spent twelve years with the Glenwood Landing Fire Department on its aerial ladder truck and was active in Rotary along with former Sea Cliff principal John French. After his father died in the mid '80s, Tom took over the firm and continues to work there full time and still does field work. His daughter Karen graduated from the University of Delaware in '86 and went to work for a Ft. Walton Beach, Florida newspaper, later moving to Ft. Collins, Colorado where her husband hosts a radio show.

Tom Wolf
7 Greely Square
Glen Head, NY 11545
Suziq2@optonline.net

Serge Yonov

Photo by Nik Epanchin

Over the course of his life, Serge (Sergey in Russian) completed many journeys in thought, time and space, but the most important was his journey in time from the Soviet Union to America and back. Except for a small administrative problem in the Russian Orthodox Church, Serge's family would have become Argentines instead of Americans. Before the US entered WWII, Stalin made his infamous pact with Hitler and the Germans took over the Baltic republics of Lithuania, Estonia and Latvia. Since neither leader was a reliable keeper of treaties Stalin's armies were soon pushing into Latvia where Sergey's grandfather had established a church and where his father, The Right Reverend Alexis Yonov had a church in Riga. The Soviets arrived with a price on Father Yonov's head for having re-opened churches on Soviet territory. The family stayed as long as possible. Serge's younger brother Cyril ('59) remembers bursting shrapnel and bombs blowing out church windows.

The Yonovs had no choice but to leave with the retreating German armies. They boarded an overloaded ferry from Riga to Danzig, a German and now Polish port on the Baltic. They went overland to Berlin. As the Soviets were closing in on Berlin, they made their way south into Austria. In the small village of Mondsee south of Salzburg Father Yonov held Orthodox services in the St. Maria of Pilzburg Catholic church when its masses finished. When the war ended, the Yonovs took a place on the immigration lists for Argentina because the quotas for the US were full. As they traveled north toward the departure port of Bremerhaven, word reached Father Alexis that the Orthodox Metropolitan in New York needed a replacement for the old and retiring priest at Our Lady of Kazan in Sea Cliff, the small brown shingled, onion domed church near the bottom of Littleworth Lane.

The family boarded the SS Marine Swallow with some 600 other passengers and set out across the north Atlantic in hurricane season. The ship narrowly missed a head on encounter with a category 4 hurricane by increasing normal cruising speed to 21 knots, but seas were heavy and all the furniture was lashed down. Capt. Elisha Cooper said of the spectacular red skies, Such skies are seen in the Orient, but it was the first time I ever saw them in the North Atlantic." (NY Times, 9/17/48)   The Yonovs disembarked into the cavernous reception hall of Ellis Island.   In New York City with the staff of the Metropolitan the boys, Cyril and Serge had their first American meal—Nabisco Shredded Wheat.   A few days later they arrived in Sea Cliff.

Nine year old Serge had attended first grade in Germany, but to learn English he started a few grades behind and joined our class a year or two later.   By graduation he had participated in half the clubs the school offered, served as Student Council treasurer, and earned his letters in track, soccer, and wrestling. In soccer he made the all-scholastic team.

He left Sea Cliff with a full four year scholarship from the Li Foundation, one of two given that year, and entered Colorado School of Mines.   For his junior year he transferred to Washington University in DC and, with an International Relations major, he began the intellectual part of his life's journey.   To take him physically as well as intellectually on the journey he joined the US Navy.   While earning his Masters of Science degree he met his future wife Gail who had finished her bachelor's in French Literature and returned to her home in nearby Pebble Beach.   They married in June 1970.   With Serge often at sea on destroyers, they lived wherever he was based whether that was California, Rhode Island or Hawaii.   In Rhode Island he served alongside Commander Pete Marnane ('55) and Lt. Commander Todd Allen ('59), Jane Allen's brother. Their daughter Helen Alexis was born in 1979 and enjoyed the domestic and foreign travel the Navy required.   Between sea duties, Serge began to serve as Naval Attaché at US embassies.   He was our first naval attaché in Kuala Lumpur.   His last foreign duty he served as naval attaché in Moscow under ambassadors Robert Strauss and Jack Matlock, thus becoming our last attaché in the USSR and the first in the new Russia.

Serge also taught at the prestigious Naval War College from 88-90 and again at the end of his career in '92-3, and he was an invited lecturer at Brasenose College, Oxford.   He had the special honor of attending the Naval Command College which gathers together one participant from the highest naval ranks in a variety of countries from Africa, Asia, Europe and Latin America.   They participate as equals to learn about US naval thinking and explain their own thinking.   Serge's wife, Gail Root, serves as a regional director of the Naval War College Foundation and says the Command College is "One of the few places where, if there's a possibility of peace in this world, men from dif countries can meet each other in a neutral ground."   Many participants go on to become admirals and even chiefs of state.

When Serge was naval attaché in Moscow he went back to Latvia.   In Riga and on the train to the town where his grandfather had a church he met people who remembered both his father and grandfather.   In '92 Cyril and his wife Carol visited Serge in Moscow and traveled to Latvia where they met by cousins, visited Cyril's birthplace, and attended a memorial service memorial at their grandfather's grave.

After retiring from the service, Serge began consulting for businesses exploring trade with Russia. Serge and Gail's daughter Alexis, after graduating from Emerson University in Boston went to Los Angeles where she learned the film business and has become a writer and director. Although Serge met an early death in 2004, he had had the satisfaction of returning to his roots as a free man, reuniting with his family. He continued serving his country while watching the Soviet Union that had launched him on his path to American citizenship and all his achievements fell apart under the weight of its own oppressive system.

Below four people who knew Serge well remember him.

John Storojev.

We had a complicated relationship that swung between affection and dislike. I guess we were very competitive in those days: for girls, for honors, for sports. You name it. It wasn't much fun, in retrospect. Serge came from a strict Russian Orthodox upbringing, which was my background as well. So we understood each other on a deeper level I think. I was an alter boy at his father's church, and I remember him lording it over us because of his status there. He had a lot going on with the pull of his strict father and the demands of the school and an American society. At one point he was very close to my younger sister and there was a real danger that he could have ended up as my brother-in-law. Imagine that! I am glad he made a name for himself in Naval intelligence and as a commander of a naval vessel. I tried over the years to find out what he was doing, but only got snatches of information from the effort. I was distraught to learn of his untimely death.

Peter Rose ('59).

[Peter sent the following vignette in notes about athletes. Peter was a classmate of Serge's younger brother Cyril. Peter graduated from college and became a Green Beret before embarking on a lifelong career as a journalist.]
Wearing my Army Class A's and beret, about to ship out to Europe, I was with Charlie Hartman in Greenwich Village and ran into Serge and his girlfriend in one of those little places that doesn't have a sign on the door. I never forgot the girl. Absolutely gorgeous and so sad about Serge leaving, also for an overseas assignment.

Pete Marnane (Class of '55):

"I knew of Serge Yonov's death and actually attended his funeral. We saw Serge and Gail frequently when we were both stationed here in the Newport RI area. At one point in the early 80's, we had command of sister ships in Newport and later both of us had tours at the Naval War College."

Peter Basilevsky (NSHS, younger brother of Helen)

" I remember in 1990 having lunch with him, my mother and Gail at their apartment in Moscow where he regaled us with his various adventures including being in Tehran during the Khomeini revolution. He was also gracious enough to invite me, my wife and my son Alexis (then 5 and 1/2) to attend a change of command ceremony in 1982 in Newport as he was leaving command of his frigate. Our tour of his ship made a deep impression on my son who still has the autographed picture of Serge's ship."

Peter also passed on this:

Serge was a NILO (Naval intelligence liason officer) in Vietnam and served in the Mekong Delta region. He nearly bought the farm while shaving one day in the field when a RPG buzzed by his head. But his worst time according to him was when he was invited to a dinner honoring the local Vietnamese Army commander. Apparently, as he entered the restaurant he was required to pop a "thousand year old egg" into his mouth and eat it. Apparently, this was an egg with a chick in it about ready to be born which is then buried so that it can "ripen". Obviously to have declined would have been a great insult and a loss of face so poor Serge went ahead and consumed it. He told me it was one of the worst experiences of his life since throwing up would have been much worse than declining the invitation to imbibe the delicacy. Clearly his diplomatic skills surfaced early in his career.

Stories of Captain Serge A. Yonov by Pietro Savo

I reported for duty on-board the U.S.S. Connole (FF-1056) around late January 1980. Captain Yonov took command February 1980 while dockedin Catania, Sicily. The previous captain, Captain Fijak kept to himself; he did not interact with the enlisted crew. This had been my first shipboard deployment, and I genuinely thought that was normal. Once Captain Yonov assumed command this all changed. The line was still drawn between enlisted and commissioned. However, something had changed. True leadership creates positive change and a positive environment for change. Captain Yonov would speak with us not only about our duties on board the Connole, he would talk about family, hobbies, and things that were important to us. He understood the utmost importance of relationship and true team building. He understood that creating a closely bound community like a naval ship, depended on mutual binding relationships.

On a small frigate like the Connole you knew quickly who you liked or disliked, who you trusted, or distrusted. Captain Yonov encouraged trust built on relationships, from shipboard duties, to the ship's softball team, and the daily news briefing we called *Fish-Eye News*. *Fish-Eye News* was televised on the ship network; it was more crew members making fun of other crew members than real news. Sometimes very funny, sometimes not so funny. We worked hard and played hard and that was the Captain's and our definition of the team.

We spent a great deal of time at sea, and it seemed an equal amount of awesome time on the beach in port somewhere. . . . When we ran into the Captain during liberty, he always did not want us to fuss over him. We would jump to attention or attempt to solute him, he would wave us off. I remember on a liberty boat in Naples Italy, I had shore patrol duty that night; we had a sailor spread across four seats. The captain came on board, when I attempted to clear a seat for the captain, he said don't bother, I can stand. That is the type of leader he was, mutual respect was the norm and we all felt it.

On Connole's Bridge, you knew who was in charge; his leadership style was to encourage others to lead, from the officer of the deck to the enlisted crew members. During port entry and port exit I was the Combat Information Center (CIC) Bridge Phone Talker. My job was to take information from the radarscope operator in CIC and track, plot surface ship contacts. Yell out this information officer of deck and Captain could navigate around them. Early in my career as a CIC Bridge Phone Talker Captain Yonov told me it was not necessary to yell out all the surface contacts, only the ones I felt were important and posed a threat to the ship.

The Captain's request went against my training. What I did not realize until later, the Captain always encouraged his crew to think on their feet. He motivated us by trusting us. I can to this day remember him asking me with his slight Russian accent, "What do you think Petty Officer Savo, should I be worried about that contact?" One particular morning while transiting the Strait of Messina, I had just come off the mid-watch. Attempting to get some rest, I was summoned to the Bridge; Captain Yonov apologized for waking me up. He said that not having me on the Bridge during the Strait of Messina transit made him uncomfortable. He also gave me the next 72 hours off when we were done. Respect created respect and our crew protected each other at sea and on the bridge.

Captain Yonov often discussed our families and my future in the United States Navy. I told him I was engaged to be married and felt the Navy would be difficult on a marriage. My fiancée's dad was a WW2 Navy Sailor and Captain Yonov invited my future father-in-law to ride aboard the Connole from Manhattan to Newport. Harold Gorman was invited to the Bridge by the Captain, sat in the captain's chair and Captain Yonov began explaining why it would be a fantastic career for Petty Officer Savo to stay in the Navy. A little background on Harold Gorman, he has never been shy or soft spoken. Harold told the Captain that he was speaking to the wrong person. The person you want to have the Naval career discussion with is my daughter Patty. The Captain smiled and went to his business of guiding his ship up the east river into Long Island sound into Newport.

Chasing a Foxtrot Russian submarine, the last story, when this occurred I was on duty in CIC. I remember the Captain asking the CIC duty officer if he thought the Foxtrot we were tracking knew we were here. Absolutely said the duty officer. I agree, said the Captain.

The Connole had an underwater telephone. The captain went over to it and asked in Russian, that the Foxtrot surface and the sub did. That is where the famous U.S.S. Connole (FF- 1056) shadows a "Foxtrot" class submarine photograph came from.

Photo by: ET2 Bruce Chalk
Text by Petty Officer Second Class, Pietro (Pete) Savo, U.S.S. Connole (FF-1056)

Pietro (Pete) Savo is the President / CEO at Mont Vernon Group. LLC.

www.montvernongroup.org

Pietro is the Author of:Root Cause Analysis System for Problem Solving and Problem Avoidance and *PERFECTION - 10 Secrets to Successful Lean Manufacturing Implementatio*

WE WERE NOT ALONE
NOTES ON OTHER STUDENTS IN OUR CLASS
OR IN OUR ACTIVITIES

Bob Bostrom

From John Storojev:

I was good friends with Bostrom who was at Sea Cliff until his Sophomore year. We shared a passion for art and we both attended the Brooklyn Museum of Art School for a brief time, going into The Big City. I took my first live model class there. I remember trying to draw this rather unattractive naked woman and yet having a hard time concentrating. During that era there weren't many places that you could see a naked woman except through those old-style (by today's "standards") girlie magazines. Nothing like it is today for young people. We can do a whole research paper on the subject of sex education and the awakening or repression of that primal instinct during that era. Anybody read Winesberg Ohio by Sherwood Anderson? Just put Sea Cliff in place of Winesberg and you'll get the picture. Bostrom had family problems which forced him to move out of Sea Cliff. He visited one time thereafter, but I never saw him again. He became an artist in The City and I still have one of his line-art pieces somewhere in my pile of stuff.

From Wallace Kaufman:

Bob and his family lived at the bottom of Tilley Place at the top of a long flight of wooden stairs that led to Tilley's boathouse and which formed one boundary of the wooded hillside everyone called "The 18 Trails". Bob's stepfather was an amateur radio operator who taught me how to build a rectifier to change AC to DC current, and demonstrated to my great interest how he could talk to people in Australia or Japan or Europe on his radio.

Bob and I and maybe Pete Swanson once decided we should try to make the old flash powder that late 19th and early 20th century photographers used before flash bulbs. In Bob's bedroom we mixed the necessary chemicals, placed them in a plastic tray, and ignited them. They produced acetylene gas. A thin column of brilliant white flame leaped up to the ceiling and quickly died, leaving the room filled with a white smoke.

When we looked up, we saw a large black spot on the ceiling. Where the tray had been was a hole scorched into the rug. Bob's mother called up, "What are you doing up there?" Bob called back, "Nothing."

In high school I had written a notebook full of poems that I hope no one will ever read. I keep them for two reasons. First, I think I write much better, but I want to remind myself how a teenager usually writes. Second, I asked Bob Bostrum to illustrate the notebook for me and I won't throw out that first-ever writer/illustrator collaboration.

Anita Hamilton

Photo by N Epanchin

Anita Hamilton left our class along with her friend Priscilla Bowden after the sophomore year, but many remember her as a smart, thoughtful girl whose father was Thomas Hamilton, a correspondent for *The New York Times*. I have seen her twice since then and each time has been a reminder that despite our general unconsciousness of caste and class, events sometimes brought out the lines very distinctly.

Late in our junior year Nik Epanchin and I received invitations to attend a coming out or debutante debut at the Piping Rock Country Club. Our invitors were Anita and Priscilla. On the appointed evening Nik and I dressed in our best Buddy Holly era Sears Roebuck or Filene's charcoal gray suits with pink shirts. We motored to one of Long Island's most exclusive clubs in his father's '51 Plymouth, one of those cars that looked something like a motorized machine gun pill box. We showed our engraved invitations and the door opened on a darkened room filled with music and people our age. The famous Lester Lanin's Band of Reknown was making the music, and the audience was a crowd of prep school kids, the male portion wearing dinner jackets, bow ties and cumber buns. The rest I don't remember.

In 1999 a Duke classmate who was serving on Clinton's National Security Council invited me to attend a wedding reception with her at DC's stodgy, fabled, and exclusive Cosmo Club. Her friend, a lawyer with the CIA, was getting married or remarried. We found our name tags for the dinner at a large round table. The boy-girl-boy-girl seating placed to my right a woman with a Polish name and a face that somehow said, "Horsey set." (Not that such faces always know which end of a horse is forward.) We talked. She was a reporter for the *Hartford Courant*, usually covering education, but here because the bride was an old school or college chum. I mentioned having published an article in the *Courant*. The follow up revealed that she was once Anita Hamilton. The rest I don't remember.

Richie Loftus

Richie became one of my first close friends in Sea Cliff when I was in third or fourth grade.   His family lived in chaos and squalor, at least as I remember it.   A typical afternoon I still relive clearly.   I was at his family's little cottage on Altamont Ave. near the present North Shore High.   The yard had a few bushes and trees, no grass, but a lot of junk.   The house was what people in the South call a "dollar down" house, a cheap pre-fab or quickly built low roofed bungalow with tiny rooms, thin walls, no basement, a tiny kitchen, and small windows.   We sat on the doorstep side by side.   Richie's little brother toddled up behind him sucking milk from a glass baby bottle.   Suddenly he raised the bottle and brought it down hard on Richie's head.   Richie exploded in curses, holding his head and spitting with anger.   His mother started cursing back at him and at the baby.   She stood there telling us to get out of the house, holding the wailing baby on her hip.   She wore a soiled thin shapeless housedress.   Her hair hung down in greasy ropes.   Maybe for the first time in my life I felt deeply sorry for someone my own age.

A few years later, still before we had become teenagers, I remember reading a book that I believe was called *The Hidden Garden*.   This was not the famous English story of the little girl in a big house.   This was about a poor boy whose father was a drunk.   The garden somehow helped the boy understand his burden and redeem his father.   I was excited because the story seemed to be a perfect parallel to Richie and his father, maybe a cure for his troubles.   I urged him to go to the library and get it.

Richie and I roamed around Sea Cliff and up into Brookville and Glen Cove.   We liked to find places to hide, build a campfire, catch frogs, whack trees with a hatchet, carve our names with a knife.   One day he called me from in front of my house, and when I came out and asked what he wanted to do, he said, "Let's go break some windows."   I didn't like the idea, but I agreed.   We went down Central Avenue and up into a wooded area behind the big old houses until we were behind a backyard garage with a window facing us.   Richie decided that was one we could break and get away.   He heaved a stone square through the window and we ran.   Over 50 years later I asked John Storojev if he remembered his family's garage window being broken.   He did.

Read Betty Sprague's biography page or Jane Allen's and you will see other evidence that Richie was both a bully and subject to fits of rage.   I was wary of those fits of rage because I had seen them turn him into a windmill of flailing fists that devastated other kids as much by their fury as by their power.   But Richie wanted to be something more than a bully and hothead.   I have always been grateful to him for spending a lot of time trying to help me make the JV basketball team by deciding if I couldn't run fast or jump high, I might become a specialized corner shooter.   He made me practice.   In scrimmages he passed up his own opportunities to throw the ball to me in the corner where I could try to prove my worth.

The second or third short story I ever sold was about a character who was no more than a thinly disguised version of Richie, and it attempted to explore the reasons why I ended up at Oxford and the Richie character ended up in jail.   I don't know what Richie did when he left our class and school before graduation.   Reliable reports say that years later he was found in his garage, in his car with the motor running.   He had given up the life I believe he had struggled to leave in better and less fatal ways.

R I P

Bob "Mugsy" Myles

I am indebted to Peter Rose ('59) for first mentioning the story of Bob Myles and the essay on Bob's life written by Peter's classmate Don Drott.

Mugsy the Ivy Leaguer
By Don Drott ('59)

There was a story about Bob that I heard on two occasions, which I considered to be probably apocryphal, and not truly that meaningful. Until later. After the transmogrification. Then I wondered. Could that have caused it?

The story was that when he had been playing football for Brown, an undersized secondary defenseman, he had been struck quite hard on the head. Despite the helmet, he had spent several weeks in the infirmary, in a darkened room, and they had been concerned about him. He was a big-man-on-campus - class officer, football star, and a bit of a hell raiser. He was noticed, as he had been in high school, where I had played with him. Baseball. Bob played four sports, the classic football, basketball, baseball trinity, and track and field, where the really gifted where given a chance to shine despite not practicing much because of the overlap with the other more important sports. I *played* at the games, and sometimes did rather well, but Bob was an *athlete*. Despite being small. Really small. That was what made him special. He performed against bigger boys throughout, and he was a star. Not at cross country, or soccer, the traditional refuges of the vertically challenged, but in the arenas where the big guys hung out.

When I returned to the home town, as some of us do, after my obligatory cavort with the more adult games of Manhattan, he was pushing forty. We got together for some beers and double dating. Nothing is quite as large later, as it had appeared in high school, including the stars, for we, the normal kids, have grown. In terms of experience, and sometimes success, certainly with the self-confidence, unless you're simply not making it. Still, being with Bob Myles, that Bob Myles, was always a bit different. On my small scale, the parochial one that we always carry with us, I was quaffing one with a legend.

And the legend had continued to impress. At least that was the initial impression.

After Brown, where he had done well, it had been off to Stanford Law. Now we in the East tend to think that if it wasn't Yale or Harvard, or possibly Columbia, it wasn't that prestigious. But it was. So Mugsy had Brown University and Stanford Law under his belt, and was now a practicing attorney. I remember sitting there with him, feeling the warm hospitality of the beer filtering in, and thinking, "Not bad for a shanty Irishman from the home town. "

Perhaps I should explain "shanty. " Oh, and "Mugsy."

I never met his parents.   But everybody had met his brother.   And if you met Frankie Myles at the wrong time and place, especially in a bar, you might never forget that meeting.   Frankie was one of the tough guys that every small town has.   Fighting was his forte, and the foundation of his persona.   Apparently the only foundation worthy of comment, for he was not an athlete like his brother, and he didn't give two hoots about education, and who knows what became of him, or cares.   Based on Frankie, and a few rumors, I always imagined that Bob's father was the type that would sometimes come home with a snootful, haranguing the neighborhood with IRA songs, and scaring the bejesus out of his wife, as they say.   Perhaps unfair to the father, I admit, but if shanty did not fairly apply to the paternal influence, it certainly did to the hard fisted, hard drinking, trouble pursued older brother.   And the Ivy Leaguer, Stanford Law guy, my friend, indeed had inherited at least a bit of it.

My junior year, Bob's senior, a high school party in a suburban home with no parental oversight visible.   I watch as he measures a big kid from a rival town, unpleasant looking brute who seems to have the same reputation and attitude as brother Frankie.   The brute is unaware that the small guy next to him is pissed. .   Pissed at what?, who cares. He's had a few, and he's small, and if he were bigger he would be headed for the Major Leagues, and this is what you do when the social inhibitions are released by the ethyl alcohol in certain circles, and who gives a shit anyway.   I see him adjusting his position just to the side of and out of the peripheral vision of the brute, and then looking down at a large knobbed ring on his right hand, swiveling it slightly so the knob, the striking knob, is centered just above the knuckle.   I know what's going to happen.   I can still see, so vividly, the blood flashing up towards the ceiling, a slashing cut appearing magically on the brute's forehead, just the size of the knob, and that large kid toppling backward towards the deck.   Cold-cocked by a midget.   Bob had jumped upward as he threw the punch, to make up the foot difference in height.   And therefore *Mugsy.*

So there I am, ordering another round with Mugsy the Ivy Leaguer, reminiscing about our double play combination and the girls who did and the less interesting ones who did not, and at some point I become aware that something is not quite as it should be with him.   Subtle.   Shielded by what he was, and the present accouterments of normality. Successful normality? I didn't probe, but the signals came.   A nervous flick of the eye. He seemed wary, like the guy who hasn't paid his bookie and the bookie drops in here sometimes.   A lower order nervousness.   Not that of a Stanford lawyer.   And the legal matters that he discussed seemed, surprisingly, rather trivial.   At this stage in his career, with his background, he should be talking of big-time business deals, or cause celebre trials, or judgeships.   Bob appeared to be an ambulance chaser.   And not the chaser who flies his own jet to the next mass tort meeting.   I remembered my first start at second base. The consummate shortstop next to me had fielded four groundballs with that easy aplomb of his and hit the pivot man chest high each time, long before the runner had a chance to disembowel me, as I had feared, and I had completed four double plays.   I was a starter for the rest of my high school career.   What's wrong, Bob?

He was riding a bike.   *Bicycle*, not a Harley.   And he was going to work.

The courthouse was ten miles away, through a lot of traffic.   Automotive traffic. And the suit, although clean, was like the ones you see on a retarded kid attending a wedding.   The suit should not be on this person.

I pulled up alongside and stopped, stepped out of the car.   It was summertime, and the suit which should not have been there was soaking down with sweat.   Large black splotches assaulting the tan.   Want a lift, Bob? A certain embarrassment, but he did not quite understand his own embarrassment.   There was a fog between he and I.   During the brief conversation I realized that the fog interceded not just between the two of us.   It was cutting him off from the world.

"Business in Mineola, Bob?" The county courthouse.

"Yeah.   I pick up DWI cases there. "

With a saturated suit that rides up above your socks, and a bicycle, and eyes that look like a head-lighted deer.   I looked away.   "Where you living now, buddy. " The next day I paid a month's rent in advance for him at a place where people live who other people don't want to be visible.

The next time I saw him, probably half a year, although I had inquired to no avail, was at   night, on a heavily wooded road.   Secluded.   And he had a car.   I caught sight of his small but distinctive figure bent over the opened hood of a relic pulled off into the brush.   I turned around and pulled over with my lights shining into the engine compartment, helpful I hoped.   But as I approached I saw him tense into the attack receiving attitude, and I stopped.

"It's me, Bob.   Don.   See you replaced the old bike with some wheels. " Big smile, reassuring I hoped.

In truth, I don't know if he knew who I was.   He had aged impossibly.   I was staring into the eyes of an old man.   I didn't recognize the eyes.   They were not actually vacuous, although that word lept out at you.   More accurately, they lacked that full sense of awareness, of intelligence, that defines a human being.   A sane human being.

"They've been following me. "

"Who?"

Unlike now, when America's *bete noire* is an Islamic fundamentalist, these were Cold War years.   "Russians. "

I didn't know how to respond to that.

"And the fucking niggers."

Now coming from Frankie Myles this might not have surprised me.   But Bob Myles had embraced gentility, in part, I'm sure, to separate himself from his brother.   The sophistication of the Eastern establishment, and Brown had become the institution of choice for the Kennedys, did not permit this.

"Can I help you get it started, Bob?"

Driving home, I considered the concept of atavism.

From time to time over the next few years, I saw him.   Walking along the sidewalks of my suburbia.   No car.   No bicycle.   But an increasing assortment of things. Stuff.   You noticed the bums in Manhattan with a lot of *stuff.*   I tried, but he would never make eye contact.   Except when you would turn suddenly, and catch him stating at *you.*

Did he know me? Do people like Bob know what is happening to them? Is there a Reaganesque retreat, measured, with an unbearably heroic stoicism, that elevates them beyond what they seem?

And what causes such a thing to happen to a man like this? A small man who never seemed small.   Whose life was, until it happened, anything but small.   Did God do it? The same God who gave Ireland the priests and the alcohol and the potatoes that failed? Or simply a cellular thing that happens sometimes, and bad luck to you as you decline into cerebral chaos?

 You know what I think? You played a hell of a shortstop Mugsy, and if you were bigger I would have watched you on television, and sometimes they throw a curveball on three and two.

ADMINISTRATION, TEACHERS, AND STAFF

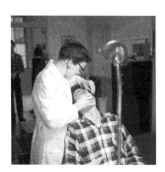

All photos by Fred Feingold

We were separated from the Spartans of ancient Greece by more than 2,000 years, but the idea of the public school is rooted in their radical innovation—take the children from their parents and family and subject them to an authority that will treat them all alike and train them to think of themselves as part of something larger. That larger society required quite different responsibilities and offered much greater freedoms. Spartans, of course, began by weeding out and killing those thought unfit for training while our school took everyone. Spartan training was physically and mental brutal and uncompromising. Over the millennia Western education had developed compassion and inclusiveness and flexibility. The purpose, however, remained the same—develop a citizenry that has a common understanding of national history, political values, and sense of purpose; in short a citizenry with an identity that survives and is more important than the family identity.

Those who have inherited this tradition begun in ancient Greece do not think of themselves as limited by their membership in a caste or class or religion or clan, but by the customs and laws of their country. These other identities exist and even thrive under the umbrella of national identity. The fit has been seriously flawed in the past and continues to have flaws. Nevertheless, it is because of these other identities that we have democracy, and because of democracy we can enjoy these other identities. Every adult in Sea Cliff School had been employed to play a role in our civilizing process and forging our identity as citizens. Some understood their role this way. Maybe a few came for the job only and did not care or did not think much about history or purpose or even results. When I look at the faces of all these people in our yearbook, I remember each one, and I cannot name one who didn't care at all.

This section of our class history recognizes those adults and their authority and records how what we thought about them and their work. As I organized the information for this chapter, I happened to read an Internet Blog that is written by Dr. Norman Ross who came to Sea Cliff in our junior or senior year to teach English, World Literature and coach junior varsity soccer. In response to an invitation to the Class of '58 reunion, which he had to decline, he noted some facts about himself that none of his classes knew. That solid little, freckle faced, red haired cock-of-the walk, in-command teacher had flown 60 combat missions in World War II as a tail gunner in a bomber, winning two Distinguished Flying Crosses and 11 Air Medals.

That revelation moved me to ask him why he never told us that he had even served in the military. And furthermore, I asked if what seemed like a wall between teachers' personal lives and students was official school policy, an accepted part of teaching practice, or the result of something else.

Dr. Ross replied, *"In my own case, the war was still too close in my memory. I tried with great difficulty to forget it and to press on with my life. My brain was still littered with scorpions...and to this day I still mourn for my buddies who did not return. This failure to reveal one's war experiences in the classroom was not due to any "school policy" nor was there any real "wall". It was just the way it was and will always be."*

This is not the place for an argument with Dr. Ross over whether the divide will always be that way or whether it is that way today. But certainly it was that way.

After retiring from public school teaching Doc wrote a memoir of his time in the Air Force, *Memoirs of a Tail Gunner*. A little summary and a few passages give the full sense of just how much we never knew.

The young Norman Ross signed up for the Navy. He expected to be assigned an office job because he could read, write and type well, but found himself doing kitchen duty in Chicago. He asked to see the list of training programs and signed up to be an aviation radio operator. That training led to gunnery training. And for a month or two the war was fun.

"Aerial gunnery school was more fun for me and the other sailors than we could have possibly imagined. It was truly dulce et decorum! It was four weeks in a Penny Arcade. We learned how to shoot, take apart and put back together 30 and 50 caliber machineguns and how to clean them; we went skeet and trap shooting using shotguns that wrecked havoc on my shoulder. Nevertheless, through all the pain, I became very adept at blasting those clay pigeons that flew out from every angle; we hit golf balls for exact timing. What was really exciting were the leather jackets we were issued and the white scarves and aviator's sunglasses. The jackets even had fur collars! While wearing them

Ifelt like Snoopy ready to take on the Red Baron!   (But, of course, back then there was no Snoopy but if there were, I felt like him)."

Then in July 1944 Doc's unit was ordered into the war in Europe.   His pilot flew over their family home in the Bronx and dipped his wings to where Doc's mother should have been waiting in the street below.   Doc arrived in England still 'flying high.'   "We were hot—a bunch of teenagers who, though not in college, could legally be riotous by creating havoc with the enemy!   How cool was that?"

During the following year the war grew grim and real for Doc and his crew.   They were flying out of Dunkleswell, England.   From that field 67 Liberator aircraft like his never returned to base.   With them 222 airmen died.   When Doc returned home to begin the rest of his life it didn't seem worth living at times.   Here is what he went through before he could go to college and arrive at Sea Cliff to teach was as much kept from us as any word of his military experience.

"At home, when my mother and sister were out, I would sit on my bed and stare blankly at the window which overlooked an alley precipitously below.   I would get up and violently punch holes in the wall above my bed.   This behavior was not lost on my mother and perhaps I wished her to notice it as a non-verbal request for help.   And finally one night while they were occupied in another room, I opened my window and decided to try to end my life & to join my friends who never came back to fulfill their own lives.   I felt guilt ridden about my own survival; I was completely numb and felt as though I were anesthetized. The war had caught up with me.   Three years of existing on adrenalin and high levels of testosterone had come crashing down.   My mind was filled with scorpions."

"My sister heard the window open and sensing something wrong, rushed in, screaming and sobbing, and grabbed me by my belt and somehow succeeded in pulling me back into the room.   My mother sat me down and insisted that Igo to the VA hospital the next morning.   I told her I was OK   "It's OK, mom.   I'm OK.   I'll go but I'll be out in a couple of days. It's all right.   Not to worry."It didn't work out that way.   My mother accompanied me to the VA Medical Center in the Kingsbridge section of the Bronx.   After registering and seeing a doctor, I described my symptoms, and my mother recounted my feeble aborted attempt at suicide.   The doctor diagnosed my condition as battle fatigue and insisted that I had better be admitted immediately to prevent something beyond feeble.Battle Fatigue is the World War II name for what is now known asPost-Traumatic Stress Disorder or PTSD."

Most teachers kept the complexity and depth of their lives from us.   Maybe it was that way and should be that way because that way is in harmony with the ideals of our nation.   A teacher should have attention and earn respect not for being a war hero, a genius, a comedian, a musician, a great dancer, a beauty, the descendant of nobility, or the relative of a performing star; he or she should have attention and the chance to earn respect for being a teacher.

Who was Freda Kittelberger, after all? A big buxom older woman who lived in a modest apartment above a hardware store by herself. She didn't tell jokes. She didn't play the ukulele. She didn't have a past. We didn't care if she had a future or any ambitions or dreams. She wanted to teach math. She wanted us to learn math. She was strict. She was fair. She inspired fear. And not every person who has talked about her has praised her. And the only thing they have to praise her for is being a teacher.

Keeping in mind how little we knew of our teachers outside the classroom, you can be sure that the impressions, memories and judgments that follow may well be examples of feelings and opinions shaped by a lack of crucial facts. If so, that too provides food for thought and possibly some insight into the complexity of education and the difficult humility required of a good teacher.

I have not tried to analyze, interpret or comment on any of these contributions. I have no special talent in educational theory or practice. I thought this section worth doing because the contributions taken as a whole may add something interesting or useful to our understanding. This is not a complete list of faculty and staff. I have included those who have been mentioned by class members and who had a lasting influence on at least some of us.

The Pioneer: Teacher's Christmas Wishes, 1954

The December 22 issue of the pioneer in 1954 listed a few things that teachers told reporters that they would want for Christmas. Here are a few examples:

Miss Maple: another bicycle trip to Norway

Mr. Pinkard: GOOD WEATHER for December 22nd and 23rd

Mr. Thompson: a drill to drill holes in the heads of my math students, a pitcher full of knowledge, and stoppers to hold it in until after Regents.

Miss Tibbets: all students to a member how good they are.

Mr. Potter. A big lab, with room for all the students.

Dr. Hartman: a supply of anesthesia which study hall teachers can draw from if the occasion arises.

Mr. Ross: all students to pass, movie cameras, skates, a pencil that rights on the water for my underwater work, and a permanent pizza pie.

Sciene teacher Royal Potter and coach Ray Conlin

INDIVIDUAL FACULTY AND STAFF NOTES

ROBERT F. ALLEN, 6th grade

Bob Allen was a former Marine who taught some of us in 6th grade, the first male teacher we had.   He was lean, wiry, and intense as both a disciplinarian and sometimes an entertainer.   We called for many repetitions of his imitation of Victor Borge's verbal punctuation—reading something and making funny sounds and gestures for the punctuation marks.   As he was teaching he was also pursuing his Ph.D. in psychology at Columbia University and practicing on the class.   He selected several members, including Allan Schwartz and Richard Loftus to take the Rohrschach Ink Blot tests, and Allan says that was the beginning of his interest in psychology and his lifelong career in teaching and clinical work.

Betty Sprague: And what about the eraser game on rainy days in Mr. Allen's class?   I even seemto recall spitball fights!   Gosh, grade school was fun . . .   My mother really liked him!   Of course I thought he was cool too and also took those crazy inkblot tests - the only time I ever did - and remember thinking how weird they were.   So a psychologist was a natural for him I guess.
Pat Mills: I thought Mr. Allen was very handsome, but MEAN!

[excerpts from a letter from former 6th grade teacher Robert Allen to Wallace Kaufman]

June 19, 1956

[after thanking me for some notes about him as our 6th grade teacher]   I remember those days very vividly And I gained immeasurably from them.   I am afraid I wasn't the best teacher in the world at that time (and I'm still not).   But I sure did have a grand group of boys and girls to work with.   I frequently feel that I learned a great deal more from my teaching than I ever managed to teach.   I guess that it was sort of like your archaeological experiences with people being the really important things.

Do you remember the poetry we used to write?. . . . and how we tried to do that play The Friendly World and it didn't quite come off.   I was proud of the good work we did on that.   And I still am.   The student council was a lot of fun too.   Can you remember those elections and those campaigns that we had on the playground during the noon hour?   They were hectic, weren't they?
. . . . . .
I was sorry to hear about Rich Loftus however.   Have you been able to give him a hand at all?   Sometimes a good friend is more than 1000 policemen to help keep the guy out of trouble.   Please tell him that I was asking for him and would like to hear from him if he ever could find the time to write.

Also, I wish that you would tell Mr. Palmer, that I was asking for him.   He was (and still is I'll bet) one of the nicest guys that I ever had the opportunity to meet.   He helped me a whole lot while I was in Sea Cliff although I guess I probably never took the opportunity to let him know about it.
As for my activities since I left Sea Cliff, I guess that they are summed up pretty well in "Who's Who in American education."   Did you notice that I was married?   This is the biggest news since last I saw you and Elaine (my wife, who is also a sixth-grade teacher) and I are very, very happy together. . . .   We live in Long Beach, directly across the street from the ocean, and it is great fun.
My work is very interesting.   I am the director of psychological services for the Oceanside Public Schools.   It manages to keep me pretty busy, but I like it a great deal.

MR. BOOKHAGEN, Head Custodian

Mr. Bookhagen along with his deep voice, square build, and Germanic passion for order often struck fear in the hearts of students who violated his rules.   At least one punishment fit the crime.   Under his guidance one day students gathered in the cafeteria, turned over the tables and set to work scraping off the bottoms of tables and chairs all the wads of gum they had stuck there.
Betty Sprague: Mr. Bookhagen's daughter is my sister's godmother.   We lived with them upstairs apt on Cromwell place.   Elsa is my sister's godmother.   Mr. Bookhaven was always very nice to us.

MS. DOROTHEA COMFORT, Spanish, English

Photo by Fred Feingold

Dorothea Comfort ranks alongside Freda Kittleberger as a teacher feared by most and respected by many, and also as a stern teacher who occasionally revealed a hidden but genuine compassion, at least for some students.

As with all stern or tough talking teachers, she inspired occasional acts of retribution or rebellion.   Pete Swanson recalls that he and Pete Muttee "wrapped leaves around a rock and put it in the exhaust pipe of her car.   It blew the muffler out. We made the mistake of returning to the scene of the crime.   The next day we were in Furlong's office."

Sandy Gleichmann: Dorothea Comfort mocked my lack of answer to an English question - it may have inspired me to go onto do some serious writing later on. Sometimes adversity is the best teacher. Used positively it becomes a challenge.

Dave Schweers says Ms. Comfort "Used to come over and have dinner with us a lot.   In my mother's generation having teachers over for dinner was a regular thing."   Ms. Comfort however did not give grades for hospitality.   Dave says, "In spite of the fact that I was a very poor Spanish student, Dorothea Comfort wrote a recommendation for college that probably got me in. And I flunked out in a year."

Fred Feingold: I was one of the few people who liked Miss Comfort.
Pete Merkel thought of her lessons in Spanish what many of us thought about learning a foreign language: "I don't know why the hell I'll ever have to use it."   He now says he understands her insistence that a foreign language is important.   Pete, who worked overseas for the CIA and then for Hewlett Packard, says, "If it wasn't for the fact of her insistence on me learning and learning the correct way I probably wouldn't have done as well in my travel."   Whenever he goes to a country he says, "I've constantly tried to learn. At least enough that people know you are trying."

Mickie Vaccaro: At the end of my freshman year I was very good friends with Barbara Bollenbacker and her family.   Her mother was an art teacher.   I was having lunch in the cafeteria, and one of the kids came over and said, 'Did you hear the latest?'   I asked what it was.   'Barbara Bollenbacker died.'   I went up to the nurse and the nurse told me that was true. I was in a state of shock.   I didn't realize I was in shcok.   I was 13 or 14 years old. I went into Spanish class and sat down.   When Miss Comfort was asking questions I couldn't answer.   I just couldn't.   I just wasn't talking. She saw that I wasn't really there. She knew better than to admonish me.   She took me out in the corridor.   She asked me what was wrong and I told her and she just hugged me.   She said, 'Now you're not going to my class.'   She gave me a pass so that I wouldn't get in trouble.

Mickie later became a librarian and teacher and remembered Miss Comfort's example. "In Providence I made sure I never confronted a student in class. I would take them outside the classroom to talk.   A lot of kids were not trouble makers but something happened at home.   If they were just being nasty I had robbed them of their audience.   I used Miss Comfort's example. I remember how she did that.   She was so kind.

COACH RAYMOND "HOOKER" CONLIN

Ray Conlin was a Sea Cliff native whose parents lived a block from the school.   He taught generations of reluctant students how to do a simple forward roll on our musty canvas mats, and patiently watched as only a few of us ever climbed the thick manila ropes to the gym ceiling.   His PE classes included tumbling, marching drills, rope climbing, and the usual outdoor sports.

MISS ALICE DALDRY, 7th grade

Miss Daldry was old when we reached her class, one of those bright women born in the late 19th Century who followed one of the few professional paths open to women.   Short and white haired and slightly stooped, she brooked no nonsense in her classes where we studied New York State history.   She also ran the Camera Club and taught hundreds of Sea Cliff students how the basics of taking pictures, developing film, printing, coloring and enlarging.   The expensive technology for developing, printing and enlarging she put at our disposal and taught us the rudiments, if not the art.   For many years after school I developed and printed my own pictures and gave thanks that the school had provided a darkroom and Alice Daldry had patiently taught us the craft.

PAUL "Pop" DRISCOLL, Industrial Arts, basketball coach

Paul Driscoll with his chiseled firm jaw, tightly curled salt and pepper hair, and eyebrows that seemed black epaulets demanded order, attention, and precision in shop and on the basketball court.   In both places he barked not spoke instructions.

The Class of 1955 dedicated its yearbook to him, and the dedication captured some of the reasons why, despite his stern manner, he won great respect.   "Those of us who have taken his industrial arts courses know Mr. Driscoll as a fine instructor.   Besides acquiring skills in shopwork, his students have learned to value seriousness of purpose and to give undeviating attention to the problems at hand. . . . By his many contributions to our school and his genuine interest in us as individuals, Mr. Driscoll has won the admiration and respect of the entire student body."   On the basketball court and in shop, he did indeed give "undeviating attention to the problems at hand and made students proud of the results.

Mike Stanton, who floated into our senior year with an air of being his own man and immune to discipline he didn't like and whose height, grace and street smarts made him a formidable basketball player, said, "For Mr. Driscoll I behaved."

Tom Wolf who was our tallest basketball player and would later go into land surveying says, ""He was tough but fair and made sure you were learning what you were supposed to learn."

Artie Hall rates "Pop" Driscoll as the best teacher he had in Sea Cliff.

ELSIE DURBIN

In modern vocabulary, the slight and soft spoken Elsie Durbin was the school's first responder from K-12 when someone had a cut or abrasion, twisted an ankle, fainted, or vomited.   She had a small voice and a quiet manner that usuallytransformed what seemed a crisis to the victim into a passing inconvenience.

FRANK W. ELLER, Physics substitute

Photo by Fred Feingold

Our senior year we walked through the door and were surprised to find behind the desk not the familiar old bald pate and rimless glasses and tweed jacket of Royal Potter, but a much younger man with a long face, plaintive eyes, and a shock of black hair wearing a white lab coat.   Mr. Potter had begun the decline that would lead in a few years to his death from heart disease, and Principal John French had recruited a friend from North Carolina to stand in.   He not only stood in but the very first day set us to work with an intensity that seemed designed for a physics special forces boot camp.   That day we were told to measure everything from desks to containers of water in the metric system.   We griped but we realized how fast we could learn something new.   To our relief and misfortune his inspired teaching came to an end after a few weeks with the return of Mr. Potter. Nevertheless, his brief ministry taught some of us that we were capable of much more than we thought, and so were schools if they had the right teachers.

Fred Feingold.   If that guy had stayed, my life would have gone a different way.
Feingold: Dr. French brought him in and said this is an old friend of mine and treat him right.

ELIZABETH "Betty" FRENCH

Betty French endowed hundreds or thousands of students with the ability to type that they continue to use today.

Sandy Gleichmann Thompson: "For years I kept in touch with Betty French. She lived with husband Bob in Naples and we were in touch by mail at least at Christmas. We never did play that game of golf that we spoke of when she knew she would be living just across the state from me. But I was honored and pleased to be invited by her daughter Valerie to surprise Betty on the occasion of her eightieth birthday which was probably seven or eight years ago. She had many other attendees - folks who loved her as much as I did. She was a great gal, very strict teacher who demanded respect and results. She is the one who most inspired the writing that I have accomplished starting with her statement that writing a letter is easily done - simply write as you would speak to a person. I certainly used that technique in the memoirs I helped people write. Also taking typing from Betty was a really productive enhancement for job- seeking right out of high school."

Kay Parks won a string of awards for typing and shorth and thanks Mrs. French. "She would spend her lunch hour timing me so I could take shorthand and typing tests." The senior year Kay, an avid sports enthusiast, injured a finger playing ball and couldn't use it. Betty French wrote in her yearbook, "To my only 9 fingered shorthand student." When students took over the school, as we did one day a year, Kay became the shorthand class teacher.

Gail Capobianco took parenting classes in 1959 when she became pregnant and found herself in a class practicing on dolls alongside Betty French. She was intimidated at first finding herself next to a teacher who had been an authority figure, but soon they were just expectant mothers talking about baby names.

Dr. WILLIAM HARTMANN, Citizenship

Dr. Hartmann came to Sea Cliff from much more difficult schools in the City. If any of us knew this, we certainly did not know that his experience there had left its mark. Dave Schweers found out. "I called Hartman a silly joker in class one day, and he failed me in history, and I had to repeat it in summer school. It turns out he left teaching in NYC because of threats from students and I had hit a button. After a week in summer school the teacher told me not to bother showing up and passed me."

JOHN "BIG JOHN" HENDERSON, Citizenship

Rosalie Greenfield: Don Henderson was wonderful and he was a wonderful teacher. I read the Story of Philosophy and he was thrilled by it. Even thou Mr H gave us forms but when you would write a paper for him and you raised questions he would love it. He would encourage you to read.

FAITH KELLER, Nurse

Sandy Gleichmann: Faith Keller school nurse was a neighbor on 8th Avenue and may have inspired me because when my children were in Middle school I volunteered one day per week to be nurse -I was not made to be a nurse - lacking common sense in this department but at least I could listen to complaints and make phone calls. Faith Keller was kind and compassionate.

FREDA KITTLEBERGER, Math

Miss Kittelburger and her stern discipline had been a fixture in Sea Cliff School for at least two generations. She is one of the most remembered teachers of our time, first for her fear inspiring discipline and later in appreciation of both her ability to teach math and the love of students that expressed itself in the discipline that made us learn.

Betty Sprague: Miss Kittleberger taught my father! I swear she had eyes in the back of her head, especially when she was sharpening a pencil!

MARJORIE MAPLE, Physical Education
(see notes from Sandi Freedman's interview with her, below)

Sept. 13, 2008, Class Reunion,
Photo by Wallace Kaufman

Miss Maple seemed everywhere in the schools and gym, almost always in her gym costume with her whistle around her neck.   She believed passionately in the contribution of physical education to girls' health and character, and despite her diminutive stature, she projected an authority that intimidated many boys and allowed girls to learn and participate without harassment.   She attended two days of our 2008 reunion, age 93, and accompanied us on the school tour, up and down the four flights of stairs. She and her friend Miss Mack who taught at Roslyn High still live in Sea Cliff and often take their exercise walking to the beach and back.

Betty Sprague: I loved sports and Miss Maple was great if you were good at sports or didn't do something to cross her.

Judy Brown: I didn't like gym. I wasn't very good and she had favorites.

Sandy Gleichmann: I loved Marjorie Maple -- she was *my* inspiration where sports came into* my life as such a major activity.
Caroline Berthoud, our star violinist, says Miss Maple once asked her, "How do you hold your violin up so long.   She was interested from the gymnastic point of view."

Sandy Gleichmann Thompson: "I was so delighted at the reunion to see Marjorie Maple another favorite of mine due to the fact that sports played and still play a very important role in my overall enjoyment of life.   Once an athlete always an athlete."

Getting to Know Miss Marjorie Maple, AgainInterview material provided by Sandi Freedman
August 29, 2008

Miss Marjorie Maple came to Sea Cliff to visit a friend as war still raged in Europe and the Pacific and we had just begun kindergarten. "I just fell in love with Sea Cliff and accepted a position here," she said. "There were so many similarities to where I grew up." Although she retired from 44 years of teaching in 1971, she is still there. And she is still very much the Miss Maple we knew--friendly, alert, in command and personable.

The hometown that Sea Cliff reminded her of was Pennington, New Jersey, a small community about five miles from Princeton. After attending a state college and working as a gym teacher nearby for two years, she answered her friend's invitation to visit in Sea Cliff. Soon she had her master's degree from a New York teacher's college.

Sea Cliff started her at $1,000 a year with following raises of $25 she remembers. She was 'the' girl's gym teacher for fourth grade through seniors. After district consolidation in 1958 she devoted her entire teaching time to high school physical education. Her favorite memories are of intermural competitions and the annual Sports Night. Team captains took charge of the events and randomly picked the members of their teams. This eliminated favoritism, Miss Maple says, and the process encouraged each person to do her best, whether or not she was athletic. She graded her gym students one-third on effort, emphasizing that it was "most important for them to try.". Miss Maple frowned upon teachers who teased their students in front of others.

She did not take a vacation from teaching in summers but worked as a camp counselor in Pennsylvania's Poconos Mountains and other area camps. She speaks most highly of working on the waterfront in Lake Oswego at the Ethical Culture Camp. [The Ethical Culture Society was a national organization devoted to the study of religions and ethical thinking.] "During those four years, we never knew the backgrounds of any of our campers," she recalled. "Their upbringings were quite diverse, but each child was treated equally." North Shore High brought a few changes to the routines that had been a familiar part of physical education in Sea Cliff. The girls' intermurals were just for varsity, and she notes that a lack of room in the new building eliminated Sports Night. The one-piece, maroon-colored, cotton uniforms required at Sea Cliff disappeared at North Shore Schools, and the students were free to wear whatever they wanted to gym class.

"During my years in the Sea Cliff School, the atmosphere was so wholesome," Miss Maple said. "Kids didn't smoke or take drugs. The teachers intermingled, and everyone was so neighborly." When she purchased her house she recalled how the principal's wife, Mrs. Furlong, and Ed Nelson and his wife [Mr. Nelson taught business and Driver's Ed] insisted on helping move her furniture in. Miss Maple has never moved from that home near the shore. She enjoys long walks to and from the Tappen Beach. Sea Cliff long ago became part of her heart, just as she became for students an inseparable part of their years at school.

DONALD MATTHEWS, English and Latin

Photos by Fred Feingold

Don Matthews was a very big man, a former Marine, who still had a lot of Marine presence in him and a quiet sense of humor.   In the days when teachers could touch a student in the course of discipline, Matthews sometimes applied his strength in just the right way to awe without pain.

Dave Schweers found out the first year we entered high school.   "I was being a smart ass in study hall in our freshman year and Don Mathews took me out in the hall and picked me right off the floor by my shirt and verrrry quietly told me to behave. I did."

Joan Imperiali: I loved Matthews.   He was so smart and he was witty and he made Latin fun and there was just enough of the Marine sergeant that made him interesting.   He would come up with these very erudite remarks.   There was such a contradiction there.   He was always fair.

Fred Feingold: Donald Matthews, for my 13th birthday went out and got a collection of great books, and I never opened one of them.   To this day I feel absolutely horrible about it.

Caroline Berthoud remembers Mr. Matthews repeated admonition, "speed and accuracy."   During tests, she says, "He used to talk all the way through.   'It makes it easier in the final exam.'   I used to get so cross with him."

Barbara Gilson: In class, when we first encountered the subjunctive, Mr. Matthews would start with the first-person, plural--*Gaudeamus igitur,* and would refer to it as the "salad subjunctive" as it began with "Let us." Silly, but a good mnemonic.

EILEEN McNAMARA, Speech and Dramatics, Librarian

The Class of 1954 dedicated its yearbook to Mrs. Mac with a short inscription "in recognition of her faithful guidance, boundless friendship and inspirtation. The Class of 1955 recognized her talent by calling her "our own Elia Kazan" who "spent long hours preparing 'Father of the Bride' for a Pulitzer Prize." Many students did consider her a personal friend, and our own class members testify to her inspiration.

Mickie Vaccaro. She became a librarian because of Mrs. Mac. "She made me think of myself not as a little Italian girl who was going to get married and have lots of children. The one person behind all of it, who gave me the guts was Mrs. Mac.

Rosalie Greenfield, who writes lyrics for musicals, has always been grateful that Mrs. Mac took the play cast to NY "to see what acting was all about."

Kay Parks: "We tried to get everybody involved in the Senior Play, *Stage Door*. I was prompter and Mrs. Mac asked me to be the off stage screamer but I was no good at it. She tried out several and Marge [Repucci] had the best off stage scream and belted it out."

Sandy Gleichmann: Eileen McNamara was my Drama teacher. . She took us into New York to
see Eugene O'Neil's *Long Day's Journey Into Night* and perhaps inspired my great interest in the theatre - I enjoy live theatre particularly drama to this day due to Mrs. Mc's inspiring leadership

EDWIN "Big Ed" NELSON, Business, Drivers' Education

Ed Nelson came to Sea Cliff from Columbia Teachers' College. His reddish hair had largely left him by our time and the most prominent feature were his large glasses through which he often stared menacingly at students before telling them what they should be doing.

Sandy Gleichmann: Edwin Nelson taught me to drive up and down hills in Sea Cliff. To this day I still drive a stick shift manual automobile and love the type of driving terrain found in Sea Cliff.

Carole Brown: I had Mr. Nelson for four periods in a row. 3 business and driver's ed. Pete and I would would stand in the wing talking and along would come Ed and clip the back of Pete's head and tell him, "Get back in class."

DOROTHY O'KNEFSKI, Art

Mrs. O had a long angular face that should have lent itself to someone's graphics, and she was good enough to have a few exhibits of her work. Mainly she lent herself to finding and encouraging student artists.

VICTOR OLSEN, 7th Grade

Mr. Olsen came down with tuberculosis about 1951 and doctors sent him to a sanitorium in the Southwest, part of the standard treatment in that era.   He was the first of the seemingly invincible adults who taught us and provided order in the chaos of growing up who was stricken by a power he could not defeat.   The school took up a collection to help and our class sent him a subscription to *Readers Digest*.

STUART PALMER, English

Photo from Newsday

Stuart Palmer with his courtly manners and slow, precise speech and elegant vocabulary might have been hounded out of a rougher school than Sea Cliff.   In our school students made him the butt of only mild mockery, though most appreciated his gentle patience, and in some vague way sensed and respected his learning.   He was the sponsor for *The Pioneer*, the student newspaper.   I remember no advice he ever gave me in English class or when I edited the paper. I do remember his quiet and welcome encouragement and his soft laugh.

John Storojev: Steward Palmer was a big influence on my literary taste. He was a gentle, intelligent man (Princeton or Yale?) who brought Shakespeare to life for me. I still recall reading the parts of Julius Caesar and realizing how great it was. This helped me later at NYU when I took this highly concentrated Shakespeare course where we had to read all his poetry and plays. One of the most challenging courses I ever took, yet very memorable in the end.

Kay Parks: Mr. Palmer was my tennis teacher at the Glen Head School near the railroad tracks. [Sea Cliff school had no tennis court. His friend was Burl Ives.

Sandy Gleichmann: Stewart Palmer was just so relaxed and sweet.

Richie Smith liked Mr. Palmer, "as wacky as he was about his cats and all. He used to get carried away with them sometimes."

GUY T. PINKARD, Biology and Chemistry

Photo by Nik Epanchin

From the unreformed rural South came Sea Cliff's most controversial school reformer, at least in science. Guy T. Pinkard grew up in the tiny town of Milltown, Alabama where most people grew cotton or tobacco or worked in the nearby textile mills across the border and kept two clocks on their mantles—one for fast time in Georgia, the other for slow time on their side of the time zone line. His father ran a traditional general store in a one story pine clapboard building sitting off the road on pilings with an outhouse behind it that straddled a small creek that served as a sewer. Guy T had graduated from New York University and, as I recall, he was doing graduate work on fish biology. To our surprise and delight he opened the usually locked school laboratory and instituted lab work and student experiments as a regular part of the biology and chemistry classes.

He also founded the National High School Biology Exchange Club with Sea Cliff as the alpha chapter and Milltown as the beta chapter. Dotty Gerroir designed the club logo. We began to send Milltown dried horseshoe crabs and marine specimens and they sent us things like prickly pear cacti. For Easter vacation 1955 Pinkard took Serge Yonov, John Storojev, Nik Epanchin and I on a trip to Milltown, rocketing down 700 miles of pre-interstate, two-lane highways from Sea Cliff to Alabama stopping only for gas, a sandwich and 10 minutes in Virginia to do a few jumping jacks to keep him awake.

For all of us Southern culture was as strange as being in Borneo or Lapland. The South still enforced rigid segregation. Most Milltown houses had outhouses. I thought an old lady we visited was eating plums and spitting the pits back into the can with the label of plums on it, but soon saw she was chewing tobacco. John, Nik and Serge all attended Our Lady of Kazan, the Russian church, and I went to St. Luke's Episcopal, and we had not seen or heard anything like the Southern Baptist preaching of Pinkard's pastor, Brother Friday. Pinkard's brother Rayford, a WWII veteran and Highway Department laborer, gave us a new repertoire of bawdy jokes. I listed them: The Quickest Pet in the World, Lost Girls, A Drunk and the Fly, Pushups, Ants, Soldier's Grenade and Outhouse, Horse Collar, The Specimen, Two Boys and the 75 cent Brothel, HT and HT Brown, and Archibald Barisol. Looking back, the trip was the happiest kind of education. We learned a lot about America, sex, and religion.

Whatever can be said about Pinkard, what we did not see at the time was his extraordinary achievement in being able to inspire students across a wide range of cultures and economic conditions. Although the fight with Little Duffy may be most vivid, he befriended many students in a way teachers had never done. That included visiting the sick and wounded. In my journal I note that on Feb. 5, 1955, ". . . went down to the hospital with Pinkard, Geecho [Joe Bellafato, '59] & Dougie [Andrews] to see Porky."

Pinkard went on to develop the National High School Biology Exchange Club and wrote an article about it for The American Biology Teacher. Henry Goldman ('58) followed me as president, but as far as I know the post did not win him any southern kisses. By the end of his term the club included Sea Cliff, Milltown, Alabama, Vashon Island in Washington state's Puget Sound, Huntington, NY, Atlanta, GA, Wheaton, IL, and Hackettstown, NJ. Sea Cliff's David York served as the first national president. Sea Cliff lawyer Richard Siegel served on the first board of directors.

Pinkard left Sea Cliff a few years after our graduation but went on teaching. Why he left, I have not found out. While writing this book I talked to people who still live in or visit Chambers County, Alabama where Milltown once stood. They include the 1955 president of the Chambers County High School Biology Club—the girl I fell in love with and who was the reason I chose a university half way between New York and Alabama. One person who knew the family well said, "That whole family was controversial." That source said one of Guy T's brothers was a notorious wife beater and was in turn killed by his wife who was committed to a mental institution. The other Pinkards saw that their children were educated and graduated from college. The widespread "gossip" about Pinkard said that Guy T. was gay. He never married and returned home to restore and old mill building. My one-time girlfriend, who now has a farm a mile from where she and I sat day after day on her porch swing shelling peas, said, "Guy T bought Flat Rock [an old mill site] and done a lot of work there, and eventually sold it. And that was the end of Guy."

John Storojev:
"Pinkard was an unusual man, a dynamic and charismatic personality who turned out to be a bogus teacher with no real credentials. Somehow my father became friendly with him. My father was friendly with every race, gender and personality. A most unusual and enlightened being he was. Pinkard at one point needed someone to take care of his laboratory rats during one summer. Since we had a large basement at the time, guess who got elected? We installed this large-size metal structure with multiple cages. I was given instructions for the care and feeding of several rats. Sure, I love looking after rats all summer. Not!

It was kind of my own experiment. I didn't know that if you didn't feed the rats that they would start cannibalizing each other. Needless to say (I love that phrase), the rat population decreased, but the smell factor increased. I am surprised to be alive today because one of those bastards bit me. I put a bandage on the cut and God looked out for this young idiot. My sister reminded me that they bit her as well. Goes to show that God covers much younger idiots as well.

"On the positive side, I recall going down with him and a bunch of us, including Buster, to his home town of Milltown, Alabama. If you were driving down a two-lane road in a rural area and you passed some homes and a store or two on the side of the road, that would be his home town. I do recall the hospitality of his kinfolk and neighbors, specially the hot biscuits served at one home. Never forget how fantastic they tasted! But I am sure that Wallace has more detailed information on that trip somewhere else in this book of recollections. Strangely, I came back with a slightly Southern accent, which I can which I can turn on and off at will. Comes in handy during social occasions or on stage."

We had five or six Jewish members of the class and one recalls that Pinkard was "truly anti-Semitic" and "made fun of me in class. It was really cruel". Fred Feingold, however, recalls that his parents liked Pinkard, saw him as a new and lonely man and enjoyed having him come to dinner.

In my journal for June 6, 1955 I wrote, "Pinkard had a fight with Little Duffy [Billy

Duffy] & was hit in the head, bleeding all over chem. Lab." Dave Schweers remembers some of the detail of that incident, which for most of us was the first time a student ever assaulted a teacher. "Pinkard heard Billy Duffy swearing and they began to argue. The words got rough and Pinkard said 'I won't have you using that kind of language with girls in the room.' No one paid much attention until, in an attempt to get Duffy to leave the room' the argument got physical. Duffy shoved Pinkard who fell and hit his head on the radiator."

The incident left an indelible impression also on Pat Walter who was one of the girls in the room. She remembers the "running, screaming argument, and hearing language she had not heard before. Among other things Duffy had told Pinkard, "You're so full s**t it's coming out of your ears."

In my journal for the next day I wrote, "Pinkard apologized for his actions yesterday."

Joan Imperiali: Pinkard was always very nice to me. I remember my science project. He once brought a friend up from Alabama who was going to Auburn at the time and introduced me to him and we dated.

Sandi Freedman:
"Judy Olson and I, who were best of friends throughout, both had a crush on Mr. Pinkard. I remember sitting in the balcony once during an asembly he ran and giggling together because he was, so we thought, 'so cute!'"

Anne Pascucci.
"I remember seeing him in a store and reminded him that he failed me in bio. He replied that I had "failed" myself. How true."

ROYAL POTTER, Science

Royal Potter had been in Sea Cliff for many years by the time we arrived in his chemistry and physics classes. He was a quiet, slightly stooped man with a fringe of gray hair around a bald dome and given to wearing tweed jackets with leather elbow patches. For many years when he was the only science teacher the school's laboratory was seldom opened for student use.

Dave Schweers: "I will never forgive Royal Potter(like he cares) for throwing me out of Physics because I wasn't smart enough. I didn't care if I passed or not, I just loved that subject. Who knows what I might have become?" [Dave, of course, was smart enough to become a diesel mechanic, English teacher, commercial boat captain, and a registered land surveyor.]

Ted Vladimiroff who became a professional chemist remembers his struggles in Potter's class. "He didn't really give me a grasp of mass and force."

DR. NORMAN ROSS, English, soccer coach (See article below)

Norman R Ross
6515 Kensington Ln, Apt 403
Delray Beach, FL 33446-3019

"The fact is that my experience in a war was the biggest influence in my life . . . " is how Dr. Ross explained why he entitled his autobiography, *Memoirs of a Tailgunner* instead of *Memoirs of a Teacher* or *Memoirs of a Thespian.* It was the biggest influence, yet despite his showmanship, he never told us that he had flown 60 combat missions that would win him two Distinguished Flying crosses and eleven Air Medals.

Dr. Ross wrote the following for the Class of '58:
I have led a good life since your graduation. I stayed at North Shore until 1982 when I retired and moved to Florida. Prior to that, I had taken a sabbatical leave, bought an Around-the-World airline ticket from SAS and traveled around the world for a year. When I returned, I married Rhoda after a divorce from my first wife. Rhoda and I just celebrated our 25th Anniversary. I raised four children who also graduated from North Shore. Robin, my eldest daughter retired from the US Marine Corps as a Lt. Colonel. Her husband, Richard Higgins, was a Marine Corps Colonel who was captured by the Hezbollah in Jordan in 1988 and was murdered by them. There is now a guided missile destroyer with his name on it, the USS Higgins. We are proud of that. My other three children also are now leading distinguished careers and you can read all about them and my whole life in my book, "MEMOIRS of a TAIL GUNNER". (Just go to Google, type in "Norman Ross, 'Memoirs.'"). . . . I'm happy to apprise you of that right now that I am 84 years old. Back then I didn't see what the war had to do with Shakespeare. I can't get around very well, anymore. Difficult walking, but I do have a scooter. . . . With fondest love,Dr. Norman

Ross
http://homeoftheredbaron.blogspot.com/2008/08/of-all-kids-ive-known-before-who-walked.html

Also by way of biography I quote this from Dr. Ross' blog, about his youth during the Great Depression:

I remember disheveled men and women selling apples for a dime on the street, and the concomitant lyric "Brother, can you spare a dime?" I remember how humiliated I felt when the mayor of Miami stopped at our door on Thanksgiving Day one year with a donated turkey. It was then that I realized how poor we really were. And I was eight or nine.

(Please read the article that follows the comments.)

Dr. Ross came to Sea Cliff High in 1954 to teach English.   He says he was glad to supplement the $4,800 salary with a little money from coaching junior varsity soccer and track.   Dr. Ross's daughter Robin attended Sea Cliff and then North Shore.   She has written a very moving book about her husband, *Patriot Dreams: The Murder of Colonel Rich Higgins*.   Robin Ross married Rich Higgins and both served in the US Marines Corps.   Most Americans remember Col. Higgins as the member of the UN peace keeping force in Lebanon 1988 who Hezbollah kidnapped, tortured, killed and dumped on a road.   Dr. Ross told me in 2001, "Anyone who reads this book must know the agony and the ecstasy that went into the writing of it.   Robin has been making speeches for a long time now, about the threats of terrorism in America, but few have heeded her warnings.   If you would care to comment to her personally, her email is: robin@higginspage.com ."   When Dr. Ross and I reconnected in 2001 he was teaching Shakespeare to senior citizens in Florida.

If any teacher could be said to be polarizing, Dr. Ross qualified.   He didn't polarize students against each other, but in their opinion of him, that led to two unfortunate thefts.

John Storojev: I was glad to see that Norman is still alive and at his cantankerous best on his blog.   He was an influential writing instructor for me, since I went on to become an English major in college and did a lot of writing, and then later earned my living as a copywriter.   There was one exercise during which he had us write a micro-detailed description of some very banal action, like buttoning your button.   I recall it forced me to really envision the situation. Very Zen, Norman.   He was a great English teacher, but not too hot in the athletic department, which he was obviously assigned to by the school.   I hope he got extra for that.   Turns out he was a war hero. I was glad to learn that recently, but he should have told us very impressionable teenagers.   He would have gotten tremendous "street cred" and we would have obeyed him without question.

Fred Feingold: "Ross' jazz record collection was stolen and broken. My attitude toward my own class was poisoned." Fred saw it as , "A senseless act of vandalism against authority."

Dave Schweers was among those who had a strong reaction to Ross' strong opinions and remembers the other theft. "I was pretty abusive in his classes and made fun of him a lot. Somebody stole a lot of research he was going for a degree. He was just adamant it was me, until he found out it was [names withheld]." I liked him but he was kind of a snotty little guy. But so was I."

Bob Clarke recalls, "Norman Ross told me one time, 'Listen Clarke, you'll never get more than a C in college English.' " When Bob's college composition teacher helped him make big strides in his writing Bob sent a thought message to Dr. Ross, "You didn't teach me how to write. You only criticized me. You get a C in teaching English."

Ro Greenfield found Mr. Ross to be a wonderful teacher. "He loved literature and he loved people who loved literature."

Dr. Ross was Jane Allen's favorite teacher. "I still have the world literature book. He allowed us to buy it and I still read it occasionally." Ross had students pick out a passage from world literature to memorize, and Jane can still recite lines from a Pushkin poem about winter and snow.

Kay Parks. I was in Norman Ross's class and we had to do a book report. I stood up and said mine was on *Foxes of Harrow* by Frank Yerby. He said "Sit down Kay."

Kay Parks also remembers that Buster Kaufman got away with writing an essay on drawers that was deliberately ambiguous about whether the word meant furniture or underwear.

Mickie Vaccaro, who became a teacher and librarian says, "I remember that Ross opened up the door. I came from a Catholic school with limited exposure. He introduced us to Faulkner. He introduced us to Hemingway. He had us sitting down and really talking about it."

Mike Stanton, the "bad boy" in our senior year says he welcomed Dr. Ross's encouragement in track.

In soccer practice one day Dr. Ross, kicked a ball at Ted Rydzewski by surprise and caught him hard in the groin. Ted reared back and kicked the ball right back at Coach Ross. Probably wearing his famous broad grin.

Nearly 60 years later, Delray man gets his due

WW II vet receives 11 medals for flying in 60 combat missions
Published Friday, January 24, 2003 by The Boca Raton News
by Aaron Shea

War is hell. Norman Ross can vouch for that. The South County resident spent his last few years as a teenager shooting down enemy fighter planes and blasting Nazi submarines from the back of a B24 bomber during World War II. During his service in the U.S. Navy from 1942 to 1945, Ross flew in an incredible 60 missions as a tail gunner over the Pacific, English Channel, North Sea and Bay of Biscay.

But in the chaos of war, Ross' heroism went relatively unnoticed. He received only one Air Medal for his courage.
Nearly 60 years after the fact, Ross, 79, got his just due Thursday afternoon during a ceremony held at the clubhouse in the west Delray Beach community of Huntington Lakes where he lives. Before Ross's family and friends, Navy Capt. Thomas Hunnicutt presented the retired high school English teacher and father of four with nine more Air Medals and two Distinguished Flying Crosses, which recognize an individual for extraordinary achievements and heroism in aerial flight.

"We are a bit late," said Hunnicutt, deputy director of analysis and simulation for the U.S. Southern Command. "We're actually over 57 years late. We will offer no excuse – just a humble apology."

Accepting the Distinguished Flying Crosses, Ross came close to tears. "One is for me," said Ross, as he fought back his emotions. "The other is for the boys I left behind." Ross said there is only one other living member of his squadron, which was based in

Dunkeswell, England. One of the men in Ross' squadron was the brother of President John F. Kennedy, Joseph Kennedy, who was killed during the war.

After reading a story in a newsletter about a veteran who had petitioned the government for his medals, Ross decided to do the same.

A former resident of the Bronx in New York who had enlisted straight out of high school, Ross had kept a log of all the missions he had flown in. He sent the 50-page log to the Pentagon and wrote a letter to another Kennedy brother, Democratic Sen. Edward Kennedy of Massachusetts.

Also in his favor, his daughter, retired Marine Lt. Col. Robbin Higgins, is an undersecretary in the U.S. Department of Veterans Affairs and the former executive director of the Florida Department of Veterans Affairs. Higgins' husband, William, was kidnapped and murdered by Middle Eastern terrorists in Lebanon in 1988 while on a U.N. peacekeeping mission.

Six months after writing the letter, Ross got the word he would receive the medals he had earned during the war.

"After a combat mission of 11 to 14 hours, a pilot is not too anxious to make reports. First thing everyone did was go to the pub." said Ross, who said his father had both of his legs and an arm amputated from injuries sustained in World War I, dying at age 33.

"I kept a detailed log book of every operation and held on to it in my closet," he said.   Not only did Ross hang on to the log, he also held on to the painful memories of the war.   "War was never discussed at home," said Ross's son, Joel, who attended Thursday's ceremony. "Despite his enthusiasm for life, there was always a dark light behind my father's life."

Following the war, Ross spent six months in a Bronx veteran's hospital suffering from what was then called battle fatigue, known today as Post Traumatic Stress Disorder. His illness, however, didn't stop him from earning a doctorate degree from Columbia University and teaching high school for more than 30 years.

Being in a war "is like having a split personality," explained Ross, who moved to Florida in 1982. "One part of you doesn't want to be there. You're terrified. The other side of you wants to use the training [provided by the Navy] to shoot down planes. You go into mission mode and do things automatically. You don't think about the danger. It's after the missions you think about what could have happened." Although it took nearly six decades to get the medals, Ross holds no animosity toward the Navy.   "Better late then never," he said. "This puts an exclamation point on the life I've lived since World War II."

THEODORE RYDER, Director of Music

In 4th grade for reasons I don't remember, I decided my instrument would be the violin, and my parents paid the necessary rental fee.   Mr. Ryder fitted me to an old violin and bow.   The embrace of the violin has an intimacy that no other instrument has.   You grip its neck with one hand, and lay your cheek in its broad black cup with your ear almost on its sounding board.   But I could never make it a friend or lover the way I saw Serge Yonov do it when his wrist would vibrate or as Caroline Berthoud did when she coaxed from it something like a human voice.   In orchestra Mr. Ryder stopped rehearsal and asked, "Buster, why are you bowing down when everyone else is bowing up?"   And in one of our lessons, he stopped my recital and said, "That's b flat, not natural."   He put my finger in the flat position and I bowed, then in the natural position and I bowed.   "Can you hear the difference?"   No, I couldn't.   He kept trying to help me. He couldn't.   I dropped the violin in 5th or 6th grade.   Caroline Berthoud went on to play in symphony orchestras in her native England.

Pat Mills: I wanted to play the violin, but the only instrument we could get "free" was the saxophone, so, I took it.   I played the piano by "ear" and one day Mr. Ryder had me play for him.   He wrote a note to my parents telling them I had talent and should take lessons. It never went further than that, since we couldn't afford dues (a nickel a week) for Brownies at that time. I used to go to lessons with Sandra Freedman and watch her teacher.   Then, I would go home and practice her lesson on our broken down piano that had only about half the notes playing.

Ginny Parks loved playing the clarinet and that was also Mr. Ryder's instrument of choice. Ginny's parents engaged Mr. Ryder to give her private lessons.   "When Mr. Ryder would come over, we'd play popular tunes.   And the neighbors would hear us and ask, 'Who's playing?'".

SAMUEL SCHIFFER, Physical Education, soccer coach

Mr. Schiffer came to Sea Cliff four or five years before our graduation.   He was an energetic and methodical coach.   Initially he bored some players by insisting on a lot more drill in fundamentals than we were used to.

ELIZABETH SCOTT, Language (French)

Betty Sprague: Miss Scott taught me French so well "I used to be able to think in French."
Rosalie Greenfield: Miss Scott for her persistence and her use of exercises which really taught me how to conjugate. All those teachers really loved their subjects.
Betty's good friend Jane Allen had the opposite take. "I couldn't stand our French teacher Miss Scott. She was the one who cracked me over the back of the knuckles because I couldn't conjugate verbs." The rapping especially hurt because "Don Rockwell was in my class and he was my boyfriend. I ran out of the room crying."

Kay Parks: The teacher I had the hardest time with was Elizabeth Scott. I was running for junior class secretary, and she was asking me right before the bell a question. I didn't know the answer and when the bell rang, I said, 'Saved by the bell.' She was kind of beating my head against the hooks in the coat room and said 'I'll see you never run for anything.'"

DR. BERNARD   SHULMAN, English, guidance counselor

Allan Schwartz with Bernard Shulman, Photo by Fre d Feingold

Dr. Shulman taught English, but more important to students interested in writing, he taught the basics of style. He also understood that a larger vocabulary meant a larger scope for thought. He would have liked to teach a wide spectrum of writers, but the curriculum and the range of student interest and ability did not permit it. He settled for listing the names and chief accomplishments of writers he thought an educated person should know and read. In the last few years he has suffered from a variety of health problems and the weekend of our reunion he was in the hospital for heart surgery. He was back on his feet shortly afterward and still lives in Greenvale.

John Storojev: I understand he is still with us but in ill health. I wish him well. Shulman was a character out of some sitcom, with his laidback behavior and preternaturally old demeanor. I guess it was the baldness factor. I enjoyed his class and remember one particular assignment. It was a research paper, with footnotes, about a subject that was to be dear to our young hearts. Well, I chose the subject of "Frustration." I read extensively in psychological and philosophical books about this very obviously real subject. As I recall, I did a good job but he was flummoxed by my choice of subject matter and thought it odd. Well, Bernie, that's what I was at that age: frustrated! But after this exegesis, I felt better and understood my life situation. I believe I got a decent grade, otherwise I would remember that also.

Betty Sprague: Bernie was at my father's funeral. My mother worked for him.   It was her favorite job.

Pat Mills: Some of my teachers made me think deeply.   Norman Ross and Bernie Shulman used the Socratic method.

Rosalie Greenfield: Mr S was wonderful. He was a good teacher and a great sense of humor and he had a passion for American optimism and democracy. I think he was a real liberal and was very upset when the "under God' portion of the Pledge was inserted.

Dave Schweers, who we voted "Teachers' Trial" certainly tried the quiet doctor's temper, beginning when a teacher shortage moved Shulman into algebra class.   Dave was nonchalant to negligent about doing homework. Shulman was not happy, but since Dave "pretty much aced every test," however, he went on to the regents exam. There too, his only blemish was forgetting to bring his scratch sheet up to the desk with his exam, at which point Shulman denied him the chance to retrieve it and Dave got docked for the last two answers and scored 98.   The next year he entered Shulman's senior English "with an attitude."   As usual, Dr. Shulman introduced us to the required senior thesis saying, "I'd just like to warn you people no one has ever graduated without writing this paper."   Dave didn't.   By dint of excelling in public speaking and winning the Glen Players award in drama, he gathered enough credits for English to graduate.   That summer as he took weekly piano lessons from Mrs. Shulman in the Shulman home, the welcome felt a bit frigid.   All that notwithstanding, Dave rates Shulman a good teacher.

Rosalie Greenfield: Mr S was wonderful. He was a good teacher and a great sense of humor, and he had a passion for American optimism and democracy. I think he was a real liberal and was very upset when the "under God' portion of the Pledge was inserted.

Peter Merkel gives English teacher Bernie Shulman credit for recognizing that what Pete could not put in writing, he could speak.   "After an oral presentation Shulman said,

'Merkel, I don't understand why you're not getting As in this class.' Nobody ever said anything like that to me before. Usually people said the opposite, 'Why can't you spell cat?'"

Anne Pascucci: I had him for English my senior year. I was in a class i shouldn't have been placed in. But, again, my fault. (I didn't take school seriously for a while there.) Anyway, the class was too easy and we'd kid about the 10 vocabulary words he gave each week. During that time I was accepted t o college and he was unsupportive. I was disappointed later to find he had been made a guidance counselor.

JOHN STERLING, Vocal Music

John Storojev: I took chorus for four years. I got to know the very talented and energetic Sterling during that time. SCHS was fortunate to have his caliber of teaching. It was a highlight of my education. I still have the record (78 long-playing) they made at the All-State Chorus to which I was privilege to be nominated. That was the big time for me at school. A very fond memory. The music helped me later to learn piano jazz, and later still to have one of my daughters consider a singing career.

Anonymous: John Sterling made me feel safe enough to sing in the chorus and church choir. Something I did for years afterward and enjoyed immensely.

Ginny Parks: Sue Izzo used to bring classical records to Mr. Sterling's musical appreciation class. He was very interesting talking about pop.

KATHRYNE STROHE, Art (see full interview with her below)

Sandy Gleichmann: Dorothy 0 'Knefski and Kathryn Strohe were VIPs - led to my being accepted at Cooper Union - which led to a career early on in commercial art and then at 65 becoming fully engaged in owning and operating a gallery of fine art in Palm Beach. !

Miss Strohe encouraged students who loved art to find their medium and method. Bette Gildersleeve says Miss Strohe inspired her with a desire to go into design.

Notes from an Interview with Kathryne Strohe, 28 March 2001
By Wallace Kaufman
She is from Bethlehem, Pa and when she retired she thought of returning to that town where she grew up with her father traveling the US, opening quarries for Bethlehem Steel.

A friend of hers who has been an artist cannot understand why people no longer listen to what she says. Strohe says that's the way it is. "I know who I am and what I've done and that's good enough."

Strohe started teaching in her late 20s at the end of the Depression in a Dutch community near Patterson, New Jersey. Her salary was $1,300 a year "but we had a hell of a good time." She lived in Greenwich Village and early every morning she took the ferry to Jersey and the train to the town where she taught. "On the train home I would often fall asleep. I smoked a little then and all my clothes had burns in them because I fell asleep smoking." She read somewhere that a Prince George, Maryland district that had an innovative new art program and after 3 years in NJ she applied and took the job in Maryland. "I found out they didn't have a program at all." Nevertheless she was there the three years required for tenure then began looking at the agency ads for teachers. "When you wanted a job in those days, you went to one of these agencies. They had a principal who was looking for teachers who might want to move back up north, she says. "I had had it in Maryland."

She made an appointment to meet Remington Furlong, the principal of Sea Cliff School. That was in June or July and she put on the customary suit and stockings and hat and took the train to Sea Cliff. She was to meet Furlong in Schoelles Drugstore, and he had arranged for Sea Cliff's only taxi to pick her up. "This old rattletrap car came up and this drunk got out in his overalls, and I said to myself, 'Oh my God!'" The driver was Mr. Tenke, a Greek or Italian immigrant who had a small shoe shop in back of Mom Longo's Bar and a grape arbor over the walk that led to the shop.

Furlong took her to see the school and when it was time for him to take her back to the train, "He took me down along the water, the long way. He knew what he was doing. All the way back home on the train I said, 'Please let me have that job.'" She was about 33 years old.

She moved to Sea Cliff shortly in the late 1940s and lived with two other teachers in an apartment near the summer theater. Sea Cliff had nothing for them to do and nowhere to eat. "Schoelles had a soda fountain where you could get a sandwich or a hamburger."

"There was nothing for us teachers to do, so we had to make our own entertainment." The teachers themselves were divided between the 'Cocoa Set' of more "reserved and unworldly" teachers and the 'Cocktail Set'. "If you were in the Cocktail Set, you were considered 'fast'."

Soon she began to meet people in Sea Cliff who were as interesting as people she had known in Greenwich Village. Mary Holler, Peter Lawler's mother, became a fast friend. Mary was a hard drinker who operated a kind of art salon in her home.

When she moved to the third floor of a building whose street level was occupied by Nelson and Rhinas Hardware store, she lived above the second floor apartment where math teacher Frieda Kittelburger had been living for a long time. Miss Kittelburger "kept tabs on me and knew what time I came home in the evening." When Kittelburger took a shower Strohe's water pressure fell to nothing. "I learned to keep some water handy to brush my teeth when my water was off." Nevertheless she loved her attic apartment overlooking Sea Cliff Avenue. "Sort of like being in Paris or something."

She later moved to an upstairs apartment in "The Towers," a small brick apartment building below the Methodist Church on Summit Ave The landlady was very strict and prohibited pets. When a friend gave Strohe a stray kitten every morning she took it in a market basket to church and put it in a storeroom at school. "The kids would run down to the kitchen and ask the ladies there for milk and food for it." Late one afternoon, climbing the steps to her apartment when she was very tired, she tripped on the stairs and fell, dropping the kitten's basket and spilling out the kitten. The landlady saw it and demanded she or the kitten leave. The town's well known and habitually drunk lawyer (name?) asked Strohe, "What are you paying over there?" She told him and he said, "I happen to have a little bungalow I moved from the power plant to Kissam Lane and you can have it for $1,000 down." Strohe had saved that huge amount and the cottage became her home for most of her career.

Among the people who became her friends was Mae Mezzerow, the wife of jazz critic Milt Mezzerow and mother of my friend Milton who lived a few houses down 17th Ave from our first apartment. Jazz was Negro music in the 1950s, and Milt had tightly curled wiry reddish hair and tan skin and we considered him part Negro. Strohe says that other teachers asked her, "Why do you go down to their house?"

"Because I'm very fond of Mae," she told them. "I was so mad at the teachers who were nasty to Milton." Mae was often alone while her husband was in Paris or on the road in the States. They had covered the walls in their home with signed pictures of famous musicians.

 Strohe also became good friends with the Powers family, and Miss Kittelburger disapproved because the two boys, Donny and Michael, were not shy about exhibiting all the flamboyant and campy behavior that said without saying that they were gay. Michael, Strohe says, was often in and out of mental institutions.

Another woman in town, a woman whose father was a famous writer (names she has forgotten) also became one of Strohe's friends. The wife had a widely known habit of ending up in the police station for drunk and disorderly conduct or running into power poles with her car.

In the end other teachers allowed Strohe her odd friends and habits. "Well it's because you're an artist, they'd say."

She also thought very highly of Mark Thompson, the grouchy waiter who rented the boarded up first floor store beneath Willet Tilley's living quarters. He opened a second hand bookstore in the early 50s and kept it open seven days a week from 3-5 and 7-9. "He was a much smarter man than people gave him credit for," she says. "When you felt lonely it [the bookstore] was a place to go." She once suggested to Thompson, "Why don't you get a coffee urn in here?"

He answered, "I got enough nuts coming in here as it is." He was gruff, she says, 'but he saw to it that every kid could afford a pair of ice skates even if he had to give them away. He cared a lot about the kids." She was also impressed by how alert he was to everything going on in the shop. She remembers him catching a kid reading an adult book he had forgotten was in the store. "Give me that book," he ordered. "It's not fit for you. I'm going to burn it."

Strohe also welcomed the big influx of Russian immigrants. She remembers one woman, a widow, who had been royalty in Russia but in Sea Cliff earned her living as a dressmaker. I was so fascinated with what she told me I began to study icons and read about Russia."

In school Strohe was always popular with students. She let them burn incense in art class. One day she saw a pair of eyes looking through the little window in her door and she went out to speak to the teacher who was looking in with disbelief. "They are burning incense," he said.

"So what?" Strohe replied.

The other teacher said this was part of the drug world.

"Not for these kids, it's not," she told him.

"Why do you let them do that?" he asked.

"Because they want to, and as long as they get their work done, what difference does it make?" she replied.

She also took classes to Our Lady of Kazan Russian Church to look at the building and the icons.

"We were considered 'far out'," she says of herself and a few of her friends.

She was glad when Stan Goodwin became assistant principal when Remington Furlong moved up to district supervisor. Miss Beulah Hayner felt she had been promised the job and 'was very upset."

"Stan was a good man," Strohe says. "When he wanted to know something he would ask people like me, 'Have you heard anything about so and so, because I know they talk freely in your class."

"We really liked the kids. It was a whole other ballgame then." She felt she was part of her students' lives. "We were all one bunch," and that if anything as serious as today's school shootings had been brewing, she would have known about it before it became dangerous. Her friend Madelein Kle told her, "The reason you are so popular with those kids is because you still have a trace of the child in you."

One of her greatest satisfactions is that, "The kids have remembered us, and that's great."

Eileen McNamara, "Miss Mac," librarian and drama teacher, lives in Sea Cliff and travels to California to visit her son. Also alive: Marjorie Maple (phys ed), Bernie Shulman (Eng), Don Thompson (math and track).

BEATRICE THOMAS, Junior High Citizenship

From John Storojev: Miss Thomas was probably my earliest and most influential teacher. You can usually identify the teacher that was crucial to your development. She was to mine. Miss Thomas was in Junior High at the time and taught Citizenship, which was really government and political science (which became my minor at college). She encouraged me and helped me (a newcomer to this country) learn the basics of government. In the end, she awarded me some prize at graduation for which I was unprepared and forever grateful. A great teacher whom I keep in mind as I teach now at a university. I went on to minor in political science, the get an MA in international relations. Now doubt, her influence and support gave me the confidence to study this field in depth.

DONALD "CREEPER" THOMPSON

Photo by Fred Feingold

Don Thompson taught geometry, algebra, trig, and advanced algebra—no escape for those who wanted to or pursue math. That was fine by some, a prison to others. His outgoing personality and his fascination with sports equally divided class opinion. Our yearbook, however, we dedicated to him. The inscription reads: *A good teacher is one who gives to his students more than a textbook and explanations. We dedicate this book to such a person, one who has also played an important part in our lives, Mr. Donald Thompson.* We note that the inscription avoids the division of opinion illustrated below.

Bob Johnston: I seem to remember coach Thompson always wore those crepe soled shoes. Thus the nickname "Creeper". He was one of my favorites. My best math teacher after Ms. Freda Kittleberger.

John Storojev: Mr. Thompson, aka "The Creeper." to whom our yearbook was dedicated was a good, kind teacher who kept his students foremost in his heart. I had him in Geometry class and I enjoyed concocting complicated theorems that Euclid would never dream of devising, let alone Mr. Thompson. I still think I posited some unique combinations that were unbeatable, at least that was my fantasy. But it was as a track coach that Mr. Thompson made his reputation. I devoted four years to track and set some records in low hurdles which stood for a couple of years, anyway. This was my love, if anything could be said to be that. He didn't know much about how to condition athletes, or how to motivate them, or how to equip them, or any of the aspects that over the course of 50 years we have associated with athletic excellence. I tried to pole vault and nearly killed myself using a defective aluminum pole which broke on the way up. I don't even want to mention the so-called "sand" on which I landed after vaulting. Anybody notice the foam padding that is now used for this purpose in most athletic meets? Hazardous is a mild description of what our amateur athletes had to endure. Glad we survived.

Jim McKinley: I give Mr. Thompson kudos for being a no nonsense individual who really emphasized the value of taking up the challenge of mathematics. He was a quiet type but he kept me pretty much on the straight and narrow.

Joan Imperiali had a slightly different understanding of his nickname. "Don Thompson was a really nice fellow. He was very fair. Creeper because of the way he walked and his general demeanor. I thought the name was appropriate."

Fred Feingold who has been a teacher most of his life reflects: "Thompson's math class was all discussing track and at the time I was rock hard anti-athlete. Also the math was all by rote, cookbook. If we had gone out taking solar shots, trig would have made sense. All this crap was theoretical.

Jane Sessler (math teacher): I remember what Mr. Thompson said because he used to talk through the tests. You should be able to work under any conditions. He would talk about the track.

Anonymous: Mr. Thompson did me bad. In my junior year. He said I wasn't qualified to do advanced algebra instead of encouraging me. I wanted to go on in math because I liked math.

In the Class Will, we find this entry: "We, Jane Sessler and Diana Djivre, leave to any girl brave enough to take solid geometry next year a well thumbed through stack of magazines to occupy her time while Mr. Thompson gives his spiel on track."

Obituary: Donald R. Thompson (Glen Cove News and Record)

Donald Thompson, resident of Sea Cliff since 1947, died June 25, 2009 at age 94. He was a math teacher and track coach at North Shore High School until his retirement in 1975. Donald grew up in Valhalla, NY. He attended Furman University and Columbia University where he majored in education. He served in the Army Air Corp during WWII; he was a sergeant working in enlistment and classification of recruits.

In 1947, Don got a job teaching mathematics at Sea Cliff School. He and his wife Virginia bought their own home in Sea Cliff in 1952, where they lived the rest of their lives. When the local high schools were consolidated into North Shore High School he taught there until his retirement in 1975. He enjoyed coaching track and cross country for many years.

Don and Virginia raised two children – Jeanne (now of Sea Cliff) and Norman (now of Louisville, CO). He and Virginia were active in the Glen Cove Presbyterian Church and then the Sea Cliff United Methodist Church, where Don served on the Board for a number of years.

After his retirement, they traveled extensively around the U.S., visiting all of the 48 contiguous states. They enjoyed visiting their many friends and relatives who were scattered around the U.S. and having them visit in Sea Cliff.

Don was a nature lover and avid bird watcher, eventually identifying over 500 birds in his travels around the U.S. For many years after his retirement, he and Virginia volunteered at Muttontown Preserve, where they shared their knowledge of nature with groups of school children. He was an accomplished travel and nature photographer, shooting thousands of slides. He also enjoyed camping, sailing on Long Island Sound, collecting stamps, gardening, painting watercolors, and playing bridge and Rummikub. He loved being active, with always another project to carry out or another place to take a bird walk. But he also enjoyed his snoozes on the couch, with a cat curled up on his stomach.

Don had a great love of life. He was always an optimist who felt that he had been blessed in his life. He loved to laugh. He loved to spend time with people. He loved to share his knowledge with others. He brought these characteristics to his teaching, his coaching, and his relationships with his family and friends. Virginia died in 2002.

Services will be held Saturday, July 11 at 3 p.m. at the Sea Cliff United Methodist Church. All are welcome.

Donald Thompson, math teacher at Sea Cliff School, surrounded by his students. The photo was probably taken in the 1950s.

JEAN "Mother Tibbits" TIBBITS, Citizenship

Photo by Fred Feingold

For many of us she was our first introduction to the Constitution, portions of which we had to memorize. She often required memorization, perhaps at the expense of understanding, but it was not because she didn't care. Because students knew she did care the Class of '56 dedicated its yearbook to her saying, "having been our homeroom teacher for three years, in which capacity she has, in effect, become a member of the class, we feel that Miss Tibbits is an unforgettable figure in our yearbook and in our lives." Katheryne Strohe, our art teacher and Jean's friend told me about Jean Tibbits' death. "She had a sad life and a drinking problem. She was deserted by a man she was madly in love with or something like that."

Bob Clarke: "Her technique was to BS during the first half of the year then cram for the Regents exam."

Sally Colgan had tried Driver Ed with Miss Tibbets, but the manual shift stymied her. "Miss Tibbets hated to get in the car with me."

ELEANOR "Mrs. Zip" ZIPPERIAN, Business

Mrs. Zipperian had two daughters, Lee who was ahead of us and Dottie who was behind us. They lived in a modest house on a postage stamp sized lot on Maple Avenue behind Carl's shoe shop. The girls were as popular as Mrs. Zip.

Carole Brown: I took all business course. She was just a real nice person, and if you were stuck on something she would take the time to sit down with you.

WISDOM

When I have ceased to break my wings
Against the faultiness of things,
And learned that compromises wait
Behind each hardly opened gate,
When I can look Life in the eyes,
Grown calm and coldly wise,
Life will have given me the Truth,
And taken in exchange—my youth.
(by Sarah Teasdale)

ADDITIONAL PICTURES: THEN AND NOW

Figure 2 Senior Class Trip, '57. (Scan by Nik Epanchin)

Figure 3 51st Reunion, September 2008.   Approximately the order in which they appear in
the class trip photo.

Glenwood Landing 8th grade graduating class
First Row: ??, ??, Karen Wignes, Valerie DeVeuve, Barbara Ferris; Second row: Soren Hansen, Jane Sessler, ??, Judy Olsen, Arlene Maass; Third Row: ??, Peter Merkel (?), ??, ??, Fourth row none identified.   Standing: Richie Smith and teacher.

1944 Barbara Ferris and friends.   (Photo from Barbara)

COMMENCEMENT PROGRAM

- 1957 -

FACULTY ADVISORS

Dr. William Hartman
Mrs. Dorothy O'Knefski
Mrs. Eileen McNamara

Mr. Bernard Shulman
Mr. Donald Thompson

SENIOR CLASS OFFICERS

President: Nicolas Epanchin
Vice President: Robert Lucas

Secretary: Linda Lloyd
Treasurer: Lois Ann Delgado

Class of 1957

Valedictorian . . . . Diana Esther Djivre
Salutatorian . . . . Allan James Schwartz

Ruth C. Ahearn
Jane Sanford Allen
Douglas Andrews
Virginia Louise Arnold
Nancy L. Baker
Helen Basilevsky
Albert Behrmann, Jr.
Blanche R. Bennett
Loretta Berroyer
Caroline Helen Berthoud
John P. Broderick
Carole A. Brown
Judith Burk Brown
Phoebe Rose Burdick
Frederic Thomas Burns

Cherry D. Campbell
Gail A. Capobianco
Annette F. Caselli
Patricia Ann Cavanaugh
Robert Anthony Clarke
Sarah Kathleen M. Colgan
Lois Ann Delgado
Valerie Ann DeVeuve
Diana Esther Djivre
Douglas Alan Elton
Nicolas Vladimir Epanchin
Marilyn Gloria Fehr
Frederic John Feingold
Barbara Edith Ferris
Sandra I. Freedman

Leslie Frost
allo
Jane Gelling
y Marie Gerroir
Lou Gildersleeve
a Gilson
L Lee Gleichmann
.e Carole Greenfield
a Mary Grella
ine June Grote
ine Sonja Hallberg
Hansen
Luise Henninger
ine Rita Herman
e H. Hincula
rick Scott Hughes
Marie Imperiali
ica Sue Izzo
t Alfred Johnston
slaw Kalakoc
ce V. Kaufman
rd E. Klein
hy C. Klenk
er A. Kotoski
A. Kreidemaker
LaJoy
anne LaPierre
A. LeFebvre
Anne Lloyd
t William Lucas
e Jeannette Maass
Malkin
Edward Maloney
d Francis McAdams
Michael McGrady
Dennis McKinley
r George Meier, Jr.
Louis Merkel

Carol Ann Moffat
John Richard Murray
Peter A. Muttee
Edwin Robert Neice
Lola Virginia Norminton
Richard S. Norwich
Judith Anne Olsen
Janice Soutar Painter
Kathleen Marie Parks
Virginia Louise Parks
Anne Lucille Pascucci
Daniel Edward Pawul
Robert E. Platt
Douglas A. Ransweiler
Margaret Reppucci
Theodore Rydzewski
Nancy Jane Samuelson
Ronald James Santonastasi
George E. Schmersal
Allan James Schwartz
David Schweers
Jane Virginia Sessler
Cecilia Marie Snayd
Robert Scudder Soper III
Betty Joan Sprague
Richard Louis Stack
Michael Stanton
John Vladimir Storojev
Charles Swanson
Catherine Sydow
Michelina Vaccaro
Mary Ann Helen Vanek
Theodore Vladimiroff
Patricia Irene Walter
Karen Anne Wignes
Thompson E. Wolf
Serge Yonov

Color Bearers and Ushers - Members of the Junior Class

COMMENCEMENT
EXERCISES
Class of 1957

NORTH SHORE SCHOOLS
Sea Cliff High School

Auditorium   8:30 P. M.   June 24, 1957

COMMENCEMENT PROGRAM
- 1 9 5 7 -

Selection . . . . Orchestra

Processional-"Pomp and Circumstance" . . . . Elgar

Invocation . . . . Mr. Horace Klenk

Flag Salute . . . . Wallace Kaufman,
Student Council President, 1956-57

Star Spangled Banner . . . . Audience

Announcement of Awards . . . . John E. French,
High School Principal

Community Scholarship Awards . . . . . . F. R. Furlong,
Li Scholarship   Supervising Principal

Senior Class Gift . . . . Nicolas Epanchin,
Senior Class President

Acceptance of Gift . . . . Peter Rose,
Sophomore Class President

Graduation Program . . . . Class of 1957

Presentation of Diplomas . . . . . . Board of Education
Mr. Robert Dixon, President

Alma Mater-"Sea Cliff Victorious" . . . . . . Audience

Benediction . . . . Reverend Alexis Yonov

Recessional-"War March of the Priests" . . . . Mendelssohn

Pavilion in Flood Tide, 1954, Photo Fred Feingold

Made in the USA
Middletown, DE
11 July 2015